# Interracial Justice

# Critical America

Richard Delgado and Jean Stefancic
GENERAL EDITORS

*To Be an American: Cultural Pluralism and the Rhetoric of Assimilation*
Bill Ong Hing

*Negrophobia and Reasonable Racism: The Hidden Costs of Being Black
in America*
Jody David Armour

*Black and Brown in America: The Case for Cooperation*
Bill Piatt

*Black Rage Confronts the Law*
Paul Harris

*Selling Words: Free Speech in a Commercial Culture*
R. George Wright

*The Color of Crime: Racial Hoaxes, White Fear, Black Protectionism, Police
Harassment, and Other Macroaggressions*
Katheryn K. Russell

*The Smart Culture: Society, Intelligence, and Law*
Robert L. Hayman Jr.

*Was Blind, But Now I See: White Race Consciousness and the Law*
Barbara J. Flagg

*American Law in the Age of Hypercapitalism: The Worker, the Family, and
the State*
Ruth Colker

*The Gender Line: Men, Women, and the Law*
Nancy Levit

*Heretics in the Temple: Americans Who Reject the Nation's Legal Faith*
David Ray Papke

*The Empire Strikes Back: Outsiders and the Struggle over Legal Education*
Arthur Austin

*Interracial Justice: Conflict and Reconciliation in Post–Civil Rights America*
Eric K. Yamamoto

Eric K. Yamamoto

# Interracial Justice

Conflict and Reconciliation in
Post–Civil Rights America

New York University Press
New York and London

NEW YORK UNIVERSITY PRESS
New York and London

Library of Congress Cataloging-in-Publication Data
Yamamoto, Eric K., 1952–
Interracial justice : conflict and reconciliation in post-civil
rights America / Eric K. Yamamoto.
p.   cm.—(Critical America)
Includes bibliographical references and index.
ISBN 0-8147-9674-5 (cloth : alk. paper)
1. United States—Race relations.   2. Minorities—Civil rights—
United States—History—20th century.   3. Minorities—Legal status,
laws, etc.—United States.   4. United States—Social
conditions—1980–   5. Social conflict—United States—History—20th
century.   6. Reconciliation—History—20th century.   I. Title.
II. Series.
E184.A1Y36   1999
305.8'00973—dc21            98-39108
                     CIP

New York University Press books are printed on acid-free paper,
and their binding materials are chosen for strength and durability.

Manufactured in the United States of America

10 9 8 7 6 5 4 3 2 1

For
Ed Nakamura
and
George and Tamiko Yamamoto

# Contents

# Acknowledgments

I dedicate this book to the late Edward Nakamura for his inspiration and lifelong commitment to social justice and to George and Tamiko Yamamoto for their enlightened guidance. I offer special thanks to Angela Harris, Harlon Dalton, Kehaulani Lum, Jo Carrillo, and Sumi Cho for their insight, critique, and encouragement and to Richard Delgado and Jean Stefancic for their editorial help and overall support.

I also appreciate the hard work of many others. Susan Serrano provided invaluable research and editing assistance and coordinated student researchers. The principal researchers were Isaac Moriwake, Jen-L Wong Lyman, and Bonita Chang. Also providing valuable research were Lia Sheehan Dwight, Camille Sirivatha, Jason Shimizu, Rowena Sommerville, Kirstin Hamman, Bridget Palmer, Dan Mueller, Carrie-Ann Shirota, Jeannie Jang, Mark Murakami, Mona Bernardino, Reid Yamashiro, Janet Lee, Paula Henderson, Dana Nakasato-Nejmi, Regan Iwao, and Arlene Jouxson. Sherri Ritter, Stacy Aluag, Melissa Vincenty, Thomas Aiu, Jamae Kawauchi, Catherine Awakuni, Anyaa Vohiri, Glenn Melchinger, Gordon Yang, Mei-Fei Kuo, Dayna-Ann Mendonca, and Geri Amparo also provided needed assistance. Helen Shikina worked tirelessly and carefully on the technical aspects of the manuscript.

Finally, my special appreciation goes to Joan Ishibashi for her many ideas and dedicated support and to the William S. Richardson Law School, University of Hawai'i, for providing me a working home.

# Prologue

## The PNT Grocers Boycott in New Orleans

How do communities of color heal their racial wounds? How do they reconcile so they can live together peaceably and work together politically in America at the millennium? We begin our exploration of these questions with a brief account of the PNT grocers boycott.

In the hot New Orleans summer of 1996, neighborhood tension erupted in a street brawl between Tho Nguyen's son and Ulysses Narcisse. Upset by the fight, which featured a crowbar, a baseball bat, and an unfired gun, African American residents boycotted the Nguyens' grocery store. They accused the Nguyens of "refusing to accept pennies, taxing food stamps, and allowing neighborhood drunkards to loiter on the corner." After an angry meeting, the Neighborhood Committee for Justice, composed primarily of African American residents, supported the effort to oust the Nguyens. The committee—whose goals included abolishing drug use and tobacco sales to minors and supporting community economic development—circulated a flier accusing the Nguyens of physical and verbal assault and discriminatory hiring practices. The Nguyens denied the accusations and brought charges of their own, particularly disrespect by African American customers and neighborhood residents. The Nguyens resented the regular barrage of obscene language and the repeated taunts about "going back to your own country."[1]

Shortly after the boycott, the Nguyens agreed to sell their business to Adel Zughager. But African American residents opposed the sale and threatened to continue the boycotts unless the store was sold to an African American. Zughager dissolved the sales agreement.[2]

Later in the summer, the Committee for Justice sponsored a rally at the Greater Antioch Full Gospel Church and demanded that African American proprietors take over the store. A spokesperson for the committee asserted, "It's time to reclaim the community from a stream of foreigners who invade a neighborhood and bleed it of money." City and federal officials were invited to the rally; the Nguyens were not. The committee's spokesperson reportedly refused to speak publicly with the Nguyens. "Now they [the Nguyens] want to talk to us, to find out what did they do to offend us. If they don't know what they have done over these past eight years, we say it's eight years too late." In support of the committee's efforts, a state politician encouraged African American protestors to "fight on" and not "give up the ship." In addition, a minister proclaimed his hope that the "campaign against outside shop owners in African American neighborhoods will spread all over the city."[3]

## The Failure of Mediation

The city's Human Relations Commission and the U.S. Justice Department offered to mediate the escalating dispute. Both worried about heightened neighborhood tensions and potential picketing of other Vietnamese immigrant–owned stores. The senior conciliation specialist for the Department of Justice believed that mediation would help both sides find common ground. The Committee for Justice, however, declined to participate in the mediation. Instead, it wrote to the City Council and accused the executive director of the Human Relations Commission of abusing his power in the mediation process and siding with the "mean spirited grocer" who "operated a reign of terror" and who should be rendered "penniless."

Mr. Jackson had aided and abetted a vicious storekeeper that operated a reign of terror in our community. Our plan is to drive this mean spirited grocer out of our community, if necessary penniless. This is our right. He came into our community, took our dollars, mistreated the community, now he must pay. We have told Mr. Jackson that we don't need any of his brand of "mediation." He is clearly on the side of these mean grocers.[4]

In light of the committee's refusal to participate in the government-sponsored mediation and the African American residents' promise of continued boycotts, the Nguyens turned to the legal system for help.

The Nguyens closed their store permanently and filed a federal lawsuit against the committee and the Greater Antioch Full Gospel Church, alleging that the committee and church demanded that the Nguyens sell only to African Americans and attempted to devalue the business so they could buy it at a severely reduced price. "The defendants are not merely exercising their First Amendment right to peacefully assemble and protest. [R]ather, they are engaged in a pattern or practice of economic terrorism."[5]

Although people on the periphery framed the incident in nonracial terms,[6] the Nguyens and the Committee for Justice told a different story. The Nguyens' legal complaint alleged that the African American residents were motivated by a racial animus against Vietnamese immigrants. African American spokespersons, on the other hand, characterized the neighborhood as theirs and described the Nguyens as foreign shopkeepers who came into their community and stripped them of financial resources.[7]

Why did the Nguyens pursue the lawsuit? Their attorney said the suit was the only way to compel the parties to talk to each other, and it did in fact bring the parties together to address the legal claims and the specifics of the immediate dispute. It failed, however, to encourage deep analysis of the preexisting intergroup grievances that transformed the initial altercation into an interracial controversy. The complaint failed to offer, and the parties failed to develop, a thoughtful, complex narrative of African American and Vietnamese American relations in New Orleans.[8]

Instead, stock stories carried the day. The Committee for Justice described the altercation as part of a pattern of Asian foreigners' exploitation of African Americans. An African American responded to the media criticism of the boycott by saying, "It is clear that some groups just arriving in America see us as the bottom of the pecking order and intend to use us as stepping stones to their own prosperity."[9] By contrast, the Nguyens' legal filings portrayed Vietnamese immigrants as victims seeking fair treatment and African Americans as perpetrators seeking economic destruction of another racial minority.

Constrained by narrow notions of legal relevance and by institutional practice, the legal proceedings did not delve into the historical roots of the black residents' perceptions of the Nguyens as members of a just-arriving group exploiting African Americans. Nor did the lawsuit bring the Nguyens closer to correcting racial misconceptions about African Americans as shortsighted and untrustworthy.

Mindful of the earlier failed government agency mediation and the difficulties of litigation, the federal district judge ordered the case to formal mediation by a magistrate judge. The magistrate, the parties, and their attorneys met privately several times over two weeks. The mediated meetings, however, focused unsuccessfully on a quick resolution of the immediate dispute—the sale of the store. They produced little in the way of healing.

## An Unenforceable Settlement Agreement

The magistrate's mediation efforts did, however, get the parties' attorneys talking. Eventually, after the mediation, the attorneys, the Nguyens, and Willye Jean Turner of the Committee for Justice negotiated a settlement. No African American buyer was available, so the Nguyens agreed to sell the business to Nguyen's son-in-law and a Mr. Hamdan. The Nguyens planned to complete the sale by transferring all their interest in the store in exchange for the defendants' agreement to cease picketing. The sale was never consummated. The Nguyen's attorney cited technical defects in the settlement agreement. Some in the community wondered whether the transaction was a "sham" (simply transferring ownership to the Nguyens' relative).[10]

Despite pressure from the city's Human Relations Commission and the Justice Department and despite the subsequent intervention of a federal magistrate judge, three attempts at private dispute resolution failed. In hindsight, these attempts appeared doomed from the outset, as they each targeted only the immediate conflict. That is, "relief" meant the sale of the business in exchange for the permanent termination of the boycott. Those dispute resolution efforts, however, failed to address the interracial grievances underlying the immediate dispute or to stress public analysis and community handling of the deeper intergroup tensions. These grievances and the tensions they generated were linked to the harsh and, in important respects, unique effects on African Americans of southern slavery, Jim Crow apartheid, and present-day white racism; the extensive poverty in both the black and Vietnamese communities; the recent violence against Vietnamese immigrants in Louisiana and Texas; and the publicized conflicts in inner cities nationwide between Asian American merchants and African American customers. These grievances and tensions also were connected to New Orleans's history of racial hierarchy, including its middle positioning of Creoles (and potentially Asian Americans) below whites and above African Americans.[11] The dispute resolution techniques employed, it appears, looked past the healing of racial wounds and the rebuilding of broken relationships.

## Resolution?

Seven months after the initial altercation and five months after the failed settlement, the Nguyens found a buyer acceptable to the Committee for Justice. African American residents celebrated the grocer's departure. The buyer was Palestinian. The African American residents welcomed him, they said, because Palestinian store owners in other communities treated blacks well. Respect for the customers, they said, had always been the issue, not the owner's race.[12]

The picketing stopped, but the lawsuit's claim for damages and the interracial distrust remained.

For this and related reasons, shortly after the Nguyens sold their business, 350 Vietnamese Americans and African Americans from five community churches gathered to pray for and promote "understanding of cultural and ethnic heritages." Leaders from various churches encouraged participants to nurture a twenty-year relationship (Vietnamese refugees first settled in New Orleans in the mid-1970s). "Let us celebrate the possibility of what we can become," said Rev. Thomas G. Glasgo, pastor of St. Brigid Church. Monsignor Dominic Luong, pastor of the May Queen

Vietnam Church, hoped the prayer service would help unify multiracial eastern New Orleans.[13]

Similar sentiments were echoed by many at the gathering. Fourteen-year-old Hoang Tran "liked how they all came together as a community. There was no fighting or anything like that. It was without racism." Songs, prayers, and Scripture readings in English and Vietnamese allowed the groups to share religious heritages. The community prayer service revealed genuine desire for intergroup healing.[14]

The warm feelings and momentary sense of harmony, however, were largely ephemeral. The prayer service glossed over or ignored altogether difficult racial issues. It made those there feel good but appeared to provide few tools for critically examining and acting on the PNT grocers controversy and others like it. Yet the service was a start. People were talking, and hoping. Healing? False grace? Or something in between?

In the fall of 1997, the new Palestinian owner of the store was shot and killed during a store robbery.

# Introduction

[Alliances between groups of color] require a knowledge and
wisdom that we have yet to attain. It is painful to see how
prejudice, resentment, petty competitiveness, and sheer ignorance
fester.

> — ELIZABETH MARTINEZ,
> "Beyond Black and White:
> The Racisms of Our Time," 20 *Soc. Just.* 22 (1991)

By the year 2000, the familiar characterization of white and black will no
longer describe race relations in the United States. In crucial respects,
twenty-first-century America will be a nation of minorities. This demographic change necessitates a change in how we think about race relations
and how we think about racial justice. With the prologue's account of
New Orleans's African American and Vietnamese American immigrant
controversy as a backdrop, I suggest we rethink the material and theoretical foundations for groups living together peaceably and working together politically by exploring issues of justice among nonwhite racial
groups. That exploration of race, culture, and responsibility both focuses
on interracial relations and implicates broader concerns for all in multiracial America.[1]

The epigraph captures two racial realities seemingly on a collision course. One reality is the desire of nonwhite racial groups, in a multitude of contemporary situations, to build interracial alliances.[2] The broad multiracial coalition opposing California's anti–affirmative action Proposition 209 is an example. Others include New York's Korean American–African American Mediation Project and Los Angeles's alliance between the Latino Association of Elected and Appointed Officials and the Korean American Coalition (formed to advance interracial cooperation by undertaking joint projects and handling intergroup tensions).[3]

The other racial reality, explored in chapter 1, is the intensifying conflict and distrust among communities of color amid shifting racial and class demographics. The rapid dissolution of African American, Asian American, and Latina/o coalitions following the South Central Los Angeles rebellion-riot in 1992, fueled by intergroup accusations and countercharges, is one instance. The failed PNT grocers mediation in New Orleans between African American church and community organizations (charging exploitation) and a Vietnamese store owner (countercharging "economic terrorism") is another.

Intergroup conflict and distrust militate against the building of workable, lasting alliances.[4] How, then, are racial groups to deal with this complex, dissonant reality—a movement toward interracial alliances characterized at least partially by anger, resentment, and bitterness?

As framed, this question is one that many racial communities prefer to avoid. By focusing attention on interracial conflict, the question can be twisted to obscure the reality of what David Roediger calls the "wages of whiteness"—the effects of continuing white dominance in most aspects of American life and its impact on all racial interactions.[5] By acknowledging interracial grievances, the question also airs dirty laundry, with no easy, affirming answers. Indeed, the answers "require a knowledge and wisdom we have yet to attain."

Nevertheless, the question is worth the candle. By avoiding it, racial communities risk having someone else frame the concepts and language of interracial conflicts and reconciliation. Controversy abhors a vacuum, and ready to fill the void are those standing outside the communities in conflict, including media reporters, social service professionals, lawyers, and academics, each with his or her own interest and agenda. A recent news article headline, for instance, coarsely framed interracial conflict as

"Asians, Blacks and Intolerance." Although the article's text raised news-worthy issues of Asian immigrant perceptions of African Americans, it lacked balanced perspectives, overstated causal connections, and employed sweeping language: "Given Asian prejudice against blacks, it is not sur-prising many blacks resent Asian Americans."[6] This journalistic framing of interracial tension appeared more inflammatory than informative.

By addressing forthrightly the difficult question of how to deal with the dissonant realities of interracial alliance forging and distrust, racial communities can begin to fill this near void in ways and on terms reso-nant with their past experiences and future hopes. Seeing the tense mix of intergroup distrust and hope and hearing the swirling sounds of inter-group accusations and optimism expands the inquiry into justice beyond white on black and even white on color (although they both remain im-portant) to encompass color on color. This expanded inquiry means con-tinuing to address the wages of whiteness. It also means developing ways to inquire into and act on justice grievances underlying many present-day conflicts among nonwhite racial groups—grappling with the reality that amid changing racial and economic demographics, racial groups can be simultaneously oppressed in one relationship and complicitous in op-pression in another.

With these sights and sounds, these contemporary racial realities, the question for communities of color is not so much "can we all get along" but, rather, "how" can we all get along?

Critical interrogation and sensitive handling of justice grievances among nonwhite racial groups, I suggest, are one response to the question of "how." In many instances, interrogation and handling of these griev-ances are predicates to intergroup healing and, in turn, to forging alliances and building coalitions—to getting along socially and politically. This healing dynamic lies at the core of the approach to interracial justice developed in part 3.

## What Is Interracial Justice?

What is interracial justice? In brief, interracial justice entails hard ack-nowledgment of the historical and contemporary ways in which racial groups harm one another, along with affirmative efforts to redress justice grievances and rearticulate and restructure present-day relations. So conceived, interracial justice is often integral to building (or rebuilding) relationships among communities of color—the establishment of "right relationships, the healing of broken relationships."[7]

In substance, interracial justice draws broadly from the disciplines of law, theology, social psychology, ethics, and peace studies and from indigenous practices. Its guiding principle for relationship building is reconciliation. Transformation through reconciliation involves messy, contentious, continuous, and often localized processes of recognition, reconstruction, and reparation. For racial communities, it means "facing history, facing ourselves."

In terms of method, interracial justice embraces a praxis methodology, or what I call *race praxis*. Race praxis is a critical pragmatic process of race theory generation and translation, practical engagement, material change, and reflection. It grounds justice at the juncture of progressive race theory and antisubordination practice—to integrate conceptual inquiries into power and representation with frontline struggles for racial justice. In so doing, it seeks to avoid the backward-looking approach of traditional legal justice analysis (focusing on past events) as well as the forward-looking but abstruse moral and philosophical arguments about justice cast entirely in terms of law's legitimacy. In short, it seeks to avoid the scholarly penchant for "theory [that] begets no practice, only more theory."[8]

In substance and method, interracial justice offers conflicting racial groups a way to conceptualize, ruminate on, and act on grievances underlying present-day tensions. It does so by presenting four praxis dimensions of combined inquiry and action—dimensions I call the four "Rs."[9] The first dimension is *recognition*. It asks racial group members to recognize and empathize with the anger and hope of those wounded; to acknowledge the disabling social constraints imposed by one group on another and the resulting group wounds; to identify related justice grievances often underlying current group conflict; and to critically examine stock stories of racial group attributes and interracial relations ostensibly legitimating those constraints and grievances. The second dimension is *responsibility*. It suggests that amid struggles over identity and power, racial groups can be simultaneously subordinated in some relationships and subordinating in others. In some situations, a group's power is both enlivened and constrained by specific social and economic conditions and political alignments. Responsibility therefore asks racial groups to assess carefully the dynamics of group agency for imposing disabling constraints on others and, when appropriate, to accept group responsibility for healing the resulting wounds.

The third dimension is *reconstruction*. It entails active steps (performance) toward healing the social and psychological wounds resulting from disabling group constraints. Those steps might include apologies by the aggressors and, when appropriate, forgiveness by those injured and a joint reframing of stories of group identities and intergroup relations. The fourth dimension, closely related to the third, is *reparation*. It seeks to repair the damage to the material conditions of racial group life in order to attenuate one group's power over another. This means material changes in the structure of the relationship (social, economic, political) to guard against "cheap reconciliation," in which healing efforts are "just talk." Although framed here in terms of communities of color, the four "R" dimensions may also aid in rebuilding relationships within a racial group as well as between white and nonwhite Americans.

These dimensions of interracial justice are described here, and developed in part 3, as separate (albeit related) analytical categories. Cast in this manner, the descriptions lack the dynamism, the feel, the intensity of real-world reconciliatory efforts. Interracial justice contributes to reconciliation in ways that exceed the sum of its analytical parts. Indeed, each of the varying disciplines sketched in chapter 7 reaches beyond analytical categories for an enlivening idea to better capture the overall tumultuous, energized feel of actual intergroup healing experiences. Those disciplines speak of "spiritual transformation," "catharsis," "reconstituting community," *ubuntu* (Zulu for community restoration), and *pono* (Hawaiian for righteousness).

In its broadest sense, interracial justice embraces what the disciplines describe through these ideas—the kind of recognition and redress of deep grievances that sparks a joint transformation in consciousness, diminishes enmities, and forges new relational bonds. Restorative justice. Because interracial justice is about reestablishing relationships, about reconstituting a type of community, it requires something special from racial group members—their commitment both to act in their group's self-interest and to transcend it. Because of this required commitment, I use here the descriptive term *reconciliation* (with its connotation of transformation) rather than *conciliation* (which suggests dispute resolution).

The specific dimensions of interracial justice inquiry, the analytical categories, the bits and pieces, are best viewed as interactive parts of a larger "complex process of 'unlocking' painful bondage, of mutual liberation"—a mutual liberation that "frees the future from the haunting legacies of the [distant and recent] past."[10] It is this larger complex process that links interracial justice to intergroup healing and connects healing to reconciliation and new alliances.

It is also this "unlocking" process that points to a way through the dilemma of history—how, in struggling to form alliances, racial communities can recall the pain of historical grievance while releasing its present-day grip. On the one hand, in light of the historical legacy of white supremacy in the United States and the current conflicts among communities of color rooted partially in perceptions of past grievance, a "never forget" view of history pays appropriate attention to power and domination in race relations. This aspect of intergroup history illuminates societal connections of race, power, and privilege and links history with groups' current socioeconomic conditions and psychological outlooks. The attention to power and pain responds to those who want to deny the present effects of group history, who want to say, "I personally never enslaved or interned anyone or destroyed sovereign native nations; the past is past, let's just forget it."

On the other hand, a never-forget approach to intergroup history can bolster the destructive side of identity politics by separating communities unnecessarily. Racial groups sometimes frame identities around historical harms, clinging to collective memories of ancestral wrongs, and thereby poison reconciliatory possibilities. History, at worst, can create permanent victim group status and ostensibly justify the oppression of others.

Interracial justice inquiry offers racial groups a critical pragmatic approach to recalling the pain while releasing it, to dealing with collective memory while moving toward a more peaceable, productive future. It suggests that only then can groups begin to unlock—to let go of perpetrator and victim identities, to move beyond both the destructive side of identity politics and wishful neoconservative individualism, to affirm the salience of group identity in American life while embracing broader bases of community action.

## Who Should Be Interested?

Who should be interested in grappling with interracial justice in this fashion? Certainly, members of racial groups whose daily efforts to forge alliances and build coalitions are often undermined by simmering and sometimes smoldering justice grievances—those in a conflictual relationship who desire to move beyond those grievances toward productive working and living relationships. (This, by definition, excludes from the interracial justice realm those who want not to move on but to perpetuate oppression by preserving power and privilege, thus engendering resistance rather than rapprochement). In addition, race scholars, public policymakers, judges, civil rights lawyers, clergy, teachers, social workers, community leaders, and dispute resolution practitioners of all races—those struggling to heal racial wounds at a time when many in post–civil rights America are "retreating from racial justice."[11]

These people, I suggest, should be interested in an interracial justice praxis for several reasons in addition to those already mentioned. First and specifically, interracial justice provides practical points of inquiry—recognition, responsibility, reconstruction, and reparation—for both assessing and guiding specific interracial healing efforts. It helps assess an Asian American church's controversial resolution of apology to Native Hawaiians and guide an ongoing denominational process of racial reparations. It helps evaluate Cuban American and Haitian struggles in Miami and the Latino and Asian American contractors' discrimination suit against African Americans for exclusionary city contracting practices in Oakland. It also aids in a deeper understanding of international racial conflicts and healing efforts: for example, South Africa's Truth and Reconciliation Commission's conciliatory approach to apartheid human rights abuses, including black-on-black harms inflicted by apartheid resisters.

Especially in light of the worldwide trend of race apologies, a workable framework for the assessment of particulars is crucial because even though some healing efforts are genuine, others are specious; some are well conceived, but others are a mishmash; and some point toward rebuilding while others signal deepening divisions.

Second, at a general level, interracial justice inquiry opens a window into the complex dynamics of interracial conflict and healing. Drawing on diverse scholarly disciplines, it offers insight into the relational dynamics of African Americans and Chicanos, Cuban Americans and Haitian immigrants, and Asian Americans and Native Hawaiians by wrestling with larger, often ignored, social and jurisprudential questions about intergroup grievance and reconciliation. It examines (1) in what ways unstated intergroup justice grievances underlie day-to-day conflicts; (2) how the traditional white-black, civil rights framing of racial justice misconceives interracial grievances; (3) how, in attempting to assess interracial harms and redress grievances in post–civil rights America, racial communities can reclaim from neoconservatives ideas of group agency and responsibility; and (4) under what conditions apologies, reparations, and forgiveness interact to transform consciousness and forge new relationships.

These levels, the particular and the general, which suggest wide-ranging interests in intergroup reconciliation, form the broad terrain of interracial justice. In this book I map that terrain and highlight its implications. The landscape, as I see it, is vast, rough, and largely uncharted. Although religious scholars are rekindling general interest in reconciliation and others are struggling with white-black healing, no body of work tackles the subject of this book—a multidisciplinary, praxis approach to conflict and reconciliation among communities of color in post–civil rights America. My mapping covers a lot of ground and, at times, necessarily generalizes broadly, overlooks nuance, and raises more questions than it answers. This is intentional. I make no claim to expertise in many of the areas I explore. Rather, I take this approach because of the real-world urgency of the subject and because there is no similar multidisciplinary mapping to guide present-day interracial justice practitioners and future racial justice cartographers. By providing concepts and language, by working with both theory and concrete stories, by embracing praxis, I hope to aid frontline justice practice and stimulate further scholarly exploration.

## Mapping the Terrain

To chart the contours of interracial justice, this book is divided into three parts. In part 1, chapter 1 describes intensifying conflicts among U.S. racial communities in local politics, business, education, and immigration and examines ways in which those conflicts sometimes erupt into legal disputes framed in civil rights terms. The chapter also identifies the often vaguely articulated intergroup justice grievances of exclusion and subjugation undergirding many of those immediate, face-to-face conflicts. It looks at how those grievances exacerbate specific conflicts and sometimes inflate localized disputes into larger racialized controversies.

Chapter 2 locates both those grievances and racial groups' colliding impulses of distrust and alliance forging in an exploding national and international trend of race apologies. This trend reflects the sometimes meaningful, but sometimes fatuous, phenomenon of perpetrator groups (or individuals) apologizing for historical or contemporary racial harms. The trend encompasses everything from the Florida legislature's reparations for African American victims of the murder and mayhem in the town of Rosewood to the South African National Party's tepid apology for racial abuses during apartheid. Chapter 3 provides an in-depth look at one such apology in its social and historical setting—the Asian American churches and United Church of Christ's apology to and reparations for Native Hawaiians for their participation in the cultural and economic oppression of Hawai'i's indigenous people.

Part 2 explains concepts of race, culture, and responsibility—concepts I use in the final part to explain interracial justice. Chapter 4 refines my use of race, culture, and grievance. It explores how ideas about culture often are intertwined practically with understandings of race but are separated conceptually (and legally) from race in contemporary discussions about discrimination, and why the concept of systemic oppression, although controversial, explains many interracial grievances.

Chapter 5 develops the dynamics of group power crucial to an understanding of interracial justice. These dynamics, framed in terms of agency and responsibility, are particularly important in locales across the United States where some groups seek to preserve the prevailing societal order and others seek to "dismantl[e] . . . a system in which one culture dom-

inates another . . . [and] to provide for a new order that does not reproduce the social structure of the old system."[12] The chapter posits that
amid social structural shifts, racial groups may be, in varying ways, simultaneously privileged and oppressed, empowered and disempowered,
uplifting and subordinating. This means understanding the continuing
impact of America's legacy of white racism. It also means understanding
the ways in which nonwhite racial groups contribute to and are responsible for the construction of their own identities and sometimes harmful,
sometimes affirmatively transforming intergroup relations.

Chapter 6 concludes part 2 with the praxis methodology mentioned
earlier—grounding justice at the juncture of progressive race theory and
antisubordination practice. This race praxis has several implications for
interracial justice—that legal justice for racial minorities (in the form of
black-white antidiscrimination law) is increasingly limited in post–civil
rights America; that justice is rooted in concrete racial struggles rather
than abstract arguments; and that justice claims, including those aired in
court, can be viewed as part of a larger process of cultural performance.

Part 3 is the book's center. Chapter 7 sketches multidisciplinary approaches to intergroup healing. It starts with law and critiques its potential
and limitations in terms of individual and group healing. It then broadly
examines the disciplines of theology, social psychology, ethics, peace studies, and indigenous healing practices and identifies points of commonality.
Those points of commonality address intergroup dynamics for "unlocking
painful bondage"—for mutual liberation that helps build relationships.

Chapter 8 offers a praxis approach to interracial justice. Drawing on
multidisciplinary common points, it translates theory and racial community experiences into the practical framework for interracial justice
inquiry and assessment described earlier. This chapter develops that
framework through a detailed description of and theoretical support for
the four "R" dimensions. Most important, it employs those analytic categories collectively to describe the dynamics of and practical possibilities for intergroup reconciliation—linking grievance, redress, material
change, and forgiveness to mutual liberation, to transcending the dilemmas of history.

The next three chapters use these praxis dimensions to help assess three
concrete interracial justice controversies. Chapter 9 continues the story

recited in chapter 3, updating and critiquing the Asian American churches/United Church of Christ apology to and reparations for Native Hawaiians. The chapter looks into the intricacies of an actual group-to-group apology based on historical grievances and pain across many generations. It explores ways in which a group's reparatory efforts may have a salutary effect on one relationship (in the church polity) and a chafing effect on another (the church and the larger Hawaiian community).

Chapter 10 addresses a local controversy with far-reaching impacts, between a Korean American hat store merchant and African American political and religious organizations in Los Angeles. Interracial justice inquiry reveals that unlike the United Church of Christ/Native Hawaiian situation, this controversy started with relatively confined individual-to-individual interactions that, owing largely to smoldering intergroup grievances, escalated into full-blown interracial conflagration. Asking questions about recognition, responsibility, and reconstruction, the chapter dissects the apparent failure of reconciliatory efforts that concentrated mainly on the resolution of the interpersonal dispute and not on the dynamics of interracial healing.

The final chapter explores an ongoing formalized nonlegal process of reconciliation beyond U.S. borders—the South African Truth and Reconciliation Commission's highly praised yet controversial postapartheid handling of human rights abuses. The chapter employs all dimensions of interracial justice inquiry to assess the difficulty, potential, and risk of a process of storytelling, confession, amnesty, and limited reparations, a process designed to repair a nation's psyche through reconciliation between whites and blacks and also among blacks.

## Perspective

I close this introduction with some comments on the perspective of this book. In advancing my ideas about interracial justice, I acknowledge the possibility, or even likelihood, of their mischaracterization. The many anti–affirmative action initiatives in the Congress, courts, and voting booths offer opportunities, as do popular discussions, to blame racial minorities for all their ills as well as many of society's economic and racial problems. And flat-out racial animus still exists. Senator Daniel Akaka from Hawaiʻi delivered the opening address to the 1997 Senate investigation into foreign political campaign contributions. Significantly, he did so shortly after President Bill Clinton's call for a reasoned national dialogue on race. Akaka, who described himself as an American of Chinese and Hawaiian ancestry, first recalled the United States' history of racism against Asian Americans and America's indigenous peoples. In carefully measured words, he then expressed his worry about the public's failure to distinguish between Asian nationals and Asian Pacific Americans and cautioned against anti–Asian American bashing. The virulence, swiftness, and volume of reaction to his speech, some of it denying America's racist history and disparaging Asian Americans, was both startling and telling. The United States remains a scary place for racial minorities speaking thoughtfully and openly about race.

With this backdrop, an exploration of interracial justice as a basis for alliance forging that examines how racial groups sometimes harm one another can easily be yanked out of context. First, such a discussion can be mischaracterized to overstate the extent of racial group agency and therefore to blame racial communities for all their own and one another's social and economic difficulties. "It's all their fault. If the problems persist, it is because of their cultural values and practices and their inability to get along." I have anticipated this possible mischaracterization in chapter 5 by describing racial group agency as "constrained" by the dominant rhetorical, institutional, and economic powers. The limited "power over" one another that racial groups sometimes exercise in damaging ways does not begin to approach the breadth, depth, and duration of historical white domination in the United States.

Second, and related, a discussion of interracial conflicts can be misused to absolve whites of responsibility for the continuing systemic subordination of racial minorities and to recast whites as the primary victims of racism. I have addressed this by acknowledging the continuing influence of white racism in shaping interminority conflicts while nevertheless centering the discussion on interracial dynamics.

Finally, an exploration of interracial grievances, even as a predicate to intergroup healing, can be misused simply to sensationalize divisions among racial groups, to mis-imply pathology in all interracial interactions.

I have addressed this possibility by locating that exploration in liberatory and reconciliatory efforts to build coalitions and forge alliances.

Despite these attempts to anticipate possible mischaracterization and misuse, the risk persists. Nonetheless, I have addressed agency and responsibility in interracial relations with a mix of skepticism and hope, because the time is now for communities of color to face ourselves and one another. In this spirit I look closely at Asian Americans, a group often ignored in race discussions, the group with which I am most familiar.

Facing ourselves and one another does not mean forgoing good relations with the many white Americans of goodwill or abandoning struggles against those of ill will. That work remains important. Rather, it means that the time has come to grapple with issues of interracial grievance and reconciliation if we are to live together peaceably and work together politically as part of the American polity in the coming millennium.

# Part 1

# How, Then, Can We Deal with Our Grievances?

[By] candidly confronting the past, expressing genuine regret, carefully appraising the present in light of the past, agreeing to repair that which can be repaired, accepting joint responsibility for the future, and refusing to be derailed by setbacks and short-term failure.

— H A R L O N  L  D A L T O N ,
*Racial Healing: Confronting the Fear between*
*Blacks and Whites,* p. 100

# "Can We All Get Along?"

Justice Grievances among Communities of Color

Despite being linked to each other, we remain hostile strangers.

— J O H N   P O W E L L ,
"Talking Race," *Hungry Mind Review*,
Fall 1994, p. 15

[Asian American settlers are] either ignorant of, or hostile to
understanding, Hawaiian history and present-day Hawaiian claims.

— H A U N A N I - K A Y   T R A S K ,
"Coalition Building between Natives and
Non-Natives," 43 *Stan. L. Rev.* 1197, 1205 (1991)

Can we all get along?

— R O D N E Y   K I N G

John Powell observes racial groups in the United States linked as "hostile
strangers." Haunani-Kay Trask charges immigrant racial groups with ignorance of or hostility toward indigenous peoples' current legal and political self-determination claims. During the violent clash among African
Americans, Korean Americans, and Latina/o Americans in 1992, Rodney

King pleads for all to "get along." These statements by Powell, Trask, and King raise broad concerns about conflictual relations among nonwhite racial communities, and they also pose a pointed question about reconciliatory possibilities: How, in theory and practice, can these communities address interracial grievances to enhance the prospects of living together peaceably and working together politically?

Discussion about coalition building in the 1990s has been limited. Broadly summarized, most of the discussion identifies "factors" contributing to intergroup conflict (changing racial demographics, rapid immigration, shrinking economy, cutbacks in government services) and to the formation of multiracial coalitions (ideology, interests, leadership). It then examines cultural patterns or the political and economic interests of specific racial groups and searches for "common ground."[1] Most often, this common ground is framed generally in terms of similar histories of resistance against white oppression and continuing struggles to overcome poverty, racism, and political disenfranchisement.[2]

By situating cultural patterns and group interests in predominantly white-dominated social and economic structures, this discussion provides important insights.[3] It also tends, however, to present whiteness as the singular agent of nonwhite conflict and to strip nonwhite racial communities of power over—and therefore responsibility for—interracial conflict and conciliation. By focusing on common goals, much of the discussion emphasizes joint political and economic undertakings and overlooks sometimes long-standing grievances among communities of color that often exacerbate immediate, face-to-face conflicts and undermine coalitional ties. In doing so, it misses the social and psychological dynamics of group wounds and healing and, I submit, the significance of those dynamics to the construction of intergroup alliances.[4] While white influence and common ground are relevant to all interracial relations, the near void of scholarly attention to justice grievances among communities of color informing intergroup wounds and daily conflicts obscures a key aspect of coalition building—interracial justice.

Justice among communities of color is important because intergroup alliances frequently founder on the shoals of racial grievance. Relationships sometimes splinter not for lack of common goals, not from chafing cultural behaviors. Rather, they break apart because of deeply felt but often vaguely articulated grievances each group harbors against the other. These grievances are rooted in collective perceptions, or memories, of how one's own group has been wronged by the other, either directly or with other groups. These often covertly communicated justice grievances shape, or at least exacerbate, the wary and sometimes caustic tenor of many coalitional interactions.

What kinds of conflicts and justice grievances am I talking about? And what are the contours of the near void in scholarly attention?

## Interracial Conflicts and Underlying Grievances

Concerning conflicts in local electoral politics, think about the struggles for seats on city councils and school boards in Chicago, Los Angeles, Oakland, New York, Miami, Dallas, and Houston, cities with substantial nonblack communities of color. One journalist described the increasing Latina/o and Asian populations in those cities as "imperiling black political power and confounding notions of a [national] rainbow coalition."[5] Is this comment (and other comments recited later) mere hyperbole or, more insidiously, an example of the white-controlled media creating conflict among nonwhite groups? Perhaps. But perhaps not.

Consider reported statements by those engaged in local electoral struggles. African Americans, says a recently defeated black city councilperson, have been on the forefront of struggle for multiculturalism and have welcomed other racial minorities, but these other communities "are just looking out for themselves." Says another, "It's our [black] community that has been devastated in order to advance the cause of environmentalists, women, Asians and Hispanics." And even more pointedly, a leader of the Dallas NAACP reportedly depicts Latinas/os as "vultures" who "feast on the results of our efforts."

An officer of a statewide Democratic Latina/o organization counters that "African Americans are very intimidated" by increasing numbers of Latinas/os and links Latina/o grievances against blacks to a cultural explanation of African American anxiety—the "thief judges by his own standards." African Americans "perceive that if a Hispanic is employed as superintendent [of schools] they will be left out or not treated fairly. ... There is a saying in Spanish: 'El ladron juzga por su condicion,' 'The thief judges by his own standards.' They have excluded us, and they think we will exclude them.'"[6] Feeding this interracial fire with a contorted image of southern racial apartheid, a white city councilperson representing a new, largely Asian American district in Oakland, reportedly commented, "I don't want to overstate this, . . . but it's as if African-Americans now are the ones standing in the schoolhouse door."

Concerning conflicts surrounding state ballot initiatives, think about the passage of California's anti-immigrant Proposition 187 and the nearly 50 percent support by African Americans and established Asian Americans, including many worried about Latina/o and South Asian immigrants displacing current workers and draining government resources. Was that vote connected to the substantial early Asian American support (which later turned sharply) for the anti–affirmative action California Civil Rights Initiative, Proposition 209? And what about the lukewarm African American opposition to Arizona's English Only initiative (which mainly affected Latinas/os)?

Concerning conflicts in university politics, think about a student's experiences as a co-organizer of a coalition of Latina/o, African American, Native American, and Asian American groups. The coalition formed enthusiastically to combat a university administration's plan to consolidate separate ethnic studies programs under a broad comparative studies umbrella. The plan, if implemented, would deprive each program of its unique identity and force the groups to compete for diminished funding. Despite a common goal and a common foe, the multiracial coalition was marked by dissension among its leaders. The student organizer watched the smallest disagreements escalate into sharp exchanges. She was shocked, she said, at the extent of the distrust—even though many in the coalition had never worked together previously. The distrust divided along racial group lines, and some of it also appeared gendered. "Why," she asked, "are we so angry with each other," and "why are we letting that anger move us off our target?" The questions resonated but yielded no clear answers.

Concerning conflicts in business, think about the complaint that Asian Americans are promoted to and kept in low management positions so they can do the firing of African Americans and Latinas/os, thereby immunizing their white employers from Title VII suits. After all, how can one racial minority illegally discriminate against another?[7] Think also about Cuban Americans in Miami and their tensions with not only blacks but also Haitian, Nicaraguan, and El Salvadoran immigrants. These latter groups sometimes complain about being shut out of local business opportunities by financially secure, politically conservative Cuban communities.[8] And think about Native Hawaiians' claims to water diverted for one hundred years by white-controlled agribusiness decimating Hawaiian agricultural communities, claims of continued subordination not only by Western capitalists but also by nonwhite racial groups who ignore the historical origins of indigenous claims of self-determination and self-development.

Some of these interracial conflicts are addressed in face-to-face interactions. Others smolder, either attended to poorly or ignored entirely. And the wounds ache. Some of those aches erupt in court, with one community of color asserting claims of illegal discrimination against another.

An example is the complicated Lowell High School lawsuit in San Francisco.[9] Chinese Americans are suing to invalidate San Francisco's court-ordered desegregation program for public high schools. The desegregation order was entered fifteen years ago in a suit by the NAACP charging educational discrimination by whites. The Chinese American plaintiffs are now seeking to exceed their current enrollment allotment, claiming denial of equal protection of the law and arguing the educational inferiority of African Americans and Latinas/os (and, to a lesser extent, whites and other Asian Americans). Given the volatile history of discrimination against Chinese in California, the continued socioeconomic subordination of many blacks, and the rising numbers of struggling Latina/o and Asian immigrants, where and with whom do the justice claims lie?

Another example is the recent federal court suit by Latina/o and Asian American groups to invalidate Oakland's affirmative action program in city contracting. The Hispanic Contractors Association, the Hispanic Chamber of Commerce, and the East Bay chapter of the Organization of Chinese Americans claim unconstitutional favoritism of African Americans. The plaintiffs' attorney describes the "present [black and white patronage] system" as "corrupt." A Latino politician charges that "there has not been any attempt by this city to improve the representation of Latinos and Asian and Native Americans in top management and at every level," and a leader of a Latina/o city employees association observes, "All the time I've been here I've had to work against discrimination, not by whites but by blacks."[10] The NAACP's response is "we can't have the have-nots fight the have-nots." Other African Americans decry the suit as an ill-advised power play by Latina/o and Asian American politicians. The slashing rhetoric of this lawsuit, awkwardly cast in traditional white-black civil rights language, played out against a recent volatile suit by Latinas/os against the Chicago Housing Authority on the grounds that the 90 percent black and 2 percent Latina/o tenant breakdown reflected impermissible discrimination.

My brief descriptions of interracial conflicts in local elections, state initiatives, university politics, business, and the courts barely scratch the surface of interracial dynamics. At first glance, the situations in which the conflicts arise appear widely varied in terms of place, groups, and claims. The intensity of many of the encounters among group members also rivets attention on the unique particulars of each controversy.

On closer inspection, however, the various conflicts bear common markings. The interracial conflicts are set within continuing white dominance in many spheres of social and economic life. Equally important, each of the specific conflicts—over discriminatory hiring, affirmative action, owner-customer interactions—appears to be undergirded by largely unacknowledged interracial justice grievances. Those grievances are often based on one group's perceptions of the other's exercise of power to exclude or subordinate. The grievances gain explosive strength from collective memories (the melange of observations, rumors, media images, and intergenerational stories) that link current perceptions of interracial exclusion or subjugation to the deep pain of historical memories of disenfranchisement by whites.

For some African Americans, therefore, contemporary justice grievances emerge from the perceptions of Asian Americans and many Latinas/os as latecomers aligning themselves with whites and appropriating civil rights strategies, pioneered by African Americans at great cost, to leapfrog over blacks socially and economically without concern for continuing black subordination. These grievances intensify because they recall the agonies of African American subjugation in the American polity—in which enslavement meant nonhuman, black meant noncitizen, Jim Crow meant separate and unequal, and civil rights struggles for social and economic gains for all racial communities meant black blood on the streets.

For some Asian Americans and Latinas/os, contemporary grievances emerge from vaguely articulated perceptions of African Americans squandering moral capital (accrued as a result of slavery), relying on special privileges detrimental to other racial minorities (limited affirmative action), or scapegoating more vulnerable minorities rather than addressing the root sources of black frustration. These grievances also come from images of African Americans who, after acquiring some local political clout, use their new power to exclude Latinas/os and Asian Americans from local economic and political participation. The grievances grate because in differing ways they recall the historical exclusion of Asians and Mexicans from the polity by means of the Chinese Exclusion and Greaser Acts, naturalized citizenship prohibitions, landownership and voting restrictions; the internment of Japanese Americans; English Only; and glass ceilings in business; and the stigmatizing of all as "foreign" (or, worse, foreign and illegal).

These kinds of justice grievances, heightened and twisted by collective memories and often operating largely unacknowledged just beneath the public surface, transform specific disputes between racial group members into interracial controversies. Conflicts between individuals devolve into struggles between groups. To understand the power and complexity of this dynamic, consider again the Lowell High School lawsuit concerning public school admissions. Brian Ho, Patrick Wong, and Hilary Chen, plaintiffs in *Ho v. San Francisco Unified School District*, represent "all [sixteen thousand] children of Chinese descent" eligible for San Francisco's public schools.[11] Their high-profile suit challenges the validity of a 1983 judicial consent decree desegregating San Francisco's schools. Approved in response to an NAACP class action charging educational discrimination by whites, the consent decree mandates racial and ethnic diversity in student bodies and sets for each "magnet" school a 40 percent cap for students from any racial or ethnic group. Early on, Chinese Americans benefited from the decree's diversity mandate, substantially increasing their enrollments.[12]

The Chinese American plaintiffs now seek to exceed the 40 percent cap, claiming that the cap constitutes unconstitutional race preferences for those less qualified, particularly African Americans and Latinas/os. Discrimination is demonstrated, the plaintiffs allege, by not admitting some Chinese American students to magnet schools, even though their entrance test scores are higher than those of some students of other races who are admitted. The plaintiffs observe that this form of exclusion is consistent with California's history of harsh discrimination against Chinese Americans.[13] Using ideas refined by neoconservative race scholars, their attorneys frame the suit in terms of individual rights, advance legal arguments of "meritocracy" and "color blindness" and seek to enjoin the school district "from operating under its system of racial classifications and quotas."[14] Some Chinese American supporters express more directly their perceptions of underlying racial-cultural differences: formal racism in the system has ended; Chinese Americans have elevated themselves as a group through ability and cultural values despite hardship; and African Americans have had the benefit of the decree for ten years, "and black student performance is still bad."[15] Chinese American educational superiority (measured by test scores), some plaintiffs and their supporters imply, at least partially reflects the cultural, if not the intellectual, inferiority of African Americans and Latinas/os.[16]

The plaintiffs' strategy of distancing Chinese Americans from African Americans is reflected not only in statements of supporters but also in the plaintiffs' legal filings. In those filings, the plaintiffs' attorneys assert that Chinese American students' interests are contrary to the interests of African American students represented by the NAACP and that the NAACP "did not adequately represent" Chinese Americans in the original desegregation action. The attorneys also contend that the defendant NAACP "is a proponent of the status quo, while Plaintiffs consider the Consent Decree a violation of their right to equal protection." The NAACP publicly opposes the suit and serves as the primary defender of the consent decree.[17]

Chinese American political and cultural organizations are sharply divided. Some offer support, recalling caustic discrimination against persons of Chinese ancestry and stressing the value of individual achievement and educational opportunities for Chinese American children. Others voice opposition, finding no evidence of school-choice discrimination against

Chinese American students (Chinese constitute by far the single largest group in magnet schools), questioning the framing of "merit" solely on the basis of an entrance test, and emphasizing continuing systemic impediments to socioeconomic advancement by African Americans, Native Americans, Latinas/os, and other Asian Americans.

Civil rights lawyers, Asian American organizations, and California politicians also diverge in their responses. Those supporting the lawsuit talk about quotas, injustice, and civil rights. A spokesperson for the Asian American Legal Foundation indicated that Chinese Americans "will not stand for injustice and inequality in our community." The lawyer delivering the keynote address at a plaintiffs' fundraiser declared that "we are on the right side of civil rights" and "we say 'never' to racial quotas on children." Legal supporters also talk about merit and racial differences: the NAACP "opposes us, but dropout rates for African American students have never been higher."[18] Unsurprisingly, conservative politicians embrace these positions, arguing affirmative action's harm to Asian Americans as a reason to jettison affirmative action altogether.[19]

Lawyers and community leaders opposing the lawsuit talk about practical consequences. If the plaintiffs succeed, a likely immediate consequence will be more Asian American and white magnet school students and significantly fewer African American and Latina/o students.[20] A likely longer-term consequence may be the legal dismantling of all race-based affirmative action programs in the state. In addition, the law may well affirm in the public mind the image of Asian American superiority and African American and Latina/o inferiority. In light of these probable consequences, a plaintiffs' "victory" may well exacerbate African American and Asian American tensions already heightened by negative stereotypes held by some members of each group about the other, by intergroup economic competition, and by intergroup justice grievances.[21]

Noticeably absent from the litigation strategy and legal and popular discourse is critical inquiry into what appear to be intergroup justice grievances underlying the suit and reactions to it—grievances concerning "barring the door" and squandering moral capital, on the one hand, and misappropriating civil rights strategies and gains, leapfrogging, and complicity, on the other. The anger vocalized behind the scenes about these "real wrongs" perpetuated by the other group is considerable. It is an anger conveyed through whispers in the halls and occasional public sound-bite pronouncements about civil rights. Critical inquiry and a constructive discussion of those grievances, however, are largely missing. Silence envelops key issues concerning the connection between law and racial hierarchy (including Asian Americans' purported role as "middle minority" buffers in the continuing subordination of African Americans), the political construction of notions of meritocracy and color blindness in the affirmative action debate (including the meaning of objectivity and race consciousness), the effects of economic dislocation on student performance, the dissonant understandings of "equality under law" (equality of opportunity, equality of result, and anticaste) and the limitations of the legal process for subordinated communities seeking racial justice (including the general failure of legal norms, methods, and procedures to foster intergroup healing).

Also noticeably missing from the legal filings, oral arguments, and court rulings is critical inquiry into the interminority dynamics at the heart of the case. One aspect of those unstated dynamics is intergroup power. Is affirmative action, as the conservatives argue, "discrimination against Asians in order to protect blacks"—making Asian Americans the "new victims" of racism and African Americans and, to a lesser extent, Latinas/os, the "new perpetrators?"[22] Or is this construction of interracial conflict a mask for continued white supremacy? A second missing aspect is the resort to civil rights law. Is the traditional white-on-black antidiscrimination law scheme workable for multiracial conflicts in post–civil rights America? Will it "do justice"? Is it likely to foster interracial rapprochement or exacerbate tensions? A third unstated element is context. How do the volatile mid-1980s Asian American admissions controversy and the mid-1990s California Civil Rights Initiative and the University of California's repeal of affirmative action further contextualize the African American, Latina/o, and Asian American relationships in the Lowell High controversy?[23]

The absence of critical inquiry into interracial dynamics masks deep concerns underlying *Ho*'s immediate conflict over public school admissions. What kinds of justice grievances, tied to past experiences of exclusion or subjugation, lie beneath the surface of the immediate conflict? Held by whom? Against whom? Based on what collective memories, racialized images, and current power struggles? Ostensibly legitimating what beliefs and actions? And what practical consequences flow from lack of critical attention to these grievances?[24]

I shall pause here in my description of interracial grievances. So far, I have tried to illuminate the underpinnings of racialized conflicts in local politics, universities, small businesses, state electoral initiatives, and lawsuits. In chapter 3, as an example, I discuss Native Hawaiians' interracial justice grievances and Asian American churches' confession of situational complicity in the oppression of Hawai'i's indigenous peoples. These descriptions paint an incomplete picture, of course, of the tenor and content of complex, varying African American, Asian American, Latina/o, and indigenous American interactions throughout the United States. They also do not depict the differing histories of subordination of and resistance by these groups. Broad descriptions are nevertheless appropriate because these justice grievances are the basis for many current conflicts in borderland sites characterized by shifting racial and economic demographics. Often broadly framed and informally articulated, they help shape a racial group's perceptions of the "other."

In these borderlands, characterized also by conflict and conciliatory efforts, crucial questions arise about interracial reconciliation: How do racial groups theorize about and act on both articulated and subconsciously held justice grievances often at the heart of intergroup distrust and conflict? How do communities of color comprehend the notion of racial group complicity in the subordination of other groups, of situational racial group deployment of oppressive social structures? How do scholars and justice practitioners rethink the binary white-over-black civil rights paradigm that dominates our vision of racial justice in order to promote healing among nonwhite racial groups? Looking backward, how do we assess past efforts to redress justice grievances and heal intergroup wounds? Looking forward, how do we contemplate and undertake future interracial healing efforts?

## The Interracial Justice (Near) Void

These questions stump most race scholars as well as people working to achieve racial justice in the streets, schools, community halls, courts, and city councils. We are stumped not only because we lack the "knowledge and wisdom" but also because we lack the concepts, the methods, and the language. Coalition-building scholarship following the 1992 televised African American–Korean American tensions in Los Angeles was, for the most part, limited in focus, not theoretical, and not integrated with other works. While valuable for the interactions chronicled, it did not generate sustained inquiry into multiracial coalitional theory. Legal scholarship during this period explored some of the legal facets of multiracial conflicts. As observed later in this chapter, although sometimes insightful, that scholarship had an "all over the place" feel to it. Most important, it generated relatively little follow-through. Social science studies, also discussed later, offered broad socioeconomic explanations for interminority conflict, but they did not address concrete possibilities for intergroup reconciliation.

In recent years, religious scholars have continued to develop analytical and philosophical frameworks for interreligious and interethnic healing—a theology of reconciliation for social groups. Notable works include John Dawson's *Healing America's Wounds*, Geiko Muller-Fahrenholz's *The Art of Forgiveness*, Donald Shriver's *An Ethic for Enemies*, Robert Shreiter's *Reconciliation: Mission and Ministry in a Changing Social Order*, and Gregory Baum and Harold Wells's *The Reconciliation of Peoples*.[25] For many racial communities in the United States, however, these often penetrating works are narrowly focused. Their sources of authority and inspiration tend to be uni-disciplinary—the Judeo Christian Scriptures—and the locus of healing activity for many of the works is the religious polity. Most situations examined (except for Dawson's and Shriver's books) lie beyond the United States' borders and involved horrific human rights abuses (such as the Holocaust). In addition, most of the relationships scrutinized involved white perpetrators directly supported by the government. None of the works deals with the complexities of color-on-color tensions in the United States. None deals with the overlay of civil rights law and discourse. Although they provide valuable insights—insights I later draw on selectively in fashioning dimensions of interracial justice inquiry—these works do not address the colliding racial realities identified earlier: interracial conflict and reconciliation in post–civil rights America.[26]

The near void in this arena is perhaps best revealed in two justice realms seemingly well suited to addressing grievances among nonwhite racial communities—cross-cultural dispute resolution (process) and civil rights law (substantive norms). Neither realm reflects justice scholars' or practitioners' development of the methodological and normative dimensions of interracial justice.

## Multicultural Dispute Resolution: An Emphasis on Technique

Following the Rodney King police trial firestorm in Los Angeles, cross-cultural dispute resolution centers quickly opened. Reflecting a coalescence of two burgeoning movements—alternative (to litigation) dispute resolution and multiculturalism—these centers produced useful process manuals and trained lay mediators and, when asked, helped resolve specific disputes.[27] They continue to do so. Skilled, trained, and committed mediators adjust standard conflict resolution techniques to account for cultural differences in an attempt to end often heated and sometimes destructive interactions between members of different racial groups. The operating premise of these professionals is that people in conflict are agents whose communications are sometimes impeded by cultural differences but who, aided by sensitive mediators, can become autonomous problem solvers. Mediators thus aim to make a process workable, not to render substantive judgments, but to enable the disputants themselves to bring closure to immediate conflicts.

The scholarship on multicultural dispute resolution follows the same general path, sensitizing practitioners to the need for culturally tailored methods of nonlegal dispute resolution. This scholarship also analyzes the cultural dispute-handling traits of different groups to guide practitioners in future efforts.[28]

Mediation practitioner and professor of ministry Virstan Choy illustrates the importance of this cultural sensitivity in his "alternative approach to conflict management."[29] He describes a church congregation of Asian American members to expose the problem of unstated dominant cultural norms. A lay church leader invited staff from the denomination's regional office to help the church deal with conflicts among its members. In his meeting with the congregation, the staff person employed the same conflict resolution techniques he employed with other churches in the region. He stressed "openness in communication" and the importance of airing grievances publicly, and he encouraged "face-to-face" "open confrontation" among church members. To frame the conflicts, he asked church members to present their "sides" of the problems. He then offered a "power analysis" of the congregation and presented his "findings": skewed power in favor of older members and long-lingering disagreements. The staff member closed the meeting by observing that the congregation was dysfunctional and in need of change, presented a list of recommended changes, and identified the positive results of the face-to-face confrontation technique.

Choy also describes how the staff member completely missed the culturally formed relational dynamics in the Asian American church, including the "continuous awareness of one's networks of relationships; recognition of the importance of 'face' (public self-image) for those with whom one is in relationship; and fulfillment of the obligations involved in maintaining one's relationships." As a result of this cultural blindness, on the day after the meeting, many of the members announced their decision to leave the church. Choy's depiction highlights the manner in which the handling of conflicts between specific groups in concrete settings is culturally influenced. The confrontational techniques of dispute resolution preferred by some—with their emphasis on direct interaction, assertiveness in making demands, give-and-take negotiation, and compromise—are just that: preferred techniques potentially suited to certain cultural settings but not others.

By emphasizing culturally appropriate techniques, multicultural dispute resolution scholarship and practice sometimes helps those attempting to resolve specific disputes. By its own choosing, however, this scholarship and practice is limited. By defining its role in terms of "neutral" facilitation, it does not stress the critical sociolegal analysis of underlying grievances or target social structural change. In most instances, it does not offer, nor does it claim to offer, tools to the participants for a substantive critique of social structures and ideology. Operating in the realm of "pure process," it does not seek to advance understandings of deeper intergroup grievances or the dynamics of sustained intergroup healing. For these reasons, genuine reconciliation must not be equated with the practice of conflict resolution. "Conflict resolution is a useful administrative skill

... that enables a practitioner to gather the conflicting parties ... and lead them along carefully planned steps into ... an agreement. The ethics involved in this process remains utilitarian. ... Conflict resolution does not involve conversion and forgiveness. ... [It] is not identical with [the process of reconciliation]."[30]

The problem of equating conflict resolution practice with reconciliation is revealed by the "resolution" achieved through rapper Ice Cube's apology to Korean Americans for his rap "Black Korea." In his rap Ice Cube demanded that Korean American merchants "Pay respect to the black fist, or we'll burn your store right down to a crisp"—a message presaging one aspect of the South Central Los Angeles rebellion-riot a year later. A boycott against Ice Cube's CDs launched by Korean American political organizations failed, but a subsequent boycott by the Korean Grocers Association (KAGRO) achieved results. KAGRO, composed of several thousand small store owners, refused to sell the malt liquor endorsed by Ice Cube. Searching for common ground, the liquor manufacturer pressured Ice Cube into a halfhearted apology, promised not to use him in future advertisements, and offered to create a youth scholarship fund. Case closed.

The resolution of the immediate conflict, however, left untouched the deeper intergroup grievances. Ice Cube's apology followed on the heels of the wrist-slap sentencing of Korean American store owner Soon Ja Du for her shooting of African American teenager Latasha Harlins—community service and probation, no imprisonment. African Americans reacted angrily to the Ice Cube apology, identifying papered-over African American grievances and what they perceived to be the continuing subordination of blacks, this time by Korean Americans. Sheena Lester wrote an editorial for the *Los Angeles Sentinel* chastising the liquor manufacturer and KAGRO. She described KAGRO members as "poison-pushing merchants, who are apparently more outraged about being called names than they are about a dead Black child." For Julianne Malveaux, a professor and columnist, Ice Cube's apology signaled the continuing systemic oppression of African Americans. "[Ice Cube] is saying what we all feel. Where is the space for us in this economy? Where is there space for us in this society? Can you value my life?"[31] Resolution without careful critical analysis of and action on underlying grievances, by both racial communities, seemed to inflame rather than heal interracial wounds.[32] Resolution hardly meant reconciliation.

### The Traditional Civil Rights Approach: Blindness to Color on Color

In the realm of substantive norms, civil rights law and the principle of equality are generally accorded center stage. The problem for racial minorities, however, is this: The traditional civil rights approach is markedly limited in post–civil rights America. Although of tremendous transformative power in the Bull Conner segregation era of firehoses and attack dogs, it now is sometimes as much hindrance as help to communities of color. This civil rights approach, reflected in antidiscrimination laws, is limited because it embodies increasingly conservative notions of what race is, what constitutes discrimination, and, indeed, whether racial subordination by whites still exists in the United States. Equally important, by focusing on conflicts with whites, the paradigm ignores justice grievances among communities of color—issues of interracial justice.

The prevailing white-black framing of racial justice narrowly conceives race relations at the edge of the new millennium: white over black, majority against minority, perpetrator versus victim.[33] This conception is limiting in two ways. It centers racial inquiry on white-black relations, and its either-or, win-lose framing of racial justice obscures possibilities for interracial healing. The white-black casting of race issues and the win-lose framing of justice disputes miss important complexities and possibilities in multiracial America.

The inadequacy of the white-black framing is revealed in its marginalization of issues of interminority group, or interracial, justice.[34] As part of its antidiscrimination law, the Supreme Court has not addressed meaningfully the dynamics of conflict among racial minorities. Nor has it developed a framework for analyzing interminority justice claims. Similarly, until recently, legal scholars largely have ignored this aspect of racial justice.

Although white-on-black and white-on-color relationships are integral to every discussion of racial justice, color-on-color relationships also are important.

*Sociopolitical Studies.* Social and political scientists, anthropologists, economists, ethnic studies scholars, and peace scholars are pursuing the changing dynamics of intergroup conflicts within and beyond the United States. Emphasizing theory, empirical studies, or both, these scholars examine conflicts among ethnic groups in other countries, particularly "ethnoviolence" in Eastern Europe and the Middle East.[35] They explore intergroup conflicts across national borders, implicating race, culture, and nationality. In the United States, scholars address conflicts between citizens and immigrants tied to racial demographic shifts, economic changes, and nativistic responses. In a context of continuing white dominance, they examine current tensions and reparatory efforts involving America's indigenous peoples and nonwhite groups as well as "group positioning" along a "racialized" hierarchy of Asian Americans, Latinas/os, African Americans, and Native Americans. They also study inner-city African American and Korean American cultural misunderstandings, conflict, and violence—inquiries spurred in the early 1990s by the South Central Los Angeles firestorm, the "Red Apple" African American boycott of Korean merchants in Brooklyn, the Ice Cube rap "Black Korea," and the Soon Ja Du shooting of Latasha Harlins.[36]

These works suggest a range of explanations for interracial conflict. Sociological explanations focus on assimilation (the difficulties experienced by newcomers in terms of a pattern of contact, conflict, accommodation, and, finally, integration) or on socioeconomic dislocation (the involuntary relocation of social groups, particularly African Americans, as a result of Latina/o and Asian immigration and a restructured economy).[37] Economic analyses describe race-class hierarchies with wealthy and middle-class whites at the top; poor African Americans, Native Americans, and recent immigrants at the bottom; and working-class whites and later generations of minority immigrants in the middle. These analyses debate intergroup tensions in terms of labor competition among racial minorities, including split labor markets (the empirical reality of white workers generally aligning most closely with white employers rather than nonwhite workers) and middle minorities (Korean American entrepreneurs serving as a buffer between predominantly white businesses in control of production and distribution and poor inner-city African Americans).[38] Political scientists and ethnic studies scholars advance related power-conflict theories, locating interracial tensions in differing group political and economic power and in the competition for scarce private resources and government entitlements.[39]

Consistent with these broad structural explanations for interminority conflict, the sociopolitical works suggest encompassing social structural changes to minimize conflict—for example, dismantling monopoly capitalism, expediting school integration, or promoting bilingual education. Though helpful for policymakers, these recommendations generally offer little to guide the handling of specific, immediate interracial justice grievances. That is, these broad prescriptions are of limited utility to frontline justice practitioners.

Those in the frontline struggle tend to grab for what is in easy reach—civil rights rhetoric and antidiscrimination law. The problem, however, is that this language and these norms were established in the heat of white-over-black conflict. And as the sociopolitical studies reveal, color on color differs significantly from white on color.[40]

*Antidiscrimination Law.* For this reason, Angela Harris suggests expanding, or reorienting, civil rights law's white-on-black framing of racial justice.

Should these groups [particularly Latinas/os and Asian Americans], more internally diverse than African Americans, nevertheless receive the same legal treatment as African Americans? Should the various subgroups in these "races" be treated identically despite very different material circumstances. . . . [T]he emergence of "other minorities" as a powerful political and cultural force raises the issue of "discrimination" among and between nonwhite groups. To what extent should the law recognize such discrimination, and is it the same as discrimination between whites and nonwhites?[41]

A pending African American employment discrimination suit targeting Asian American managers reveals the complexity of these questions in even "ordinary," minimally publicized, interracial justice settings.

The United Minorities Against Discrimination, an unincorporated community organization, five African Americans, and two Latinos are suing the city and county of San Francisco and its civil service commission.[42] The plaintiffs assert federal and state civil rights claims of discrimination in the hiring and promotion of African American and Latina/o personnel analysts. What distinguishes this suit from many other discrimination suits by racial minorities is that the apparent discriminators and main beneficiaries of the alleged discrimination are not white. They are Chinese Americans. According to the allegations of the complaint, "Black and Hispanic personnel analysts comprised between 29 and 44 percent of the analyst pool," and despite requests for promotion by qualified African Americans and Latinas/os between 1985 and 1990, none was promoted. The complaint also alleges that the defendants failed to follow established hiring and promotion procedures and that "certain supervisors" made "disparaging remarks regarding Blacks and Hispanics" with an intent to discriminate.

Interestingly, the complaint does not state explicitly that Asian Americans, or Chinese Americans, are the primary beneficiaries of the asserted discrimination. In fact, the complaint is silent as to the races of the beneficiaries of the alleged discrimination, saying only that they are "neither Black nor Hispanic." Nevertheless, by listing the names of the "less qualified" applicants who received the positions or promotions, the complaint implicitly racializes its claim. The people identified are predominantly Chinese American—Wong, Wong, Lum, Gee, and (Mei-Long) Sam. One is Korean American (Ko), and two appear to be white (Heurlin and McAllister). The complaint also does not list the names or races of the city's decision makers. Subsequent filings indirectly revealed that key decision makers were white (four) and Chinese American (two) and that the person assigned to conduct an internal investigation of plaintiffs' charges was Chinese American.[43]

Two noteworthy features of the dispute, which are only hinted at in the complaint, emerged in bits and pieces during discovery and briefing on motions. One feature is the interracial dynamics between the Asian American applicants, supervisors, and investigator and the African American and Latina/o applicants. The other feature is the reluctance of the plaintiffs, defendants, and their attorneys to acknowledge, let alone address directly, these dynamics. Neither the plaintiffs' complaint nor the parties' briefs on motions call attention to the interplay of color on color. None of the legal filings questions whether antidiscrimination law, originally constructed to handle white-against-black, majority-versus-minority disputes, needs to be reinterpreted. None of the filings or arguments discusses the legal implications of the apparent racial hierarchy: Chinese American and white managers accused of discriminating against African Americans and Latinas/os in favor of Chinese Americans and whites. None of the filings acknowledges other high-profile San Francisco political-legal disputes, such as the Ho case, involving Chinese Americans, African Americans, and Latinas/os.

Indeed, rather than acknowledging the volatile, socially significant interracial dynamics of the case, the parties' attorneys agreed to "protect" against public disclosure the "racial designations" of the participants in the hiring and promotion process.[44] Under threat of contempt, no one can reveal city records on race matters critical to a full, context-sensitive understanding of the controversy. Thus, by court-approved stipulation, the parties, attorneys, and judge are concealing from public view what for many may be the heart of the case—the African American, Latina/o, Chinese American, and white intergroup dynamics in a specific social-historical setting.

The apparent racial hierarchy and interminority interplay—only hinted at in the case filings and public documents—complicate the plaintiffs' antidiscrimination claims and, in important respects, lift them out of the white-black jurisprudential paradigm. Chinese Americans historically suffered at the hands of whites in San Francisco. In business, housing, and education, the Chinese were denigrated and discriminated against by law and social custom for more than one hundred years after their arrival in the mid-1800s. Even today, Chinese Americans face discriminatory treatment. Recent Chinese immigrants tend to fall below the poverty line and have to struggle to find adequate housing and jobs, particularly in the wake of California's Proposition 187. Young Asian males have been randomly photographed so that mug books can guide Bay Area police in their search for Asian youth gangs. In upscale Marin County, an unemployed white male awoke one morning in 1995 and decided to kill an Asian, any Asian. At a nearby store, he stabbed in the back Chinese American Eddy Wu, the first Asian person he saw. Some middle-class Chinese Americans perceive continuing discrimination not only by whites in terms of glass ceilings and sporadic hate violence but also by African Americans and Latinas/os by means of affirmative action.[45]

Despite past and recent history, many Chinese Americans in San Francisco are financially successful; Chinese American political visibility is rising in the Bay Area; and Asian Americans generally exceed their proportionate numbers at University of California campuses. The newly appointed city chief of police and state supreme court justice are Chinese American, as was the recent chancellor of the University of California at Berkeley.[46] Indeed, some African Americans perceive Asian Americans as a buffer between whites and blacks, as the "racial bourgeoisie"[47] or "middle-man minority" who, by their partially elevated position in the racial hierarchy, undermine black charges of white supremacy while nevertheless preserving white privilege and slowing black advancement. Some mid-level Asian American managers confirm that charge, at least in part, through their complaint that they are used by white superiors as "pacifiers" and "shock absorbers." They perceive that they are directed to fire or make unrealistic demands of lower-level African Americans and Latinas/os while absorbing the flack and insulating their employers from discrimination claims by virtue of their own minority status.

Do these complex interracial dynamics inform the United Minorities' (an ironic name choice) legal justice claims? If so, why do those dynamics remain submerged in the litigation substrata? Why are underlying sociopolitical grievances among Asian Americans, African Americans, and Latinas/os ignored? And why does no one—litigants, attorneys, media—address white racism in the city's institutional bureaucracy? One response to these questions comes in the form of other questions concerning the parties' attorneys. Why have the plaintiffs' attorneys, from a large, established San Francisco firm, limited their efforts to searching for evidence of intentional discrimination? "Because that is what the civil rights law requires" is an apt answer. The focus on "intentional" discrimination, however, misses the important institutionalized aspects of the actual hiring and promotion process. Why have the plaintiffs' attorneys cast the case in the narrow binary white-black antidiscrimination law paradigm? "Because that is how antidiscrimination law is framed." The victim-perpetrator, good-bad, either-or framing of the issues, however, belies the multilayered interminority dynamics of this and related justice controversies.

The volumes of court filings in the suit reveal the limits of legal justice and traditional antisubordination practice: the interracial dynamics that appear to be central to the illumination and handling of the justice claims are nowhere to be seen or heard. How do differing group histories, changing racial-economic demographics, and shifting group positions in a racial hierarchy both complicate and ground analyses of the *United Minorities* controversy? We do not know because no one is talking, and no one is talking, it seems, because no one is inquiring. And no one is inquiring, I suggest, because we have not yet developed suitable foundational concepts and language.

This, then, raises the larger inquiry: What languages do the law and other disciplines employ to account for, or discount, intergroup dynamics? In the realm of intergroup conflict, the language of community leaders is often assertive, even vociferous. Organizers speak to and about people in their communities in language rooted in both concrete particularities and political strategy.[48] Journalists speak to a broader audience, often eagerly reporting on intergroup tensions, sometimes with considerable sophistication.[49] As mentioned, sociopolitical scholars are studying many different aspects of intergroup conflict.

Compared with recent high-profile community and media commentaries and sociopolitical studies, the courts, attorneys, and legal scholars have said little about interracial conflict and justice claims. In the *United Minorities* discrimination suit, for instance, the judge, lawyers and parties refuse to talk about (and legal scholars have not weighed in on) what appears to be the heart of the suit's justice claims: an ostensible racial hierarchy in one part of city government, with whites at the top and African Americans and Latinas/os at the bottom, maintained by complicitous Asian Americans in the middle.

Why the silence? Is it in part because justice claims are usually cast in a traditional civil rights white-black, majority-minority, individual perpetrator–individual victim jurisprudential paradigm? The attorneys and parties clearly cast *United Minorities* within that paradigm.[50] Is the silence also because color on color is rendered inconsequential by the legal irrelevance of color distinctions? U.S. Supreme Court Justice Sandra Day O'Connor implied as much in *Shaw v. Reno*,[51] a case in which the predominantly white North Carolina legislature, at the urging of the U.S. attorney general and according the dictates of the Voting Rights Act, altered the election district lines to create the state's second black-majority voting district. Writing for the majority, O'Connor observed that all government racial classifications should be treated in the same skeptical legal fashion, regardless of whether a classification is designed to end a white-controlled racial caste system or to perpetuate it.[52] O'Connor implied that races are fungible under the law, that all racial categories should be treated as interchangeable. "Racial classifications of any sort pose the risk of lasting harm to our society," and therefore "equal protection analysis is not dependent on the race of those burdened or benefited."[53] The fact that race is involved is all that matters. Courts need not scrutinize racial identities or the history of racial subordination.

O'Connor's approach—which Justice Antonin Scalia endorsed by his pronouncement in *Adarand Contractors, Inc. v. Peña*,[54] that "we are just one race . . . American"—presents a twist on the notion of constitutional color blindness. That twist is the Court's conscious acknowledgment of interracial competition and conflict in "multiracial America" as justification for its de facto prohibition of affirmative race consciousness in governmental racial classifications.[55] Implicit in this contradictory recognition-nonrecognition of interracial dynamics is the decision not to develop a meaningful interracial jurisprudence.

How has this occurred? Over the last twenty years, the Supreme Court has used America's multiracial demographics and the existence of interminority competition and conflict to transform whites from the centuries-long historical oppressors of people of color into "just another group competing with many others." Based on the Court's rulings, whites now can be considered "a victim group with the same moral and legal claims" as other groups.[56] Although a detailed analysis of how this has occurred is beyond the scope of this chapter, a summary is feasible. In its recent rulings, the Court has attributed interminority competition and conflict to "racial factionalism," "separatism," and "balkanization," which in turn it has attributed to consciousness of racial differences. For the conservative majority on the Court, the evil of racism in intensely conflictual multiracial America is no longer individual and institutional acts of white supremacy but, rather, the recognition of racial differences in the form of racial classifications. Race consciousness leads to factionalization and separatism, which lead to conflict. In short, racial classifications "threaten

... to incite racial hostility."[57] The very existence of governmental racial classifications, race factions, and interminority conflict are circumstantial proof of the causal links.

With this description of racial reality, the Court's ostensible quest for harmony has focused on outlawing race consciousness. Only by banning consciousness of racial differences can the government avoid supporting race factionalism; only by avoiding race factionalism can the government reduce racial conflict. Of course, a ban on consciousness of racial differences would make sense only if racial distinctions were unworthy of notice—a seemingly tough conclusion to draw in light of America's history of differential white racist treatment of minorities and the continuing socioeconomic differences between whites and nonwhite racial groups. The Court nevertheless reached that conclusion by characterizing all racial groups as one and the same: racial groups, including whites, are fungible, with equivalent moral and legal claims to freedom from discrimination. What justifies this characterization? The Court pointed to the "facts" of multiracial America, where every group inflicts harm on another. When it comes to discrimination, whites are no better and no worse than any other group. At bottom, "we are just one race."[58]

Three consequences of this characterization of multiracial conflict are important. First, as Alexandra Natapoff pointed out, the Court recognizes multiracial conflicts to justify its ban on affirmative race consciousness. Second, in practice, the ban on race consciousness is being applied by courts not to promote equality for nonwhite racial groups or redress interracial justice grievances but to validate white claims of discrimination and to "reliev[e] whites of the costs of forty years of [antidiscrimination] remedial measures." Third, and returning to the point of this discussion, the Court's acknowledgment of multiracial conflicts serves ironically as the foundation for its jurisprudential blindness to interracial claims.

These consequences suggest explicit and implicit rationales for the Court's recognition of multiracial conflict without an articulated position on how to analyze or address justice claims arising from those conflicts. Explicitly, an interracial jurisprudence that is attentive to historical and current racial differences is at best unnecessary to dispensing racial justice and at worst inimical to the nation's interest in racial harmony. Implicitly, jurisprudential blindness to the dynamics of interracial justice claims enhances the legitimacy of the Court's overall ban on race consciousness.

If this at least partly explains the federal judiciary's constricted approach to interracial justice claims, what explains the silence of justice scholars? Until very recently, why have legal scholars, in particular, like the courts refrained from pursuing the jurisprudential underpinnings of intergroup justice claims?[59] One possible reason is that the courts' reluctance to acknowledge, let alone act on, the interracial justice issues has deprived scholars of legal records to scrutinize.

Another reason for the comparative silence may be that no theoretical core has coalesced. Early efforts at developing an interracial jurisprudence seem fractured and sometimes even at odds. Some scholars examine court treatment of interminority rights issues and search for an intergroup jurisprudential base for adjudicating Title VII and equal protection antidiscrimination claims. Others study the process of adjudicating antidiscrimination claims, the potential for lawyers' exacerbation of intergroup conflicts, the possibility of intergroup reconciliation predicated on "doing justice," and monopoly capitalism and the fostering of interminority economic competition.[60] Still others tack in the opposite direction, cautioning race scholars about the distracting potential of interracial inquiry: the diversion of attention from the structural source of intergroup conflict in America—white supremacy.[61] Perhaps this all-over-the-map feel to the few articles on interracial jurisprudence simply means that interminority jurisprudence is in its early stages, but perhaps it indicates scholarly ambivalence.

A final explanation for the lack of attention to interracial justice issues, which applies to the courts and litigants as well as legal scholars, may be political. Discussion of interracial conflict is considered taboo, a subject too explosive for whites who do not want to be perceived as saying simply "see, they're racist too" and for people of color who do not want to detract societal and legal attention from the whites' position atop the racial hierarchy.

## A Call for Practical Theory

For these reasons, it is not surprising that interracial justice concepts, methods, and language have yet to emerge. Beyond the recent work of a handful of theologians and religious scholars addressing the biblical basis for reconciliation, cited earlier, there has been little sustained intergroup healing scholarship. And even those scholars acknowledge the limited practical impact of a theology of reconciliation—that even though "reconciliation and peacemaking are part of the Christian calling . . . [t]hat churches and Christian people have failed in their efforts almost entirely is all too evident."[62]

The near void, although understandable, is highly problematic. Workable concepts, methods, and language—a "theoretics of practice"[63] that builds on and moves beyond theological ideas—are needed for four related reasons. First, they are needed to challenge our overall blindness to color-on-color justice grievances, including the courts' jurisprudential myopia in post–civil rights America. Second, they are needed to address theoretically and practically the justice grievances underlying myriad interminority conflicts—the kinds of grievances mentioned earlier that are often handled, or mishandled, in haphazard, ad hoc fashion, without a guiding vision of the problem or a way of achieving peaceable and productive interracial relations. Third, the absence of suitable language, concept, and method opens the door to those with agendas other than reconciliation to shape the discourse and future possibilities.

Finally, a practical theory is needed to facilitate the formation of durable interracial alliances and coalitions. Prominent race scholars Manning Marable and bell hooks, speaking to teachers, political lawyers, and community activists, see the only hope for African Americans and other racial minorities in the formation of interracial alliances, whether those alliances are created to enhance cooperative working and living arrangements or to combat white racism.[64] Marable's "theory of liberation," which is built on a "transformationist redistribution of resources and the democratization of state power along more egalitarian lines," and hooks's "practical model for social change," which speaks to the inducement of enlightened whites to surrender race privileges, both depend on political power mustered through coalitions of racial groups that are, at some deep level, mutually distrustful. The problem with this vision, as George Fred-rickson points out, is that neither Marable nor hooks offers a persuasive view of "how to"—that is, how to employ concepts, methods, and language to construct interracial alliances or form and maintain coalitions in a distrustful post–civil rights America.[65]

I suggest that theorizing about and acting on concrete interracial justice grievances is one aspect of the "how to." In the face of increasingly complex intergroup grievances and the limits of legal justice, the call for alliances and coalition building underscores the need for developing a sophisticated interracial justice theory with practical implications. This theoretics of practice, developed in parts 2 and 3, must unravel the ideological strands of the Court's recognition of multiracial conflict to justify its ban of affirmative race consciousness, to interrogate the complexities of group agency and responsibility for disabling intergroup constraints, to integrate group healing insights from various disciplines, and in doing so, to respond to justice grievances among communities of color that undermine alliance-forging efforts.

# 2

# "When Sorry Isn't Enough"
## A Worldwide Trend of Race Apologies

In Racial Healing,[1] Harlon Dalton describes racial injuries as "wounds." The metaphor of woundedness is apt. It expresses pain and dysfunction—the fear, anger, mistrust, and self-doubt of people subordinated on account of race. It also signals the need for regeneration—or healing.

Healing racial wounds is messy and complex. It means not only handling current problems and conflicts but also restoring the psyche and the soul.[2] In part, suffering is social and psychological. Long-term pain is often experienced not just physically but also as a reflection of one's relationships and perceptions of societal norms. For example, how society treats people with AIDS in terms of medical research, direct care, and social stigma and how family and friends interact with a person with AIDS contribute significantly to how that person experiences suffering.[3] Cultural representations of the infirmity (its social meaning) and the collective experiences of those with the infirmity (insider narratives) combine with physical pain to inform a person's suffering. Those cultural representations and collective experiences connect the body with the self and society. Therefore, the treatment of suffering, and certainly healing, must reach beyond the body into the social self and the personal soul.

Healing racial wounds—those inflicted by groups on other groups through culture, politics, economics, and sometimes violence—requires at least as much. For Dalton, healing these wounds entails engagement and struggle. The engagement must be mutual, with the groups in conflict committed to rebuilding relationships. And the struggle must be political and cultural, with the groups interacting on the rugged terrain of image and power. Rather than the pseudohealing advanced by politicians— "those who counsel smoothing over our differences and pushing our fears to the side"—meaningful racial healing requires "unadulterated struggle" among and within racial groups. For as Frederick Douglass observed, "If there is no struggle, there is no progress. Those who profess to favor [racial justice] and yet deprecate agitation, . . . want crops without plowing up the ground, they want rain without thunder and lightning."⁴ That struggle, that agitation to heal racial wounds, means facing ourselves and one another.

Race apologies are one form of engagement and struggle. Indeed, race apologies among groups apparently trying to restore broken relationships exploded as a worldwide phenomenon in the 1990s. In important respects, the phenomenon signals the growing recognition of healing as a social imperative for the new millennium. Those recently apologizing for historic and contemporary racial wounds are national, state, and local governments; religious denominations and missionary groups; businesses, politicians, and entertainers. The apologizers are mainly, but not exclusively, white. Those to whom the apologies, and in some cases reparations, are directed include African Americans, Asian Americans, Native Americans, Native Hawaiians, Jews, Korean women, black South Africans, New Zealand's Maoris, and Australia's Aborigines. The apologies address a multitude of oppressive behaviors, ranging from violence by wartime regimes, to colonialists' destruction of indigenous culture as a method of social control, to the enslavement of Africans, to the systemic exclusion and denigration of racial minorities, to public racial slurs.

The apologies thus vary widely in tenor, scope, time, place and reception, and their diversity raises questions about social meaning and impact. In what situations have groups apologized for inflicting racial harms? Under what kinds of social pressure? To heal what wounds? According to what notions of responsibility or justice? With what immediate and long-term effects? With what backlash? And why now?

For some, the apologies are concrete manifestations of a mounting desire throughout the world for racial healing—a recognition of the societal dysfunction caused by the still prevalent effects of racial oppression.[5] For others, the apologies in many instances are empty; they merely mask a desire by those in power simply to release pent-up social pressure generated by identity politics and thereby maintain the institutional status quo.

I introduce the race apologies phenomenon not as the subject of inquiry but as the setting for the narrower focus of this book—interracial justice and its potential for healing among communities of color. This chapter catalogs a wide range of recent national and international race apologies and describes varying responses by recipients and the public.[6]

## National

Since the United States' 1988 apology to and monetary reparations for Japanese Americans wrongfully interned during World War II, America has experienced a spate of race-related apologies. In the business world, the chairman of Texaco apologized for the company's use of racially derogatory terms. The racial slurs were caught on tape during a meeting of senior Texaco executives who were planning to destroy documents in a class action discrimination suit by African American employees. In Florida, a Yellow Cab Company manager apologized for the company's policy of not picking up young black males. At the behest of his liquor manufacturer sponsor, rapper Ice Cube apologized to Korean American merchants for his rap "Black Korea" that threatened to burn down Korean stores.[7]

In political and educational arenas, U.S. Senator Alfonse D'Amato issued a tepid apology on the Senate floor for his mockery of Judge Lance Ito's Japanese ancestry. U.S. Senator Ernest Hollings apologized for implying that African leaders were cannibals. Rutgers University President Francis Lawrence apologized for his remark that blacks lacked the "genetic hereditary background" to succeed on standardized testing.[8]

In the religious arena, churches have been primary exponents of apologies for past wrongs. Among the broad apologies covering many events over a period of time, the Southern Baptists apologized to African American church members for the denomination's endorsement of slavery; the Evangelical Lutheran Church of America apologized for founder Martin Luther's damaging anti-Semitism; and descendants of Congregationalist missionaries apologized for their ancestors' part in the overthrow of the Hawaiian monarchy. Among apologies for specific actions, the deacons of the Barnett Creek Baptist Church in Georgia apologized for asking the mother of a biracial baby to exhume her dead child and move her to an all-black cemetery; and the United Methodist Church apologized to Native Americans for the 1864 actions of John Chivington, a Methodist lay preacher who led the United States Army Colorado Volunteers in a post-treaty massacre of the Cheyenne and Arapaho.[9]

Governments have been apologizing, too. In the United States the trend began in the early 1970s when through the Alaska Native Claims Settlement Act, Alaska's indigenous peoples received nearly $1 billion and more than 44 million acres of land as reparations for wrongfully taken land. As mentioned, in 1988 the United States apologized and paid $1.2 billion in reparations to Japanese Americans unlawfully interned during World War II. Recent government apologies (some with and some without accompanying reparations) include President Clinton's apology to Native Hawaiians for the illegal overthrow of the Hawaiian nation in 1893 (discussed in the next chapter); President Clinton's apology to victims of the "Tuskegee experiment," in which African American men with syphilis were left untreated so that the Public Health Service could determine the disease's long-range effects; and the Florida legislature's 1995 decision to compensate survivors of the 1923 government-backed massacre of black men, women, and children in the town of Rosewood.[10]

What is the genesis of these American race apologies, and what have been their effects? For example, the Rosewood massacre is a racial wound still raw after seventy years. In 1923, Frances Taylor, a white resident of nearby Sumner, Florida, falsely accused an unknown black assailant from Rosewood of sexually assaulting her. More than two hundred white men gathered, some traveling great distances. After four days of lynchings, executions, and torture, more than one hundred blacks were dead, and all of the town's structures had been destroyed. The surviving residents fled, leaving Rosewood a ghost town.

For years after the massacre, the survivors kept silent. Overwhelmed by the trauma, their silence shielded children from the deep hurt. It put the past far behind them. But not the pain. Two generations later, when the few survivors and grandchildren of former residents began to talk, the pain reemerged, and the reparations movement gained momentum.

The process was slow and painful. The former residents of Rosewood initially presented a claims bill of $7 million to the Florida legislature for the loss of personal liberty and life. The legislature rejected the claims, arguing that the Rosewood massacre had taken place seventy years earlier and that any pending legal claims were barred by the statute of limitations. The survivors persevered, however, comparing their experience with that of the interned World War II Japanese American internees. The Rosewood survivors finally piqued the interest of the Florida legislature by refashioning their liberty claims as property claims. The claimants argued that although the government did not take title to their property and possessions, it did support the displacement of the residents and the destruction of their property. The legislature ultimately agreed and authorized monetary reparations. It declined, however, to issue an official apology. The ceremonial announcement of the release of the money to the survivors and their descendants was, for some, a tremendous source of release from unresolved grief. For others, though, partly due to the lack of an official apology—that is, some ceremonial form of repentance—the grieving continues.[11]

In addition to these recent race apologies in the United States, other apologies and demands for reparations are pending. Native Hawaiians have made international law–based claims for reparations against the United States and the state of Hawai'i. Peruvian Japanese, abducted from Peru by the United States during World War II and interned in America's concentration camps, recently filed suit claiming entitlement to reparations under the 1988 Civil Liberties Act.

The most volatile proposal calls for a federal government apology for slavery and reparations for African Americans. Although African American reparations have been debated for years, President Clinton reignited the issue through his 1997 "Initiative on Race." "Surely every American knows that slavery was wrong and that we paid a terrible price for it and that we have to keep repairing that. [T]o say it's wrong and that we're sorry about it is not a bad thing. That doesn't weaken us."[12] Congressperson Tony Hall sponsored a formal apology resolution that stated simply, "Resolved . . . that the Congress apologizes to African Americans whose ancestors suffered as slaves under the Constitution and laws of the United States until 1865."[13] Hall, one of twelve white representatives introducing the resolution, explained its rationale: "Though no one alive today is responsible for slavery, all Americans share our shameful heritage and we all suffer from the consequences of a divided nation."[14]

President Clinton's hints at an official apology for slavery and Hall's apology resolution were quickly opposed at both ends of the political spectrum. Civil rights activist Rev. Jesse Jackson and House Speaker Newt Gingrich labeled the proposed apology a meaningless gesture. Jackson urged that "if you want to apologize for slavery, then why not apologize for legal segregation and then work to end present racial discrimination." Gingrich considered an apology redundant, claiming that "if you want to see a great apology for slavery, go to the Lincoln Memorial and read Lincoln's Second Address." For Kenneth Feinburg, who advised the government on compensating victims of radiation experiments, an apology for slavery opens a Pandora's box. He asks, "Would the American Indians request an apology? Would those workers who were victims of the Industrial Revolution—would they request an apology? Are there a series of wronged groups who would come in and similarly request an apology?"[15]

Patricia Williams offered the most incisive critique of the Clinton-Hall apology proposal:

I start to twitch when gestures, and essentially religious ones at that, appear in the empty rhetorical spaces created by the abandonment of serious political process. Love! Manners! Good Values! are all supremely attractive attributes in boy or man, but, to be blunt, we should expect more than good wishes from the House of Representatives.

It isn't just the current spate of apologizing strikes me as flaccidly nice. . . . It's that apologizing for slavery with such neon concision is . . . too easy. . . .

Slavery was a killing field . . . [I]n contrast to those cultures where apology is linked to real sorrow, intense contrition, acknowledgment, confession, explanation, acts of repentance, appeals for mercy and the restless search for balance—. . . ours is a tradition of stiff upper lips and quick "closure." . . . Forgive then forget; to forgive is to forget. . . .

Apologizing without acknowledging the broken bones is what dysfunctional families do.[16]

Williams concluded reluctantly that "black people must, I think, hand this kind of apology back—gently, but with a firm no thank you. . . . So long as that subtle legacy of slavery remains, an apology would be superficial, not reflective of the moral change truly required of America."

As evidenced by these comments, the very idea of an apology for slavery has stirred national soul searching, and linking reparations to an apology has only intensified the debate. For the last several years, Representative John Conyers has introduced a resolution entitled "The African-American Reparations Study Commissions Act." The resolution, supported by a multitude of civil rights, political, and community organizations, calls for Congress's acknowledgment of the injustice and inhumanity of slavery. It also seeks to establish a commission to examine the institution of slavery and subsequent racial and economic discrimination against African Americans and to recommend remedies. Speaking at the national convention for the National Coalition of Blacks for Reparations in America, a leading advocate group for reparations, Conyers noted that "the time is ripe now to push for a greater galvanizing of national efforts to put the reparations movement and H.R. 40 at the top of the American agenda." Conyers's resolution resonates with many African Americans, particularly in a post–civil rights, anti–affirmative action era. The promise of forty acres and a mule remains unfulfilled while other groups ask for and receive reparations. The Japanese Americans' redress movement has become a model for some African American reparations activists. "Everybody thought it was a joke for years," said Raymond Jenkins, and "when the Japanese got $20,000 each, then they stopped laughing."[17]

## International

These recent race apologies in the United States are part of a worldwide phenomenon.[18] Canada paid Japanese Canadians $230 million in reparations for their internment during World War II; Canada also returned land to indigenous Canadians. South Africa's F. W. de Klerk apologized before the Truth and Reconciliation Commission for the white National

Party's "mistakes" through its policy of apartheid. The United Kingdom's prime minister, Tony Blair, apologized for the government's involvement in the Irish potato famine. Queen Elizabeth apologized to New Zealand's Maori for the seizure of Maori lands and the extermination of the Maori people. Similarly, New Zealand apologized to the Maori for malfeasance 131 years ago and agreed to pay a Maori tribe $27.6 million for occupying its land and hanging its chief. At the Australian Reconciliation Convention, the prime minister of Australia, John Howard, referred to a human rights report that found both the Australian government and the Australian Catholic Church guilty of aboriginal genocide. Without making a full national apology, he expressed his own "deep sorrow" for injustices.

To ease the pain of World War II abuses, Russian President Boris Yeltsin recently asked for forgiveness from the families of 15,000 Polish officers murdered by the Soviet secret police The German government agreed to pay reparations to U.S. citizens imprisoned in Nazi concentration camps during World War II (without apologizing). French President Jacques Chirac apologized for the French collaborationist Vichy regime's deportation of 76,000 Jews to Nazi death camps (without offering reparations). Swiss banks, holding Jewish funds and Nazi war booty, agreed to create a $5 billion Holocaust survivors' fund for Jews and other victims.

Religious organizations are at the crest of the apology trend. Pope John Paul II asked for forgiveness on behalf of the Roman Catholic Church for violence during the Counter-Reformation of the late 1500s, for its failure this century to defend human rights in totalitarian nations, for its complicity in the African slave trade, for abuses committed by Christian colonizers against native peoples, and for the church's marginalization of women. And the Australian Catholic Church apologized for its systematic destruction of the Aborigines' spiritual and cultural life.

## Reactions

Recipients of apologies and beneficiaries of reparations have reacted with mixed emotions. Many of the Japanese Americans interned during World War II rejoiced at the announcement of congressional reparations. Redress and reparations, and the process of obtaining them, were cathartic for former internees. A measure of dignity was restored. Former internees could finally talk about the internment. Feelings long repressed, surfaced. One woman, now in her seventies, stated that she always felt the internment was wrong but that, after being told by the military, the president, Congress, and the Supreme Court that it was a necessity, she had come to seriously doubt herself. The apology and reparations and the recent successful court challenges, she said, had now "freed her soul."[19] In Rosewood, Arnett Doctor worked for compensation for his family for years. During much of the reparations struggle, Doctor felt embittered. After the reparations were awarded, however, he found a sense of peace. "I think . . . that the fact that the state of Florida has seen fit to pay at all, that they would reach into their pockets at all, speaks volumes about the state of mind of our elected legislators and how far we've come in the past seventy-three years."[20]

Other people, however, reacted negatively. For many, the Rosewood reparations process was extremely frustrating. Out of the four hundred property claim applications, fewer than seventy claimants received compensation. For those who received property reparations, with amounts ranging from $100 to $5,000, the money was neither life changing nor healing. In addition, tens of thousands of state dollars remain unclaimed, and hundreds of acres of Rosewood property are unaccounted for. Descendants of residents who could not prove their families' losses were left empty-handed—with no property, no compensation, and no apology. For some, it hardly seemed worth the battle.

African Americans also experienced a backlash. Many in Rosewood today, the majority of whom are whites, resent the payment of reparations. As one resident complained, "All these people, all these reporters. I'm sick of it. That happened in 1932 or 1923 or whenever it was. That is history and every person in the state of Florida is paying for this, and that just don't cut it. That's our tax money." Rosewood today is a story about a community and a government attempting to come to terms with a painful past. Good intentions, long-awaited apologies, and minimal reparations are steps—but small steps at best—toward healing.

What potential does the worldwide wave of race apologies hold for the redress of justice grievances among racial groups in the United States? For interracial reconciliation? When do apologies lead to a meaningful restructuring of intergroup relations? When are they simply trendy? Or masks for continuing oppression? What insights guide ongoing and future apology efforts? In the words of one African American worker, "We get so many apologies; apologies for this, that and the other, you know? And I'm looking for a difference in other words. What difference is this apology going to make?" Part 3 of this book responds to these questions by developing a critical pragmatic framework for assessing and shaping interracial justice efforts.

The overview of the worldwide apology trend just recited hints at an important reality: For African Americans, Latinas/os, Native Americans, Asian Americans, and white Americans across the United States, each racial grievance and each proffered apology has a complicated history that warrants careful scrutiny. To ground the dynamics of interracial justice developed in part 3, I turn in the next chapter to one particular apology—an attempt to heal racial wounds—in its sociohistorical setting.

# 3

# Asian Americans and Native Hawaiians

## Apology and Redress

> I . . . apologize for the support given [for the illegal overthrow of the Hawaiian monarchy] by ancestors of ours in the church now known as the United Church of Christ. We do so in order to begin a process of repentance, redress and reconciliation for wrongs done. We are here not to condemn, but to acknowledge. We are here to remember and ask [for] forgiveness.
>
> — REV. PAUL SHERRY,
> President of the United Church of Christ,
> an apology statement to Na Kanaka Maoli, January 17, 1993

## Apology and Redress

Rev. Sherry apologized to Native Hawaiians for the United Church of Christ's participation in the United States–backed overthrow of the Hawaiian nation one hundred years earlier and for the ensuing economic and cultural devastation of the Hawaiian people. As part of a "process of repentance, redress, and reconciliation," the apology posed a challenge to

1.5 million members of the United Church of Christ: How will each member accept responsibility for the church's injustices, and what must they now do collectively to heal the continuing wounds of injustice within and beyond the polity? The apology also posed a challenge to Native Hawaiians: Under what circumstances might they no longer condemn but forgive?

Sherry's apology on behalf of the denomination, recited in part in the epigraph, responded to the organizing and educational efforts of a multiracial alliance led by Hawaiian clergy and activists. The apology and those efforts stirred Asian American churches in the United Church of Christ's Hawai'i Conference (one of several regional conferences) to propose their own apology to the Native Hawaiians.[1] The Asian American churches proposed an apology along with multimillion dollar reparations for Asian American complicity in the economic and cultural oppression of Native Hawaiians following the overthrow. The Asian American churches presented their formal resolution of apology and call for reparations at the Hawai'i Conference's 171st 'Aha Pae'aina (annual meeting) in 1993. The resolution complemented a broader resolution calling for the conference's apology for the participation of its white missionary predecessor in the overthrow of the Hawaiian monarchy.[2]

In their resolution, the Asian American churches recalled the Asian disapproval of the dethroning of Queen Lili'uokalani in 1893 by white business and religious leaders supported by United States officials and an American warship. They acknowledged "a certain bond" between Hawaiians and Asians during the first half of this century as social, economic, and political outsiders in a white oligarchically controlled Hawai'i. They also acknowledged one hundred years of oppressive group interactions—confessing that "we as Asians have benefited socially and economically from the illegal overthrow" of the sovereign Hawaiian government and that "many Asian Americans have benefited while disregarding the destruction of Native Hawaiian culture and the struggles of Na Kanaka Maoli."

The Asian American churches then addressed current relationships arising out of those historical interactions—"[a] particular dynamic ... between Native Hawaiians and Asian Americans, rooted in mutual misunderstanding and mistrust," that has encouraged the "use [of] stereotypes and caricatures to demean and dehumanize" and foster "racist attitudes and actions." Finally, while acknowledging the interpretive and perceptual ambiguity of "motives, results, characterizations and causes," the Asian American churches focused on "the anguish of our Native Hawaiian sisters and brothers" in the conference and beyond. They sought to begin a process of redress and reconciliation with Native Hawaiians and to offer support for the larger Hawaiian struggle for justice.[3]

By proposing an apology and reparations, the Asian American churches sought to put into practice their religious beliefs about "peace and justice." As recited in their resolution, those beliefs were grounded in theology ("repentance," "confession," and "reconciliation,") and law ("demands of the law," "illegal overthrow," "due process," "restitution," "reparations," and "justice"). Moreover, the churches attempted to alter Asian American relationships with Hawai'i's indigenous peoples by scrutinizing "how structures and strategies of domination created under colonialism are transferred and redeployed by the formerly colonized."[4] Through the resolution, Asian American churches attempted to build bridges with Native Hawaiians.

Anonymous hate phone calls and heated debates preceded the formal presentation of the finished resolution to delegates from 120 churches at the 'Aha Pae'aina. The resolution's attempt to cast reconciliation in terms of relations between Asian Americans and Native Hawaiians met immediate challenge. Ministers and congregations contested any unified meaning of Asian American. One congregation composed primarily of third- and fourth-generation Chinese Americans was outraged by the resolution, finding it both demeaning to Hawai'i's Chinese Americans and lacking in moral ("I didn't do anything wrong") and legal ("what right do they have") justification.[5] The largely Korean American churches tended to express indifference, hinting that any responsibility for complicity in the white-controlled oppression of Hawaiians in the first half of the century lay with Japanese and Chinese Americans. The Samoan American churches remained silent, leaving unexpressed their feelings about the continuing discrimination against Samoans by others, including some Native Hawaiians. Clergy of the self-identified Hawaiian churches and congregation members, most of whom were of some combination of Hawaiian, Asian, and white ancestry, expressed wide-ranging views about the significance of, and need for, an apology and redress from the conference generally and Asian American churches specifically. Others observed that mixed ancestry drew nebulous lines between "Hawaiians" entitled and not entitled to benefit from reparations.[6]

Thus, even before the formal testimony on the resolution at the 171st 'Aha Pae'aina, a conflictual, shifting picture of Asian American identity emerged, undermining the potential for an Asian American apology.[7] "Asian Americanness" fractured into various amorphous, dissonant sub-parts, ostensibly dividing various Asian American ethnic groups along vague lines of responsibility.

The passionate testimony of Rev. Richard Wong revealed the complexity of the intergroup justice issues raised by the Asian American apology resolution. Rev. Wong, an eighty-year-old Chinese American minister and former pastor, was highly respected by conference clergy and laity. Through his dedication and skill in handling latent interracial tensions, he revived a historically significant yet struggling Hawaiian church on O'ahu. Owing to a lingering illness, Rev. Wong presented his response to the apology resolution by proxy. In his letter to the 'Aha Pae'aina, he partly opposed the resolution because the term *Asian American* encompassed Chinese Americans whom he believed were not legally or morally culpable.

As an Asian/Chinese, we Chinese look back at our [relations] with Native Hawaiians. We feel that we have not exploited nor dehumanized them. But in fact, we have accepted them enough to marry them. Today, the so-called "Hawaiian name"—Apaka, Ahuna, Achiro and so on are unions of Chinese [and Hawaiian]. . . . Please do not clump Chinese with other Asian-Americans who may have taken advantage of these Oahuans [Hawaiians on O'ahu]. Secondly, if the Asian-Americans fear they have deeply denied Native Hawaiians, they should offer their own apology [and reparations].[8]

Rev. Wong's short testimony garnered considerable attention. He raised a host of complex interracial justice issues concerning the contested nature of identity politics, the situated nature of racial group agency and responsibility, the historical roots of contemporary interracial tensions, and the difficulties of and possibilities for intergroup healing.

For many in the conference, racial misunderstanding and sometimes antipathy among member churches needed to be acknowledged. Only when present pain rooted in past harms was addressed and redressed could there be justice. And only when there was justice could there be reconciliation and a foundation for genuine hope and cooperation. As stated earlier, the Asian American churches' apology resolution initially generated heated debate within and beyond those churches. That debate, often challenging the racial categories and racial politics of the resolution itself, ranged from strong endorsement to ringing denouncement. The participants at the Hawai'i Conference's annual meeting earnestly discussed the Asian American churches and conference apology resolutions but could not agree on what had happened historically, who was involved, who was culpable, and what redress, if any, would be appropriate.

When it appeared that the conference polity could not reach a consensus on the appropriate action, Rev. Kekapa Lee, a Hawaiian-Chinese American pastor of a small church on Maui, stood and spoke: "I would like to ask all those willing Hawaiians to please stand." A dozen of the four hundred conference delegates in the room stood. Acknowledging the divergent views of history, Rev. Lee then spoke about the significance of the apology—recognizing the deep hurt so that the Hawaiians "might move on."

Those of us who are standing are Hawaiian people—people who lived in this archipelago called Hawai'i for generations. . . . Some of us are hurt deeply by what took place 100 years ago. Some of us have not a consensus on the role of the [church in the overthrow of the Hawaiian nation]. That is not the point. What the call for apology [does is] . . . to sever this pilikia [troubled feeling] that we might move on. We want to put this behind and we call on all of you who are not Hawaiian to kokua [cooperate]—even though some of us Hawaiians are not totally [with] this.

Another thirty Hawaiians rose, slowly. Lee spoke again.

And I have a very heavy, heavy, heavy heart because I don't understand why an apology is such a big thing. . . . Some of us are hurting and in pain because of this, and we're asking your support and kokua . . . because there are many things that face our church and community as Hawaiians and we want to move on but feel that this apology is so important.[9]

As Rev. Lee finished, many more Hawaiians rose. At first sixty, then eighty, perhaps one hundred; almost all the Hawaiians in the polity, including those who earlier spoke against the resolution. The emotion was palpable. After days of fractious discussions, many non-Hawaiians there (including white and Asian Americans) finally grasped the depth of the continuing pain experienced by Hawaiians in their own conference. For the first time, many began to understand how their refusal to acknowledge that present pain and its historical context had erected huge barriers between the groups in the conference and hindered collective efforts to address the "many things that face our church and community." This new understanding signaled a turning point for the conference. Earlier disagreements about specific historical facts suddenly emerged in a softer light.

The members of the conference polity by consensus adopted an amended version of the conference's apology resolution, incorporating key aspects of the Asian American churches' apology resolution (particularly its call for reparations). The polity directed the Hawai'i Conference to apologize formally to Native Hawaiians for its predecessor's participation in the overthrow of the Hawaiian nation. It also called for creation of a local task force to begin a process of reparation.

A difficult year-long study followed. Disagreements continued about the extent of historical participation of the conference's predecessor in the overthrow of the Hawaiian nation and about the appropriateness of reparations. In 1994, the task force work culminated in a solemn apology service and ceremony at the Royal Mausoleum with a commitment to land and monetary reparations.

In 1996, after two more years of intensive study and following raucous debate at the 173rd 'Aha Pae'aina, the Hawai'i Conference approved an extensive monetary and land reparations package. In 1997, each of the forty-eight Hawaiian churches worshiping in 1893 (or its successor) received $28,000. In addition, the conference committed $1.5 million in trust to a newly created foundation for the benefit of the Hawaiian community generally (augmenting a denominational contribution of $1.25 million). Finally, as part of the reparations package, the conference transferred six improved, valuable parcels of land on five islands to Hawaiian churches and to the foundation.[10]

The conference has apologized. The lengthy, difficult redress process is nearing completion. Has interracial justice occurred? And if so, has it fostered racial reconciliation? There are, of course, no clear answers, just more questions. What are the likely effects of the United Church of Christ's denominational apology? What about the Hawai'i Conference's apology and reparations? And what about the Asian American churches' resolution and the tumultuous processes surrounding it? What, if anything, will have changed in terms of individual feelings, group relations, and church structure? In the larger community and throughout the state, how will images and structures of interracial relations have changed, if at all? Is what appears to be interracial healing meaningful to Native Hawaiians, and if so, will it be lasting? How will participation in the apology and reparations process change the Asian American churches and Asian Americans generally?

These questions, revisited in chapter 9, merge into what may be a task of paramount importance for all communities of color in twenty-first-century America: healing the wounds of grievance through interracial justice.

## Justice Grievances

When we speak of healing these wounds of grievance, what kinds of grievances do we mean? More specifically, what Native Hawaiian justice grievances underlay Asian American worries over contemporary intergroup "mistrust and misunderstanding" and the use of "stereotypes to demean?" The apology resolution described those grievances in terms of partial Asian American complicity in the destruction of Hawaiian culture and the socioeconomic devastation of Hawaiians following the 1893 overthrow of the Hawaiian nation.

Some Native Hawaiians feel aggrieved by Asian Americans because present-day Asian Americans or their ancestors came from abroad and are now living, working, and politicking on ground that "belongs" to indigenous people and because as "settlers" they have not forged meaningful understandings of the historical harm to and current struggles of Native Hawaiians.[11]

Some consider Asian Americans unwanted or hostile foreigners because they have, or appeared to have, situationally redeployed colonialist structures of oppression. Rhetorical, institutional, and economic structures are situationally redeployed when groups formerly or even currently disadvantaged by those structures exercise some degree of emergent power to use those structures to disadvantage other groups.[12] For example, some Hawaiians point to the redeployment of rhetorically and economically oppressive structures by some Asian Americans who acquired varying degrees of political and bureaucratic power in Hawai'i. Those Asian Americans are seen as former outsiders who now champion private property development and economic liberty, ideas once employed by the white oligarchy to dominate all aspects of their lives. In redeploying those structures, they "cannot truly understand this cultural value of malama 'aina [caring for the land]" and are "either ignorant of, or hostile to understanding, Hawaiian history and present-day Hawaiian claims."[13]

Others see subconscious Asian American participation in the redeployment of institutional and economic structures oppressing Native Hawaiians. Political scientist Michael Haas first defines institutional racism historically in terms of white ["haole"]-controlled institutional "policies, practices and procedures [that] favor some ethnic groups [haole] over others even when persons in the institution harbor no ethnic prejudice." Those policies, practices, and procedures roughly disguised discrimination in jobs, business, education, and housing, among other things. Haas then observes, "Today . . . few props of institutional racism have been dismantled, and many forms of institutional racism that place the kanaka maoli [Hawaiian] at a disadvantage have been defended in our own day by non-haoles [that is, Asian Americans] who claim not to be motivated by . . . racism."[14]

Rev. Abraham Akaka reflects views of rhetorical and economic oppression held by some Native Hawaiians opposing a legislative "land reform" law. This law enables residential leaseholders to force landowners, principally large charitable trusts whose beneficiaries are Native Hawaiians, to sell underlying fee interests to the leaseholders, including many upper-middle-class Asian and white Americans. Akaka worries that the rhetoric of "the fundamental right" to private landownership legitimates a second "mahele" (or private land divide), thereby enhancing non-Hawaiians' economic power and further separating Hawaiians from Hawaiian lands.

Memories of the Great Mahele of 1848 come to mind. We feel that pressure for land reform then [through legal recognition of private property ownership and alienability] was due more to a rising generation of Western investors than from the native Hawaiian himself. We cannot but feel that pressure for land reform now is due not to the poorer man—among whom are a great many Hawaiians—but from a new generation of investors from East and West.[15]

A cartoon and editorial in a university newspaper aggravated these and related Hawaiian grievances against Asian Americans. In 1993 the University of Hawai'i approved 280 tuition waivers for Hawaiians who, as a group, continue to struggle in Hawai'i, according to all socioeconomic indicators. As part of a larger recruitment program, the university was seeking to change the vast underrepresentation of Hawaiians in its student population. Many celebrated the tuition waiver decision, seeing it as both a recognition of history and a step toward leveling the higher educational playing field for Hawaiians.

Some, however, viewed the university's action at best as culturally biased against non-Hawaiians and at worst as an illegal race preference. The editor of the campus newspaper, a Japanese American, claimed in an editorial that the university set a "poor example" in making a race-based decision. Implying that scholarships would be awarded to undeserving Hawaiians, she argued that academic meritocracy would be the only appropriate policy. "The only way to have a truly fair distribution of the resources available to students would be to eliminate any consideration of race. Whatever happened to scholarships based solely on someone's academic abilities? Why is it necessary to create these distinctions between the races?"[16]

Interestingly, the editor appeared unperturbed by the many other kinds of university scholarships not "based solely on someone's academic abilities"—for example, athletics, economic need, and military service scholarships. She also missed the irony of her position. Only two or so generations ago, many of her male Japanese American ancestors, returning to Hawai'i from World War II service for America, received veterans' scholarships (not based solely on "academic abilities"). Those scholarships enabled young men formerly disabled by finances and societal racism to attend mainland professional schools—which in turn helped prompt the democratic revolution in the 1950s, which politically ended the white oligarchy's iron grip over all facets of Hawai'i's social and political life.

Perhaps most important, the editor failed to engage the critical question she raised, "why scholarships for Hawaiians?" She acknowledged that "many part-Hawaiians come from disadvantaged families" but stopped there.

A cartoon accompanying the editorial illustrated its message about racially privileged Hawaiians taking away opportunities from deserving non-Hawaiians. The cartoonist, a Chinese American, depicted a group of "Happy Hawaiians" singing and dancing with their tuition waivers (but no books) in hand, wearing shorts and sandals and sporting a local "shaka" hand-sign signifying "everything's cool." In the background, a long line of faceless students are waiting to pay their tuition. In the foreground, a nicely dressed Asian American with a full backpack, sitting on the ground and looking depressed, says "Tuition BLEEDS ME DRY." The cartoonist thereby underscored the editorial's point about undeserving Hawaiians by resorting to the age-old caricature of Hawaiian students as nonintellectual—recall the pre–Civil War cartoons of the simple, "happy," southern slaves—and by juxtaposing that image with that of the (similarly, but favorably, caricatured) image of the diligent, unfairly deprived Asian American student.

Both the editor and cartoonist chose to make their point about tuition waivers without acknowledging the historical and contemporary educational realities. Neither revealed an understanding of why the university administration and board of regents approved the waivers, what historical circumstances and current conditions might justify them (including continuing group socioeconomic disadvantage and underrepresentation in higher education), or what valuable societal impacts the waivers might have by leveling an educational playing field then sharply tilted by historical injustice. By not engaging in this inquiry, by uncritically intoning meritocracy and color blindness, and by using derogatory cultural images of Hawaiians and complimentary images of Asian Americans to make their point, they appeared to do what members of groups with some degree of newly acquired power tend to do through institutions and media—valorize their group while denigrating the other to justify continuing inequalities between the two. They thereby exacerbated the Native Hawaiian grievance of Asian American complicity in the subordination of Hawaiians.

Consider, now, the backdrop to these racialized events.

## Sociohistorical Conditions

> I plead with you, please come . . . and hear the many voices who cry out and get no help.
>
> — ALICE  ZENGER,
> *A Broken Trust* (1991)

> All of you may be asking, How is this possible? Simply put, . . . that I and many Hawaiians have yet to return to the land indicates the government's gross neglect in abiding by their own laws, laws established as a result of the government's attempt to make right the original wrong, the illegal seizure of the Hawaiian kingdom, the total annihilation of our religion, our culture, language, and our lifestyle.
>
> — LEHUA  NAPOLEON,
> *Joint Hearings Transcript*, U.S. Senate Select Committee
> on Indian Affairs, August 9, 1989

> We've got the rights. But we've got no justice.
>
> — ALICE  AIWOHI

Alice Zenger, Lehua Napoleon, and Alice Aiwohi are Hawaiians. They also are American citizens, although not necessarily by choice. In crucial ways, their stories are like those of many outsiders and especially native peoples in the United States. Their voices bespeak particularized, long-submerged narratives about the destruction of culture on account of race and nationality.[17]

Alice Zenger made her plea to "please come" in 1988 to members of the U.S. Civil Rights Commission's Hawai'i Advisory Committee.[18] Please come "in physical body," she meant, to see and touch the *'aina,* the homelands of Hawaiians. Please come "in spirit," she also meant, to feel the mana or spiritual power of the 'aina and Native Hawaiians' special relationship to it. *Malama 'aina*—caring for the land.[19] It is a spirit that suffered first in 1848 when American businessmen and Calvinist missionaries shepherded through a radical legal reform, the "Mahele," which imposed Western concepts of private property ownership and led quickly to non-Hawaiian ownership and control of vast tracts of 'aina;[20] and again in 1893 when American businessmen and missionary descendants, with the support of the U.S. military, overthrew the Hawaiian monarchy under the threat of force and confiscated all government and crown lands;[21]and again in 1898 when the United States annexed Hawai'i as a territory and acquired control of all nonprivately owned Hawai'i lands; and again starting in 1921 when 200,000 acres were returned to Native Hawaiians in trust, only to have most of the lands, and the best lands, given by government trustees to non-Hawaiian private businesses, politicians, and the U.S. military; and still again when much of the comparatively little land returned to Native Hawaiians was stripped of vitality by government-approved diversions of water by non-Hawaiian businesses.[22]

Hear the many "voices who cry out," Alice Zenger said. Hawaiians suffer in their homeland. By all social-economic indicators, especially those of health, housing, employment, and incarceration, Hawaiians are the most disadvantaged of Hawai'i's racial and ethnic groups.[23] And Hawaiian culture has suffered as well. From the mid-1800s through the early 1970s, native language, religion, agriculture, art, concepts of property, and methods of communal dispute resolution, among other things, withered from direct institutional repression and subtle private coercion.[24] Come hear the life and death in people's voices, the struggle for "malama pono" (to make righteous), Zenger meant, beyond the statistics and sociological facts.

Born amid the 1960s civil rights and black nationalism movements, a cultural renaissance and political awakening in the 1970s and 1980s turned Hawaiians both inward, through group introspection into identity and culture, and outward, to group activism in political and economic arenas.[25] Many different, and sometimes discordant, voices emerged. Sometimes with blame, sometimes in pain, sometimes with pride, sometimes with demands. Crying out for the United States' and the world's acknowledgment of historical wrongs, for the recognition of continuing cultural and spiritual harm to a racial group separated from its land, for remediation by the United States, for acceptance of responsibility by the state.[26]

For Alice Zenger, however, Hawaiians cried out for return of homelands but "got no help." At the time of her testimony in 1988, the "track record in helping us is zero." The United States formally annexed Hawai'i as a territory in 1898, acquiring 1.5 million acres of government land. In Hawaiian, one meaning of "annexation" is *'aihue 'aina*—"to steal the land." Seventy-seven years ago, in recognition of this "theft," Congress initiated the 200,000-acre Homelands program. Yet fewer than four thousand Hawaiian families have received homelands parcels and occupy less than 20 percent of the designated land. Non-Hawaiians occupy more than 60 percent. Tens of thousands of acres of remaining homelands lie fallow mainly because of the absence of infrastructure and water. Twenty thousand Native Hawaiian families are waiting, with some having been on the eligibility list for more than twenty years. The federal statute admitting Hawai'i to the United States and the Hawai'i Constitution explicitly create Hawaiian rights to live on homelands and use water for self-sufficient homesteads.[27] The federal act and state constitutional provision, as part of the covenant of statehood, identified Native Hawaiians as trust beneficiaries, designated the state of Hawai'i as the trustee, and spelled out the state's fiduciary obligation to develop the homelands and place Hawaiians on them.

All recent investigations into the Homelands program reached the same conclusions: from admission to statehood in 1959 to 1990, the state, with complicity of the federal government, woefully and sometimes willfully, failed to discharge its trust duties; the federal government in effect renounced all trust responsibility and refused to carry out its oversight role; and far too many Hawaiians are waiting for land, thereby continuing the cycle of disenfranchisement, pain, and frustration.[28] Despite their rights, the state's generally acknowledged breaches of its trust duties and the federal government's neglect of supervisory responsibilities, Hawaiian voices fell on deaf ears; they "got no help" from politicians and bureaucrats.

For a time, they turned their voices toward the courts. From the late 1970s through the early 1990s, Hawaiian groups sued in federal court to enforce their federally created, state-acknowledged rights. They did not charge discrimination or seek equal treatment according to mainstream norms. Although framing their claims formally in the language of civil rights, as required by federal law, they sued to compel the state's discharge of its fiduciary obligations to homeland beneficiaries and, more important to some, to develop a land base to transform a paternalistic program rooted in historical conquest into a foundation for cultural self-determination and political sovereignty.

The federal courts, however, refused even to hear, let alone comprehend, those messages. They employed a panoply of procedures to block or severely limit consideration of Native Hawaiian claims—subject matter jurisdiction, nonimplied rights of action, sanctions for frivolous filings, standing, statutes of limitations, Eleventh Amendment limitations on remedies, and, indirectly, administrative estoppel.

As I described in an earlier article, in case after case—with one exception later sharply limited—the federal courts' procedural rulings precluded them from reaching "the merits" of Native Hawaiian claims— merits, according to traditional legal principles, compellingly revealing breaches of trust.[29] Of even greater significance, this maze of rulings created a procedural labyrinth that blocked official, public scrutiny of key social relationships and cultural messages at the heart of the Native Hawaiians' claims. Those rulings precluded inquiry into the relationship of Native Hawaiians and the United States as a former conqueror and land trustee and continuing military occupier of Hawaiian homelands; of Native Hawaiians and the state as the successor sovereign, land trustee, and proprietary user of the homelands; of the state and the United States as co-covenantors in the operation of the homelands trust; and of Hawaiians and the 'aina as a source of spiritual and economic sustenance.

Collectively, those rulings narrowly shaped—and in crucial ways distorted—popular and legal discourse about Hawaiians' drive for cultural and political self-determination. It made what was for many the heart of an indigenous people's claims irrelevant to court business. The Hawaiian legal claims offered a counternarrative to the melting-pot, Pacific-paradise, immigrant-success narrative embraced by many. Their claims recounted the social effects of conquest and the continuing cultural subjugation of indigenous people. Hawaiians cried out to the courts to halt the "annihilation of our . . . culture" and to allow Hawaiians themselves to repair the harm. The procedural labyrinth, however, swallowed their voices. They "got no help." From the courts, as Alice Aiwohi observed, they "got no justice."

The cycle of pain, frustration, and feelings of injustice continued. A fuller recitation of Alice Zenger's statement captures some of the feeling about a pressing need to reach beyond the established governmental authorities.

Breach of trust? This voice calls out, yes, yes, yes. . . . And why? Because the powers [that] be in the Department of Hawaiian Home Lands [state trustee] are not acting exclusively for the beneficiaries. There is a definite conflict of interest. When [a major sugar company] can dictate what happens to all that water that comes down by the ditch . . . ; when the act of 1920 (HHCA) specifically spells out that . . . I am entitled to surplus water, and I do not have adequate water to even flush my toilet; I do not have adequate water for my troughs for my animals. . . . And I go to the [trustee] DHHL, and I write to [two] Governors, with copies to my legislators, and I talk with the powers that be in the DHHL. . . . And all this time, through two generations, 33 years and 8 months, and their track record in helping us is zero. . . . I plead with you, please come to Kaua'i and hear the many voices who cry out and get no help.[30]

Nor could Hawaiians look to the federal executive branch for justice in the early 1990s. Although indigenous Hawaiians are appropriately designated, like Native Americans, as a political minority in the United States,[31] the U.S. government framed the discussion of Native Hawaiians in racial terms. In 1991 then President George Bush's Justice Department temporarily halted the disbursement of federal funds allocated to the Hawaii Department of Hawaiian Home Lands for housing construction. The Justice Department argued that targeting federal funds for Hawaiians constituted an illegal racial preference, terming it "reverse discrimination" against whites. In 1993, in a contorted, retroactive effort to avoid federal responsibility, and only hours before Bill Clinton assumed the presidency, the Interior Department proclaimed that the federal government had never entered into a trust relationship with Hawaiians concerning their homelands. The department did so by distorting the history of the 1921 Hawaiian Homelands Act and renouncing a 1979 Interior Department declaration directly to the contrary.[32]

In Hawaiian faces, the U.S. Justice and Interior Departments then saw only a racial group asking for benefits on account of its race; they ignored a history of conquest and subjugation. In Hawaiian voices, the Justice Department heard demands for government largesse; it ignored the unlawful seizure of Hawaiian land according to international human rights norms and the creation of the Homelands trust as partial reparation. In Hawaiian legal claims, the Justice and Interior Departments perceived only illegal race preferences; they ignored historical and ongoing disenfranchisement and the quest by many for cultural revival and political and economic self-determination.

Yet Hawaiians continued to speak. In the nine years following Alice Zenger's testimony, Hawaiians intensified their broad-based educational, political, and legal challenges to existing social and economic arrangements in Hawai'i. With a three-year, million-dollar grant, they brought together more than forty pro-sovereignty organizations under a single umbrella. With state money, they conducted a controversial vote of the Hawaiian people on whether to convene a convention to establish the structure for Hawaiian self-governance. They participated in and received support from international human rights organizations.

Now, in the late-1990s, with wide-ranging support from Hawaiians and significant if sporadic support from non-Hawaiians, Hawaiian groups are making increasingly sophisticated demands for some form of governmental sovereignty for the Hawaiian people. The voices cry out, in Lehua Napoleon's words, "to make right the original wrong, the illegal armed seizure of the Hawaiian Kingdom"—a wrong officially acknowledged at the turn of the century by President Grover Cleveland[33]—and the "annihilation of our religion, our culture, language, and our lifestyle." It is a cry beyond the demand for equal opportunity in day-to-day activity, beyond the pain of discriminatory treatment. It is a cry familiar to many native peoples in America and throughout the world and, in important ways, to African Americans and Mexican Americans—a cry for the resurrection of culture and the reclamation of the group self. It is an affirming cry in opposition to the melting-pot and assimilation narratives embraced by many. It is an intensifying cry finding both emerging institutional support and stiffening establishment resistance.

In 1993, support for Hawaiian self-determination came directly from

Congress and the president. Responding to Hawaiian calls for justice, Congress passed a resolution directing the president to apologize for the United States' role in the overthrow of the sovereign Hawaiian nation and for the resulting harm to the Hawaiian people.[34] Support from the federal government now comes indirectly through program aid to Hawaiians for education, health, job training, and home mortgage financing for the homelands.

State support comes in varying forms. The 1994 legislature sponsored the hotly contested Hawaiian vote on whether to hold a convention to determine the structure of a self-governing Hawaiian entity. Financial support comes mainly in the form of compensatory payments to the Homelands Trust in settlement of the state's fiduciary breaches as the homelands trustee. The Hawai'i Supreme Court has weighed in with controversial decisions under the state constitution affording protection for traditional and customary Hawaiian religious and subsistence practices.[35] The court is also currently reviewing a lower court ruling that the state owes the Office of Hawaiian Affairs, a body created by the state constitution in 1978 to represent Hawaiians, an amount possibly in excess of $1 billion for nonpayment of revenues from the state's Ceded Lands Trust (of which Hawaiians are one-fifth beneficiaries).

These recent governmental initiatives have generated discomfort and, in some instances, a backlash. The court decisions in particular, which recognize indigenous practices and depart from traditional Western property law tenets, have greatly unsettled some lawyers, businesses, title insurance companies, land developers, missionary descendants, and media. Members of the general public also are discomfited by huge payments from the state treasury and the possible transfer of large tracts of state land to a Hawaiian entity in settlement of Hawaiian claims. The backlash has taken the form of strong and sometimes vituperative media commentary, controversial legislative proposals to whittle down court pronouncements, and political organizing for a state constitutional convention to repeal or limit Hawaiian rights.

The sentiments of Alice Zenger, Lehua Napoleon, and Alice Aiwohi are part of this larger story about the historical and continuing subordination on account of race and political status. Those sentiments are also about political and legal movements—and resistance to them—to repair resulting wounds so that Hawaiians can rebuild for their future.

It is in this setting of governmental and public support and opposition, amid the strong Hawaiian sovereignty movement, that the Asian American churches proposed their resolution of apology and reparations. And it is in this setting that the Asian American churches endeavored to redress what they perceived to be Hawaiian justice grievances underlying sometimes strained, present-day interracial relations.

## Why Examine Asian American and Native Hawaiian Conflict and Healing?

Before concluding, some lingering questions call for a response. Why examine Asian American and Native Hawaiian relations in such detail? Why look at race in Hawai'i? What is the relevance of this inquiry to interracial justice issues in twenty-first-century America? These are important questions, for I have not, as have others, described Hawai'i as a race relations model. This "race relations model" label carries two dubious meanings. As a descriptive model of race relations, it falsely essentializes the complex interplay of location, institutions, cultures, and people, glossing over myriad subtle and overt racial conflicts. Moreover, as a guidance model for race relations, it unduly valorizes Hawai'i, in effect saying "be like Hawai'i" without carefully teasing out the complexities of race relations and explaining the relevance of one locale's experiences to another's. I thus do not look at Hawai'i as a model of, or for, race relations.

I do, nevertheless, find the dynamics of Asian American and Native Hawaiian relations in Hawai'i to be particularly relevant to a more generalized inquiry about interracial justice. Despite many important differences, Hawai'i now and several parts of the United States in the near future share a critical resemblance in terms of racial demographics. Asians and Asian Americans (including many recent immigrants from Southeast Asia) comprise a politically and economically significant portion of Hawai'i's population. They are of diverse cultures and disparate socioeconomic classes and have multiple identities. Documented and undocumented workers from Mexico are among the state's fastest-growing immigrant labor groups. Hawai'i's indigenous peoples are asserting historically rooted claims to land and self-governance and are rapidly becoming players in the state economy. African Americans, although few in number, continue to suffer overt and institutional discrimination.[36] Although whites are the largest single racial group, they are a numerical minority and no longer dominate elective political offices. They do, however, continue to exert dominant control over private business and the media.[37] Hawai'i is transforming its economic base from agriculture and military to service and light industry, with many lower-end jobs filled by recent immigrants. Group stereotyping addresses not only culture but also institutional power. For example, an anti–Asian American backlash has developed from a "mythology" of Asian American dominance, particularly by Japanese Americans. Even though Japanese Americans are highly visible in elective offices and are overrepresented in public-sector employment, "contrary to popular misconception," they "do not have the highest occupational status . . . [and are] especially absent in terms of corporate power."[38]

Predictions about demographics for cities in California, Washington, New York, Florida, Illinois, and Texas for the year 2020 bear important similarities to and differences from Hawai'i's current demographics, as do anticipated demographic changes throughout the country.[39] One commonality is the significance of "borderlands" (discussed more fully in chapter 5). My use of "borderlands" has two meanings; one territorial, the other representational. Defined territorially, borderlands are areas in which situations historically oppressive of racial minorities are changing sharply in terms of demographics, economics, and politics. Defined representationally, borderlands refer to the locus of cultural or ideological contention over identities and images, the representations of groups engaged in struggle over systemic oppression.[40] In both usages, borderlands are characterized by continuing contests over identity and power. A second commonality in these borderlands is the intense interactions *among* racial groups generally and interracial grievances and healing efforts particularly—issues of interracial justice.

# Part 2

# Race, Culture, and Responsibility

How are we to deal with the problems of interracial grievance described in part 1? More specifically, how can we develop a practical approach to interracial reconciliation through justice? To develop an approach that is both sophisticated and workable, we need basic theoretical concepts, and that is the task of part 2. How are race, culture, and grievance linked for racial communities in post–civil rights America? Why are prevailing views of group agency and responsibility outdated, and what alternative understandings might be offered? Finally, how might we think critically and pragmatically when shaping interracial justice practice? These are the questions addressed next.

4

# "It's Sanitized, Guiltless Racism"

## Race, Culture, and Grievance

Behind the mountains lie other mountains.

SALLY FALK MOORE,
"Treating Law as Knowledge," p. 26

In 1995 dozens of African American churches in the South burned. A presidential candidate, who earlier declared that America was engaged in a "culture war," encouraged Americans to "lock and load"—and many understood his statements as favoring white American supremacy. Consistent with this understanding, a flier circulated on the University of Southern California campus "alert[ed] all the whites that the niggersare [sic] taking over. Take up arms and defend yourselves, my brothers." At Emory University in Atlanta, African American students found a note under their door saying, "You niggersnever [sic] sleep," and a Jewish student's shirt was marked with a swastika—in her closet.[1] In Flint, Michigan, four white youths hitched a train ride into a economically depressed area inhabited mainly by blacks and were sexually assaulted and shot. A

Northern California white man, frustrated with his lack of job prospects and with America's changing cultural face, awoke one morning, decided to kill the first Asian American he saw, and stabbed Eddy Wu in the back at the neighborhood grocery store. Anti–Asian American harassment and violence in Northern California jumped 113 percent between 1993 and 1995, and following the recent media frenzy over Asian political campaign contributions and the broad-ranging investigation of Asian Americans, additional harassment is predicted.[2] Indeed, some people worry that the United States is becoming "irredeemably racist."[3]

How does this perception square with America's self-image as the melting pot and home of the free or with perceptions of a now-level racial playing field (the "end of racism") and the call to repeal civil rights laws?[4] How do we grapple with these colliding perceptions? With what tools?

Notions of race, culture, and conflict are changing rapidly. Traditional assumptions, "usually so deep as to seem natural or incontestable, are newly open for discussion."[5] Persisting socioeconomic differences between white Americans and other racial groups, emerging white anger, increasing conservatism, shifting political alignments, and intensified scholarly debate about the meaning of racial justice encourage us to "dig deeper into cultural presuppositions." We are catching a glimpse of other mountains behind the mountains. That glimpse, seen through changing theoretical frames, deepens our understanding of the kinds of racial harms addressed by interracial justice.

## Types of Race Controversies

What many Americans of all races desire is peaceable relations. Instead of mutual goodwill, however, what many feel about racial conditions today is angst. Indeed, President Clinton identifies anger and confusion about race as America's number one problem.

Angst is revealed in white American perceptions of communities of color. Many whites (and some nonwhites) perceive immigrants—primarily those from Asia and Mexico—as economic problems at best and cultural threats to mainstream America at worst.[6] Conservative politicians and media personalities blame racial minorities for many of America's social and economic ills.[7] Traditional liberals send mixed messages of support for affirmative action, saying perhaps we should consider class disadvantage, but not race, in the school admissions or job-hiring calculus. White frustration with racial minorities "playing the race card" simmers at a slow boil. Susan Smith blamed the abduction of her two boys, whom she murdered, on a dark colored man, and America willingly believed her. O. J. Simpson's acquittal outraged whites throughout the country.

At the same time, angst is revealed as racial minorities bristle at what they perceive to be a white backlash against their small educational and economic gains. Socioeconomic conditions for African Americans overall have declined, yet a sizable majority of whites favor the repeal of affirmative action.[8] The small yet significant emerging African American middle class expresses consternation at the continuing discrimination in housing, mortgage financing, and employment and in social clubs and restaurants. Native Americans face state taxing and regulatory encroachment on gaming, the first tribal economic ventures to succeed at lifting reservation communities out of poverty. Latina/o immigrants are angered by constant mainstream suspicion about the legality of their presence, and Southeast Asian immigrants complain about their high group poverty rate coupled with their exclusion, as Asians, from government programs for the disadvantaged.[9]

Finally, racial angst is reflected in the heightened prominence of conflicts among nonwhite racial communities. Interracial tensions occupy center stage. Social scientists observe that interminority relations in the United States have "undergone a dramatic shift since the mid-1980s. They have become more tense, more provoking, and more confusing."[10] That shift, they observe, is tied to a shrinking economic pie, continuing Asian and Latina/o immigration, worsening inner-city living conditions, differential minority group power, neoconservative political backlash, and expanded media attention. Small face-to-face conflicts become full-blown intergroup controversies—"more provoking, and more confusing." The intensifying interracial conflicts described in chapter 1, along with expanding coalitional efforts, mark the late 1990s racial landscape.[11]

Given the public injunction against racism and the legal ban on intentional race discrimination, why is there so much racial angst, so much confusion and anger, and so little harmony? I will not attempt to offer an encompassing answer, but I will, in this chapter, explore one aspect of that question relevant to interracial justice: What are the differing types of race controversies contributing to this confusion and anger, and how are they addressed?

One type of race controversy emerges from an individual's or institution's present-day acts of invidious racial discrimination. Those acts are directed at and inflict ascertainable harm on specific individuals. Examples include racial hate violence on the criminal side (burning down a church because its congregants are black) and racially motivated discrimination on the civil side (purposely rejecting qualified Latinas/os for jobs or housing). Legislatures and courts try to address these kinds of actions through laws targeting identifiable perpetrators of ill will. Hate crime statutes mandate harsher sentences for race-motivated crimes. Courts sometimes block ongoing intentional job discrimination and order monetary payments or compel settlements—witness Texaco's sizable settlement of a federal court employment discrimination class action on the revelation of overt racism by high-level officials. Civil rights statutes and court process, however, provide only limited aid to racial minorities in these kinds of situations. Litigation costs and delay, labyrinthine procedures, narrow remedial options, and a politically conservative federal judiciary make civil rights enforcement, even in clear cases of ill will, a difficult and uncertain process. For this reason, further developed in chapter 7, many instances of this first type of race controversy are not brought to the attention of, let alone redressed by, the courts.

When these contemporary acts of discrimination are unredressed—when one group perceives another as "getting away with it"—intergroup grievances are exacerbated. One such example arises out of the U.S. Supreme Court's refusal to apply a state racial hate sentencing law. The white defendants burned a cross in the front yard of an African American family's home, recalling symbols of race hatred and Ku Klux Klan intimidation tactics. The Court held unconstitutional the Minnesota statute enhancing sentences for race hate crimes because the law unduly prohibited the defendants' freedom of speech.[12]

I will not debate the propriety of the Court's ruling other than to note the shock and dismay of many African Americans at the apparent unwillingness of judges to enforce legislative mandates punishing blatant acts of race supremacy. Indeed, embittered, exhausted, and confused is how an attorney describes her clients after civil rights enforcement efforts.

A second type of race or ethnic controversy involves acts of group oppression that inflict long-lasting trauma on group members, sometimes for generations. International examples of these historic acts include the Jewish Holocaust; the "cleansing" of Croats and Muslims in Bosnia; the killing fields of Cambodia; the confiscation of land and the decimation of culture of New Zealand's Maoris; and the kidnapping and forced prostitution of Korean women by the Japanese military during World War II. National examples include the enslavement of African Americans for southern plantations; the mass internment of innocent Japanese Americans during World War II; and the U.S. military massacre of American Indians at Sand Creek, Colorado. Social justice movements organized by political groups focus on these controversies by making justice claims against governments and established institutions. Redress, if any, usually comes in the form of the limited apologies and reparations—symbolic acts of atonement.

Between these two types of race controversies lies a third. It involves neither present harms intentionally inflicted on individuals because of their race (grievances sometimes handled by criminal and antidiscrimination laws) nor the horrific acts of domination that darken the pages of modern American and world history (the focus of social justice efforts). Rather, this third type of controversy involves members of different groups seeking to live together peaceably and work together politically who are stymied by the continuing effects of racial wounds inflicted by one group's participation in public or private systems subordinating the other. This kind of controversy is marked by group relationships broken not by individual discriminatory acts or historical trauma but largely by a group's sometimes sharp, oftentimes mundane deployment of subordinating social, economic, and political structures. Criminal law punishment, antidiscrimination law remedies, and social justice movements overlook the grievances generated by these racial conditions.

What are those subordinating structures, and what is the nature of the wounds inflicted? In brief, this third kind of controversy usually arises between whites and nonwhites when societal structures that historically enforced a racial hierarchy (for instance, social segregation in clubs or neighborhoods) continue to exert an influence. It often arises among communities of color when racial groups with some emergent power participate in (or at least support) and benefit from structures tending to exclude or subjugate members of other racial communities, recalling for those communities memories of painful oppression by whites.

## Systemic Exclusion and Subjugation

Social structures are the collective norms, rules, practices, and routines—the systems—that shape the operations of governments and private institutions. These structures influence the social, economic, and political life of groups in a polity. How and when those structures become subordinating is explained in part by the concept of oppression.

*Oppression* is an explosive term that easily evokes a defensive reaction. I use the term carefully and acknowledge its many meanings. Rather than use *racism* (which is diffuse in meaning and even more publicly explosive) or *discrimination* (with its narrow legal meaning), I use *oppression* to elaborate on the systemic grievances of exclusion and subjugation underlying many face-to-face interracial conflicts. I do so not to label "good" and "bad" groups—for oppression at times is multifaceted—but as a tool for examining interracial grievances that arise less often from individual acts of bigotry than from the collective operation of societal organizations and institutions.

For Iris Marion Young, understanding group oppression and its companion concept of domination is the starting point for achieving justice for those most often subject to society's "disabling constraints"[13]—racial minorities, women, gays and lesbians, and the differently abled. Traditionally, oppression meant tyranny by a ruling elite. A prime example is the pre-1993 overtly racist apartheid regime in South Africa, engineered and controlled by the white National Party. Young broadens this definition of oppression to include "structural phenomena." Oppression can be systemic; it can be built into institutional structures such as schools, churches, businesses, law, medicine, media, and government bureaucracies. Some groups benefit disproportionately from the operation of those structures. The disadvantages that some groups suffer result not from the tyrannical acts of a dominant ruler but from the daily practices of a generally well intentioned society—disadvantages "embedded in unquestioned norms, habits, and symbols, in the assumptions underlying institutional rules and the collective consequences of following those rules."[14]

In broad terms, those disadvantages are oppressive when they, collectively, exclude group members from full participation in the polity or subjugate those members through inferior treatment in the polity. These "disabling constraints" of racial exclusion and subjugation are particularly insidious in post–civil rights America because they are informed by unquestioned norms of group behavior and unexamined assumptions about institutional rules.

For this reason, critical race theorists identify the dominant group's self-interest, rather than ignorance or enmity, as a major factor in the conservative federal judiciary's narrowing of civil rights doctrine. They describe how "areas of law ostensibly designed to advance the cause of racial equality often benefit powerful whites more than those who are racially oppressed."[15] Along with critical sociologists, cultural anthropologists, and cognitive psychologists, they move inquiry into the sources of racial oppression away from "a coherent, discrete cluster of beliefs and attitudes held by individuals and social groups and toward the study of how racial meanings are implicated in discourses, institutional power arrangements, and social practices that may or may not be explicitly marked as racial."[16]

The U.S. Commission on Civil Rights adopted this systemic view in its highly regarded 1970 study.[17] The commission perceived racism as America's most complicated and important problem. Despite the existence of overt racial animus, the commission identified subtle systemic racial oppression as the more pervasive problem. It identified the economic, psychological, and political benefits derived by whites from racism institutionalized in government, business, and private life and concluded that "almost every white American supports some form of institutional subordination." A recent U.S. Labor Department study found that institutionalized racial subordination persists in the marketplace. Owing to "attitudinal and organizational barriers," the glass ceiling for racial minorities exists "at a much lower level than first thought."[18]

The circumstances of the death of Cynthia Wiggins, an African American, are instructive. Wiggins, a single mother and engaged to be married, was struggling to stay off welfare by working as a cashier at a restaurant in a suburban shopping mall in Cheektowaga, New York. She commuted round-trip for almost two hours a day by public bus from a largely black downtown Buffalo neighborhood. Although charter buses from the region deposited shoppers on the mall premises, mall owners refused to allow inner-city buses to do the same. Thus Wiggins had to walk three hundred yards from the nearest bus stop and cross a busy seven-lane highway without traffic lights. While crossing on a day with snow mounds on the highway shoulder, she was hit by a truck and killed.

Why had the mall owners vigorously resisted eight years of efforts by city transportation officials to move the bus stop to a safer spot on the mall perimeter? According to one report, a mall owner underscored the mall's attractiveness by assuring a store operator that "you'll never see an inner-city bus on the mall premises."[19] What was it about the culture of the area that enabled both the mall owner and the store operators to understand that statement as a racially coded, class-based message? Businesses and housing developments in many predominantly white Buffalo suburbs had attempted in various ways to exclude outsiders, ostensibly to preserve racial homogeneity. (Racial exclusivity is one reason that many whites have left increasingly diverse and increasingly socioeconomically troubled cities.) An observer viewed the mall owner's bus stop decision in this context as "sanitized, guiltless racism." That seemingly mundane decision, and many others like it, made by businesses and tacitly accepted by white customers, maintained a system of exclusion. As another observer noted, the use of seemingly neutral rules and regulations "doesn't directly say no blacks are allowed, but the effect is the same."[20] Cynthia Wiggins, who tried to break through the wall of exclusion by getting a suburban mall job, paid (albeit indirectly) the ultimate price.

According to Young's definition, whites in the United States have consistently oppressed racial minorities, not only through the horrors of slavery and Jim Crow violence, for instance, but also thereafter through cultural denigration and legalized and informal segregation in schools, jobs, housing, and politics. Also by Young's definition, under certain circumstances, nonwhite racial groups have acted oppressively toward other racial minorities, although not in the same way that whites have. Racial groups with a degree of social or political power and with at least intermittent access to institutional operations and means of communications can participate directly or complicitly in the oppression of others. Oppression can be perpetrated, or aided, by still partially subordinated groups with emergent, fluctuating power, particularly in times of rapid sociodemographic and economic change, through what I term in the next chapter the redeployment of oppressive structures and strategies.

Racial groups attain some degree of power by winning city council and school board elections, operating small businesses, publishing community newspapers, entering the lower and middle ranks of government bureaucracies, and producing small numbers of professionals. In particular locales, these groups can be simultaneously oppressed by more dominant groups and oppressive of those struggling in similar ways but with less socioeconomic or political power. Oppression in those instances is multidirectional.

Native Hawaiian grievances against Asian Americans, for example, center not on bigotry or acts of a tyrannical ruler. Rather, they focus on the perceived Asian American redeployment of oppressive rhetorical, economic, and social institutional structures. For scholar and activist Haunani-Kay Trask, the United States, reflecting dominant white interests, still holds Hawai'i as a virtual colony. She perceives partial Asian American complicity in the United States' subjugation of Hawaiians through their redeployment of oppressive systemic structures. Those rhetorical and economic structures include the championing of economic liberty in the form of private property acquisition and development—structures once used by the controlling white oligarchy in Hawai'i to subordinate Asian Americans. Rev. Akaka particularized the grievance by linking the 1848 Mahele (privatization of Hawaiian lands) with the "new Mahele" of the 1970s and 1980s. The current divestiture of Hawaiian (and other private) lands is grounded in rhetoric concerning an individual's fundamental right to landownership. Framed in those terms, state legislation facilitates the divestiture of land primarily from large landholding Hawaiian trusts and transfers ownership to individual homeowners (many middle-class Asian Americans and whites) at moderate cost—thereby further distancing Hawaiians from Hawaiian land.

Thus the injuries of systemic oppression are often real, yet diffuse. They are sometimes temporally unconnected to specific acts. I define those injuries in the following way: Racial group members suffer systemic oppression when they are subject to disabling societal constraints on their self-determination regarding participation in the economy and in political decisions affecting conditions of group life (exclusion) and on their self-development regarding identity, community, and culture (subjugation). Such disabling constraints occur when "systematic institutional processes . . . prevent some people from learning and using satisfying and expansive skills in socially recognized settings, or . . . inhibit or prevent people from participating in determining their actions or the conditions of their actions."[21] These group constraints and their consequences over time, including a lower group status and material well-being, give life to intergroup grievances.[22]

## Influences of Culture

In the conceptual scheme just described and alluded to earlier, culture is integral to racial oppression and the ensuing intergroup grievances. "[The dominant]culture has always marked cultural difference by producing the [racial] other; it has always been comparative, and racism has always been an integral part of it: the two are inextricably clustered together, feeding off and generating each other."[23] How does this occur? Let us step back.

The emerging scholarly consensus is that "culture ought to be regarded . . . 'as the signifying system through which necessarily (though among other means) a social order is communicated, reproduced, experienced, and explored.' "[24] Culture informs how racial minorities think about themselves and others in social settings. For racial minorities, culture is a complex matter: a group may identify and separate its own (historically rooted) culture from a dominant (out there) culture, even as the minority culture is being reshaped by influences of a dominant culture and even though those influences defy easy description.

Despite their complexity and ambiguity, cultures are significant parts of the social landscape. Group membership is often determined initially by race, as are group members' attributed traits. Initial social connections and disconnections are indeed affected by appearance and presumed ancestry. A racial group's internal structures for building relationships and ascertaining the meaning of interactions, institutions, and social norms, however, are located at a deeper level. These internal structures are rooted in that group's historical and contemporary cultural practices. In this view, culture gives a social meaning to race. Culture is not simply shared practices or values. It is a "system of inherited conceptions expressed in symbolic forms by means of which [group members] communicate, perpetuate, and develop their knowledge about attitudes toward life."[25] Although in crucial respects multidimensional, shifting, and regenerating, a racial group's culture "provides the framework, the anchor, in which a range of choices and values can be considered and evaluated."[26]

Culture also informs how dominant groups think about and act on race. The still-thriving English Only movement, for example, is cultural in its normative emphasis (all people in America should conform to the mainstream culture) and racial in its manifestation (nonwhite racial groups are the focal point of mandates to conform). The recent California initiatives on affirmative action and unlawful immigration were defended in economic and cultural terms but were racially coded in their conception and impact.[27] As a white proponent of the reclamation of "American culture" revealed, "There's something happening in our favor for a change."[28] In these instances, culture becomes a surrogate for race. The protection of mainstream culture stands in for the protection of whites in the mainstream. The socially unacceptable derogation of a racial group is recast as an acceptable criticism of the group's culture. At an unconscious level, cultural denigration does the dirty work formerly done by overt racism.

Cognitive social psychology therefore connects culture to "unconscious racism." The dominant cultural belief systems embracing largely negative images of nonwhites influence us all. Culture transmits beliefs and preferences not as explicit lessons but as what seems to be part of a person's rational ordering of society. In most instances, people fail to recognize the influence of cultural experience on their racial beliefs or the ways in which those beliefs shape their actions.[29]

The unconscious cultural assumptions of well-meaning people supporting oppressive systemic acts are revealed in the reported opinion of the United States Court of Appeals for the Ninth Circuit in *In re Halladjian*.[30] Four Armenians sought to become naturalized citizens. To do so under the federal immigration statute, they had to prove they were "free white" people. Government officials opposed their naturalization, claiming they were not white. First, the government officials argued that white "is the equivalent of 'European.'" Second, and more significant, the officials contended that white was used in the statute as "a brief and convenient designation descriptive of the prevailing ideals, standards, and aspirations of the people of Europe." White was thus presented as the superior cultural and "mental development of a people" and, by contrast, it defined and thereby excluded from citizenship lesser developed (that is, nonwhite) groups. The court determined that Armenians should be deemed white, and thus eligible for citizenship, because they had assimilated European culture to a far greater degree than had other groups marked by American society as unassimilable and therefore nonwhite—the Japanese and Chinese.

Linda Krieger deepens this view of the unconscious, culture-based creation of the racial other by offering a cognitive social theory account of group stereotyping and the manner in which stereotyping contributes to intergroup discrimination.[31] While her account explores the misunderstandings embraced by prevailing federal antidiscrimination law, its implications extend beyond legal justice. Krieger posits, correctly, that the prevailing antidiscrimination law views discrimination as a racially motivated act, an intentional bad act reflecting deviance from "normal" ways of thinking. The current civil rights adjudicatory process therefore searches for a bad motive—that is, for overt stereotypes reflecting prejudice, for something abnormal. Krieger argues, however, that this intentionalist view and the law tied to it misunderstand the actual cognitive dynamics of intergroup discrimination.

Social cognition theory holds that ordinary cognitive structures and processes "involved in categorization and information processing can in and of themselves result in stereotyping and other forms of biased intergroup judgment" and that discriminatory actions based on racial stereotypes occur regardless of motivation. This theory plays out in four parts.

First, stereotyping itself is nothing special. It is an ordinary form of categorizing used by all people as part of the sifting and sorting needed to handle huge quantities of incoming information. Without categories, we would be overwhelmed and unable to make even the simplest decisions. Second, and perhaps most significant, people give substance to a stereotype by creating a mental prototype of the typical category member. Krieger's discussion does not identify how that prototype is defined other than to indicate that it reflects "a person's accumulated knowledge, beliefs, experiences... and expectancies." I attribute that "substance giving" largely to culture. As discussed in detail earlier in this chapter, as circumscribed by place and time, group culture gives contours and content to racial categories. Culture, or more accurately multiple cultures, generates prototypical images of the mid-western American farmer, or inner-city Asian American merchant or unwed African American mother. Culture analysis and social cognition theory thus intersect in describing the dynamics of substance giving to racial categories.

Third, once fleshed out, a culturally generated prototype, or social schema, functions as a filter that biases "in predictable ways the perception, interpretation, encoding, retention, and recall of information about other people" we actually encounter. If a decision maker determines that a job applicant falls into a particular social category, then her prototypic vision of members of that category kicks in and determines how she processes and interprets information about that person. Schematic biases, which sneak up on the decision maker, distorting the data on which her decision is based, are cognitive rather than motivational. Fourth, because they function as social schema, stereotypes often operate without the awareness of the decision maker. Cognitive bias may be both unconscious and unintended.

According to cognitive social theorists, this often unconscious process of stereotyping and information organizing contributes to intergroup discrimination in several ways. In terms of ingroup/outgroup behavior, studies reveal that even without a factual basis for differentiation, people perceive those described as "members of their group as more similar to them, and members of different [groups] as more different from them."[32] People also tend to "perceive outgroup members as an undifferentiated mass [they all look and act the same], while ingroup members are more highly differentiated."[33] Finally, in part due to stereotyping, people tend to be able to recall the undesirable behavior of outgroup members better than the similar behavior of ingroup members and to favor ingroup members in the allocation of rewards. In terms of decision making, stereotyping contributes to discrimination by narrowly shaping how we process information about other people. Information is filtered through the preexisting and culturally generated schema. Information that does not fit the schema is unconsciously manipulated or recoded according to systemic biases, resulting in social judgments that tend to favor those seen as ingroup members and to disfavor others. For cognitive social theorists, these errors of social judgment by decision makers generate intergroup discrimination even in the absence of discriminatory intent or racial animus. As implied by the foregoing descriptions, culture plays a key role in racial exclusion and subjugation and the grievances they generate, by influencing both the material conditions of racial groups' lives and the representations, or depictions, of racial groups.

*Materiality.* Culture suppression affects the material conditions of racial group life by dislodging a racial group's anchor to self-understanding. This occurs when a racial group's framework for understanding itself and guiding its relations with others is distorted or destroyed by the intentional or unconscious acts of those with some social, economic, or political power. In this way, cultural domination becomes a disabling mechanism that constrains a racial group's self-development.

Behavioral constraint occurs through a racial group member's reluctance to act assertively because of fear of violence, disorientation resulting from prohibitions on language and religious practices, or self-doubt rooted in the mainstream's disparagement of group customs, work practices, and family relations. Psychological constraint occurs as communal interactions among group members become attenuated when cultural practices are suppressed. When group members' cultural anchor is dislodged and they are not fully accepted by the dominant culture, they experience a loss of identity that results in feelings of alienation and anxiety. Their framework for understanding events and relationships disintegrates. Culture negation of this sort thus simultaneously fractures the framework through which racial communities "make sense of their lives" and facilitates systemic acts of exclusion and subjugation—acts experienced in tangible, concrete ways by racial group members. Under these conditions, oppression is perpetuated practically and justified paternalistically. In these ways, culture plays a material role in racial oppression.

Thus when Lehua Napoleon testified that through the overthrow of the Hawaiian nation and the confiscation of land and the suppression of Hawaiian religion and language, the United States annihilated "our way of life," she was identifying behavioral constraints on Hawaiians' capacity to act affirmatively, confidently, and cohesively in a semiforeign social structure—the results of which are revealed in Hawaiians' current highest rate of prisoner incarceration, poorest health, highest infant mortality rate, low median income, and on. Napoleon also identified psychological constraints in the disorientation arising from the loss of identity, communal ties, and common frameworks for understanding events and relationships.

*Representation.* Culture also plays a closely related representational role in racial oppression. Through language, particularly social narratives, culture constructs societal "truths" about groups which in turn legitimate public and private actions. Language thus links culture to knowledge and power. Albert Memmi, a Tunisian Jew, developed this linkage in his exploration of the foundational structures of racism in colonial settings.[34] Building on the insights of Edward Said and Frantz Fanon, and in important respects echoing Krieger's cognitive analysis of racial discrimination, Memmi posited the central significance of discursive, or representational, strategies.

For Memmi, the maintenance of the material conditions of racial oppression depends on a discursive strategy composed of four main components. First, in viewing the minority racial group, the dominant group (through its institutions) describes aspects of cultural difference, whether real or imagined. These differences can be cast in terms of physical appearance, intelligence, language, religious practices, work habits, character, and family relations. Second, the dominant institutions attribute value to those differences, elevating the dominant group's traits while denigrating those of the racial minority. Third, dominant institutions extend, or generalize, these value differences concerning particular traits to overall qualitative differences between the two groups, thereby valorizing the dominant group while demonizing, or at least diminishing, the racial minority group. In contrast with the enhanced humanity of the dominant group, the racial minority loses humanity and becomes an object, the "other." Finally, the dominant institutions draw on perceptions of qualitative group difference, and therefore differential human worth, to justify the paternalistic treatment of the "other" at best and harshly unequal, exclusionary, or violent treatment at worst. (Here, the material and representational dimensions of oppression connect most clearly).

In this fashion, racial representations differentiate the culturally superior subject from the inferior other and, in so doing, legitimate racial exclusion or subjugation. During Reconstruction after the Civil War, freed African American slaves moved into formerly all-white cities and sought work and housing, their presence building pressures for social and economic integration. In reaction, whites began to characterize African Americans culturally as uncivilized, lazy, lascivious, and violent. This characterization contrasted sharply with cultural representations of African Americans during slavery, in which docile slaves were depicted as happy with their situation. The post-Reconstruction representational denigration of black culture allowed whites to exclude African Americans from the American polity (through Jim Crow laws) and, in certain areas, to destroy their communities (through lynchings and other forms of violence).

More recently, racially coded references to "a semipermanent welfare constituency" and "welfare queens" disparaged African Americans in cultural-economic terms in order to justify cuts in welfare for families. Similarly, before World War II, Japanese Americans were described as posing a threat to American security for cultural reasons. They were characterized by media and the U.S. Supreme Court as inscrutable, Shinto worshipers inherently loyal to Japan by reason of culture. As "yellow peril," they were excludable by means of mass incarceration. Characterized as savages and heathens by American businessman and religious leaders, countless Native Hawaiians, like Native Americans, died because of Western diseases and, in Lehua Napoleon's words, the "total annihilation of our religion, our culture and language, and our lifestyle"—that is, the destruction of their framework for behavior and meaning-making, the denial of conditions for self-development and self-determination.

In sum, in certain situations, the articulation of cultural differences distinguishes the dominant racial group (or groups) from the racial minority. It also provides a basis for judging that group superior and the racial minority inferior. In this fashion, culture constructs racial differences and supports the imposition of disabling constraints on the racial minority. These constraints of exclusion and subjugation are imposed sometimes through intentional exclusion or violence by bad actors and more often through the unconscious, culturally formed assumptions of ordinary people engaged in daily interactions.

In these ways, race, culture and grievance are linked. And from this linkage, often just beneath the public surface, comes racial angst—that knowable yet undefinable dis-ease that racial communities experience in post–civil rights America.

# 5

# "Who's Hurting Whom?"

Reframing Racial Group Agency
and Responsibility

Does the linkage of race, culture, and grievance and the mounting angst of racial communities help explain the Asian American churches' resolution of apology to Native Hawaiians? Some Hawaiians complain of Asian American ignorance of indigenous culture and hostility toward Hawaiian self-determination claims. Ignorance and hostility are serious charges, especially when an accused group, like Asian Americans, itself continues to be the object of false praise, discrimination, and violence in American society. Discussion of these charges can easily be distorted or taken out of context by those who want only to say "people of color are racist" without inquiring into the dynamics of interracial conflicts and without self-critical analysis.

These charges, and similar complaints among racial communities, nevertheless warrant careful attention. They challenge those inclined to think about race only in black and white terms to think more deeply and broadly across other racial lines. They also challenge racial groups, amid changing demographics and social structure, to look both at and beyond their own struggles with predominantly white-controlled institutions, to inquire into the identity, claims, and goals of other racial groups, including America's first peoples.[1]

For instance, these charges challenge Asian Americans to think about Asian American agency and responsibility in the context of interactions with African Americans, Latinas/os, Native Americans, and Native Hawaiians, to see diverse Asian American communities (and others) sometimes as simultaneously privileged and subordinated, empowered and disempowered. Framing agency and responsibility in these terms opens for scrutiny the extent to which Asian American groups—themselves subject to almost continual stereotyping, discrimination, and violence over the last 150 years in America—have, in Rev. Wong's words, at times situationally "exploited and dehumanized" and "taken advantage of" indigenous peoples and other racial groups. It opens for scrutiny the apology resolution's perceptions of a "particular dynamic . . . of mutual misunderstanding and mistrust, . . . the use of stereotypes and caricatures to demean and dehumanize . . . and the persistence of racist attitudes and actions."[2]

This scrutiny expands the field of vision for Asian Americans to encompass both daily interactions with other racial groups and the larger social dynamics attracting public attention. The former includes encounters in the classroom, at the grocery counter, in the mortgage finance office, and at the political meeting. The latter includes the "violent discourse" between Korean Americans and African Americans in South Central Los Angeles and other locales; the historical foundation, current impact, and social meaning of the Chinese Americans' civil rights challenge to a court order desegregating San Francisco's public schools in the Lowell High School case; and the perceptions, attitudes, and understandings underlying Asian Americans' evenly split vote on California's Proposition 187 concerning the treatment of undocumented, primarily Latina/o and recent Asian, immigrants.[3]

Expanded scrutiny of this sort grounds the inquiry into racial group agency and responsibility in two ways. It situates interracial relations and justice issues in "highly fluid, highly contested . . . borderland site[s] of continuing struggles for identity and power."[4] Contested borderland sites are the terrain, the sociopolitical context. It also calls for a dynamic conception of racial group agency and responsibility.

## "Highly Fluid, Highly Contested Borderland Sites"

By "highly fluid, highly contested borderland sites," I mean specific phys-ical borders over which groups struggle for control and power, whether neighborhoods, streets, or former national territorial boundaries. I also mean figurative borders circumscribing group identity and the social meanings attached to those identities. The former are spatially oriented, the latter discursively represented. For both, contested borderland sites in post–civil rights America are characterized by rapidly changing racial demographics due largely to Asian and Latina/o immigration and by shift-ing economic structures due to the decline of heavy industry.

Those changes are marked by the "proportional decrease of Euro-Americans, the widespread phenomenon of racial and ethnic mixing . . . and even the dissolution of fixed boundaries in the 'conventional black and white dialectic.' "[5] They also are marked by interracial conflict and the increasing media coverage of interracial tensions. The media's com-paratively newfound emphasis bears watching. Some observers perceive that the media's attention to interracial and interethnic conflict "performs in part the cultural work of suppressing awareness of the way the struc-tures of white racism intensify conflict between racial and ethnic others."

With this in mind, those observers nevertheless argue against redivert-ing the entire media (and scholarly) focus back onto white and nonwhite relations. In evaluating the discourses that emerged after the Rodney King police trial uprising in South Central Los Angeles, Susan Friedman, for example, suggested the development of an interracial narrative that sup-plemented rather than displaced the narrative of white racism. Specifically, she called for "a more complicated discourse, one that acknowledges the ongoing impact of white racism but also goes beyond [it]," that is, a discussion that moves beyond fixed categories of good and evil, victims and victimizers.

Indeed, race and gender analysis at the "crossroads of different systems of stratification requires acknowledging how privilege and oppression are often not absolute categories but, rather, shift in relation to different axes of power and powerlessness." Power in multiple social systems flows in many directions. Social actors in the borderlands of those systems assume multiple, sometimes dissonant roles. Victims "can also be victimizers;

agents of change can also be complicitous, depending on the particular axis of power," for "new relationships emerge chiefly at the point where some . . . or postcolonial power is attained."[6]

The intensifying attention to new interracial relationships in highly fluid, highly contested borderland sites underscores the need for a theory of racial group agency and responsibility that accounts for both the relational and the conflictual nature of power among racial groups. How do we comprehend racial groups as social actors in their continuing struggles for identity and power and in light of their potential during those struggles both for liberating action and for redeploying oppressive rhetorical, institutional, and economic structures?

## The Inadequacy of Prevailing Approaches to Racial Group Agency

Interracial conflict has sparked considerable attention. Only a small portion of that attention, however, has focused on understanding nonwhite racial groups as social actors. By "social actors," I mean agents with the power and opportunity to participate affirmatively in the construction of racial identities and intergroup relations. And by "affirmatively," I mean action that involves some degree of creative choice, that involves the recognition of group subjectivity—or put in spatial terms, movement toward a vision of how things should be rather than solely movement in opposition to how things are.

Two divergent approaches to minority racial group agency and responsibility emerged in the 1960s and 1970s civil rights era. One approach drew on "neoconservative ethnicity theory;" the other on colonialism or related nationalism and class-based theories.[7] The former engaged in a form of social scientific cultural analysis; the latter in structural analysis. Those two approaches tended to polarize discussions about racial group agency and responsibility, often along political lines. Those approaches frame contemporary thinking, and their continuing influence is deeply problematic because they fail to reflect sharp changes in America's racial demographics, economic structure, and political views of civil rights. More important, they fail to account adequately for the complexity of racial group agency in the structuring of group identities and intergroup relations. As we shall see later, neither provides foundational insight into the fluid, situated nature of racial group agency, and neither illuminates in meaningful fashion group responsibility for interracial harms and prospects for interracial healing in post–civil rights America.

Ethnicity theorists focused on ethnicity rather than race, using culture principally to describe processes of ethnic immigrant group assimilation. They also used culture ideologically to argue normatively for immigrant assimilation into the dominant Anglo-American mainstream. In crucial respects, early ethnicity theory provided the foundation for the 1950s and 1960s civil rights movement's emphasis on integration and equality of opportunity.

The social upheaval of the late 1960s and early 1970s, accompanied by the rise of black nationalism and colonialism race discourses, facilitated the reworking of ethnicity theory. This reworked ethnicity theory continued to focus on culture but offered a new methodology and a new ideology. Its methodology centered on racial group agency concerning negative cultural practices and values and on racial group responsibility for the consequences of those practices and values. Its ideology rejected group-based equality and emphasized the dangerous radicalism of race-conscious policies.

In this neoconservative form, ethnicity theory tended to overstate the extent of racial group agency.[8] It concentrated on the impacts of culture on immigrant racial group assimilation into a mythic white American mainstream. Assimilation, and therefore group success, depends on each group's characteristics, including cultural practices and values regarding education, work, and family. By virtue of these characteristics, each racial group controls its destiny. Failure to assimilate fully is the fault of the group and its culture. This neoconservative version of ethnicity theory, prevalent today, draws its conclusions about racial group agency and responsibility from the immigrant analogy. America opens the same general path for all immigrants—contact, conflict, accommodation, and finally assimilation.[9] Ethnic Italians and Irish, for example, because of their cultural characteristics, assimilated after early conflicts.

By equating white ethnic immigrants with more recent immigrants of color, however, the immigrant analogy overlooks unique and often insurmountable institutional and attitudinal barriers facing nonwhite immigrant groups.[10] By ignoring these barriers, ethnicity theory over-determines immigrant racial group agency and responsibility concerning group socioeconomic status and intergroup relations. It tends to blame racial minorities for all group disadvantages and thereby masks the influence of social structural factors beyond a group's control.

In his book *The End of Racism*, Dinesh D'Souza extends this neoconservative version of ethnicity theory to a horrendous extreme.[11] He builds on this version of ethnicity theory to justify "rational discrimination" against African Americans—that is, the rejection of African Americans for mortgages, jobs, taxi pickups, and housing rentals. D'Souza agrees with most observers that African Americans as a group are struggling socially and economically. He also acknowledges the statistics concerning overall African American employment, education, housing, and health, noting their comparatively high levels of poverty, unemployment, welfare, and prison incarceration.

To explain these statistics, D'Souza first declares the end of racism. Few people, he asserts, with a disapproving nod toward Richard Herrnstein and Charles Murray, authors of *The Bell Curve*,[12] now adhere to the racist ideology of biological determinism. That ideology links racial superiority or inferiority to genetic traits—attributes over which groups have no control. D'Souza instead connects African Americans' socioeconomic problems to their own cultural and moral failings—attributes over which they do have control. Like the recent ethnicity theorists, he cloaks African Americans and other racial minorities with unbounded agency and therefore total responsibility for their socioeconomic group situations.

From this point, D'Souza makes a short jump to the conclusion that the continuing discrimination against African Americans reflects not prejudice but, rather, rational discrimination. Inferior African American culture and lax morals, buttressed by three decades of interventionist government, are the cause of the overall harsh African American socioeconomic conditions. Those conditions give rise to images of welfare dependents, criminals, and drug addicts. For D'Souza, these images legitimate the adverse white reaction to and discrimination against African Americans.

Although whites cannot rationally discriminate on the basis of a false belief in the biological inferiority of a racial group—that would be racism—they can and do rationally discriminate on the basis of their "true" belief in the cultural inferiority of nonwhite racial groups. That discrimination, according to D'Souza, is not racism; it is rational reaction. Whites will stop discriminating when racial minorities uplift their culture and improve their culture-based behavior. Until racial minorities do so, continuing discrimination by whites—at least in the private sphere—is legitimate. D'Souza therefore calls for the dismantling of affirmative action programs (racial minorities' subordinate status is "their fault") and for the repeal of the 1964 Civil Rights Act (private discrimination is rational).

D'Souza's arguments are intensely problematic. I will address only those problems pertaining to racial group agency and responsibility. D'Souza employs the notion of cultural inferiority of racial groups to justify the continuing societal subordination of African Americans and other racial minorities. By talking about culture, he avoids talking about race. More important, by talking about racial group culture (which he finds socially constructed) instead of biologically determined racial traits, he is able to explain group inferiority and subordinate status as a matter of group choice, or agency. When a racial group has choices, as it does over its own culture, it bears responsibility for the consequences of its choices. Bad group socioeconomic conditions, according to D'Souza, reflect bad cultural choices, not racism.

D'Souza substitutes cultural inferiority (real) for racial inferiority (false) to both explain and justify continuing racial oppression. In doing so, he explicitly endorses as rational a cultural hierarchy that places white-European culture alone at the top and implicitly supports, as one D'Souza critic terms it, "cultural racism."[13] He ignores ways in which the dominant institutional structures (for example, English Only laws) and racial animosity (for example, that displayed following the O. J. Simpson verdict) constrain the field of cultural choices for minority racial groups. Consistent with ethnicity theory, D'Souza's approach thus sharply exaggerates the agency of African American and other racial groups.

In contrast, colonialism, nationalism, and economic theories, from the left and right, tend to minimize racial group agency. According to those theories in their many permutations, dominant institutional structures determine racial identities and racial group relations for largely economic reasons, eliminating racial group agency and, by implication, racial group responsibility.

Colonialism theory tend to view race as an institutionally employed mechanism for devaluing conquered racial groups in order to justify white imperialist control over land and resources.[14] It addresses the ways in which racial discourses helped legitimate European colonial domination. Racial differentiation and stereotyping by colonizers created the dehumanized racial "other," which in turn justified continuing white conquest. In related fashion, internal colonialism theory links all racial minorities in America with formerly colonized "Third World" groups internationally in opposition to continuing Western capitalist domination.[15] According to these colonialism views, the main identity and action options for minority racial groups are oppositional. The focal point of social action is resisting the socioeconomic structures created and maintained by dominant Western powers. Interracial distinctions are submerged and interracial conflicts are attributed to dominant power strategies of divide and conquer. Racial group agency in the formation of interracial relations is minimized.

Nationalist movements in the late 1960s emerged as one response to colonialism analyses and the perceived failure of the civil rights movement's integration strategy. African Americans, Mexican Americans, Native Americans, and Native Hawaiians each reconstructed their racial identity around notions of group sovereignty and control over land, language, and culture. With some exceptions in the later movement phases, however, nationalists linked group agency to oppositional politics.[16] Freedom from white racism meant fighting against white-controlled institutions. Racial group agency, again with some later exceptions, was seen as largely reactive. In this way, both nationalism and colonialism theories, which retain some continuing vitality for indigenous groups, tend to minimize the idea of nonwhite racial groups as social actors in the formation of positive intergroup relations.

Class-based economic theory also minimizes racial group agency. Monopoly capitalism, for example, is perceived as structuring the "violent discourse" between African Americans and Korean Americans. The structures of large-scale capitalism impel Korean American immigrant entrepreneurs to exploit African American consumers in their neighborhoods and Korean American workers in their community. This is explained in terms of Asian American "middleman" minority status. As objects of mainstream discrimination in obtaining jobs, loans, and commercial and residential leases, minority entrepreneurs find it extremely difficult to begin their own enterprises. They therefore locate themselves between "producer and consumer, employer and employee, . . . and elite and masses" in areas deemed undesirable by mainstream businesses.[17] In this setting, for example, immigrant Korean subcontractors feel compelled by competition and discrimination to accept minimum price payments from manufacturers. These "middle" firms then sometimes operate in substandard conditions, pay less than the minimum wage, and view fair wage and safe working conditions laws as threats to razor-thin profit margins. Minority businesses operating under these circumstances are "perceived as callous, . . . oppressive, and exploitative, allowing the actual employers to remain essentially invisible."[18] This invisible structure of monopoly capitalism, controlled largely by whites in America, creates and maintains conditions that lead some African Americans to view Koreans in America as the "new economic exploiters." From the other side of the economic theory spectrum, law and economics observe conflicts among social groups over scarce material resources and posit that "the very mechanism that facilitates greater intra-group cooperation [in a fight for resources] will ensure a new form of conflict: competition for inter-group status." In other words, a group's members will band together internally to elevate the group's status publicly to enhance the group's ability to compete against others. From this perspective, the economic-political system structures zero-sum competition among racial groups over scarce resources, thereby fostering both cooperation within groups and conflict between groups. These are useful, although not particularly startling, structuralist insights.

This analysis breaks new ground in law and economics because it draws on these insights to offer a status-production model of race discrimination. Whites discriminate not because of inherent evil but because "whites gain status by discriminating against blacks." The exclusion of blacks from workplaces and social organizations, for example, enhances white privilege and therefore white stature.

According to this analysis, discrimination is status driven, and those resisting it often employ "status defense mechanisms." The first mechanism is the "enraged victim's" response in kind: "attempting to disparage and subordinate the original discriminator." Because of power differences, this mechanism often fails. The second mechanism, and relevant to this inquiry, is the victim's attempt to "regain status by subordinating someone other than the original discriminator. If whites present too difficult a target, other minority groups [or those in one's own group] may be within reach."[19]

Interracial group conflict and the agency of nonwhite racial groups are thus defined structurally. Whites discriminate against racial minorities to enhance white status. White economic and political dominance means that white discrimination forces racial minorities to compete for an inordinately small piece of the economic-entitlement pie. Racial group anger at systemic discrimination and status loss is sometimes vented directly against whites, both to claim vengeance and to recapture status. But more often, that anger is transformed into efforts to regain status by subordinating other racial groups. Apart from its theoretical or empirical soundness, this structuralist approach is relevant to our inquiry because it tends to erase racial group agency. Conflict among racial groups is viewed as the product of white economic-political dominance and white discrimination. Racial groups are social actors only in direct or skewed opposition to white dominance.

Ethnicity theory and nationalism, colonialism and economics theories—described here broadly without attention to nuance—occupy opposite positions in the discussion of racial group agency. Those positions create an either/or dualism, polarizing the debate often along conservative-liberal political lines. Either racial groups have the power of self-definition and socioeconomic attainment, or they do not. If they do, continuing racial group problems will reflect their cultural choice—it is their fault. If they do not, continuing group problems will be structurally determined by institutional racism—it is not their fault. The former embraces culture and group choice while ignoring the structural constraints of racialization; the latter emphasizes institutional structures to the exclusion of group agency and responsibility.

Colliding views of Asian American agency underscore the inadequacy of these prevailing polar, and polarized, approaches to racial group agency and responsibility. Some contemporary ethnicity theorists point to Asian Americans as the example that proves the rule. Asian American assimilation into society's mainstream, and the model minority image that accompanies it, proves that cultural values and practices determine racial group "success." Hard work, family cohesion, value of education, and entrepreneurial spirit are all that is required. Asian Americans dispel the notion that race itself poses a structural barrier for immigrant groups of color. Racial groups are the agents of their own destiny.

For other observers, Asian American assimilation and the model minority image are largely myths that disguise high levels of poverty among Asian immigrants, particularly those from South and Southeast Asia, and continuing discrimination against Asian Americans in education, housing, electoral politics, and the upper levels of business. Those myths also deflect attention from increasing racial hatred of and violence against Asians in America, who are lumped together by many as "foreigners."[20]

For these observers, dominant largely white-controlled institutions maintain the assimilationist norms by which Asian American "success" is measured while at the same time restricting Asian American capacity to succeed. Those institutions, including legislatures, courts, corporate business, churches, government agencies, and the media, continue to shape relations between Asian Americans and other racial minorities through the subtle, often unconscious maintenance of a racial hierarchy. This hierarchy places whites at the top, Asian Americans in the middle, and other racial minorities in competition with one another at the bottom.[21] Viewed this way, Asian Americans lack meaningful agency in the forging of intergroup relations and are being "used" by dominant white society to blame African Americans, Latinas/os, and Native Americans for their social and economic struggles.

In the construction of racial identities and interracial relations, Asian American agency is thus portrayed in contradictory ways. On the one hand, Asian Americans are autonomous members of a social group with unfettered agency. On the other hand, they are the objects of structural constraints imposed from above, with severely limited or nonexistent agency. This conflicting portrayal tracks the opposing positions in the agency debate continued today.

## Reframing Racial Group Agency

I offer a different approach to racial group agency. My approach more explicitly addresses the idea of situated racial group power, or group agency both enlivened and constrained by multiple, shifting contexts. It also recognizes the capacity of racial groups, amid changing racial demographics and socioeconomic structures, to be simultaneously oppressed and oppressive, liberating and subordinating. This dynamic and contextual approach to agency is cast here in a preliminary form to aid the discussion of interracial justice in chapters 7 and 8. The approach reflects my commitment to a critical pragmatic methodology of race praxis, described in the next chapter. It emphasizes key points of inquiry—simultaneity and differentiation.

*Simultaneity*

The exploration of group agency in the tension between polar positions is aided by aspects of postcolonial theory. With its initial roots in the critique of traditional historical accounts of British control over India and India's transformation into a nation-state, postcolonial theory encompasses initial colonial domination (including the control of land and the suppression of culture), indigenous resistance and dominant reaction, formal decolonization, and the complexity introduced by partial adaptation of indigenous peoples and immigrants to colonial social structures.[22] More particularly, it addresses cultural representations of colonized and former colonized subjects and examines the ways in which those subjects construct group identities and social structures, in part through resistance against dominant powers and in part through affirmative group actions.[23] In this way, postcolonial theory interrogates the transformation of power and group agency.[24]

Of what relevance is postcolonial theory to post–civil rights America? Certainly, the reconstruction of knowledge about interracial relations and the transition of racial group power in America are relevant to interracial justice. And certainly, postcolonial analysis resonates at some level for America's indigenous peoples—Native Americans, Native Hawaiians, and

Native Alaskans who live with the continuing effects of varying forms of colonial domination by the United States and European powers. But as a whole, America's history of relations between whites and racial minorities does not fit neatly into the East Indian/British model of colonialism.

Despite its limitations, postcolonial theory is relevant to this section's discussion in one important respect: postcolonial theory addresses shifting power and identity among groups amid changes in racial demographics and socioeconomic structures, amid still prevalent but nevertheless apparently declining white dominance, and amid borderland sites. One aspect of postcolonial theory observes how historically subordinated groups with a degree of newly acquired power sometimes situationally redeploy dominant structures of control and adopt oppressive attitudes toward subordinate other groups. The redeployment can occur even though the groups themselves remain objects of enmity and violence. This is what I term *simultaneity*, which is itself shaped by three concepts: redeployment, positionality, and alignment.

### Redeployment of Structures of Oppression

At the moment of power transition in the decolonization of India, resistance efforts and discourses tended to "become enmeshed in concepts . . . that redeploy[ed] ideas of surveillance, control, and development in post-independence politics."[25] Racial communities in the United States sometimes experience similar transitional dynamics. As multiculturalism and "rhetorical claims to political change and difference" are advanced, "many deep-rooted, politically reactionary forces return to haunt us." The "new solidarities" generated by these forces "are often informed by a strategic attitude which repeats what they seek to overthrow." Old ideologies are often reproduced by groups with emergent power, including "essentialist notions of culture and history; conservative notions of territorial and linguistic propriety, and the 'otherness' ensuing from them; unattested claims of oppression and victimization that are used merely to guilt-trip and to control; sexist and racist reaffirmations . . . in the name of righteousness."[26]

This aspect of postcolonial theory posits that a central challenge facing any movement dismantling "a system in which one culture dominates another . . . is to provide for a new order that does not reproduce the social structure of the old system."[27] In this light, Lisa Lowe rereads the influential work of Frantz Fanon as a critique not only of colonial domination but also of nationalist resistance. Fanon observed newly empowered nationalist groups that pursue bourgeois assimilation and produce the same structure of cultural domination that they overthrew. In this rereading, Fanon warns against "nationalism practiced by [emerging] bourgeois neocolonial governments [that] . . . can be dictated easily into racism, territorialism, separatism, or ethnic dictatorships of one tribe or regional group over others."[28]

This warning against the redeployment of structures and strategies of oppression, reflected in the phenomenon of simultaneity, also emanates from other disciplines. The Torah enjoins long disenfranchised Jews, "When you come into your land, do not oppress the stranger. Remember that you were strangers in the land of Egypt." That injunction recognizes the tendency of those with newfound power to oppress a different "other" as part of the psychological phenomenon of "repetition compulsion[,] a tendency of most human beings to act out on others that which was done to us."[29]

This phenomenon is also cast in social science terms. "How can resistance to oppression avoid mimicking oppression? How can people seek equality and justice without becoming what they hate?" Recent psychological research suggests that "some [young] African American males develop an exaggerated conception of male power and devalue females, apparently as a coping response to racial and economic disadvantage," and postcolonial theory names this kind of internalized dominance—a "piece of the oppressor . . . lies in each person."[30]

In sum, postcolonial theory, complemented by other disciplines, including feminist legal theory (discussed later), opens for scrutiny the rhetorical, institutional, and economic ways in which racial groups, amid struggles to recast identity and remake social structure in borderland sites, work with and against, lift up and oppress, other groups. And by recognizing a capacity to oppress in those settings, it reclaims the concept of racial group agency.[31]

In this sense, agency is not conceived in terms of either freestanding individual autonomy or straitjacketed structural determinism. Instead, agency is the existence of affirmative group power to self-define and interact with other groups, the exercise of which is both facilitated and constrained by sociopolitical circumstances—choices are exercised "not by free agents or autonomous actors, but by people who are compromised and constrained by social context."[32] By recognizing simultaneity and the dialectic between continuing racial group subordination and emerging group power and by locating racial group agency in that tension, postcolonial theory provides a dynamic yet constrained view of group agency.[33]

Positionality

The dynamics of how racial groups can be both oppressed and oppressive in borderland settings are illuminated theoretically by feminist ideas about intersecting systems of oppression. In addressing women's agency at the juncture of race and gender, feminist legal theorists inquire into how white women, subject to patriarchal oppression, possess largely invisible white privilege and sometimes exercise attendant power in ways harmful to women of color.

Some perceive a tendency among white feminists to discount the significance of the racialized experiences of women of color. Even though white women may condemn the harm to women of color from overtly racist acts, they sometimes fail to see how they, as whites, benefit from systemic racial oppression. They fail to recognize their comparatively privileged position as members of the socially dominant race; they receive the advantages of race without having to think about race. By contrast, women of color, who suffer the disadvantages of systemic racism, cannot ignore race—even when race is not foremost on their minds, it remains a backdrop, coloring their world.[34]

White privilege, in this sense, is largely invisible because of the way that women's agency is often conceived. According to Martha Mahoney, for some prominent feminist theorists, gender is constructed entirely by male sexual oppression of women. And when "harm [alone] defines gender[,] . . . identifying any authentic women's action or vision" is difficult.[35] She worries that a women-as-oppressed-by-males construct in law erases women's agency. Like neoconservative ethnicity and nationalism/colonialism theories of racial group agency, it encourages an "all-agent or all-victim construction in which one either does or is done to, and women have gender oppression done to us."[36] The all-victim approach makes it difficult for some white women to see the extent of their own privilege, and agency, in terms of race and racism.

Mahoney and other feminist legal scholars maintain that although all women struggle with varying forms of male domination, the sole focus on "the sexual exploitation of women hides both racist oppression [by men and women] and the strength, struggles, and multiple interests of women of color."[37] Thus they argue generally for the recognition of women's agency in the construction of gender and race, and they argue specifically for the recognition of women of color's multilayered experiences with oppression and multiple consciousness.

A key to understanding women's agency in this way is the idea of relational positionality. Women engage in many kinds of relationships in multiple contexts, with power flowing simultaneously in several directions. Each context is itself shaped by the ongoing interactions of various factors, including gender, race, class, sexual orientation, disability, immigrant status, and culture. The "position" of the actor in each relationship, in each context, is the focal point of inquiry into the actor's collective agency. For example, a middle-class, straight, light-complected African American women in Tulsa lives in sometimes colliding systems of social power. She is positioned differently in each system, depending on the particular relationship. She may be comparatively disempowered in relation to a white, upper-middle-class woman—even though both struggle with patriarchy in the workplace. Yet she may be comparatively advantaged in relation to an immigrant, primarily Spanish-speaking Latina, or a dark-complected, lesbian African American woman. Women as social actors assume multiple power positions simultaneously, and depending on the context, "an individual may be an oppressor, a member of an oppressed group, or simultaneously oppressor and oppressed."[38]

In this way, relational positionality significantly complicates fixed categories of good and evil, of victims and victimizers. Relational positionality acknowledges that "the flow of power in multiple systems of domination is not always unidirectional. Indeed, "victims can also be victimizers; agents of change can also be complicitous, depending on the particular axis of power one considers."[39] A women's potential for both victimization and domination thus depends on her relational position with other social actors. She may be oppressed under one system of domination (patriarchy) and oppressive through others (race and class). In terms of social agency, women (like racial groups) can be simultaneously privileged and subordinated, empowered and disempowered.

Social Alignments

The ideas of redeployment and positionality thus fill out the simultaneity dimension of racial group agency in the borderlands. They do not, however, illuminate the power dynamics of racialized social actors who are situationally disempowered in relation to some groups and empowered in relation to others. Those dynamics can be cast in terms of a question connecting power to oppression: How does a group disempowered in one intergroup relationship acquire and maintain a position of power over another group?

As pointed out earlier, feminist legal theory at the crossroads of race and gender is revealing. It examines the microdynamics of intergroup power, or more particularly, the ways in which a social actor, with multiple identities, can be simultaneously subordinated and privileged. Relational positionality provides a method for inquiring into this dialectic by focusing on the actor's often shifting power position in each context. The idea of alignment, as part of Thomas Wartenberg's notion of situated power, deepens this understanding of positional power.

Wartenberg's theory of power addresses a social actor's "power over" another. It locates each relationship in a larger "field" and thereby expands the traditional power analyses beyond two groups engaged in the primary relationship in order to emphasize the broader nature of social power.[40] By situating the primary relationship in a broader social field, the theory recognizes that agents external to the primary relationship— outside agents—contribute significantly to the allocation of power in the primary relationship. One group's power over the other in the relationship is enhanced or even created by the outside agents' differential responses to these groups. That is, the outside agents contribute to the power of one group while disempowering the other.[41]

Through these alignments, one group in the primary relationship gains some control over the other group's action alternatives in terms of self-definition and self-development. It is thus the coalescence of outside agents and their temporal alignment with one of the groups in the primary relationship that contributes to that group's power over the other.

When Chinese Americans sued to invalidate court-mandated affirmative action in San Francisco's public schools and other Asian Americans initially supported the California anti–affirmative action initiative, white journalists, scholars, university administrators, and politicians supported the suit's and the initiative's goal by characterizing Asian Americans along with whites as victims of racial preferences for African Americans and Latinas/os. The alignment of influential white individuals and institutions behind these Asian Americans in the arena of affirmative action contributed to limited Asian American power over African Americans and Latinas/os. At the same time, in the racialized debate about immigration, many whites and a near majority of Asian Americans (mainly later generation and middle class) aligned with a majority of African American voters in support of California's Proposition 187, creating a nativist citizen–versus–foreigner discourse and locating middle-class whites, Asian Americans, and a cross section of African Americans against Asian and Latina/o immigrants. This alignment gave even socially and economically struggling African Americans some degree of power over recent Asian and Latina/o newcomers.

This notion of social alignment adds depth to the idea of simultaneity in three respects. First, it gives concrete meaning to amorphous idea of "context." Context matters in articulating power in a relationship not because social setting exudes formative vibrations but because outside actors align themselves in varying ways with one central agent rather than the other. It is through these alignments that "context" empowers one agent over the other in the primary relationship and shapes possible courses of action. Second, it highlights the salience of alliances (general alignments) and coalitions (task-directed groups) to group agency.

Third, the idea of social alignment offers a dynamic view of intergroup power as fluid and changeable. Since in any single relationship, each group may be aligned with several outside agents in the field, one group may have some limited form of power over the other under certain circumstances and may have power over it exercised by the other in other circumstances. This means that power in a given relationship, and certainly in multiple relationships, is shifting and colliding, often operating at cross-purposes. Power in intergroup relationships is an "ongoing social process" rather than a simple "static social distribution."[42] Understood temporally, power in a relationship changes continually as alignments outside the relationship shift according to the vicissitudes of politics, the economy, and social demographics. Groups therefore continually reproduce power relationships by maintaining or developing new social alignments. This dynamic view of power suggests the contestability of power in every intergroup relationship in the borderlands.

*Differentiation*

Simultaneity, deepened by the notions of redeployment, positionality, and social alignment, addresses the ways in which oppressive institutional structures are sometimes dismantled and sometimes redeployed. And it explains how groups can, at least situationally, be simultaneously oppressed and oppressive. It does not, however, explain why racial groups in borderland settings differ in terms of identity and status or why different racial categories acquire different racial meanings. And it does not tell us how constructed racial differences might affect the comparative agency and responsibility of groups.

The sociolegal concepts of differential racialization and differential disempowerment do, however, begin to answer these questions, implicating the idea of differentiation. Race is understood as an "unstable and 'decentered' complex of social meanings constantly being transformed by political struggle."[43] The concept of "racialization signifies the extension of racial meaning to a previously racially unclassified relationship, social practice, or group."[44] Political, cultural, and legal conflicts racialize groups and thereby form and re-form racial identities and relations. For example, in the late 1960s and 1970s, diverse Asian groups in the United States seized on a government census classification and articulated a new encompassing racial identity, "Asian American." They did so to raise political consciousness about common problems and to assert their collective demands on government. By minimizing group differences among distinct Asian cultures and political outlooks, the racialization of Asian Americans aggregated political power among formerly disparate, relatively powerless groups.[45] In doing so, however, as revealed by Rev. Wong's

testimony on the Asian American churches' apology resolution, the racialization process also generated internal instability in the Asian American category and falsely represented an essentialized Asian American
identity.

The concept of differential racialization responds in part to the problem of group essentialism and in part to questions of group power. It
acknowledges that historical and contemporary influences racialize different racial groups and subgroups differently. Michael Omi explains how
differences in a group—class cleavages, for example—differentially racialize members of the group, thereby creating different racial statuses
and power for subgroups.

The problems encountered by a rich entrepreneur from Hong Kong and a recently
arrived Hmong refugee are obviously distinct. The sites and types of discriminatory acts each is likely to encounter, and the range of available responses to them,
differ by class location . . . [A] differential racialization has developed between and
in different Asian American communities with important consequences for individual identity, collective consciousness, and political organization.[46]

Although Omi attributes the differing racialization of Asian American
groups principally to class divisions, he also acknowledges other factors,
such as the extent of isolation. Pat Chew adds country of origin, length
of U.S. residence, and gender to the differential racialization calculus.[47]

The concept of differential racialization, extended to encompass racialized differences between groups as well as within groups, furthers inquiry into comparative racial group agency. Differential racialization of
groups creates differing racial meanings for racial groups and subgroups,
and those meanings bear not only on "individual identity [and] collective
consciousness" but also on "political organization." They affect the
"range of available responses." More established immigrant groups, with
greater resources and access to political power, for example, may organize
around mobility issues (glass ceiling), and recent immigrant groups may
focus on survival issues (funding for language classes and job-training
programs).

Indigenous groups may embrace these issues or pursue radically divergent agendas. Native Hawaiians, for example, recently have been re-
racialized in complex ways, with significant political-legal consequences.

The long-term stereotyping of "happy Hawaiians" has given way to an acknowledgment that some continue to suffer from land dispossession and culture destruction and are now a group that seeks self-definition and self-governance. The re-formation of meanings of Native Hawaiian from racial minority to politically subjugated group have provided a foundation for the recent return of large tracts of formerly native lands and payments of hundreds of millions of dollars to Native Hawaiian public trusts.[48]

Racialized group differences, especially in borderland settings, implicate differing social perceptions and goals. They also implicate differential power. For this reason, in light of the "growing multiplicities of race and culture, further complicated by class," Jeff Chang suggests "a notion of 'differential forms of disempowerment' amongst communities of color" to grapple with complex interracial conflicts. He observes that in constructing identities and ascribing racial meanings, the racialization process fixes status and allocates power differentially among and within racial groups. Differential group power, or perceptions of power or lack of power, often underlies intergroup conflict. He therefore argues for localized analysis of differential power among communities of color.[49]

To illustrate how this agency analysis works, Chang describes politically organizing racial minorities in South Central Los Angeles after the Rodney King police trial. The organizing followed two different, sometimes compatible, sometimes conflicting, approaches. Many African American groups organized under what Chang terms an *anticolonial approach*. This "approach is rooted in the idea that [all] racial minorities in America are, and have historically been, colonized peoples who share a similar situation of oppression and because of which have a common natural unity against the white colonizers." The goal was broad-based coalition building. Chang observes, however, that the anticolonial approach was problematic. Many Korean Americans could not relate to the approach's colonizer/colonized framework. As recent immigrants, they had not experienced the same type of white oppression as had African Americans and earlier generations of Chinese and Japanese Americans. They therefore did not share a feeling of intergroup solidarity rooted in common oppression. Rather, they more often perceived African Americans to be oppressors—as a result of neighborhood clashes concerning employment, over-the-counter interactions, threats of violence, and occasional economic boycotts.

Some Korean Americans rejected the African American and Latina/o overtures and attempted to organize on the basis of ethnicity—concentrating on Korean American merchant problems and sources of support. Chang notes that such an approach, which he terms *nationalist,* also was problematic. It turned on organizing for Korean Americans alone, without regard to other groups, calling for the empowerment of Korean Americans through limited ethnic solidarity.

Thus the sweeping anticolonial approach faltered because it failed to account for racial differences in experience, outlook, and power and the need to attend to these sources of intergroup conflicts. The "go it alone" nationalist approach also faltered because it failed to link with other groups and build coalitional support. In addition, it ignored the need to examine historical sources of contemporary intergroup conflicts and thus exacerbated lingering African American resentments toward Asian Americans perceived as "jumping ahead" of their place in the economic line.

Chang argues that differential disempowerment provides a more relationally sensitive approach than either the anticolonial or nationalist approaches. It focuses on recognition of power differences among racial groups and sees power in terms of racial history, locale, politics, and economics. Only when racial groups recognize how and why they are differentially empowered or disempowered can they begin to address their own power imbalances and work in coalition.

The related differential racialization and disempowerment concepts are significant for two reasons. First, an acknowledgment of differential power in and among racial groups, however unstable and shifting, is also an acknowledgment of some degree of group agency and responsibility. It raises questions similar to those raised by postcolonial theory: To what extent do groups in a given situation have power over one another? And what ethical responsibilities attend the exercise of that power? Second, differential racial group power analyses historicize and localize inquiry into contemporary group relations and lay the sociopsychological groundwork for intergroup empathy. They encourage groups to ask: To what extent are this other group's formative experiences similar to and different from ours? By viewing this other group through the lens of our experience, in what ways have we overlooked or misunderstood their racial wounds and justice grievances as well as their cultural vibrancy?

For example, in pre-statehood Hawai'i, white oligarchical control, Asian immigration, and Hawaiian separation from land and traditional cultural roots constructed differing racial identities. Native Hawaiians, as former citizens of a conquered sovereign, and Asians, then as first- or second-generation immigrants, were differentially racialized. This typology distinguishes "voluntary" citizens who are Americans by choice (for example, most Asians) from "involuntary" citizens who are Americans by force (native peoples and African Americans). The typology provides beginning insight into relevant historical patterns of differential racialization. Despite many similar hardships, most Native Hawaiians and Asian Americans were differently situated. Internally, the sense of culture destruction, the impacts of the large-scale death and dying, and the spiritual suffering attendant to the dispossession of land characterized Native Hawaiian but not Asian American experiences. Externally, the rhetoric describing group characteristics; the market distribution of labor; and the opportunities for education, housing, and economic advancement by mid-century lifted Asian Americans above Native Hawaiians. Each group, differently situated, was racialized differently in the context of white oligarchical control.

In each group, class and urban/rural differences and differences in attitudes toward assimilation also meant differential subgroup racialization. Thus even though most Hawaiians suffered the cultural-economic consequences of the overthrow of the Hawaiian government, some Hawaiians did well—in comparison with both other Hawaiians and Asians. In the three decades following the United States' annexation of Hawai'i, some educated Christian Hawaiians became Republicans and lent political support to white oligarchy leaders. In return, urban elite Hawaiians came to occupy many government civil service positions and commissions and professional positions and were admitted into racially exclusive white social clubs. In contrast, Asian immigrants, denied the right to vote during that period, lacked political influence and were excluded from most government jobs, private schools, and social organizations. Asians, like many rural and underclass Hawaiians, were disenfranchised and disempowered, finding their language schools closed and "their unions savagely broken and nearly all avenues of economic, political and social advancement blocked."[50]

Differential racialization historically affects current group identity and group claims. Describing differential effects precisely, however, is difficult. In contemporary Hawai'i, the voluntary-immigrant-American versus involuntary-American typology becomes less useful. As indicated by the discussion of urban Hawaiians and Asians in the 1920s and 1930s, real-world lines of distinction are less than clearly drawn. Asian Americans have no essential history or culture. Some Asians, especially those from Southeast Asia, are in the United States more or less involuntarily as refugees forced out of their homeland. Recent Asian immigrants differ greatly in culture and identity from third-, fourth-, and fifth-generation Asian Americans. Many persons of Hawaiian ancestry also are of Asian ancestry. Mixed blood not only complicates identity issues, it also creates legal problems concerning the distribution of resources reserved for 50 percent blood Hawaiians.[51]

Despite problems of precise description, the concepts of differential racialization and disempowerment show the effect of differing racial conditions on racial group agency. The vigorous Native Hawaiian sovereignty movement has revealed the historic injustice of the overthrow of the Hawaiian nation in 1893 and the continuing harm of the land dispersal and Hawaiian culture destruction that followed. The movement has also conveyed to the people of Hawai'i the deep pain, the profound sense of cultural loss, passed from generation to generation of Native Hawaiians— a pain and a sense of loss beyond the experience of most others. In doing so, it has distinguished the experiences of Native Hawaiians from those of other racialized groups in Hawai'i. It has compelled those other groups to examine the extent to which they were complicit over the last one hundred years in the denigration of Hawaiians as business people, workers, teachers, students, and leaders. The sovereignty movement, with its claims of self-governance and control over homelands, has also compelled other racial group members and government leaders to think seriously about rectification and reparation; to think about healing.

The sovereignty movement itself speaks with a less than unified voice, and it faces both support and resistance from a gradually but steadily growing Hawaiian middle class. Some experience continuing harm from the overthrow of the Hawaiian nation and yet also accept Western values, institutions, and patterns of behavior.

It is thus in light of, and not despite, complex historical group and subgroup interactions, and the power relations underlying them, that we can begin to understand and empathize with deeply felt beliefs about group oppression and complex claims for group justice, that we can begin to understand the conflicts, claims, reparatory efforts, and resistance characterizing contemporary Asian American and Native Hawaiian relations. Without historicizing contemporary intergroup power relations and grounding them in concrete particulars, racial groups facing real-life intergroup grievances and claims of injustice are likely to assume the understandings of "others." Those understandings are likely to be based on societally constructed racial meanings linked to essentialized, albeit often internally dissonant, group identities—for example, the Asian "opportunistic settler" and "yellow peril," the "happy Native" and "virulent Hawaiian nationalist." Without attention to differential racialization in the context of both national and localized struggles for identity and power, racial groups cannot begin to address issues of "mutual misunderstanding and mistrust" that result in the "use of stereotypes and caricatures to demean and dehumanize" and give rise to the persistence of "racist attitudes and actions"[52]—issues of interracial justice. Without addressing foundational interracial justice issues, rooted in forms of subordination, the search by coalition builders for a common ground, the calls by community leaders for multi-racial unity and cross-cultural understanding, and the claims to empowerment by racial groups "can become tools to maintain historical forms of subordination."[53]

In sum, simultaneity and differentiation are points of inquiry into complex interracial struggles over power and identity. These aspects of racial group agency enable us to ask questions about interracial conflict and healing because they focus on ways in which history is linked to current conditions and perceptions. They enable us to ask questions about contemporary interracial relations because they recognize that differing sociohistorical contexts contribute to differing group images, goals, memories, and group agency. By understanding the extent of a group's agency, constrained by context, the extent of its responsibility for harm to another can be roughly evaluated.

## Group Responsibility

Informed by the ideas of simultaneity and differentiation, constrained group agency suggests a corollary to group power—group responsibility. Responsibility is each group's commitment to exercise its limited agency without oppressing other racial groups. This framing of racial group responsibility is informed by ethical or moral principles. Cornel West offers a "prophetic" approach to a mature racial identity. For blacks in particular, that identity is rooted in self-love and self-respect and is based on "the moral quality of black responses to undeniable racist degradation in the American past and present." Notions of responsibility inform the moral quality of black responses. Black responses are moral when they assess "the variety of perspectives held by black people" and select "those views based on black dignity and decency that eschew putting any group of people or culture on a pedestal or in the gutter." The mature black identity is cast in terms of agency ("specific black responses" to racist degradation) and responsibility ("responses such that the humanity of black people does not rest on . . . demonizing others").[54]

Responsibility is thus each group's commitment to recognize the hierarchical structure of power in race relations and to advance socially, politically, and economically without denigrating or otherwise subordinating other groups. When steps toward self-definition or material advancement nevertheless denigrate or subordinate others, responsibility is discharged through acts of restorative justice—that is, some form of racial healing (discussed in chapter 8). This general framing of group responsibility is sharpened by Wartenberg's notions of dominance and transformation.

### Dominance/Transformation

As mentioned earlier, group agency is derived in part from the alignment with others in the larger field. It is a racial group's choices in the exercise of its power over another—to either dominate or transform—that determine whether that group has discharged its responsibility as social agents to act in a nonoppressive manner.

In a given situation, power over another can be exercised through dominance. Dominance is the exercise of one group's power over another to create or maintain oppressive systemic structures. Subordinate group members are dominated when they are subject to disabling societal constraints on their self-determination (exclusion) and self-development (subjugation).

Power over can also be exercised transformatively—acknowledging and redressing past wrongs and restructuring current power imbalances in the relationship. Although the lines of demarcation between domineering and transformative uses of power are rarely clearly drawn, distinguishing between the two is important. A transformative use of power inures directly to the subordinate group's benefit and indirectly to the dominant group's benefit. It "seeks to bring about its own obsolescence" by empowering subordinate groups in a way that undercuts the power differential between them and the dominant group. When group power is used to transform the relationship in which it is exercised, the subordinate group expands its powers of self-determination and self-development.

In a transformative relationship, the more dominant group not only advances and develops itself without denigrating or subordinating the other group, thereby discharging its responsibility to act in a nonoppressive manner. It also acts to repair the damage of oppressive exercises of power over the other, thereby discharging its responsibility to rectify past injustice in the relationship.

Transformative power also may be exercised when the less powerful group suffers from harms inflicted by others. In this instance, part of the more powerful group's responsibility may be to aid in intergroup healing, regardless of the source of harm. This responsibility means a commitment to assist in healing the other group's wounds, not necessarily for purposes of redress but for purposes of community building.

In sum, dominance and transformation begin to address the roots of racial group responsibility: the mutual implication of institutional structure and group agency and the exercise of group choice in a field of hierarchical power. These multilayered notions of responsibility are further developed and illustrated in part 3's treatment of interracial justice.

## Individual Responsibility for Group Actions

Implicit in this discussion of group responsibility and in chapter 7's sketch of multidisciplinary approaches to intergroup healing is the idea of an individual's responsibility for harmful group actions. Social psychological, theological, and political theory approaches to intergroup healing recognize some form of group member responsibility for actions by other group members. By virtue of the benefits of group membership, individual members bear responsibility for repairing group-inflicted harm. This notion is integral to understanding group responsibility for healing group wounds.

In his 1990 New Year's address as the first democratic president of Czechoslovakia in a generation, Vaclav Havel explained that no one would be held accountable for the past: "All of us are responsible, each to a different degree, for keeping the totalitarian machine running. None of us is merely a victim of it, because all of us helped to create it together."[55] This clean slate view of universal guilt is one way of avoiding the complicated and imprecise task of assessing individual responsibility for group wrongs. How can specific people shoulder the blame for societal conditions more properly attributed to group dynamics rather than individual action?

Indeed, the Western ethic of individualism, supported by the law's emphasis on individual rights and personal culpability, weighs against individual responsibility for collective wrongs. Western law generally, and American antidiscrimination law particularly, embed this ethic in concepts of individual rights and duties. The individual harmed possesses the legal claim, and the individual actor directly causing the harm bears the responsibility. Even when group identity plays a large role in harmful interactions—for example, racism and sexism—those group identities are irrelevant to determining responsibility for consequences. Only individuals act, and only individuals are harmed. Culpable individuals, not groups, bear legal responsibility.

The disciplines described in chapter 7 nevertheless distinguish between guilt for group wrongs and responsibility for righting them. Although oppression often is grounded in systemic structures and assigning individual culpability may be difficult, social psychologists, among others, recognize that group members may appropriately deny personal fault "without denying our collective responsibility for racism's eradication."[56]

The notion of individual responsibility for group actions extends this understanding of responsibility by asking, Who belongs to the group? This question is difficult in part because differing situations raise group responsibility issues in different ways. The easier situation involves specific, identifiable acts of group harm. For instance, consider an angry mob of otherwise law-abiding people who attack defenseless individuals largely because of their group identity. The people in the mob at least temporarily renounce personal responsibility for the group's action—the group is something with a life of its own. Of course, the group takes its life from the individuals comprising it. In this situation, attributing responsibility to those in the mob, even if they did not by their own hands harm the individuals, is readily understandable. Their voluntary participation in the group facilitated, or empowered, those in the group who acted.

The harder situation involves systemic oppression. For intergroup conflicts arising from disabling constraints, the individual is one step removed from collective actions. "The greatest wounds in human history, the greatest injustices, have not happened through the acts of some individual perpetrator, rather through the institutions, systems, philosophies, cultures, religions and governments of mankind. Because of this, we, as individuals, are tempted to absolve ourselves of all individual responsibility."[57]

Systemic racial oppression, lying "embedded in unquestioned norms, habits, and symbols," presents difficulties because of its pervasive yet subtle method of operation. The very existence of institutionally generated oppression often eludes individual awareness, leading to the denial of its effects ("America has achieved racial equality of opportunity"), as well as causality ("minorities are the source of their own problems") and intent ("I've never discriminated against anyone"). The space between individual and group responsibility widens in cases that also involve a temporal dimension—when a prior generation initiated the injustice. The nature of historical group oppression thus adds to the complexity of individual responsibility for group wrongs.

Despite varying situations, individuals always stand amid the fray of intergroup strife. Critical race and feminist legal theorists underscore the concrete social benefits and harms accompanying group membership. Their scholarship on white privilege shifts the traditional focus of discrimination inquiry from an individual's bad intent and personal culpability to the individual's group-derived privilege and corresponding responsibility. Individuals may deny or be unaware of their group affiliation and the benefits conferred. A fundamental element of privilege is the luxury to attribute advantage to personal merit or ignore its existence altogether.[58]

Religious scholars take a different route to the same point, observing that most people grasp the notion of individual responsibility for group actions—that "every heritage comes with both benefits and responsibilities, including the responsibility to right past wrongs." People simply choose to suppress that understanding. John Dawson identifies different reactions to unresolved collective guilt over white privilege, including "defiantly defending their ancestors and vilifying their victims." Dawson stresses that to overcome this common form of aggressive denial, individuals need to identify with the sins of the group. Group wrongs must be atoned for by individuals' acceptance of responsibility for their own sin, as well as "confess[ion] of the shortcomings and transgressions of relatives and predecessors." Dawson therefore urges a practice of "identificational repentance," in which the "intercessor freely chooses to identify with and confess [the sins of the group]" in order to foster healing.[59]

In sum, from these vantage points, individuals bear responsibility for intergroup healing. Individuals often unconsciously enjoy concrete advantages by virtue of their group membership. Group-based benefits carry with them responsibility for disadvantages unfairly imposed on members of other groups. Individuals are thus responsible through their participation in and benefit from often subtle systems of oppression that serve both to capitalize on intergroup injustices and perpetuate their existence.

# 6

# Race Praxis

## A Developing Theory of Racial Justice Practice

At a gathering of law teachers of color in 1995, Robert Williams Jr. called for a future critical race practice. Wondering how professors unconnected with actual antiracist struggles could produce meaningful progressive theory, he urged race scholars to spend less time on abstract theorizing and more time on actual community law–based antisubordination practice.[1] He encouraged scholars' involvement in setting up legal clinics, working with community organizations, guiding student activists, advising local tribunals, speaking with politicians and bureaucrats, and drafting regulations.

Similarly, in *Rebellious Lawyering*,[2] Gerald Lopez argued for antisubordination theorizing that focuses on practical community-centered lawyering. He offered a foundation for progressive lawyering grounded in the particulars of peoples' lives, supportive of community members' problem-solving skills, and sensitive to the dynamics of neighborhood, local, state, and national politics. In related fashion, Luke Cole called for environmental justice for poor people and people of color. He suggested "practicing law in a way that empowers people, that encourages the formation and strengthening of client groups, and that sees legal tactics in the context of broader [political] strategies."[3]

Williams thus called for a critically informed race practice, Lopez for community-centered rebellious lawyering, and Cole for legal tactics by racial minorities and the poor cast in the context of broader political strategies. I move a step further. I suggest for progressive race scholars, political lawyers, and community activists—for race healers—an explicit race praxis characterized by reflective action: infusing antiracism practice with aspects of critical inquiry and pragmatism and then recasting theory in light of practical experience. *Race praxis*—or what I have elsewhere called *critical race praxis* because of its grounding in and extension of critical race theory insights[4]—means for many theorists enhanced attention to theory translation and deeper engagement with frontline action. For many political lawyers and community activists, it means increased attention to a critical rethinking of what race is, how civil rights claims may be both empowering and debilitating and whether legal process and its alternatives foster or impede racial healing.

Race praxis shapes the approach to interracial justice developed in part 3. It attempts to put theory to practical use, to avoid the problem of theory's begetting more theory but no practice. It informs this book's aim to speak to both racial justice scholars and practitioners and, more important, to encourage scholars and practitioners to engage one another in racial healing efforts.

## A Working Definition

Race praxis combines critical pragmatic analysis with political lawyering and community organizing to practice justice by and for racialized communities. Its central idea is racial justice as antisubordination practice. As recognized in the pathbreaking empirical studies of Lind and Tyler, in addition to ideas and ideals, justice is something experienced.[5] Grounded in concrete and often messy and conflictual racial realities, it is something that people struggle with viscerally and intellectually.

Race praxis provides structure to justice practice. It means understanding justice in terms of both process (experience-rethinking-translation-engagement) and norms (first principles of antisubordination and rectification of injustice). Race praxis thus directs theorists, lawyers, and activists to the specifics of the immediate grievance or claim (for example, the race-infused interaction between merchant and customer, a promotion-denial Title VII claim) and, at the same time, pushes them to probe further. It instructs them to use theory to investigate subtext to identify the disabling cultural representations and exercises of group power underlying or exacerbating the specific conflict and to assess critically the institutional dynamics (limitations and potential) of the setting in which justice is practiced. It encourages them to translate the insights from critical inquiry into operational ideas and language for individuals and groups working to redress grievances. It also means, in appropriate instances, critiquing and moving beyond notions of legal justice pragmatically to heal disabling intergroup wounds and forge intergroup alliances.

I offer the beginnings of a framework rather than a fully developed race praxis. Drawing selectively on insights of critical race theory, pragmatism, prophetic theology, feminist legal theory, and environmental justice scholarship, I suggest four aspects of race praxis inquiry: the conceptual, the performative, the material, and the reflexive. They are not offered as a universal theory of justice, nor do they prescribe what racial justice is, or should be, in any particular situation. Rather, for those confronting concrete racial conflicts in an attempt to construct "right relationships," these aspects of race praxis inquiry offer guideposts toward collective, reflective, antisubordination practice. They provide the foundation for the four "R" dimensions of interracial inquiry developed in part 3. The earlier discussions of the Lowell High School and United Minorities cases provide a glimpse of their use in actual controversies, as both a critique of ongoing justice practice and a guide to future reflective action.

The "conceptual" aspect of race praxis inquiry encompasses critical sociolegal analysis and translation.[6] Critical sociolegal analysis examines the racialization of a controversy and the interconnecting influences of heterosexism, patriarchy, and class and locates that examination in a critique of the political economy. It thus focuses on both the particulars and the context of a relationship in conflict.

The analysis starts with an examination of the claim's traditional sources of authority, supporting arguments, evidence, and requested remedy—more or less a traditional investigation of a legal claim. The analysis then identifies in detail both the neoconservative and liberal (including civil rights) lines of argument on the claim.

Most important, sociolegal analysis then deploys tools of critical inquiry in two respects. First, it assesses the justice setting and the implications of the potential "legalization" of the conflict—the way in which substantive norms and procedural rules are likely to be construed and applied in light of both methodological constraints and the interests of and power alignments among storytellers, advocates, mediators, and decision makers, on the one hand, and politicians, businesses, governmental bureaucrats, and community groups, on the other.[7] Second, critical sociolegal analysis identifies larger grievances possibly underlying the specific claims. It aims to break apart distorted cultural representations undergirding intergroup tensions; to challenge group deployment of oppressive rhetorical, institutional, and economic structures; and to rearticulate group identities and conceptualize the redress of justice claims, when appropriate, to support intergroup healing. The sociolegal insights from these inquiries by theorists, lawyers, and community leaders are translated into operational language for individuals and groups undertaking "actions" to redress grievances and forge alliances.

Action is part of the "performative" aspect of race praxis. Performance comes in at least two parts. The first involves the question of what? What practical steps are responsive not only to the specific claim but also to subtext—the underlying disparaging cultural images and exercises of group power that intensify historical intergroup grievances? This means acting on the operationally translated insights of critical sociolegal analysis, that is, "performing" in the specific setting to dismantle subordinating social structures and to rectify injustice.[8]

The second part of the performative dimension involves the question of who? Who should act? More specifically, given the assumption that political lawyers and community activists will participate, should scholar-theorists join the lawyers, activists, organizations, and institutions and try to influence the storytelling and decision making of a controversy? The praxis response is a definite yes. One conclusion I draw from interactions with political lawyers and community activists is that theoretical insights into race, culture, and law and that critical sociolegal analyses of particular controversies are unlikely to be developed and translated for frontline antisubordination practice unless theorists personally deal with the difficult, entangled, shifting realities of that practice. A disjuncture between progressive race theory and political lawyering and community activism, I suspect, not only chokes useful theory development and translation but also stifles the contemplation of multilayered actions designed to produce material change.

The "material" aspect of race praxis is the counterpart of performativity—the intended consequences of conceptual analysis and performance. It means inquiring into changes in the material conditions of racial oppression. Without those changes, analysis and translation are "just talk," and actions little more than tilting at windmills. Change is material when it occurs simultaneously at two levels. Change must be social structural; it encompasses fair access to housing, educational, and job opportunities; the redistribution of societal goods; and the remaking of the democratic structure of public institutions. Change must also be representational, as it entails the reassessment of group cultural traits and the rearticulation of racial identities and relationships.[9] The material aspect of race praxis inquiry thus directs antisubordination practice toward both the structural and the discursive.

Finally, the "reflexive" aspect alerts theorists, lawyers, and activists to reintegrate their experience into a theoretics of practice. It signals the continual rebuilding of theory in light of the practical experiences of racial groups engaged in particular antiracist struggles, thus recasting the conceptual, performative, and material aspects of race praxis. These aspects of race praxis inquiry resemble the United Church of Christ's prophetic "see-judge-act" methodology. Drawn from Latin American and South African liberation theology, this praxis cycle starts with the "see" phase. Seeing begins with concrete experiences, the stories, of those involved in a justice controversy; not just stock stories repeated by those with media control, but also stories from the inside expressing human reactions and interpreting social information. Collected stories, which provide the often varying histories of the controversy, are then subjected to critical social analysis. That analysis probes into core questions, asking why one group apparently is suffering at the hands of another, challenging assumptions underlying common beliefs about the groups involved and their relationship, and scrutinizing social structures (political, economic, social) for the "root causes" of problems. The goal of this analysis is group awareness, or acknowledgment, as a communal base for informed group action.

The "judge" phase is discernment—the identification and integration of guiding and, for the United Church of Christ, theological principles and values. Judging is not so much ascertaining right or wrong as discerning "what needs to be done" in light of those principles and values. Discernment thus takes the results of critical social analysis and asks what these principles or values reveal about appropriate courses of action and responsibility for undertaking those actions. The third phase, "act," involves engagement, or goal setting, planning, and affirmative steps. In bureaucratese, it means plan implementation; in drama-speak, it means performance. The see-judge-act cycle closes with evaluation—determining how the three phases played out in the actual justice controversy and how the process influences the experience.[10]

## Sources

Race praxis is rooted in critical pragmatism. Pragmatism first developed in the early twentieth century as a challenge to philosophical notions of universal truth. Pragmatists argued that foundational truths did not exist, waiting simply to be discovered. There were no grand narratives, for example, that explained justice for all situations for all time. Rather, what we call truth at any given time emerges from the interactions of people in particular situations, the values they hold, and the experiences they bring to bear.

Pragmatism implicated a rethinking of law and legal method. The traditional legal method, or legal formalism, misconceived the actual operations of the legal system. Its pseudoscientific reasoning process (abstract principles applied to proven facts) did not, in itself, lead to predictable and, more important, just results. As revealed by the work of legal realists, who drew on pragmatism's insights, legal justice was related to context and to the particulars of each situation in ways that legal formalism could not comprehend. Pragmatism's influence waned toward the middle of the century, partly because of a withering post–World War II philosophical attack on pragmatism's perceived relativism, that is, its failure to offer substantive norms to combat evils such as Nazi anti-Semitism.

As part of a critical rethinking of philosophy and law, pragmatism reemerged in the 1980s.[11] For some legal pragmatists—and here I mean pragmatism in law—practical reasoning offered a rough but workable alternative to the now largely rejected formalist method of legal reasoning.[12] For others, however, the more extreme new practical reasoning proponents suffered from the same infirmity as their predecessors did: they offered no normative baseline for decision making, and their resort to "common sense" simply shielded personal preferences and intuitive judgments.[13]

In response to these concerns about revived pragmatism's "impoverished pluralism"—while acknowledging its continuing methodological appeal—Mari Matsuda in 1989 called for a "pragmatism modified." Consistent with traditional pragmatism and more recent approaches to practical reasoning, she identified a pragmatic method that "suggests plural, provisional, and emergent truths . . . [and] is skeptical of universalized experience and absolute description." In addition, however, Matsuda also suggested transforming traditional pragmatism into a critical pragmatism that emphasizes multiple consciousness, experience, flexibility, and context; that engages the experiences and stories of those habitually on society's margins, not because those experiences and stories are more worthy but because in mainstream justice discourse they tend to be minimized; and that embraces the "rectification of past injustice and elimination of all present forms of subordination" as first principles. These suggestions bent traditional pragmatism "toward liberation." They assessed justice strategies practically: Does the strategy aid in dismantling oppressive social structures?[14]

Informed by this kind of critical pragmatism, praxis is what Paulo Freire encouraged through his program of reflective action. Freire, a Brazilian educator, worked with poor rural farmers against an oppressive government and private landholding system. He connected the role of theorists to grassroots work and popular political movements. Freire's teachers-intellectuals developed liberation theory from the experiences of the poor and, through pastoral workers and community leaders, translated theory into frontline engagement with antisubordination practice. Using reading and writing as tools of organization and action, Freire's praxis of experience-rethinking-translation-engagement produced for the farmers and their collaborators opportunities for reflective action.[15]

From the same soil that nourished Freire's praxis, liberation theology emerged in the 1970s in response to Latin American governments' oppression of the poor with the Catholic Church's acquiescence. Radical theologians reinterpreted Christian faith from the perspective of the poor, used theology to criticize oppressive social structures and ideologies, and critiqued church orthodoxy. In translating critique into practice, the theologians deepened Freire's notion of praxis. They identified a theory of praxis, meaning a theory of oppression and resistance continually reformulated by the insights, questions, and experiences of those oppressed. They also identified a theory for praxis, meaning theoretical input into grassroots action.[16]

Integrating aspects of critical pragmatism, feminist legal theory has developed a rich, practice-tested notion of praxis. Feminist legal praxis integrates theoretical notions of knowledge, language, and power into antisubordination legal practice. Feminist legal scholars thus have exposed the nonneutral legal meanings of family, work, equality, abuse, and welfare. Through those meanings, the law reinforces certain societal perspectives, devalues others, and helps shape community understandings of events and relationships.[17] Feminist legal scholars have also developed insights into how the dominant legal rules that reproduce those meanings can be challenged practically through court process, legal storytelling, and reconstruction of legal doctrine.[18]

Environmental justice scholars recently have urged a related praxis approach to "lawyering for social change" for poor people and racial communities. Studies from the late 1980s and early 1990s revealed the inordinately heavy burden borne by racial communities and the poor as a result of environmental policies and law enforcement practices. The traditional theoretical model of environmental lawyering failed to protect or advance the interests of those groups. Environmental justice scholars have thus attempted to integrate theories of race and class oppression with environmental law practice.

Environmental justice rests on many factual assumptions and theoretical insights articulated by critical race theorists and poverty law scholars. One assumption is that in general, racial communities and the poor understand both that they need access to the courts and that the legal system is stacked against them. This assumption leads to the theoretical insight of minorities' multiple consciousness about law and legal process. A second assumption is that the legal problems of the poor and people of color are often also political and economic problems. This leads to the recognition that "even if the law is 'on their side,' unless [they] have political or economic power as well, they are not likely to prevail."[19] A third assumption is that environmental problems, although most harshly burdening poor people and people of color, cross race and class boundaries. This leads to the recognition of the potential for building multiracial, cross-class political movements.

These factual assumptions and theoretical insights inform a praxis that views justice in social structural terms and embraces goals of client empowerment and group representation. It sees law as a means rather than an end and views legal maneuvers in the context of broader political strategies. In concrete situations, contextual analyses are translated into practical or operational terms through evaluative questions. For Luke Cole, the three practical questions for evaluating rhetorical and action strategies aimed at particular situations of environmental injustice are, Will it educate? Will it build political movements? Will it address root problems rather than just symptoms?

Finally, an evolving dimension of critical race theory speaks to the need for a sophisticated race praxis.[20] Critical race theorists seek to eliminate, or at least diminish, racial oppression in American society. To achieve this, they attempt to transform jurisprudential dialogue in a way that furthers antisubordination practice. The "critical" aspect of their project draws on postmodern theory. Critical race theorists deconstruct the limitations of traditional liberal legal discourse and the ways in which that discourse excludes voices on society's margins and perpetuates structural inequality. They thus reveal the social construction of legal concepts presented as fixed and natural, challenge the "efficacy of both liberal legal theory, and communitarian ideals as vehicles for racial progress, destabilize the supposedly neutral criteria of meritocracy and social order, and call for a reexamination of the very concept of 'race.' "[21]

In this fashion, critical race theorists reveal the law's blindness toward unconscious racism, the ways in which legal discourse inscribes and reproduces subordinating images of racial groups, and the ways in which legal institutions and discourse contribute to the construction and maintenance of racial hierarchies. In short, critical race theory analyzes the ways in which those processes contribute to racial oppression.

At the same time, critical race theory endeavors to develop a jurisprudence of reconstruction to contribute practically to the continuing struggles against oppression. Two clusters of critical race scholarship, explicitly embracing a critical pragmatic approach to law, introduce a practical reconstructive dimension to race writing. One cluster integrates high theory into antidiscrimination legal doctrine. A second cluster links critical race theory ideas about multiple consciousness and alternative transformative ways of legal "knowing" to practical processes of racial justice.[22]

Taken together, those clusters of reconstructive writing can be described as critical race theory's practical turn. That practical turn responds in part to the caution regarding "hyperabstract theorizing [among scholars] that makes a public debate about race and racism impossible,"[23] and in part to critical race theory's goal of contributing materially to diminishing racial oppression. It provides a beginning response not only to the limitations of antidiscrimination law (discussed later) but also to the disjuncture between progressive race theory and political lawyering practice. That practical turn itself, thus far, appears to be both salutary and limited.

On the one hand, it addresses antisubordination practice in a potentially useful fashion. It argues for judicial acceptance and the application of new, possibly racially transformative, legal rules and methods. The primary audience for those writings is judges, particularly federal judges. The secondary audience is civil rights and political lawyers, those actually "doing law" for people, those arguing the rules and working with methods of factual proof on behalf of the individual or organizational disputants involved in litigation.

On the other hand, critical race theory's practical turn, as reflected in these clusters of writing, is limited. It directs the potentially transformative antisubordination practice at judges, lawyers, legal analysis, and methods of proof. Judges and lawyers often are crucial players in race controversies.

If new doctrines and procedural rules are adopted and applied, they can assist antisubordination claimants. However, critical race theory's own analyses of doctrine and process reveal law's contingency and indeterminacy in handling race controversies, usually to the detriment of the racial group members, particularly in an era of conservative, Reagan- and Bush-appointed judges.[24] The focus of critical race theory's practical turn on legal analysis and the reframing of legal doctrine is thus useful yet limited.

In light of critical race theory's recognition of the special value of "rights talk" for racial communities, I assert something more is at play. That something more moves rights discourse beyond what judges and lawyers are traditionally thought to do in the courtroom and through case opinions. That something more is found in the practical, real-world benefits and disadvantages of modernist narratives for communities of color who are struggling politically, economically, and legally against subordination.[25] These narratives tend to embrace the language of rights, which derives meaning not from their objective truth but from how they facilitate self-definition by those often ignored and from how they galvanize and support multifaceted racial group actions against subordination in places and at levels at which subordination is experienced and contested —in courtrooms, schools, workplaces, churches, government agencies, public accommodations, and social clubs. That something more is race praxis.

## Implications

What are the main implications of race praxis for interracial justice? The first is the need to envision racial justice practice as something more than the enforcement of civil rights law; the second, the need to base justice on concrete racial realities; and the third, the reframing of racial justice claims and court process as cultural performances.

### Limitations of Legal Justice

One general implication of race praxis is the need to envision racial justice practice as something considerably more than the enforcement of civil rights laws. The post–civil rights era is marked by the narrowing of legal justice for racial minorities. In particular, nonwhite racial groups are experiencing a withering of legal justice under antidiscrimination laws. Over the last fifteen years, court decisions interpreting and applying civil rights laws have tended to define racial justice in crabbed and inverted ways. Those decisions and recent procedural reforms conceive of and administer justice in ways that clash with the ideals, perceptions, and concrete experiences of many members of racial communities, thereby dissociating law (not completely, but significantly) from racial justice.

Six general explanations for this dissociation warrant brief mention. The first is that even the courts' "progressive" civil rights rulings often reflect majoritarian interests.[26] From this view, with politically conservative judiciaries, antidiscrimination doctrine and process tend to preserve the social and political status quo. Society perceives the occasional enforcement of antidiscrimination laws under blatantly racist circumstances as justice done. Antidiscrimination law now at best offers correctives in limited situations and at worst generates illusions of systemic reordering and long-term racial justice.

A second explanation is the courts' increasingly narrow understanding of what race, and therefore racial discrimination, is. For a majority of the current Supreme Court, race is skin color. Race is thus seen as an immutable, biologically determined trait. Racism, in turn, is the "belief, held by too many for too much of our history, that individuals should be judged by the color of their skin"[27]—prejudice about something beyond anyone's control and irrelevant to human interactions. In short, color discrimination is wrong; antidiscrimination law prohibits it. By contrast, culture—language, accent, customs—is seen as changeable, socially created, and voluntarily adopted. It is seen as separate from race. Culture discrimination is not necessarily wrong and may even be rational; antidiscrimination law allows it. As Angela Harris observes, however, limiting antidiscrimination law's reach solely to color prejudice permits "discrimination against traditionally subordinated groups, so long as it is recharacterized as being based on 'culture' rather than race."[28]

A third and related explanation, developed in chapter 1, is antidiscri-

mination law's failure to recognize the distinct features of justice grievances among communities of color. The framing of those grievances in
the prevailing white-black civil rights law paradigm is, in many instances,
a mis-fit.

A fourth explanation for the increasing dissociation of civil rights law
from racial justice concerns the law's internal methodological constraints.
One such constraint is the notion of "commensurability." Substantive and
remedial legal doctrine often treat as commensurable things that the people involved would adjudge as vastly different. Law does this by first
creating categories that transform concrete matters of great significance
to the parties into abstract concepts. It then makes comparisons at a
highly abstract level in order to make decisions about justice. For example,
a person may find ludicrous a court's suggestion that her severed leg was
worth $200,000. Yet according to the legal system's abstract linkage of
damage to compensation, the jury's award may be both principled and
just. In cases of intentional institutional racism, the law deems commensurate the harm of racial harassment and a specified amount of money,
even though a monetary award may not redress human indignity, alter
relationships, or restructure offending institutions—a principled render-
ing of legal justice often deemed unjust by those suffering the racial
harm.[29]

A fifth explanation for the limits of antidiscrimination law for racial
minorities is the recent efficiency reforms in the law's adjudicatory procedures. Those reforms, ranging from stepped-up sanctions for unrea-
sonable filings to privatized dispute resolution, diminish court access for
those already at society's margins, especially racial and other minorities
asserting novel claims or theories that challenge existing social and political arrangements.[30]

A final explanation locates majoritarian influence, race-culture distinctions, the white-black civil rights paradigm, internal methodology, and
procedural reform in a specific political context. The 1980s witnessed federal court rulings narrowly interpreting legislative enactments and trim-
ming back prior liberal pronouncements. The mid-1990s abandoned any
remaining facade of liberalism. The U.S. Supreme Court jettisoned liberal
legal doctrines in favor of overtly conservative ones. In a two-week period
in 1995, by a five-to-four majority, the Court effectively dismantled federal

race-based affirmative action programs, invalidated redistricting plans under the Voting Rights Act that purposely created majority African American districts, and approved the Ku Klux Klan's right to erect a cross in a public park during Christmas. These decisions followed another 1995 Supreme Court decision ending, in effect, a school racial desegregation effort.[31] The 1995 decisions built on other Court rulings from 1988 through 1993 that sharply limited claims by people of color for racial harassment and workplace discrimination while expanding discrimination claims by whites.[32]

Most significant, a majority of the Court in 1995 for the first time effectively embraced color blindness as constitutional principle without differentiating "between a policy that is designed to perpetuate a caste system and one that seeks to eradicate racial subordination."[33] In justifying the color/blindness doctrine, the majority in effect assumed the existence of racial equality in society—color is irrelevant, since we all are on a level playing field.

The limitations of civil rights law, explained generally in these six ways, coalesce for many racial minorities in an experience of law as often irrational, as a "retreat from racial justice." A recent survey for the California Judicial Council found that a majority of African Americans and Latinas/os believe that the courts do not ensure racial fairness. One civil rights attorney describes her clients as "embittered," "frustrated and misunderstood" after "encounters with civil rights enforcement."

For racial communities, justice through law is thus a conundrum. Hope, promise, and change are its legacy, as are disillusionment, breach, and stasis. My point is not that legal justice is impossible for racial minorities in post–civil rights America. Indeed, many people continue to lobby local legislatures and file discrimination lawsuits; some obtain personal relief; and a few compel institutional reordering. My point is that in concept and current practice, the civil rights, antidiscrimination law approach to racial justice is constricted and that for many racial minorities, this constriction undermines the notion of justice through legal process. A ground-level race praxis view reveals formal law pulling away from racial justice.

*Justice and Racial Realities*

A second and related implication of racial justice as praxis is the grounding of racial justice in concrete places, events, people, and inter-actions. Rather than focusing solely on antidiscrimination law and courts, practical justice is located in the social realities people see, hear, touch, and sense, and it takes account of how subordinated racial groups experience justice efforts. "Justice cannot be left in the hands of judges and lawyers. It is too big, too important, too close to private meanings and public purposes, and too much missing to be delegated to any sub-group."[34]

Nor can it be left primarily in the hands of scholars. Traditional theories of justice tend to be highly abstract and to speak past day-to-day social realities. They embrace broad principles of political and moral philosophy, scrutinizing law's legitimacy. Traditional theories tend to translate poorly into concrete approaches to understanding and addressing real-life racial conflicts and prospects of remediation or healing.

Race praxis, with its inquiry into the conceptual, performative, and material, grounds racial justice in concrete situations. Rather than beginning and ending justice analysis with abstruse philosophy or after-the-fact opinions of appellate judges, it starts with inquiry into the experiences, perceptions, and interactions of racial groups. Chapter 3's description of the Asian American churches' apology resolution provided a glimpse of the complex, shifting racial and political dynamics lying just beneath the surface of Asian American and Native Hawaiian relations. Race praxis examines those ongoing dynamics and the people and organizations in-volved and concentrates on which theories, principles, and concepts provide workable approaches to understanding and diminishing oppressive racial conditions.

This grounding is important because it recommits interracial justice theorists and activists to each other and to making a difference by con-necting discourse analysis with the material conditions of people's lives. Progressive race theorizing tends to emphasize discursive strategies. Ideas, images, and language are often mapped as the battleground. Indeed, the way we talk influences the way we think and act. That is why, when an interracial controversy arises, print and electronic journalists, politicians, scholars, businesses, and group spokespersons clamor for opportunities to shape ideas and images.

During the post–Rodney King police trial firestorm, for example, the portrayal of interracial conflict by journalists (remember the television shots of armed Korean American storeowners atop their shops) and politicians (recall President Bush's castigation of welfare dependency) created lasting impressions of intergroup hostility and sloth. Later conciliatory coalition building efforts by African Americans, Asian Americans, and Latinas/os in South Central Los Angeles struggled not only with internal tension over goals, funding allocations, and political voice but also with overwhelmingly negative public images of intergroup relations. When Chinese Americans launched a legal challenge to the San Francisco School District's court-ordered affirmative action program in 1994, the initial battle was over competing racial portrayals of the lawsuit. Was the Lowell High School suit about "preferred" African Americans and Latinas/os displacing "better-qualified" children of Chinese immigrants and whites, or, conversely, about Asian Americans oppressing African Americans and Latinas/os by carrying out neoconservative whites' designs to dismantle all affirmative action?

At the level of ideas and images, discourses or, more precisely, discursive strategies embody power. Making a difference at least partially entails the power to tap communicative channels and the insight to reconstruct public events and rearticulate images regarding racial identities and group relations.

Progressive race theory's tendency toward preoccupation with discourse is problematic, however, because it comes at the overall expense of the concrete and particular. A quip attributed to an African American scholar vivifies the problem: understanding that race is a social construction does not help him get a taxi late at night.[35] Dismantling disabling group constraints and redressing the group harms require engagement with the material conditions of racial life. They require engagement in, and the connection of discourse analysis with, actual interactions among members of different racial groups in specific locales. At the face-to-face intergroup level, material goods, human interactions, access to political channels, and discursive strategies embody power. Making a difference requires the power and insight simultaneously to adjust the material aspects of race relations and to rearticulate intergroup identities.

The interracial justice grievances described in chapter 1 and the reconciliatory efforts examined in chapters 9 through 11 point to an important reality: the potential sites of justice interaction are many and varied and exist both within and beyond legal settings. Legal claims call forth several possible forums. Most legal claims are settled outside the courtroom through the joint efforts of parties, attorneys, and sometimes judges. Participants in a case construct and agree on the controversy's resolution. Even when claims are not settled and a court enjoins a defendant from specific future discriminatory behavior, some degree of cooperation and trust is required of the parties to prevent eruptions over the defendant's efforts at compliance. In addition, other opportunities exist, and are often encouraged, to resolve legal claims outside the formal litigation process. Methods of alternative dispute resolution, such as mediation and arbitration, with their greater informality and speed, are employed by the choice of the participants or by court order. Each of these sites for the resolution of legal claims enmeshed in racial conflicts offers opportunities for racial justice inquiry, rumination, and action.

Myriad other sites also provide opportunities for resolving justice grievances at and beyond the edges of formal law. Religious denominations, such as the United Church of Christ and the Southern Baptists, using theology, law, and social psychology, wrestle with racial conflict and healing at both national and local polity decisional meetings. Truth commissions, without the power to mete out legal punishment, work to discern the "truth" about human rights abuses and provide public forums for those suffering. Labor unions offer tolerance workshops and informally adjudicate highly charged group-based grievances concerning racism not only by outsiders but also within their own ranks. Racial coalitions sometimes coalesce and then splinter in search of political or economic common ground, foundering on unacknowledged long-held intergroup stereotypes and grudges.[36] Students on university campuses, seeking to interact across groups in dormitories and classes, bring with them from the social world intergroup baggage loaded with misunderstandings and tensions. Racially charged economic boycotts bring groups face to face, sometimes on collision courses, often at high decibels.[37]

Each of these sites, or situations, compresses the conflicting drives of racial groups. One drive is toward peaceable relations: the desire to make peace, to reconcile, to live side by side if not together; to work and play with one another. The other drive is toward separation: the desire to attack perceived misuses of group position and power by others, to distance one's group from the offending other. For each of these widely varying sites, race praxis directs scholars, lawyers, clergy, social workers, teachers, and community leaders—racial healers—to integrate their efforts and ground them in the concrete social realities of racial communities' struggles for justice.

### Justice Claims and Legal Process as Cultural Performance

A third general implication of seeing racial justice as praxis, and a deepening of the others, is an expanded vision of the courts, legal process, and justice claims as integral components of larger cultural performances. This praxis notion of justice claims and legal process as cultural performance speaks to those working with legal claims framed in broader political strategies.

Race praxis deepens the notions of community-based law advanced by Lopez and Cole, reframing the processes of legal justice for racial minorities in terms of cultural and communicative limitations and possibilities. It recognizes justice claims and legal process as integral parts of political-cultural processes that generate "structures of meaning that radiate throughout social life and serve as part of the material people use to negotiate their understanding of everyday events and relationships."[38] It searches critically for ways to locate justice processes and outcomes in larger community struggles; it searches pragmatically for resonance in racial communities.

Multifaceted justice practice for racial communities can start with judges and lawyers and legal process—most Americans, to some degree, are familiar with legal systems. It can—and, I believe, should—start with the law, because substantive legal principles of equality, liberty, and fairness and legal process values of dignity and participation, at least in the abstract, provide a strong modernist core.[39] But as pointed out, legal doctrines often are narrowly drawn, and legal principles and values are vaguely stated. Even though their abstract appeal persists, their practical manifestation for many racial minorities fails to resonate.

With its emphasis on critical pragmatism and multidisciplinarity, race praxis suggests rethinking notions of legal justice to encompass racial community understandings of conflict, redress, and healing—understandings illuminated by a mix of law, theology, social psychology, history, political theory, and ethnic or indigenous cultural practices. Reconfiguring legal justice in this way entails rethinking the functions of courts, judges, lawyers, social workers, clergy, teachers, and community organizations. Racial justice can be reframed beyond traditional institutional legal players. It can embrace the idea that courts and law stimulate sociocultural thinking about justice but that jury verdicts and narrow legal judgments alone do not necessarily define what is just for racialized communities.

Vantage point is key. From one view, courts are simply deciders of particular disputes involving specific parties according to established norms. From another view, courts are also integral parts of a larger communicative process. Particularly in a setting of hotly contested racial controversies, courts tend to help focus cultural issues, to illuminate institutional power arrangements, and to tell counterstories in ways that assist in the reconstruction of intergroup relationships and aid larger social-political movements. In those situations, the court process can be seen as a cultural performance, and justice can be viewed in part as the transformation of oppressive dominant racial and cultural narratives.[40] "In a society, there are specific places where most of the activities making up the social life in that society simultaneously are represented, contested, and inverted. Courts are such places."[41]

This observation is reinforced by the studies of sociolegal scholars that conclude that case handling by courts can be viewed as "cultural performances, events that produce transformations in sociocultural practices and in consciousness."[42] Those transformations may be repressive, legitimating harsh imbalances of power in social relationships; they may be liberatory, remaking entrenched group images or relationships; or they may reflect some complex, shifting combination of the two. Those transformations may occur as accretions over time, little noticed; or they may emerge in the jolt of a singular case-event. Of course, relatively few court cases singularly produce transformations in sociocultural practices and in consciousness. Those that do tend to occur when the legal dispute is reflective of a larger, ongoing social-political controversy. Other factors—location, media attention, community organizing, related lawsuits, and legislative initiatives—are significant.

The view of courts as dynamic sites and generators of cultural performances is supported generally by dispute transformation theory. According to this theory, each stage of the court process contributes in varying ways to a "rephrasing" of the dispute.[43] Decisions concerning the initial claim assertion followed by decisions concerning the pretrial discovery, sanctions, and overall case management—including motions, settlement maneuvering, and legal issue formulation—redefine the claimant's understanding and framing of the controversy. The interactions among parties, attorneys, judge, court personnel, community groups, and general public through the media and the trial itself further contribute to this rephrasing at the trial court level. Decisions by appellate courts, more detached and yet in some respects, more far-reaching, further solidify the court system's dispute rephrasing performance. A legally phrased claim is a "social construct which orders 'facts' and invokes 'norms' in particular ways,—ways that reflects the personal interests and values" of the describer.[44] Concerns critical to the rephrasing process thus arise: Who has court access; who controls claim development and presentation; according to what standards; from what perspectives, who reports on the contextual facts; and according to what selection criteria? What cultural values collide and emerge in the interactions of judges, parties, attorneys, communities, and media? These concerns shape the contours and content of a court system's overall cultural performance. From this view, courts in important instances not only decide disputes; they also transform particular legal controversies and rights claims into larger public messages.

These messages can be thought of as sociolegal narratives, or stories, about groups, institutions, situations, and relationships. The shaping and retelling of stories through a court process can help either reinforce or counter a prevailing cultural narrative in a given community. A prevailing, or master, narrative provides the principal lens through which groupings of people in a community see and interpret events and actions. It provides a set of basic assumptions for evaluating social-political controversies and the relationships of the groups involved.

A counternarrative challenges those assumptions and the vantage point from which they are made. By offering a framework not previously accepted, the counternarrative challenges established categories for classifying events and relationships by linking subjects that are typically separated or by elevating previously suppressed voices, thus stretching or altering the accepted frameworks for organizing reality.[45] It thereby undermines the clarity and strength of the master narrative, infusing complexity and providing a competing perspective.

Historically, for example, master sociolegal narratives about indigenous groups have tended to characterize their subordinated situations as inevitable, due to the groups' inferiority, or insignificant, due to the passage of time and past remedial efforts. Subordinating sociolegal narratives have thus long fixed blame for Native Hawaiians' physical and cultural destruction on their inferiority and "semi-barbarous face."[46]

Court rulings have reinforced such master narratives, and harsh societal actions have been justified by them. Many racialized groups are now countering master cultural narratives with narratives of their own—not only telling stories of historical and contemporary victimization but also offering normative precepts for future social structural change. These counternarratives are rooted in history and culture. And they are rooted in law.

Legal storytelling can be a powerful means for shaping and communicating counternarratives. Stories by Native Americans, "when broken from the dry legal recitation of the facts in the cases and placed in context, reveal powerfully the inadequacies of the dominant group's stories."[47] In this setting, racialized groups, and indigenous groups in particular, are asserting justice claims in narrow and expansive frameworks and rethinking the "cultural performance" role of courts in addressing race controversies.

This rethinking of justice efforts parallels the shifting perceptions of the judicial role in civil rights litigation. It reflects in part the transformation from the civil rights activity of the 1960s and early 1970s to the post–civil rights era. For racial minorities, the current post–civil rights era might be characterized generally by a reconceptualizing of the role of courts and law as part of, rather than as the pinnacle of, political strategies for social structural change; the movement away from principal reliance on narrow judicial remedies toward the additional use of the courts as forums for the development and expressions of counternarratives and for the promotion of local empowerment and community control; and the rising importance of educational, religious and community forums for developing and hearing justice claims.

# Part 3

# Interracial Justice

Interracial justice, I submit, is integral to peaceable and productive inter-group relations. When racial groups in conflict seek to live together peaceably and work together politically, interracial justice often helps bridge the chasm between currently felt racial wounds and healthy relations. It helps bridge the chasm by facilitating the healing of wounds that undergird many present-day intergroup conflicts. Its guiding principle is reconciliation, its goal the transformation of strained relations. Interracial justice thus may be characterized as an antisubordination approach to intergroup grievance that, in some instances, leads toward the establishment of "right relationships" or the restoration of "broken relationships."[1]

Part 1 discussed the problem of interracial grievance and reconciliation in local, national, and international settings. Part 2 described theories of race, culture, and grievance that shape the praxis approach to interracial justice developed here.

Part 3 reintroduces and more fully develops my conception of interracial justice. It casts interracial justice not as a universal theory of justice but as a critical pragmatic approach to interracial grievance and reconciliation. What do law, social psychology, theology, political theory, and indigenous customary practices say about intergroup healing? Chapter 7 sketches multidisciplinary insights, and chapter 8 distills those insights and articulates interracial justice dimensions to facilitate analysis and action in concrete controversies. How do these interracial justice dimensions work in practice? Chapters 9, 10, and 11 use them to assess and rethink three particular interracial justice controversies.

One such controversy is the continuing reconciliatory efforts in a religious-political setting—the contentious reparations process following the Asian American and United Church of Christ apology to indigenous Hawaiians described in chapter 3. A second is a localized conflict between a small businesses and community organizations—the eruption, volatile handling, and complicated resolution of a racialized dispute between a Korean American hat shop merchant and African American minister in Los Angeles. The third pertains to reconciliatory efforts in rebuilding a nation—the South African Truth Commission hearings not only concerning white-on-black human rights abuses by the former ruling National Party during apartheid but also black-on-black abuses by apartheid resistors.

My discussion of these concrete controversies provides a glimpse, and only a glimpse, of interracial justice problems and potential. This discussion is not meant to represent the entirety of interracial grievances and healing efforts. Nor is it intended as social history. The opportunities to critique, amend, and extend the mapping I offer are many.

One final introductory question. Of what interest to white Americans is this part's discussion of interracial justice? Considerable, I suggest. First, although specifically addressing healing among communities of color, the interracial justice dimensions developed here also provide guidance for white Americans genuinely interested in struggling to heal white-on-color wounds in post–civil rights America—for example, the United Church of Christ apology to and reparations for Native Hawaiians. Second, when racial communities grieve and work to reconcile, they often do so in a larger setting that includes whites; understanding the complex dynamics of those struggles better enables white Americans of goodwill to be critically aware and politically supportive.

# 7

# Interracial Healing

## Multidisciplinary Approaches

Harlon Dalton observes that public talk about race often invokes the language of healing. He is right. We hear about racial healing during public ceremonies (the replaying of the "I Have a Dream" speech on the Martin Luther King holiday), amid local conflicts (politicians demanding peace between neighborhood grocers and community organizations), and during times of public upheaval (Rodney King's plea "can we all get along"). But, Dalton says, this language of healing is used too often to squelch hard, forthright talk about race. Right again. Hard straight forward engagement, "we are told, [is] likely to produce ill will and discord. Instead of promoting divisiveness we should be promoting healing."[1] It seems, then, that we are to talk about healing racial wounds without talking seriously about racial conflict. A flawed prescription.

What, then, do groups desirous of genuine reconciliation mean when they talk about racial healing? Dalton offers a language of healing that begins with engagement and moves to "pure, unadulterated struggle." He is speaking generally of a kind of praxis.

The race praxis ideas developed earlier suggest a pragmatic search for healing understandings that resonate with racial communities. These understandings emerge in bits and pieces from the disciplines of law, theology, social psychology, political theory (particularly peace studies), and indigenous healing practices.

In this chapter, I describe general understandings from those disciplines and tease out commonalities. Before doing so, several words of caution are in order. Questions arise concerning disciplinary authority. What qualifies as a discipline's insights? Each discipline encompasses divergent, sometimes oppositional, theories and methods about harm and healing. Describing one theory, or even coalescing several, risks oversimplification, if not distortion. Questions also arise about racial group voice. In a group, or in a subgroup of a group, who speaks for the rest? In a given situation, who decides which group-healing steps are appropriate, and what are the risks of leadership co-optation? These and related questions, while important, are left for future works. Here I shall simply map the terrain—to draw out healing understandings from various disciplines as a basis for the interracial justice inquiry set forth in the next chapter.

## Multidisciplinary Insights into Group Healing

### Law

Law does not address healing directly. The actual healing of injured bodies, minds, and spirits and the repairing of broken relationships generally lie beyond the law's reach. Instead, law addresses healing indirectly through the multifaceted idea of court-rendered justice. Some conceive of legal justice in a manner that ignores healing completely. For them, legal justice simply means dispute resolution; the disposition of claims of individuals according to substantive norms through fair process.[2] The idea of commensurability allows law to dispense justice through a single substitutionary remedy (money) despite a wide range of harms suffered. This version of legal justice tends to turn a blind eye to the social and psychological impacts of dispute resolution outcomes and procedures on the participants and their communities. Many see this as the dominant legal approach to justice.[3]

For others, legal justice is something more than dispute resolution. It constitutes who we are as a people. This understanding of justice underlies James Boyd White's suggestion that law "should take as its most central question what kind of community we should be."[4] According to this communitarian view, law grounds justice in the construction of moral communities. The central facet of legal discourse should be its capacity to build, rather than destroy, communal relationships.

For still others—and perhaps in reaction to both the narrow dominant approach and broadly framed communitarian ideals—justice is both law and something beyond. Justice between people in conflict can emerge from "communication, compromise, mediation, bargaining, leadership, institutional design," supported by "virtues of openness, generosity, and wisdom." These "virtues are not . . . unique to law; they may even be undermined by it."[5] What is significant in this perspective are the ways in which formal legal process inhibits rather than encourages the restoration of damaged relationships. Testament to the popularity of this law-and-beyond approach is the burgeoning alternative dispute resolution industry, with its emphasis on mediation and arbitration, and the success of neighborhood justice centers.

Debates continue about these and other approaches to legal justice. I will not discuss them further other than to observe that for most scholars in the United States, including many advancing beyond-law prescriptions, ideas of justice remain deeply rooted in law. Notions of rights and duties, remedies, and open process still carry enormous purchase. These notions and their limitations are part of the fabric of the American polity. Procedurally, justice is commonly defined in terms of fair process—the opportunity to be heard, to participate, to be treated with dignity. Substantively, and relevant to our discussion of interracial justice, legal justice norms focus on fairness and equality. (The meaning of equality, of course, is sharply contested—one meaning is equality of opportunity, another is equality of result).[6] Remedially, in most instances, law prescribes compensation—wrongdoer payment for physical and emotional as well as economic loss.[7]

In some situations, these aspects of legal justice—procedure (encompassing participation and dignity), equality norms (including an antisubjugation principle), and remedies (primarily compensation)—generate a sense of justice for those involved. In terms of traditional roots and continuing influence, law thus provides a beginning point for the exploration of racial healing.

Even as a beginning point, however, the healing effects of legal process are limited. A brief examination of remedial options from the vantage point of those suffering reveals why. Legal justice's primary remedial emphasis on monetary compensation focuses on material redistribution and embraces the notion of commensurability; that is, monetary damages are commensurate with human loss. That remedy, however, may not address what most concerns those harmed—dignity, emotional relief, participation in the social polity, or institutional reordering. Legal remedies also emphasize the punishment of wrongdoers (punitive damages in civil cases, imprisonment in criminal cases). This remedial focus assumes—falsely much of the time—that retribution will help heal the victim's wounds. For this and related reasons, many racial communities are left embittered, frustrated, and misunderstood after efforts at civil rights enforcement.[8]

What legal doctrine, remedies, and procedure overlook is the psychosocial healing of harmed individuals and groups. The law misses the repairing of individual bodies, minds, and spirits and, equally important, the rejuvenation of denigrated group identities and restoration of broken relationships. When Carl Hansberry won on appeal to the U.S. Supreme Court in 1940,[9] his legal victory was acclaimed, and still is, as a major civil rights advance. Hansberry prevailed over lakefront landowners in Chicago who sought to enforce a covenant in deeds to lakefront lots that prohibited sales to blacks. He prevailed on procedural grounds, defeating the landowners' contention that a prior fraudulently conducted class action upholding the validity of the covenant foreclosed Hansberry's later challenge.

Hansberry's victory, however, hardly led to the repair of wounds to his body, mind, and spirit or to the rifts in neighborhood relationships between blacks and whites. These wounds were first inflicted by the landowners' efforts to exclude him from the lakefront, then through the neighborhood attacks on his family, and finally by the crush and time-delay of litigation. His daughter, Lorraine Hansberry, who later wrote the award-winning play *Raisin in the Sun* about her family's struggles for legal justice, poignantly described her father's "victory." What those who called the

case progress toward racial justice through law did not grasp, she observed, was the "emotional turmoil, time and money, which led to my
father's early death as a permanently embittered exile in a foreign country." What they did not see was that

> the "correct" way of fighting white supremacy in America [through legal justice]
> include[d] being spat at, cursed and pummeled in the daily trek to and from
> school . . . my desperate and courageous mother, patrolling our house all night
> with a loaded German luger, doggedly guarding her four children, while my
> father fought the respectable part of the battle in the Washington court.[10]

Constricted notions of legal justice failed to address, let alone redress, the
kind of harm suffered by "prevailing party" Hansberry and his family.

Nevertheless, as highlighted in the previous chapter's discussion of race
praxis implications, rights claims and justice process, sometimes and in
other ways, engender affirmation and healing. Patricia Williams opens a
window into the psychosocial dynamics of rights claims by racial minorities, even when those claims await formal recognition under law. In response to the charge that legal discourse generally and rights discourse
particularly have been employed by those in power only to mystify African Americans and thereby perpetuate their oppression, Williams points
to blacks' sometimes nurturing, empowering, and life-giving experience
with the assertion of rights.

> To say that blacks never fully believed in rights is true; yet it is also true that
> blacks believed in them so much and so hard that we gave them life where there
> was none before. We held onto them, put the hope of them into our wombs, and
> mothered them. . . . We nurtured rights and gave rights life.[11]

The assertion of rights, "so deliciously empowering to say," is a statement
of selfhood, of boundary drawing, especially for blacks long used to in-
visibility and long subjected to the "crushing weight of totalistic—bodily
and spiritual—intrusion." It is the existence of law, and the possibility of
justice through legal process, however remote, that gives rights assertion
and its statement of selfhood enhanced potency.

This view of rights assertion implies an expansive notion of racial justice. Something more is at play than legally sanctioned distributive outcomes or, during the Reagan-Bush era, the "sop of minor enforcement

of major statutory schemes like the Civil Rights Act." That something more starts with law but then moves beyond. It encompasses racial minorities' psychosocial reactions to, and perceptions of, the processes and boundaries of justice; it embraces their responses, feelings, and sense impressions stirred by symbols such as rights "deeply enmeshed in the psyche of the oppressed."

In widely varying ways, theology, social psychology, political theory (particularly peace studies), and indigenous practices address the psychosocial dimensions of conflict and reconciliation among groups. In particular, they address the healing of breaches in relationships and in communities. Each of these disciplines is internally diverse and differs from the others. Each has its limitations. Even commonalities in disciplines play out in differing ways according to cultural settings.[12] Nevertheless, the following general description of healing approaches in each discipline is useful to a preliminary discussion of possibilities of interracial reconciliation.

Let us first revisit the Asian American churches apology resolution which drew on both legal concepts and healing insights from these disciplines. Clergy drafting the resolution fixed heavily on legal concepts. Even though theological ideas of repentance and atonement provided spiritual impetus, legal concepts informed the resolution's basic structure. Legal notions of culpability ("illegal overthrow" and "complicity"), procedure ("due process"), and remedy ("restitution"), collectively embodied in the "demands of law," structured the resolution's approach to its stated goal: justice. The clergy solicited my legal advice on their draft.

Notwithstanding this legal approach, the forum for the resolution's presentation was decidedly nonlegal. It was the annual polity decision-making meeting of the Hawaiʻi Conference of the United Church of Christ. Although the resolution's drafters framed the "dispute" partially in legal terms; although many offered and refuted "evidence"; although deliberations by individual churches, committees, and breakout groups entailed sometimes heated arguments about "illegality" and "due process"; and although a modified version of Robert's Rules of legislative order shepherded the polity's final vote, there was no adjudication, no court ordering legal remedies, no formal legal judgment. The justice sought by the polity was nonlegal. It started with but moved beyond notions of legal justice into realms of theology, social psychology, and indigenous healing practice. The justice sought focused on "healing" intergroup wounds, releasing the "hurt," and "reconciling" groups in tension so that the polity might "move on" and address the "many things that face our church and community."

Why lean on legal concepts to frame notions of entitlement but not remedy? Why bypass the legal system entirely? Of course, the simple answer to both questions is that the resolution's proponents were in effect confessing historical complicity in the subordination of Hawaiians and that adversarial adjudication and legal remediation were unnecessary. Another simple answer, to the second question, is that the resolution mainly addressed relationships in internal church affairs. The annual conference meeting provided the appropriate forum. But why look beyond law for healing insights? What do other disciplines offer?

## Theology

Theology offers a developed conception of intergroup healing. A Judeo-Christian theology of reconciliation grounds healing in stories of freedom from bondage, care for the abandoned, and compassion for the outcast and in biblical notions of love, peace, and justice.[13] Among those notions, justice is key. It is the transcendent idea that connects love (the "instrument," according to Martin Luther King) with genuine peace (the goal). Indeed, for prophetic theology, justice is a precondition to peaceable relations. The Christian clergy authors of the 1985 Kairos Document rejected the white South African government's mollifying calls for unity and peace in the face of intensifying black agitation, stating that "there can be no true reconciliation and no genuine peace without justice."[14]

In the United States, Rev. King offered perhaps the most sophisticated and enlivening theological view of group healing. The open wounds of slavery and continuing segregation could be healed only by African American participation as full citizens in the polity. Rev. King recognized that full participation, and healing, could not be achieved by blacks alone. Given the overwhelming social and economic power of whites in America, African American healing required some form of reconciliation between blacks and whites. Yet many whites opposed social integration. The question that Rev. King and supporters faced was, how do African Americans engender reconciliation in the face of continuing white racial oppression?

Rev. King's response, which galvanized the civil rights movement, was to push for reconciliation through justice. He framed that response, directed to both races, in terms of the injustice of savage inequality in America, even after the United States had spilled much blood in Europe fighting for freedom and democracy. His carefully chosen method for working against that injustice—love, nonviolent resistance, and the assertion of civil rights—framed genuine justice as the heart of reconciliation. The theologian James Cone captured the power of this linkage of nonviolence and justice to reconciliation.

King emphasized that violence never creates the conditions for reconciliation; it only breeds more of the same. The American dream is possible only if Negroes struggle for justice with a method that has reconciling power built into it. Nonviolence [in King's words] "helps you to work for something that is morally right, namely integration and the brotherhood of men, with methods that are morally right."[15]

Rev. King's theology of reconciliation, or "political ethics," spoke directly to the dilemma of history—recalling history and its present-day consequences in order to release its grip. The process of remembering and releasing, through nonviolent struggles for justice, aimed to transform white resistance into black-white rapprochement, so that, as Rev. King put it, "the evil deed is no longer a mental block impeding a new relationship."[16]

How justice fosters reconciliation in post–civil rights America and in contemporary world politics, of course, differs from situation to situation. One theological concept is atonement—to sacrifice to make up for wrongs perpetrated and thereby seek forgiveness.[17] The African American "Million Man March" on Washington D.C. in 1995 embraced atonement as its theme. The march attempted to reconnect and reconcile African American men with one another, families, and communities. For the march, Christian Protestant and Muslim theologians located reconciliation in atonement and linked atonement to justice—the acknowledgment of brokenness and harm, repentance, and acts of contrition.[18]

Another concept is reparation. To repair harm to individuals and groups and thereby rebuild the polity, theological acts of reparation must extend beyond monetary payments. For the Ecumenical Dialogue for Reconciliation, meeting in Belgrade near the end of the interethnic and interreligious Balkan hostilities, those acts must undo damage to material conditions of daily life. Reparatory acts necessarily included restoring homes, caring for the bereaved, providing jobs, reaching out to youth, promoting multicultural education, discouraging misleading media portrayals, and monitoring elections.[19]

This Christian theological notion of intergroup reconciliation through justice—atonement and reparation—embraces the "confessional character of community building." Indeed, confession and community were entwined in the Asian American churches and United Church of Christ Hawai'i Conference resolutions of apology to Native Hawaiians.

The confessional character of community building meant an acknowledgement on the part of the church members of their own deep-seated prejudice and distrust across ethnic, generational, and class lines. Only when their divisions were confessed in light of faith did the church [members] become open to a new way of relating with each other, a new way of community building.[20]

Zen Buddhism also locates reunification in reconciliation, although in a different fashion. The ultimate state of being is *satori*, or the state of enlightenment in which people and nature are experienced as one and in which conflicts are acknowledged and released. Confessions of guilt and acknowledgments of fault, however, are unnecessary. Conflicts are released and a state of Zen emptiness is attained through understandings reached in the process of mutual listening and empathy. Zen reconciliation is "to understand both sides, to go to one side and describe the suffering being endured by the other side, and then to the other side, and describe the[ir] suffering being endured."[21]

Words alone, of course, even when understood, are unlikely to heal deep intergroup wounds. The Torah enjoins long disenfranchised Jews to do justice not only by swearing by God but also by "removing your abominations" and "loving the stranger."[22] And prophetic Christian theology warns against false words of unity or, in the terms of the Kairos Document, "cheap reconciliation." Indeed, the theologians who wrote the Kairos Document charged South Africa's liberal Christian churches with "preaching reconciliation as a subtle way of avoiding resistance against evil."[23]

In our situation in South Africa today it would be totally unChristian to plead for reconciliation and peace before the present injustices have been removed. Any such plea plays into the hands of the oppressor by trying to persuade those of us who are oppressed to accept our oppression and to become reconciled to the intolerable crimes that are committed against us. That is not Christian reconciliation, it is sin. . . . No reconciliation is possible in South Africa without justice.[24]

The churches' position at the time supported white South African government officials' calls for reconciliation—to stop the resistance and maintain the status quo. The churches said: "Why must we always live with conflict and unrest [caused by black resistance]? . . . Let us all work together for national reconciliation!"[25] The Kairos theologians highlighted the danger of this repressive "peace at the expense of justice" approach to unification, a danger similarly identified by Dietrich Bonhoeffer in his attack on the cheap grace of the German Evangelical Church during the Third Reich.[26] The Kairos theologians located genuine reconciliation in a kind of continuing justice practice: sincere repentance by the oppressor, forgiveness by the oppressed, and the dismantling of oppressive societal structures.[27]

## Social Psychology

Where theology offers approaches to reunification through justice, psychology offers catharsis—to confront externally induced emotional trauma as a foundation for releasing it. The psychological dynamics of conflict and healing are complicated and, in important respects, contested in the discipline. My treatment here describes the salient points without attention to differing approaches or fine distinctions.

Generally stated, when unresolved anger and loss are internalized, deep psychic injuries cause those suffering to withdraw into passivity and depression. Western psychologists therefore seek to create a new reality for their patients by guiding them through stages of healing: denial, anger, self-blame, guilt, acceptance, and forgiveness.[28]

These stages are described collectively as *mourning* or *grieving*. When a person has experienced a psychic harm—whether from a traumatic event or successive acts of discrimination—mourning enables that person to acknowledge the anger and injustice. It begins a process of releasing the pain and moving beyond victimhood toward a capacity for trust, autonomy, initiative, competence, and intimacy. Mourning can be facilitated by affirming interactions between aggressor and subject, including the aggressor's acceptance of responsibility for the harm and an expression of contrition. When this "reaction [mourning] is worked through, something is gained: The mourner feels a new surge of energy that may be expressed in his undertaking new projects or new personal attachments. Mourning, although marking a loss, also eventually brings a kind of new power."[29]

Mourning by social groups is more complicated. Social psychologists wrestle with the translation of personal psychological concepts of acknowledgment and forgiveness into group concepts to guide intergroup (as distinguished from interpersonal) healing. The phenomenon of collective memory is central to this difficulty of translation. Group identities, group suffering, and collective accounts of historical events evade easy description. How are historical memories of group pain and loss formed by group experiences and continually re-formed by changing social circumstances? How do those group memories of racial grievances inform current conflicts and shape the ways in which racial wounds are aggravated or salved? Recent international works identify the political dimensions of memory reconstruction by both oppressors and victims, at all levels. Individuals, social groups, institutions, and nations filter and twist, recall and forget "information" in reframing shameful past acts (thereby lessening responsibility) as well as in enhancing victim status (thereby increasing power). Collective memory not only vivifies a group's past, it also reconstructs it and thereby situates a group in relation to others in a power hierarchy.

For a group in mourning, individual feelings of loss and anger are magnified. "Mythologized as well as realistic memories of hurts and psychological wounds of one generation are conveyed to the next generation . . . [as the next generation] tries to recreate a version of the event in which the self-esteem of . . . their group was damaged."[30] In this fashion, collective memory shapes racial group grievances and, in turn, determines the prospects for intergroup healing through contrition and forgiveness.

For both theology and social psychology, forgiveness signals the end of mourning and a transformation in group relations. Genuine forgiveness corrects and restores. "[Forgiveness] corrects the distortion which an act of evil establishes between two . . . groups—the distortion of stolen power. . . . At the same time such correction restores the dignity of both sides. While the perpetrator renounces his or her false aggrandizement, the victim rises from his or her induced humiliation."[31] Forgiving, however—unburdening the past to move into the future—does not mean forgetting. "Forgetting prolongs captivity," says a Jewish proverb. "Remembering is the secret of redemption."

This process of deep remembering leads both those suffering and those inflicting harm to name human hurts and acknowledge human dignity. It allows both to gain insight into their common humanity and remake a relational narrative as the basis for future relations. In this way, forgiveness connotes a mutual liberation from the bondage of past hurts with hope for a better future.

*Political Theory (Peace Studies)*

Political theory addresses group injury and healing from a different angle. In particular, political theory informing international human rights law and peace studies focuses on democratic processes and offers the concept of reparation—to repair societal harm by one entity, usually a government, inflicted directly on another, usually a marginalized social group.[32]

In concept, healing through repairing is rooted in democratic notions of participation in the social, economic, and political life of the polity. A breach in the polity through wrongful exclusion is repaired by fostering the participation of those excluded.[33] In practice, repairing the breach means lifting the barriers to liberty and equality in education, housing, medical care, employment, cultural preservation, and political participation.[34]

The African concept of *ubuntu* embraces and extends these conceptual and practical political understandings of healing. *Ubuntu*—the notion of interconnectedness, that "people are people through other people"[35]— emphasizes healing through the restoration of the polity. People suffering are not "saved" as individuals but "through incorporation into a body." The focal point is the community, whether defined by tribe, locale, or nation. *Ubuntu* thus shapes healing efforts through notions of co-responsibility, interdependence, and enjoyment of rights by all.

The South African understanding of justice is informed by *ubuntu*. It "is far more restorative [than retributive]—not so much to punish as to redress or restore a balance . . . [it is] restorative of the dignity of the people" as part of a common humanity.[36] For this reason, Archbishop Desmond Tutu, first chair of South Africa's Truth and Reconciliation Commission, emphasizes that his country cannot be healed without repairing the wounds inflicted by apartheid on the life of the community. Repairing those wounds means reintegration of the community, and reintegration means "affirming the legitimacy of victims' claims [along with reparations to] bring back into the polity those who had concluded that this government has nothing to offer them."[37] It also means forgiving those who atone for heinous crimes—those who confess, express contrition, and offer restitution. (Of course, for intensely practical reasons, former perpetrators may be incorporated into the reconstituted polity even without contrition—as a necessary exchange in the society's moral economy. Tutu observes that many white members of the former ruling National Party still possess economic and military clout, so that attempts to exclude them from the center of South African life would likely generate opposition fierce enough to destabilize the new government.)[38]

Guided by *ubuntu* and political pragmatism, South African President Nelson Mandela both exhorts and cautions that the survival of each of the many South African groups is dependent on the survival of and, to an important extent, reconciliation with the others. The transitional South African constitution, entitled "National Unity and Reconciliation," reflected this perspective. The interim constitution's postamble envisioned healing among racial groups as a key to the peaceful coexistence of South Africans: "There is a need for understanding but not for vengeance, a need for reparation but not for retaliation, a need for ubuntu but not victimization." In light of apartheid-inflicted social wounds, the postamble stressed that "national unity, the well-being of all South Africans and peace require reconciliation between the people of South Africa." Taking a cue from the postamble, South Africa's judiciary recently embraced ubuntu and reconciliation as part of South African constitutional jurisprudence. Linking social inclusion to healing, the South Africa Supreme Court highlighted South Africa's need in the rebuilding process to integrate into the polity those marginalized by apartheid.

In important respects, these South African constitutional and judicial notions of reparation are consistent with the theoretical underpinnings of international human rights norms—particularly the necessity of repairing the wounds to both the individual and the social community. In some situations, international tribunals prosecute human rights violators for crimes against society and order redress to benefit harmed individuals and to repair tears in the inter-nation social fabric.[39] Redress entails restoration and therefore "must, as far as possible, wipe out all the consequences of the illegal act and reestablish the situation which would, in all probability, have existed if that act had not been committed."[40]

## Indigenous Healing Practices

Finally, indigenous healing practices provide related yet unique insights into intergroup healing. For example, indigenous Hawaiians continue to engage in a process of *ho'oponopono* to heal physical and psychological wounds arising out of interpersonal or intergroup conflicts.[41] The process is "complex and potentially lengthy . . . [and] includes prayer, statement of the problem, discussion, confession of wrongdoing, restitution when necessary, forgiveness and release."[42] It is a therapeutic process that examines the past and uncovers thoughts and feelings leading to conflict, in order to loosen and then cut the negative entanglements of those involved and their communities.[43]

Similarly, the Navajo justice system emphasizes tribal relationships and values. In 1981, after almost a century of United States–imposed adjudicatory methods, the courts of the Navajo nation remade the legal system to better accommodate traditional Navajo practices and values in addressing certain kinds of justice grievances. The Navajo peacemaking process is called *hozhooji naat'aanii*. Its norms, or guiding principles, are "internalized" through the use of songs, prayers, origin scripture, and journey narratives. Its emphasis is the restoration of group harmony. This process resembles the Navajo physical healing process: purification through words and symbols and a reaffirmation of solidarity with the group centering on goodwill and aiming toward community reintegration. Authority is persuasive, not coercive. The focus is not on fault but on why the people are in disharmony and what can be done about it. By emphasizing their relationship in the community, justice enables them to rejoin the community spiritually and socially.[44]

## Common Points

Some of the more recently crafted approaches to intergroup reconciliation draw implicitly from the insights of the disciplines just described. Ronald Fisher, for example, offers "generic principles" of process for resolving intergroup conflicts. Those principles are reflected in what Fisher describes as a three-stage process. The first stage, *conflict analysis*, is "initial and mutual exploration, differentiation, and clarification of the sources of conflict and the processes of interaction that characterize both its history and current expression."[45] Conflict is analyzed to identify the sources and types of tensions, enabling the group participants jointly to "identify, distinguish, and prioritize the essential elements of [the] conflict." The second stage, *confrontation*, is direct interaction in which the participants engage one another, focus on the conflict between them, and work toward mutually acceptable solutions through a process of collaboration and joint public sharing. Confrontation proceeds from a basis of multicultural respect and common needs. The third stage, *resolution*, means that conflict is "transformed to a state and in relational context which is self-supporting, self-committing and sustainable for the foreseeable future."

The scheme's strength is its clear articulation of three general stages of healing. Its shortcoming lies in what it omits—in the second and third stages, a description of norms and guidelines for fashioning mutually acceptable solutions through "collaboration and joint problem solving."

Because the scheme is not clearly grounded on critical inquiry or theories of intergroup healing, its core ultimately amounts to an exhortation to "just do it together."[46]

By contrast, both John Dawson and Joseph Montville, in separate works, draw explicitly on aspects of Christian theology, Zen Buddhism, psychology, and political theory to offer "therapeutic" approaches to healing for social groups. Similarly, Donald Shriver employs Christian theology and political theory to map a "politics of forgiveness." All three scholars direct their inquiry into intergroup healing at oppressive relationships marked by white dominance.

For Dawson, author of *Healing America's Wounds* and founder of the International Reconciliation Coalition of Los Angeles, the acknowledgment of historical group harms, sincere apology, and rectifying action facilitate the healing of intergroup wounds and provide a path toward meaningful change in relationships.[47] Examining the white Christian massacre of Cheyenne Indians, the British race violence against New Zealand's Maoris, America's white supremacy, the Jewish Holocaust, and Korean and Japanese enmity, he challenges Americans to repent and reconcile not for personal salvation but for healing the nation.

Intergroup wounds, according to Dawson, are of both local and national concern. They are of localized concern because their effects— "rejection, fear of authority, rebellion . . . loneliness and isolation, fear of intimacy, withdrawal, melancholy, inferiority"—are manifested in intergroup behavior. At the same time, those wounds are "living scars marring our national face."

More specifically, the intergroup healing process for Dawson entails confession, repentance, restitution, and reconciliation. Confession is "stating the truth; acknowledgment of the unjust or hurtful actions of . . . [a] group toward other persons or categories of persons." Confession recognizes the historical roots of contemporary conflicts and examines responsibility for underlying hurtful actions of one group toward others. Repentance follows confession. It requires acts of contrition, acts reflecting the acknowledgment of responsibility for the historical roots of contemporary conflict—"turning from unloving to loving action." Confession and acts of repentance need to be supported by appropriate restitution to restore what has been destroyed. Reconciliation follows—

"expressing and receiving forgiveness and pursuing intimate fellowship with previous enemies."[48]

For Montville, a theorist and practitioner of intergroup conflict resolution, the prospects of healing interracial and interreligious wounds depend on a similar "process of transactional contrition and forgiveness between aggressors and victims."[49] This process is the joint analysis of "the history of the conflict, recognition of injustices and resulting historic wounds, and acceptance of moral responsibility." Transgenerational storytelling and the articulation of intergroup grievances help by "revising and cleaning up the published historical record of a conflicted intergroup . . . relationship [and have] become widely accepted as an essential part of a reconciliation process." The joint reconstruction of history and recognition of group responsibility for wrongdoing are crucial steps toward intergroup healing.

Montville also draws on psychological insights into the therapeutic effects of forgiveness. All therapists regularly confront injustice—the "abuse of the weak by the strong, betrayals of trust, loyalty, and innocence"—and help patients explore the past and experience repressed feelings of anger and loss[50]—for example, adults who have suffered mental and physical abuse as children. The question connecting the personal psychological to the sociopsychological is, How does a person whose injury is related in part to her group identity let go of her past humiliation, her victimhood?[51] Forgiveness, a conjunction of religious tradition and psychology, is central.

Donald W. Shriver Jr. deepens the understanding of forgiveness through theology and political theory. He approaches forgiveness in the context of human enemies who have greatly harmed one another. How can former enemies "grope toward political association again"? For those groups seeking genuine alliances, "they will find themselves practicing a collective form of forgiveness." Borrowing from Hannah Arendt, Shriver elaborates on the dialectics of this practice.

[It] calls for a collective turning from the past that neither ignores past evil nor excuses it, that neither overlooks justice nor reduces justice to revenge, that insists on the humanity of enemies even in their commission of dehumanizing deeds, and that values the justice that restores political community above the justice that destroys it.[52]

Relationships cannot move forward without the healing dynamic of re-pentance and forgiveness. "The debris [of the past] will never get cleaned up and animosity will never drain away until forgiveness enters these relationships." Intergroup reconciliation emerges from this process through the forging of a new relationship based on the beginnings of mutual acceptance and trust.

Dawson, Montville, and Shriver are self-critical. Dawson warns that repentance, and thus reconciliation, can be real or cheap. Real repentance is "taking on ourselves both the guilt and grandeur of our history and facing the implications squarely." Repentance is cheap, on the other hand, when "we can have peace with God, by pretending offenses did not hap-pen or that injustice cannot be addressed" or by "overemphasi[zing] the significance of solemn assemblies and other formal acts of confession."[53] This warning mirrors the Kairos Document's warning against cheap rec-onciliation (peace without justice) directed to churches and government officials.

Montville cautions that the psychological idea of healing individuals in a relationship through repentance and forgiveness may not be easily trans-latable to social group interactions. Clinical literature reveals little about the cathartic effect of forgiveness as a part of a group mourning process. Montville also cautions that "unilateral forgiveness"—as distinguished from a mutually engaged process of contrition and forgiveness—may be "helpful in individual therapy where the 'aggressor' mother or father may be dead, but unilateralism is rarely helpful in political conflict resolution."

Four commonalities generally emerge from the diverse disciplines of law, theology, social psychology, political theory, and indigenous practices sketched here, commonalities relevant to interracial justice. The first is the notion that group healing requires some combination of acknow-ledgment of the humanity of the other and of the sources of the conflict (including joint historical and contemporary analyses of mutual griev-ances underlying present conflicts); acceptance of appropriate responsi-bility for group harms (by recognizing the extent of group agency); re-construction of the relationship (including acts of apology, the bestowal of forgiveness, and the refashioning of stories about self, other, and the relationship); and reparation (repairing material racial harms). The second is the notion that healing of wounds from perceived wrongful acts is an interactive enterprise and, by virtue of its mutuality of effort, provides a foundation for future communal, or at least cooperative, action. The third commonality is that these approaches to intergroup healing incorporate legal concepts of equality and fairness in some fashion and also move beyond formal notions of legal justice. The fourth commonality, developed in the next chapter, is recognition of the danger of incomplete or insincere acknowledgments and ameliorative efforts—how "empty apologies" and words without institutional restructuring and attitudinal changes can mask continuing oppression.

Building on these points of commonality, the next chapter delineates four praxis dimensions of interracial justice inquiry.

# 8

## "Facing History, Facing Ourselves"

### Interracial Justice

If I am not for myself, who will be for me?
If I am not for others, what am I?
And if not now, when?

— RABBI HILLEL,
first-century poem

Interracial justice entails a hard acknowledgment of ways in which racial groups harm one another, along with affirmative efforts to redress grievances with present-day effects. Set in a larger context of the "wages of whiteness," it encompasses messy, shifting, continual, and often localized efforts at interracial reconciliation. Indeed, for racialized communities in post–civil rights America, interracial justice means "facing history, facing ourselves." And in so doing, it means looking at self-interest ("if I am not for myself, who will be") and then looking beyond ("if I am not for others, what am I").

Framed in this manner, interracial justice is an integral, although often overlooked, component of peaceable relations and coalition building among communities of color. For groups seeking to live together peaceably and work together politically, interracial justice serves in many instances as a bridge between currently felt racial wounds and workable intergroup relations.[1]

To assist in bridging, I connect the conceptual to the practical. Empirical studies reveal that in addition to ideas and ideals, justice is something experienced.[2] It is grounded in gritty racial realities; it is something racial communities struggle with viscerally and intellectually.

When those communities seek to rebuild relationships shaken by justice grievances, their struggles are illuminated by group healing insights from law, prophetic theology, social psychology, peace studies, and indigenous practices, sketched in the preceding chapter.[3] These disciplines collectively offer a rough, incomplete, yet nevertheless compelling portrait of the dynamics of intergroup reconciliation. Those dynamics reflect some combination of acknowledgment of the humanity of the other and of the sources of conflict (including joint historical and contemporary analyses of mutual grievances underlying present conflicts); acceptance of appropriate responsibility for group harms (by recognizing the extent of group agency); reconstruction of the relationship (including acts of apology, the bestowal of forgiveness, and the refashioning of stories about self, other, and the relationship); and reparation (repairing material racial harms).

Cast in this manner, these descriptions lack the dynamism, the feel, the intensity of real-world reconciliatory efforts. Indeed, each of the disciplines discussed in chapter 7 frames group healing according to its component parts and then, sensing something missing, reaches for an enlivening idea, or term, to better capture the tumultuous, energized feel of the actual intergroup healing experiences. In transcending categories, religious scholars speak of the "spiritual" rush of reconciliation—the reunification of people through God. Psychologists work toward patient "catharsis"—the entering of places of pain and its deep emotional release—and social psychologists observe dramatic "transformations" in consciousness and behavior. Political theorists speak of "reconstituting community"—reshaping the polity by breaking old barriers and reincorporating people at the margins. Indigenous Hawaiian healing practitioners search for *pono*—making right, or righteous, the broken relationship. In bringing reconciliation discourse to life, these concepts touch the heart of

South Africa's notion of restorative justice, *ubuntu*—we are people only through other people.

In its broadest sense, interracial justice embraces this notion of reconciliation through restorative justice. The specific dimensions of interracial justice inquiry, developed here, address restoration through the interrogation of and action on justice grievances undergirding immediate conflicts. Those dimensions, the categories, the bits and pieces, should be viewed as integral parts of this larger "complex process of 'unlocking' painful bondage, of mutual liberation"—a mutual liberation that "frees the future from the haunting legacies of the [distant and recent] past."[4] It is this larger complex process that links interracial justice to healing, and healing to reconciliation and new alliances.

## Four Dimensions of Interracial Justice

This chapter endeavors to translate theoretical insights into concepts, language, and methods that are useful to both scholars and frontline justice practitioners. That translation takes the form of four dimensions of interracial justice inquiry. These dimensions are not a formula for justice. How justice is conceived and experienced in a relationship is determined by the interactions of the participants and the justice setting in which they interact—by racial realities. These culturally influenced interactions vary from relationship to relationship. What follows, therefore, is neither a list of elements of justice nor a catalog of specific techniques for cross-cultural conflict resolution.

Rather, what follows are the dimensions of an approach for inquiring into and acting on intergroup tensions marked both by conflict and distrust and by a desire for peaceable and productive relations. These dimensions of interracial justice inquiry are characterized by the four "Rs." The first dimension is *recognition*. It asks racial group members to recognize, and empathize with, the anger and hope of those wounded; to acknowledge the disabling constraints imposed by one group on another and the resulting group wounds; to identify related justice grievances often underlying current group conflict; and to critically examine stock stories of racial group attributes and interracial relations ostensibly legitimating those disabling constraints and justice grievances. The second is *responsibility*: It suggests that amid struggles over identity and power, racial groups can be simultaneously subordinated in some relationships and subordinating in others. In some situations, a group's power is both enlivened and limited by social and economic conditions and political alignments. Responsibility therefore asks racial groups to assess carefully the dynamics of racial group agency in imposing disabling constraints on others and, when appropriate, accepting group responsibility for healing resulting wounds.

The third dimension is *reconstruction*. It entails active steps (performance) toward healing the social and psychological wounds resulting from disabling group constraints. Those performative acts might include apologies by aggressors and, when appropriate, forgiveness by those injured and a joint reframing of stories of group identities and intergroup relations. The fourth dimension, closely related to the third, is *reparation*. It seeks to repair the damage to the material conditions of racial group life in order to attenuate one group's power over another. This means material changes in the structure of the relationship (social, economic, political) to guard against "cheap reconciliation," in which healing efforts are "just talk."

In mapping these dimensions of interracial justice inquiry, I draw selectively from the diverse disciplines summarized in the last chapter without attention to vast internal diversity or dissonance. My aim is not to describe or critique each discipline fully but to extract commonalities among disciplines that pertain to interracial healing. This critical pragmatic method calls for further development of both the praxis construct offered and the contributions of each discipline. Although cast in terms of conflict and healing among communities of color, interracial justice inquiry at times may assist also in the process of rebuilding relationships within a racial group as well as between whites and nonwhites.

## Recognition

Recognition is akin to the first step in healing a lingering physical wound: a person's suffering must be recognized and the wound carefully assessed.[5] That assessment must include social and psychological inquiry. Long-term pain reflects not only physical feeling but also one's relation-

ships and perceptions of societal norms.[6] Cultural representations of the
infirmity (its social meaning) and the collective experiences of those with
the infirmity (insider narratives) combine with physical pain to inform a
person's suffering.[7] These cultural representations and collective experiences connect the body with the self and society. The treatment of suffering, and certainly healing, therefore must reach beyond the body into
the social self and the personal soul.

With these notions of woundedness and treatment as background, the
recognition dimension of interracial justice prompts two inquiries by racial groups desirous of peaceable and productive intergroup relations. It
asks each group to see the woundedness of the other. It also asks racial
groups to undertake critical interrogation to assess the specific circumstances and larger context of a conflict and to analyze justice grievances
undergirding present-day intergroup tensions.

Seeing into the Woundedness of the "Other"

One task of recognition is empathy. Members of each group work to
understand the woundedness of the other groups' members. The specific
goal is for groups to look beneath surface appearances to gain an appreciation for the struggles and hopes of the "other," to understand the
other's experiences of oppression and resulting pain and anger, hope and
resilience. The larger goal is to begin humanizing the other and transforming the other from object (out there) to subject (in here).[8]

Empathizing with those harmed means recognizing at least two kinds
of wounds. One kind of wound is the immediate harm. This harm is the
anger, hurt, and material loss resulting from disabling group constraints,
including the denial of a contracting job, the refusal of hotel accommodations, the physical assault over a customer-store owner dispute. A second, more pervasive kind of wound varies for all racialized groups in the
United States. It is the pain buried in collective memories of group exclusion from or subjugation within a primarily white-dominated social
structure, a deep wound for many now exacerbated by a nonwhite racial
group's apparent deployment of oppressive structures.

Empathizing also with those inflicting harm is difficult but necessary.
First, those racial groups, too, carry wounds of historical (and, more sub-

tly, current) exclusion and subjugation. Second, particularly in borderland locales, where power flows simultaneously in multiple directions, those groups can be oppressed in some relationships (perhaps even in the relationship with the harmed group in other realms) and oppressive in others. Third, these groups self-inflict psychic or moral wounds by harming, and dividing themselves from, other struggling racial communities while they themselves are struggling for social and economic survival.

How are groups to empathize in this fashion? Mutual storytelling and listening are one means of empathic communication—"perhaps the only basis for gaining an understanding of both ourselves and the hopes and fears of others."[9] Theologian James Cone suggests that sharing stories helps groups transcend day-to-day obstacles to peaceable relations.

Every people has a story to tell, something to say to themselves, their children, and to the world about how they think and live, as they determine their reason for being. . . . When people can no longer listen to the other people's stories, they become enclosed. . . . And then they feel they must destroy other people's stories.[10]

Recall Alice Zenger's words about the forcible confiscation, ostensible return, and then bureaucratic misappropriation of Hawaiian homelands and how Hawaiians "cry out and get no help." Think about the stories of Latinas/os after the passage of California's anti-immigrant Proposition 187 initiative. Legal resident immigrants and even citizens were subjected to the vilest epithets, job harassment, and violence. What was the pain of the family of the elderly Latina who suffered a fatal stroke on a public street while under verbal and physical siege by white youths whose anger was unleashed by the California electorate?

Recall also the death of single mother Cynthia Wiggins in Cheektowaga, New York. Think about the story's resonance with many African Americans and the resulting frustration: owners of a suburban shopping mall for eight years vigorously refused the city's requests to allow buses from largely black, inner-city Buffalo to stop on the mall premises (as buses from predominantly white suburban areas were allowed to do). While attempting to get from an inconvenient off-site bus stop to her clerk's job at the mall. Wiggins was killed by a truck as she tried to cross a snow-bordered six-lane freeway without a traffic light. One African American damned the mall owners' eight-year campaign to keep inner-city buses off the mall as "sanitized, guiltless racism."

Think also about a Japanese American's struggles upon his release from a U.S. World War II internment camp. His family had lost everything during their incarceration—home, business, belongings, freedom. His imprisonment with 120,000 others on account of race, without charges or trial, was later recognized by a congressional commission and the courts to have resulted from political agitation, mass hysteria, and racism. After his release, he boarded a public bus. Continuing racial apartheid in America meant that whites sat in the front of the bus, blacks in the back. Where should he sit? In the front as if he were white (or at least free to sit with whites)? Or in the back as if he were black (acknowledging African Americans in their suffering but also accepting their inferior social status)?[11]

Understandably, African Americans might not sympathize with his dilemma, since the Japanese American appeared to have a choice (front or back of the bus), and either choice for him still meant the continuing legalized subordination of African Americans. When faced with this story, African Americans nevertheless might empathize with the difficulty of his choice in light of his historical situation, wonder whether Asian Americans face similar choices today, ponder what African Americans might do under similar circumstances, and contemplate whether all communities of color at least sometimes face related dilemmas (whether some middle-class African Americans, for instance, experience an affiliational dilemma concerning poor blacks).

In short, the first recognition task is for groups to empathize, not sympathize; to listen, not analyze; to acknowledge, not blame. The result of "entering into the pain of the other," the exchange of pain, is the kind of "deepened understanding of the other and of oneself" that makes reconciliation possible.[12]

Empathy, of course, is a concept loaded with postmodern baggage. Calls for a more empathic justice system have been criticized even by those generally supportive of the concept. Toni Massaro argues that the call to context, with its emphasis on legal storytelling, overvalues empathy as an instrument of legal justice and undervalues the rule of law.[13] Although concurring with psychological insights into the significance of empathy in understanding others differently situated, she questions the methodological utility of empathy (in place of normative rules, critical interrogation, and explicit value ordering) for achieving the kind of contextual, individually tailored justice envisioned by its proponents. I agree that intergroup empathy is a valuable aspect rather than the core feature of justice among communities of color. The discussion later in this chapter about the linkage of forgiveness to healing underscores its value.

Interrogating Present-Day Intergroup Tensions and Underlying
Justice Grievances

A second recognition task complements empathy with critical sociolegal inquiry. It asks racial groups to interrogate critically both the particular/contextual and structural/discursive aspects of a relationship in controversy. This is the critical analysis of intergroup histories underlying present-day conflicts.

Interrogation begins with sometimes straightforward, sometimes complicated assessments of the particulars of a controversy. The assessments are basic journalism. Who, for example, are the principals, and who are the aligned interests in an African American–organized boycott of an inner-city store owned by a Korean American woman? What is the specific dispute about? How did it arise? In what locale? What legal claims might be asserted? How are the principals dealing with the initial dispute, and how and why is it escalating? How might it be resolved, according to what principles and with what intervention?

This inquiry also examines the agendas and reactions of those with power—politicians, bureaucrats, police, business, clergy, community organizations, and media. In related fashion, it scrutinizes the interests, histories, and methods of individuals (community leaders, mediators, social workers, lawyers) and institutions (mediation centers, courts, schools, community organizations, churches) engaged in dispute resolution.

The interrogation of these particulars then broadens to sketch the controversy's socioeconomic setting. How do the racial demographics and political economy of the area and the class and gender of the principals shape the conflict? How does the conflict relate to others in the local area, the region, the country? For instance, the inquiry into the black–Korean American conflict in South Central Los Angeles following the 1992 acquittal of the four white policemen who beat Rodney King expands to examine the socioeconomic sources of the rebellion-riot. What were the effects of police brutality, a long history of white racism, inner-city poverty, job dispersal, decaying schools, a crumbling welfare system, immigration, and limited legal justice for poor African Americans? For similarly situated Asian Americans and Latinas/os? How did tensions between African American and Latina/o workers affect conflicts between blacks and Asian American merchants? Why did a considerable segment of the public come to consider black-Korean conflict, rather than economic dislocation, as a principal source of the firestorm?[14]

The examination of the controversy's particulars and context then shifts to the stock stories that groups themselves tell to explain the conflict and justify the groups' responses. Stock stories are narratives shaped, told, and embraced by groups about themselves and others. They are usually a conglomeration of group members' selective historical recollections, partial information about events and socioeconomic conditions, and speculations about the future. Some of these narratives are tied to time and place; some transcend temporal and physical boundaries. As forms of cultural representation, the narratives create social identities for the group members. They also influence the dynamics of interracial relations by providing the lens through which group members see and understand other groups.[15]

For instance, African Americans and Korean American grocery store owners tell stock stories about their interactions. One story told by some African Americans is that immigrant Korean grocers receive government and bank financial support unavailable to African Americans and that this support enables "foreigners" to displace black entrepreneurs and exploit and disrespect black customers.[16] It is through this story's lens that some African Americans view Korean American merchants and, with limited investigation or negotiation, justify short-term store boycotts and long-term takeover strategies. A competing story told by some Korean American merchants is that young, urban blacks are not interested in getting a job, belong to gangs, steal, and threaten violence to get their way and that adult African Americans lack the business values to be successful entrepreneurs.[17] It is through this story's lens that some Korean

Americans see young African American store patrons, like Latasha Harlins, and justify their suspicious and sometimes violent treatment of African Americans.

These stock stories and others like them are constructed from a melange of direct experiences, ancestral memory, rumor, the written word, and media images. In simplified yet important ways, the stories shape how groups comprehend their and others' justice grievances, inform perpetrator-victim identities, and legitimate occasionally harsh actions toward one another—witness African Americans' apparent targeting of Korean American stores for burning after the first Rodney King police trial as well as store owner Soon Ja Du's fear of young African Americans and her shooting of Harlins.

Critical interrogation of stock stories such as these requires the unraveling of each story's "facts" (events, tenor of interactions, information omitted), its methodology (sources of information, rhetorical techniques, storyteller vantage points, viewpoints represented and excluded), its tendency to universalize (attributing a particular trait to all group members), and its range of social impacts (in creating identities as a justification for actions toward others and for delineating perpetrators and victims). This interrogation aims not to disprove the story and its cultural representations so much as unpack them—to show how they are constructed, whose interests they further, and what influence they exert over the power dynamics of interracial interactions.[18] In this way, critical interrogation may be valuable for what it reveals about the story's subjects, the story's tellers, and their perceptions of the relationship in conflict.

The decoding of stock stories informing specific interracial conflicts sometimes reveals shaky or even illusory factual bases. Inner-city Korean American store owners do not receive private bank or government financial support unavailable to African American entrepreneurs. African Americans are willing to work, and exceedingly few in inner cities are gang members intent on ripping off neighborhood stores; many, despite economic discrimination, are capable entrepreneurs. In light of the shaky and misleading factual foundations of many stock stories, Harlon Dalton asks African Americans and Asian Americans to carefully analyze each other's racial conditions and not "ignore the true circumstances in which [the groups] find themselves." His accounts are worth repeating at length. Concerning Asian Americans:

One can, of course, point to Asian-American success stories. But there are also Asian-American immigrants, including males from Korea, Vietnam, and the Philippines, who are economically no better off on average than African-Americans . . . [N]early half of Southeast Asian immigrants live in poverty with annual income below ten thousand dollars. Moreover, many of the success stories rely on incomplete or misleading data. For example, comparisons of median family income do not take account of the fact that immigrants from Japan, China, and Korea have more workers per family than do African Americans (or Whites . . . ). . . .

Moreover, it is a mistake to assume that Asian-Americans who have succeeded economically have thereby been exempted from racism. Ask anyone who has been shunted into a particular job category or denied admission to an elite school based solely on her Asian appearance and name. . . .

Not only does the bandying about of the "model-minority myth" work to keep African-Americans in their place and to sow dissension between them and Asian-Americans. It tends to keep Asian-Americans in their place as well. After all, if they are being held out as a model, how can they complain?

Concerning African Americans:

By mindlessly focusing on slavery's physical cruelty, we . . . entice White people [and Asian Americans] into a false catharsis. We permit them, with a "shudder of horror," to "turn away, smug and exculpatory, from a world" they wrongly believe to have been "laid to rest."

[The slavery narrative needs to be reinterpreted so that it is] less of a history lesson and more of a present reality. . . . Slavery has enduring significance . . . not because of the monstrous but transitory harms done to those who were enslaved, but rather because it served to indelibly link Blackness and subservience in the American subconscious. At a deep level, slavery stamped Black people as inferior, as lacking in virtue, as lacking the capacity to order their own lives. In addition, the . . . dehumanization of captive Africans made it possible for White Americans to resolve the contradiction between their professed commitment to freedom and their subjugation of other human beings. . . .

[T]he "demons" that plague the Black middle class [include]: the inability to fit in; exclusion from the club; low expectations; shattered hopes; faint praise;

presumption of failure; coping fatigue; pigeonholing; self-censorship and silence; mendacity; identity problems; guilt by association . . . [and] survivors guilt.[19]

Even when shaky or misleading factual foundations are revealed, the stories sometimes persist. Their enduring social power suggests something more at play than descriptive accuracy. At times, further interrogation of stock stories reveals that something more—long-held, deeply felt, sometimes vaguely articulated intergroup grievances. Lehua Napoleon's testimony, recounted in chapter 3, suggests that group members pass relational hurts from generation to generation. Following the imposition of Western land laws and annexation by the United States, Native Hawaiians' separation from their land nearly destroyed the cultural fabric of Hawaiian life. Hawaiians still feel the resulting pain, and many continue to mistrust groups they perceive as directly responsible for or complicit in their century-long subordination. That pain and sense of group grievance, often unacknowledged by non-Hawaiians, create contemporary interracial conflicts by providing a hidden lens through which many Hawaiians interpret current intergroup interactions.

Inquiry into these kinds of group grievances means crafting thoughtful histories of racial oppression. Those histories are more than accounts of events, people, and places. They encompass ways in which groups now in conflict have been "differentially racialized." Those histories reflect differentiation in groups' identities, power, and claims.

There are some groups—like African Americans in relation to slavery, Native Americans in relation to the genocide . . . , Chicanos in relation to conquest of Mexican territories in the Southwest, . . . and refugees from conflicts generated by particularly egregious U.S. foreign policy debacles—that justifiably see their claim to remediation as unique in the context of American history.[20]

Understanding differing group histories is important not to erect a hierarchy of racial oppression. Rather it is important for the purpose of identifying, even in rough ways, the particular and sometimes unique characteristics of racial groups' grievances and claims.

In addition to revealing shaky factual accounts and often differing historical grievances and claims, the interrogation of stock stories sometimes also illuminates purposeful distortions of history by political leaders in order to legitimate continuing oppression. For example, critical inquiry revealed a tortuous remaking of history integral to postcommunism ethnic and religious violence in the Balkan states. The International Commission on the Balkans found that Balkan leaders—Serbian president Slobodan Milosevic, Croatian president Fanjo Tudjman, and Bosnia Serb leader Radovan Karadzic—identified ancestral and religious strife as the main sources of recent atrocities. The commission also found that the political leaders' specific characterizations of ancestral strife were unsupported by historical circumstances. The postcommunist politicians deployed falsely constructed ancient enmities to "justify the unjustifiable." According to the commission, the politicians "have invoked 'ancient hatreds' to pursue their respective nationalist agendas and deliberately used their propaganda machines to justify the unjustifiable: the use of violence for territorial conquest, the expulsion of the 'other peoples,' and the perpetuation of authoritarian systems of power."[21]

Perhaps most important, the critical interrogation of stock stories often reveals the political and cultural shaping of those stories and the complexity and malleability of the group memories sustaining them. Groups often recall events, relationships, and institutional practices in widely divergent ways. Social-psychological study of collective memory suggests that groups in conflict filter and twist, recall and forget "information," both in reframing shameful past acts to lessen perpetrator responsibility and in intensifying continued suffering to enhance victim status. As implied by Dalton's deconstructed stories of Asian Americans and African Americans, collective memory not only vivifies a group's past; it also remakes group narratives and thereby situates a group's current relationships with others along a power hierarchy. It contributes to shaping the meanings of group, community, and nation[22] and attendant understandings of culpability and harm. How groups shape these meanings is integral to how groups understand disabling constraints and resulting intergroup grievances. The unraveling of stock stories, including collective memories, thus in part aims to unpack these understandings.

Empathizing with others, critically interrogating particulars and context, and unraveling stock stories advance the recognition process of interracial justice. They open fresh possibilities for exploring racial group agency in the generation of intergroup grievances and responsibility for racial wounds and for healing.

## Responsibility

The recognition and responsibility dimensions of interracial justice inquiry are linked in this fashion. "Responsibility" asks racial groups to assess group agency and accept responsibility for racial wounds. Joseph Montville suggests that after assessing the history of an intergroup conflict, groups need to acknowledge appropriate responsibility for harms inflicted by each group.[23] John Dawson similarly emphasizes the acknowledgment of historical agency and responsibility through confession. Confession is the "acknowledgment of the unjust or hurtful actions of . . . [a] group toward other persons or categories of persons."[24] It recognizes the historical roots of many contemporary interracial conflicts and examines the hurtful actions of a group toward other groups. Community building requires the acknowledgment of group agency concerning deep-seated prejudice and distrust across ethnic, generational, and class lines and the acceptance of responsibility for the consequences of that prejudice and distrust.

Sometimes the line between perpetrators and victims is brightly marked, with the group's responsibility for racial harms easily attributable and confession clearly called for. In 1997 Texaco Company's white treasurer was caught on tape making derogatory comments about African Americans while planning to destroy smoking-gun corporate documents sought by African American employees for their class action race discrimination lawsuit.[25] Texaco's president immediately apologized to African American employees and customers (later partially recanted) and settled the suit. In the 1990s Native Hawaiians called for and received "a clear acknowledgement of the United States' responsibility for the overthrow of the Hawaiian native government in 1893" and the harmful effects of the annexation of Hawai'i and the confiscation of Hawaiian government and crown lands in 1900.[26]

At other times, this line blurs with changing circumstances. Since power often flows in multiple directions in a relationship, along varying social and political axes, a racial group can be both subordinated in some respects and an agent of subordination in others. Especially in these situations, critical analysis of group agency and responsibility is in order. This line blurring is illustrated by Chinese American, African American, and Latina/o relations in the Lowell High School suit challenging a public school desegregation order, by an African American boycott of a Vietnamese American–owned store for "exploitation" and the store owner's counterlawsuit for "economic terrorism," and by the struggles of Palestinians and Israelis over homelands.[27]

Chapter 5 developed the idea of constrained group agency to sharpen this difficult analysis. Concepts of simultaneity, differentiation, and dominance/transformation facilitate the assessment of one group's exercise of power over another. Group power is derived in part from material advantages, particularly control over means of economic production. The greater the control is, the more powerful the group will be. Group power is also derived from fluid, shifting alignments with other groups and institutions in the larger social field. Racialized groups are both empowered and constrained by those multiple alignments, creating shifting, colliding spaces for power over one another. This situated view of agency recognizes the capacity of racial groups, amid changing racial demographics and socioeconomic conditions, to be simultaneously oppressed and oppressive, liberating and subordinating.

The agency and responsibility assessment starts by asking whether one group's alignments with others outside the relationship and its access to economic opportunities and public communication channels give that group power over the other in shaping racial identities and structuring intergroup relations. That inquiry then explores ways in which group-based power has been or is being exercised by group members. In particular, it examines the ways in which groups in borderland sites situationally redeploy structures and strategies of oppression. These multidimensional structures include the rhetorical (the ways in which group narratives are constructed and infused in popular consciousness, systematically uplifting some groups and denigrating others), the institutional (the ways in which formal organizations adjust individual and group relations according to societal norms, systematically advantaging some groups and disadvantaging others), and the economic (the means for creating and allocating wealth, sometimes largely on the basis of group membership).

Those structures are situationally redeployed when groups formerly or even currently disadvantaged by those structures exercise some degree of emergent power to embrace or employ those structures in order to disadvantage other groups. This redeployment harms both racial communities. The group with "power over" inflicts harm by culturally denigrating the other group and denying it specific social or economic advantages. As mentioned, this kind of exercise of "power over" both inflicts and deepens racial wounds by tapping into the other's collective memories of the pain of exclusion and subjugation. At the same time, the group self-inflicts psychic or moral harm. By denigrating and denying another subordinated racial group, the more powerful group—itself partially subject to discriminatory social and economic structures—harms itself.[28]

Only by understanding the extent of a group's agency, constrained by context, can a rough evaluation be made of the extent of its responsibility for harm to others (and self). A racial group's choices in the use of its ebbing and flowing power over another—whether it situationally redeploys structures employed to oppress its members to oppress others—determine whether it has discharged its responsibility toward those others. One pertinent inquiry is this: Especially in the borderlands, do interracial conflicts "reflect minor disagreements among subordinated groups or one group's attempt to replace one oppressive regime with another?"

Ethics connects these notions of agency with responsibility. To reiterate, racial group responsibility is situated in a racial hierarchy and enlivened by ethical and moral principles. For Cornel West, a mature racial identity for blacks is rooted in self-love and self-respect and grounded on the "moral quality of black responses to undeniable racist degradation in the American past and present." Notions of responsibility inform the moral quality of black responses. Black responses are moral where they assess "the variety of perspectives held by black people and select those views based on black dignity and decency that eschew putting any group of people or culture on a pedestal or in the gutter." The mature black identity is thus cast in terms of agency ("specific black responses" to racist degradation) and responsibility ("responses such that the humanity of black people does not rest on . . . demonizing others").[29]

Responsibility is accepted in the first instance by each group's commitment to recognize the hierarchical structure of power in race relations and to advance socially, politically, and economically without denigrating or otherwise dominating other racial groups. When efforts toward self-definition or material advancement nevertheless denigrate or harm others, responsibility is discharged through a combination of reconstruction and reparation—that is, racial healing. These ideas begin to address the roots of racial group responsibility: the mutual implication of institutional structure and group agency; the exercise of group choice in a field of hierarchical power.

Understanding conceptually how to evaluate group agency and responsibility is one matter. Grasping practically how to act on that understanding to facilitate group acceptance of responsibility in a particular situation is another. Chapter 5 explored the intricacies of and obstacles to group members' acceptance of responsibility for group actions. The Western ethic of individualism, supported by the law's emphasis on individual rights, militates against the acceptance of group responsibility. Even more important, the sincere acceptance of responsibility, or confession, reallocates group power. Laying "oneself open is nothing less than an act of disarmament. You put down the weapons you employed to dominate others; you renounce the power you gained" over others.[30] Aggressor groups, including national governments, concerned about power loss, employ the psychological device of denial to avoid moral consequences. In addition, according to Raphael Moses's account of a healing workshop attended by Palestinians and Israelis, even when group members desire some form of healing, "each side comes to a fear . . . that if they were to 'admit' mistakes and wrongdoing, this would weaken [the] position" of their group or "likely be misused for propaganda or political purpose."[31]

It is therefore predictable that for political reasons members of aggressor groups often resist responsibility for hurts inflicted on members of other groups. Cognitive psychology suggests an additional reason. Group members sometimes lack conscious knowledge of wrongdoing: "the human mind defends itself against the discomfort of guilt by denying or refusing to recognize those ideas, wishes, and beliefs that conflict with what the individual has learned is good or right." This idea is reinforced by a "strain theory" of unconscious racism—in which the recognition of one's racism collides with one's sanguine self-perception of egalitarianism, and the resulting strain causes one to deny the racism. In this view, those meanings and values that are most deeply ingrained in the culture are transmitted through tacit understandings.[32]

A final impediment to a group acceptance of responsibility of another's justice grievances is the pull of legal culture. As observed earlier, American law focuses on individual, not group, rights and duties. Equally important, the assignment of fault, rather than the acknowledgment of responsibility, drives the formal legal system. Legal remedies flow from assessments of liability that turn on judicial findings of fault. Wrongdoer acknowledgment of fault is superfluous. When legal claims are tried to judgment, juries or judges evaluate evidence and "find" culpability. When claims are settled through negotiation, the settlement agreement almost always states that the charged wrongdoer "admits no liability." When it finds fault, the legal system imposes the acknowledgment of wrongdoing, often in the face of continuing refutation. Voluntary wrongdoer acknowledgment thus lies beyond the legal conception of justice. Law, enforced by state authority, makes no claim on parties jointly to analyze historical roots of conflict, recognize injustice, or accept responsibility. This cultural predilection, or resistance, usually unspoken, presents another formidable obstacle to group acceptance of responsibility for justice grievances.

In light of these difficulties, a group's acceptance of responsibility for addressing justice grievances might, in some instances, be broadened to include responsibility for helping heal racial wounds impeding peaceable and productive intergroup interactions, regardless of their source. In this sense, responsibility is broader than a group's obligation to remedy the harms its members inflict on others. It means a commitment to assist in healing another group's wounds, even wounds inflicted principally by groups outside the immediate relationship, not necessarily for purposes of redress but for purposes of community building. It reflects the recognition of a dual reality in which racial wounds are inflicted by multiple sources (particularly in settings with a history of white dominance) and in which racial healing begins in the immediate relationship (regardless of the sources of conflict).

The Asian American churches' apology resolution, for example, apologized for Asian American complicity in the cultural and economic subordination of Native Hawaiians following the United States–aided over-throw of the Hawaiian nation. The clergy authors of the resolution committed the churches to helping heal Hawaiian wounds in and beyond the church, immense social wounds for which Asian American respon-sibility was proportionately small (compared with the responsibility of the U.S. government and the former ruling white oligarchy).

In other settings, acceptance of broader healing responsibility by Asian Americans might mean empathizing with and a commitment to assisting African Americans in their efforts to heal the continuing wounds of slav-ery and Jim Crow segregation—possibly including support for African American reparations, for affirmative action for black students and con-tractors or for African American city council candidates. For African Americans and Latinas/os, accepting some responsibility for healing Asian American wounds inflicted by historical and continuing anti-Asian sen-timent in America might include a commitment to oppose efforts to tar all Asian Americans with the brush of suspicious foreignness—efforts such as the vituperative Republican-controlled and Democrat-supported investigation into illegal "Asian" campaign contributions. For African Americans and Asian Americans, acceptance of broader responsibility might mean a greater commitment to resist English Only initiatives exclud-ing Latina/o immigrants from full participation in social and economic life. For all three groups, acceptance of this responsibility might mean supporting indigenous peoples' intensifying struggles against states and the United States over various forms of economic and political sovereignty.

*Reconstruction*

In some situations, the recognition of grievances and acceptance of group responsibility for historical wounds may be enough to promote intergroup healing. In other situations, particularly when the group harm arises from disabling group constraints, more may be needed, because "repentance without restitution is empty."[33] That something more is ad-dressed by the third, and performative, dimension of interracial justice: reconstruction. Reconstruction means acting on acknowledgments of dis-abling group constraints and commitments born from recognizing constrained yet extant group agency and responsibility. It means reaching out in concrete ways to heal.

Reconstructive action proceeds in two parts. The first is mutuality of performance, often in the form of apology by those responsible and corresponding forgiveness by those harmed.[34] The second part, frequently overlooked, is efforts to remake and retell stories about the self, the other, and the relationship.

## Apology and Forgiveness

*Apology.* In his sophisticated sociological study of apologies, Nicholas Tavuchis describes the main function of an apology in terms of restoring group membership. Membership in a community depends on validation by other community members. Immediate conflicts and underlying grievances present obstacles to validation. They generate perpetrator and victim identities and fuel long-term enmities, thereby dismembering community relationships. An apology means re-membering the community, a "painful re-membering, literally of being mindful again, of what we were and had as members and, at the same time, what we have jeopardized or lost by virtue of our offensive . . . action."[35] Part of that re-membering is recalling; part of it is seeking forgiveness for harmful acts threatening community belonging. Seen in this way, an apology is "a special kind of enacted story whose remedial potential, unlike that of an account, stems from the acceptance by the aggrieved party of [a sorrowful] admission of iniquity and defenselessness."[36]

The dynamic of this enacted story starts with a call for urgent remembering and for an expression of regret—a call usually made by those aggrieved. The response, the apology, "or, more aptly, the apologetic speech, is a decisive moment in a complex restorative project." The apology "presupposes cognitive and evaluative congruence in the form of shared definitions of the violation, its severity, history, and implications"—mutual empathy and critical sociolegal interrogation. It accepts responsibility and expresses regret for wounds inflicted and rending the community—acknowledging agency. And at least implicitly, it tries to heal both the specific relationship and the community.

For this reason, a group apology and responsive forgiveness are a kind of social contract, securing common moral ground and committing to group harmony over individual desires.[37] That commitment requires participants to give up something personal to secure a larger collective good. Aggressors must give up self-righteousness and dominating power; those harmed must relinquish resentment and victim status. Group harmony (forward looking, relationally directed) is deemed more important than individual rights (backward looking, individually oriented).

The Southern Baptist apology to African Americans, for example, encouraged group reconciliation. By apologizing for past historical wrongs, the leaders of the church spoke not only on behalf of themselves but also for others and their ancestors. Although not all Southern Baptists felt remorse or even agreed that an apology for support of slavery was appropriate, the denomination's apology allowed group members to express collective remorse for oppressive actions to begin healing historic wounds.

In a local setting, a letter by a Japanese American minister and former immigrant that recounted his apology to Chinese immigrant congregants in Los Angeles illustrates the potency of these intergroup apology dynamics.

My Personal Background

I was born in Osaka, Japan. My family immigrated to the United States in 1956. I have lived in the Los Angeles area ever since.

My Experience

I was asked to minister at a Chinese church in Westminster last November. This congregation was primarily composed of first and second generation Chinese, so that the majority spoke in Chinese and I had to speak with the aid of a translator.

Before the meeting, the Lord impressed on my heart the need to ask forgiveness on behalf of the Japanese for the atrocities committed against the Chinese people before and during World War II. After this word came from the Lord I sensed that this might be very significant, as my father served in Manchuria with the Japanese during World War II.

Thus, I asked the people at the beginning of my ministry to forgive me on behalf of the Japanese for the acts they committed. As I spoke, the Lord seemed to give me the words to speak: "You must have been hurt deeply, losing friends and family, losing property, seeing destruction and terror." As I continued, the majority of the congregation began to weep; then, I found myself welling up and deep emotions and I, too, began to weep.

I don't quite understand the dynamics of what transpired that evening, but the Lord, indeed, gave us great release.

R. Shin Asami[38]

While potentially transformative in these kinds of situations in which no formal claims are asserted, the promise of intergroup apologies is undermined by Western legal culture. In the United States, a genuine apology is neither recognized as a legitimate legal remedy nor perceived as a component of justice. Instead, Western law views an apology as an "admission of liability that complicates the process of settlement—a process in which the denial of liability serves as a lever to negotiate an acceptable level of damages." An individual may risk personal liability by electing to apologize and focus on restoring the broken relationship; hence the tentativeness of many American race apologies—"I apologize for comments you may have perceived as insensitive."[39]

In light of these difficulties, Hiroshi Wagatsuma and Arthur Rosett explore the promise and limitations of apologies in legal disputes. In their cross-cultural social-psychological study, they recognize that apologies alone for some kinds of harms are clearly inadequate. They also recognize, however, that traditional common law remedies are sometimes unsatisfactory and that an apology may help rebuild human relationships.

To explain this point, Wagatsuma and Rosett describe the differing cultural perceptions of apologies in the American and Japanese legal systems. Americans tend to view apologies as simply self-expression. They rely on adversarial adjudication and court pronouncements to determine a person's rights and duties. Paying damages or accepting punishment ends their personal responsibility. Expression of contrition is unnecessary. In addition, the absence of apology in the American legal system may be tied to the legal system's translation of psychic hurts into losses compensable by monetary awards. As a result, if "any legal authority—perhaps a judge or the police—[were] to seek an apology from an American as part of the settlement of a serious dispute, such an apology would probably be perceived as either insincere, personally degrading or obsequious."[40]

By contrast, the Japanese legal system attaches great significance to the act of apologizing as an acknowledgment of group harmony. The Japanese are less concerned about compensation than reparation—repairing harm to both the relationship and the social order. In the Japanese legal system, an offer to compensate or accept punishment without an apology is considered insincere.[41]

The American and Japanese legal systems are embedded in differing cultural systems with differing ideas about legal wrongs, injuries, and remedies. Suggestions about cross-system borrowing are fraught with the risk of incoherence. Indeed, a suggestion that the American legal system immediately and fully embrace remedial apologies is meaningless in light of the system's focus on individual rights, monetary remedies, and adversarial dispute resolution. Nevertheless, America's justice systems—including its legal system—can begin to rethink intergroup justice by scrutinizing other disciplines' recognition of selective apologies as viable means for at least partially redressing past wrongs. As described earlier, social psychology finds that when genuine, the act of apologizing has significant therapeutic value. Christian theology recognizes that the path to reconciliation begins with the act of expressing contrition. The indigenous Hawaiian practice of ho'oponopono similarly prescribes "mihi, . . . [the] sincere confession of wrongdoing and the seeking of forgiveness," as a key step toward reconciliation. Peace studies stresses the importance of group apologies for redressing human rights abuses and restoring breaches in the polity. For these disciplines, the performative "words 'I'm sorry' and 'we were wrong' can, if sincere, be profoundly therapeutic—even if made years after the offense by people who didn't do it."[42]

These diverse disciplines provide a glimpse of apologies as an affirmative step toward interracial justice. A strong caveat is necessary, however. Apologies are susceptible to insincerity, misapprehension, poor timing, and inadequacy. As revealed by chapter 2's apology catalog and by the preceding discussion of the American justice system's discomfort with apologies, intergroup apologies can become hollow words and empty gestures."[43] Two main concerns arise: are the apologies empty, in that they are based on inadequate acknowledgments or have no material affect on the participants' relationship, and given a sincere apology, has the injured group, through its members, been sufficiently healed to engender intergroup forgiveness and, in turn, transformation?

The first concern is that an apology can become an end rather than a means for relational change. Individuals and groups "routinely employ the language of apology in self-interested and exploitive ways" as "another form of impression management, an interactional gambit, or a rhetorical ploy."[44] An apology unaccompanied by changes in the apologizer's underlying belief system easily becomes "self-serving in self-renewing pursuit of the meaningless.[45] It is just talk, or in the words of the Kairos Document, cheap reconciliation.

Because of this risk of manipulation, a meaningful group apology is tied to a commitment to make amends for past wrongs and to action on that commitment; "confession is a charade unless matched with action."[46] With this in mind, Ann Calhoun examined the global apology trend, citing Japanese Prime Minister Tomiichi Murayama's recent expression of his sincere apology for Japan's World War II human rights abuses. Despite the apology, Murayama indicated that Japan would not accede to the victims' demands for compensation. The halfhearted tenor of his apology and the Japanese government's refusal to support it with concrete actions sparked continuing calls for Japanese contrition and reparations for World War II atrocities. In light of such criticism, the chair of Japan's Social Democratic Party recently urged the government to compensate Korean "comfort women," declaring that "words of apology can carry weight only if followed by deeds," for apologies and compensation are "two sides of the same coin."[47]

An apology thus is likely to be viewed as insincere, a pseudoapology, if the apologizer fails to participate in a joint analysis of the conditions of conflict and underlying grievances, to accept appropriate responsibility for injuries inflicted, and to discharge that responsibility through action. In particular, without corresponding action, the apology is devalued—it is "just talk."

The second, and related, apology concern is about slippage—that apologies will not change the relationship structure enough to bring about enduring forgiveness. This concern speaks in part to reparations, a widely recognized form of corresponding action. Indeed, when the apology is group to group and personal sorrow is difficult to communicate, the "practical and symbolic import of collective apology" is best "judged in terms of the remedial and reparative work it accomplishes."[48] Reparations in this sense complement an apology. Reparatory work covers a range of acts aimed at restoring those harmed financially and psychically and repairing damaged social relationships—by the payment of money, the return of lands, the opening or restructuring of institutions, and the like.

*Forgiveness.*    Three choices face a person who has suffered serious harm. The first is revenge. Often driven by bitterness, this option creates formidable obstacles to healing. The second choice is martyrdom or the passive embrace of victimhood. As discussed later, this option creates an initial feeling of power and entitlement but ultimately is self-defeating.

The third choice is forgiveness. Indeed, whether acts of apology and reparation help rebuild a relationship depends in part on their capacity to elicit some form of forgiveness. Forgiveness is "not an arbitrary, free act of pardon given out of the unilateral generosity of the forgiver—forgiveness is an interpersonal transaction between two parties."[49] This transactional understanding of forgiveness highlights the relational nature of intergroup grievance and reconciliation. It underscores the notion that restoration of a relationship is a struggle for all involved and that the responsive act of forgiveness furthers a difficult process of mutual transformation.

Seen in this fashion, the apology and forgiveness transaction is a "complex process of 'unlocking' painful bondage, of mutual liberation." These acts help set perpetrators "free from their guilt (and its devastating consequences)" and liberate victims "from their hurt (and its destructive implications)." When supported by appropriate recognition and acceptance of responsibility, the reconstructive acts of apology and forgiveness free both the perpetrator and the victim "from the haunting legacies of the past. Both sides are changed by this encounter. It paves the way for a better cooperation between formerly conflicting partners. A painful past opens new possibilities for the future."[50]

This process of mutual liberation transforms the relationship by altering the balance of power. The perpetrator and the victim undertake "acts of disarmament" in front of the other, a painful process that requires vulnerability and internal strength. For the perpetrator, it means relinquishing power and accepting responsibility for participation in the oppression of another group. For the victim, it means reopening and cleansing old wounds and returning to the source of painful memories to release them. Forgiveness is "more than an encounter; it is an exchange of pain. The result is a deepened understanding of the other and of oneself. By entering into the pain of the other an overwhelming liberation takes place."[51] It is the process of looking into the heart of one's pain and the willingness to release oneself from the constraints of the past in order to heal.

The transformative power of forgiveness, therefore, lies not only in its capacity to liberate but also in its power to correct and restore relationships. "It corrects the distortion which an act of evil establishes between two people or groups—the distortion of stolen power and enforced impotence. At the same time such correction restores the dignity of both sides."[52] The performative process of apology and forgiveness engages the parties in critical analysis of intergroup histories and aids in the unpacking of stock stories and cultural representations. The deepened understanding gained, in turn, encourages the remaking of relational narratives. Apologizing and forgiving do not mean erasing history and forgetting the past. They mean fashioning new stories of intergroup relations that build on the past and move beyond it.

This, of course, is easy to say and hard to do. The challenge of confronting the past and reliving the hurt is sometimes so difficult and unbearable that some victims are unable to forgive. In other instances, those suffering may withhold forgiveness to seek martyrdom or victimhood. Integrating victimhood into group identity and political strategies, sometimes for many generations, nurtures claims of group entitlement that can be employed to manipulate oppressor guilt. In effect, these are claims to power through entitlement ("you owe me"). For the most part, however, those claims serve as consolation for the lack of real social power. Over time they can be destructive, since those aggrieved must maintain a subordinate social position. By embracing victimization, the aggrieved forfeit agency. Instead of becoming actors of social change and subjects of history, they remain objects on whom history acts.[53]

Liberation therefore requires not only the release of painful memories but also the avoidance of limited, self-destructive empowerment. Through the act of forgiveness, the aggrieved wield a power affirmatively to transform the relationship. Only through "constant mutual release from what they can do can men remain free agents."[54]

So how are forgiveness and justice linked? As mentioned, in American law, an apology is not recognized as a discharge of legal obligations, as a legal remedy. Nor does the bestowal of forgiveness itself constitute justice. Justice is advanced through the recognition of multiple kinds of harms, the acceptance of responsibility for wrongs, and the reparatory acts that engender forgiveness. For Zambia's first president, Kenneth Kaunda,

Justice and forgiveness are related this way. To claim forgiveness whilst perpetuating injustice is to live a fiction; to fight for justice without also being prepared to offer forgiveness is to render your struggle null and void. Justice is not only about what is due to a human being; it is also about establishing right relationships between human beings.[55]

Kaunda's insight links "reconciliatory forgiveness" to justice and ties justice to right relationships. Thus through forgiveness and the acts that engender it, justice becomes a reality. It is only then that restoration is possible.

Retelling the Stories, Fusing Horizons

Reconstruction often means performative acts of apology and forgiveness. It also entails remaking and retelling stories about self, the other, and interactions. Of course, unraveling stock stories and jointly remaking new intergroup narratives may be impossible in some situations—for example, amid the frenetic ethnic fighting between Bosnian Serbs and Muslim Croats.

Other situations, though, offer reconstructive possibilities. Along with acts of contrition and forgiveness, reconstruction forges "partisan memories into the greater story that unites." Historical reconstruction by groups in conflict is more than an analysis of differing group memories. It is "telling our stories to one another and listening intently" as a way of "cracking the code," of "fusi[ng] horizons." This storytelling "involves reaching beyond the words and the 'facts . . . ' of gaining an understanding from the perspective of another's experience. It is a process that involves more than empathy . . . whereby we see, hear and understand in a different way."[56]

Hearing and understanding in a different way through stories is a theme of Jerome Bruner's cultural psychology. Bruner is an eminent psychologist and a pioneer in the cognitive revolution in psychological theory, and his recent, controversial work emphasizes the cultural function of narratives in the way human beings construe reality and make meaning about themselves and others. Telling stories about self and others, to ourselves and others, is the way we organize our experiences and knowledge. These stories include metanarratives about our origins and heritage, including our cherished beliefs. They also include narratives that ground our personal identity and day-to-day sense of well-being. "We represent our lives (to ourselves as well as to others) in the form of narratives. It is not surprising that psychoanalysts now recognize that personhood implicates narrative, 'neurosis' being a reflection of either an insufficient, incomplete, or inappropriate story about oneself."[57] Healing psychological wounds requires in part the completion or remaking of inappropriate, damaging narratives.

After unraveling stock stories, remaking narratives of relational history—fusing horizons—requires further inquiry and analysis on at least two levels. One level of reconstruction is remaking understandings of the particulars and the context of grievances underlying current tensions. For example, consider Dalton's reconstructed accounts of historically situated African American and Asian American racial conditions. He asks African Americans to recast the Asian American model minority story to account more fully for contemporary Asian American conditions—including violence, glass ceiling discrimination, swaths of poverty, and negative stereotyping. He also asks Asian Americans and all groups to reinterpret the African American slavery narrative. This narrative of long-ago physical cruelty must connect history with current realities, including the enduring linkage of "Blackness and subservience in the American subconscious."[58] The prevailing black middle-class success story (discrimination no longer exists) also needs to be reframed to reflect contemporary realities—including the demons haunting many because of limited acceptance by the mainstream and the continuing systemic discrimination against blacks.

For another example, in the early 1990s, the Office of Hawaiian Affairs (OHA), the legally recognized representative of Native Hawaiians, negotiated with the federal and Hawai'i state governments over a variety of current disputes. Those disputes included the continuing U.S. possession of Hawaiian homelands, the state's ongoing breach of trust in the management of Hawaiian trust lands, the state-sanctioned desecration of native religious sites, and the inhibition of customary Hawaiian cultural practices, as well as the governments' contribution to the high levels of Hawaiian criminal incarceration, poverty, illiteracy, homelessness, and ill health. To clarify the basis of its historically rooted claims and to build a foundation for reconciliation, OHA first called for jointly reframing the historical roots of current disabling constraints. More specifically, OHA and other pro-sovereignty groups called for the United States to acknowledge its participation in the wrongful overthrow of the sovereign Hawaiian government, the seizure of Hawaiian government and crown lands through annexation, and the destruction of native culture.[59]

In response to this and related calls, amid intensifying grassroots political agitation for Hawaiian sovereignty and the assertion of legal claims over Hawaiian lands, Congress passed and President Clinton implemented the Native Hawaiian Apology Resolution in 1993. In reframing and retelling the story, the resolution incorporated ideas and language urged by Native Hawaiian groups. It identified the central role of the United States' agents and military in the illegal overthrow of the kingdom of Hawai'i, acknowledged the linkage of Native Hawaiian "health and well-being" to "their deep feelings and attachment to the land" and the United States' confiscation of Hawaiian government lands "without the consent of or compensation to the Native Hawaiian people," and recognized the resulting historical injury to Native Hawaiian culture and life. Significantly, the apology resolution expressed a "commitment to acknowledge the [present structural] ramifications of the overthrow of the Kingdom of Hawaii, in order to provide a proper foundation for reconciliation between the United States and the Native Hawaiian people."[60]

A second level of reconstructive inquiry centers on a particular dynamic implicit in the first—the connection of the structural to the discursive. It addresses a group's deployment of oppressive social, political, or economic structures to subordinate another and the derogatory group cultural representations generated by the more powerful group to legitimate its oppressive actions. This inquiry aims to break apart distorted cultural representations of racial groups contributing to disabling group constraints and to reconstruct group images to foster intergroup reconciliation. Intergroup reconciliation requires the transformation of groups' harsh characterizations of one another and their often tilted rhetorical framing of historical and contemporary entanglements.

For example, healing wounds inflicted on America's indigenous peoples as described in chapter 3 requires more than the recognition of a history of specific harmful actions and apologies. It also requires the undoing of the derogatory cultural representations of Native Americans and Hawaiians as uncivilized, unmotivated, less-than-human "others" that legitimated violence then and justify continuing subordination now. For another example, in the Lowell High School lawsuit, dissolving the tensions between the Chinese American plaintiffs, on the one hand, and African Americans, Latinas/os, and some Asian Americans, on the other, involves more than rewriting the history of public school segregation, formal desegregation, and changing racial demographics since the original consent decree in 1983. It also entails the recasting the culture-laden images of African Americans as intellectually inferior and Asian Americans as yellow-peril/model minorities hidden just beneath the surface of the case discourse about merit, qualifications, and affirmative action preferences—just as diminishing inner-city tensions means recasting stock cultural images of rude, privileged Korean American store owners and thieving, slothful African American customers.

As these and other examples reveal, critical interrogation generally and historical reconstruction particularly are likely to be fraught with difficulty. Group members may be unaware of collective history or even contemporary group interactions. They may decline to decode stock stories and critically analyze racial demographics and socioeconomic conditions. Even when group members are aware of their group history and are willing to analyze it and even though the mutual recognition of an intergroup history "often elicits relief, and a more flexible position and a

willingness to compromise,"[61] group leaders may be reluctant to participate in reconstructing group stories, fearing political misuse later by others.

Sometimes racial group members may jointly reconstruct a relational
story for its own sake—the right thing to do. Or they may do so to assist
the formation of mutually beneficial alliances. At other times, however,
they may require transactional incentives. In some situations, the reframing of histories and memories is bartered for material resources as part
of the polity's moral economy. The living conditions of those socially
marginalized are materially improved (through restitution and institutional reordering) in exchange for group forgiveness (the dissolution of
dominant group guilt). When this kind of bartering occurs between perceived perpetrator and victim groups, the transaction "shapes the way
each of the parties thinks about itself, its history, and its identity."[62] By
transferring resources through restitution, the dominant group is able to
regrind the lens through which its history is assessed and recharacterize
itself as a group committed to reconciliation. By accepting restitution, the
marginalized group is able to claim acknowledgment of its suffering and
the restoration of its dignity. By treating apologies and forgiveness as
moral commodities, the exchange transaction itself demands the reframing (but not denying) of a volatile past.

Despite the risk of leadership manipulation, the difficulties of group
recollection, and the potential for bald (as distinguished from strategic)
commodification, the disciplines described in the preceding chapter consider as significant both levels of narrative reconstruction—the particular/
contextual and the structural/discursive. Taking a joint rather than an
adversarial approach to the analysis of the conflict allows both groups to
articulate feelings and perspectives omitted from stock stories or official
government versions of events. In this fashion, a joint analysis begins to
remake stories of intergroup relations and "revis[es] and clean[s] up the
published historical record of a conflicted intergroup . . . relationship [and
is an] essential part of a reconciliation process."[63]

For related reasons, social psychology recognizes the healing value of
transforming history. For groups suffering from cultural trauma, social
psychologists suggest reconstructing the events underlying continuing
wounds and unraveling the negative cultural images ostensibly legitimat-

ing the dominant group's power over the other. Cultural trauma occurs when a group is faced with events and institutional attitudes and structures that so overwhelm the group's cultural system that it can no longer provide guidance and meaning to daily existence. Cultural group members experience symptoms of humiliation and low self-worth. Working through the continuing effects of the trauma requires attention to those suffering, acknowledgment of oppressive actions, and a reframing of the denigratory group cultural images.[64]

## Reparation

Reparation is the fourth dimension of interracial justice. In its singular form, reparation means "repair." It encompasses both acts of repairing damage to the material conditions of racial group life—transferring money and land, building schools and medical clinics, allowing unfettered voting—and of restoring injured human psyches—enabling those harmed to live with, but not in, history.

So viewed, reparation means transformation. It avoids "the traps of individualism, neutrality and indeterminacy that plague many mainstream concepts of rights or legal principles."[65] Reparation is grounded in group, rather than individual, rights and responsibilities and provides tangible benefits to those wronged by those in power. Properly cast, reparation targets substantive barriers to liberty—education, housing, medical care, employment, cultural preservation, political participation. In addition, coupled with acknowledgment and apology, reparation can be transformative because of what it symbolizes: reparation "condemns exploitation and adopts a vision of a more just world."

For these reasons, some scholars argue that reparation is an essential part of redress for justice grievances. Manning Marable contends that the post–Civil War Reconstruction eventually failed because the federal government refused to support broad land grant reparations to African Americans. Without large-scale land redistribution (forty acres and a mule), the Emancipation, the Fourteenth Amendment, and civil rights statutes failed to uplift blacks socially and economically. Marable observes that because economic power was held by whites, equality in political and social relations was an illusion. Without change in the material conditions of racial life, "reconciliation [had] meaning only for the privileged in society."[66]

Without material change, acts of reparation may have regressive potential. Without attitudinal and social structural transformation, of a sort meaningful to recipients (forty acres and a mule), reparations may be illusory, more damaging than healing. No repair. Cheap grace.

Native Hawaiians voice these concerns in their drive for reparation. Hawaiians are seeking reparation from the United States and the state of Hawai'i in the form of money, homelands, and Hawaiian self-governance. Repairing cultural wounds, restoring a land base, and altering governance structures are perceived by increasing numbers of Hawaiians as essential to a functioning relationship among indigenous Hawaiians, the federal and state governments, and their non-Hawaiian citizens. Thus, even though monetary compensation may be an appropriate form of reparation in some instances, it is not, alone, deemed sufficiently reparatory by most Hawaiians. For some, monetary payments alone would not bring material change; it would likely generate only illusions of progress, "throwing money at old wounds [in ways that] do little to heal them."[67]

Thus symbolic compensation without accompanying efforts to repair damaged conditions of racial group life is likely to be labeled insincere. For instance, despite modest monetary restitution, the Japanese government's refusal to acknowledge responsibility for World War II crimes or to take active measures to rehabilitate surviving victims has generated charges of insincerity and foot-dragging. For many, the government's refusal to express regret undermines the possibility of forgiveness and prospects for healing.[68] By contrast, Germany's efforts to heal the wounds of Jewish Holocaust survivors extends beyond monetary reparations. The German government has also opened its war archives, passed legislation barring race hatred, overhauled Holocaust educational materials, and commemorated war victims.

Reparation, as repair, therefore aims for more than a monetary salve for those hurting. Multifaceted reparations are a vehicle, along with an apology, for groups in conflict to rebuild their relationship through attitudinal changes and institutional restructuring.[69] In terms of changed attitudes, making apologies part of a group's public history—as the Southern Baptists did through their formal apology to African Americans—is one means of reparation. Committing to end derogatory stereotyping of racial others—as the Asian American churches' proposed apology resolution did—is another.

In terms of dismantling disabling social structures or supporting empowering ones, reparation might mean, as it does in South Africa, the government's new struggling but active Reconstruction and Development Programme aimed at redistributing land; changing education, health, and housing policies; and establishing public and private affirmative action programs.[70] In the United States, it might mean supporting rather than challenging affirmative action programs in education and employment whose primary beneficiaries are from other communities of color. It might mean politicians appointing and local businesses hiring members of other racial groups. Or it might also mean the formation of inner-city business and political coalitions to expand entrepreneurial opportunities.

Reparations that repair are costly. They require change. Change means the loss of some social advantages by those more powerful. For these reasons, those responsible for repairing the harms always resist initially. In addition to the plea of lack of available resources, those resisting reparations generally raise four objections shaped by narrow legal concerns: the existence of factual ambiguity or justification for illegal acts (employing the criminal law notion of "excuse"), the difficult identification of perpetrator and victim groups (raising the procedural issue of "standing"), the lack of sufficient connection between past wrong and present claim (invoking the tort notion of "causation"), and the difficulty of calculating damages (applying the tort concept of "compensation").

These concerns are shaped by the common law paradigm of a lawsuit—an individual wrongfully harmed by the specific actions of another in the recent past is entitled to recover damages to compensate for demonstrable personal losses. The prototypical situation is the two-person car accident. That paradigm, however, is inapposite when the actions and harms occur over time and are rooted in group membership—when, for example, different members of a group act to preserve the group's system of dominance and privilege by denigrating other groups and excluding those groups' members from housing, business, job, and social opportunities.[71]

The limited purchase of narrow, often-repeated legal objections highlights reparation critics' underlying social and political objections. Will the reparation process reopen old wounds and allow them to fester for new generations? Where will reparation resources come from, and will reparatory steps sufficient to "do justice" disrupt the economy? Will there be a social and political backlash against the reparations' beneficiaries and political leaders? Not only by disgruntled dominant group members but also by marginalized groups who have not received reparations? Will the benefits to recipients have a lasting or only a temporary effect?

These questions raise serious concerns worthy of careful consideration in every situation in which specific reparations are contemplated. In most instances, no clear answers will be forthcoming. It is possible that opponents will use the complexity of the analysis, the difficulty of the search for answers, as a tactic for delay. Although there is no simple way to cut through the morass of analytical questions and practical concerns, I suggest combining several key concerns into one question about healing: will reparation help heal intergroup wounds and establish or restore right relationships?

Joe Singer identifies a dilemma of reparation that bears directly on this concern about reconciliation. He asks, "Will reparation right a wrong" and aid healing, or "will it create further victimization of the oppressed group," exacerbating the wound?[72] Seeing those dual possibilities in all reparation efforts, Singer explores the potential for further victimization in two contemporary situations.

Singer describes Jews' highly publicized demands in 1997 that Swiss banks account for and restore Jewish money and gold held by the banks for Nazis during World War II. Acknowledgment and restitution by the banks would treat Jews as worthy human beings with rights, including the right to own property. Restitution counters the anti-Semitic myth of Jews misappropriating the property of others. Jewish "victimhood is acknowledged, but Jews are not treated as mere victims, but as agents in calling Swiss banks to account." One problem, however, is that Jews' claims for monetary restitution resurrect for some the harsh historical stereotypes of them "as money-grubbing, as having both accumulated secret bank accounts in the past and as caring now about nothing more than money." Another, and broader, problem is that continuing Jewish reparations claims spark reparations claims by other groups (such as the

Hungarian gypsies who were exterminated by the Nazis), breeding resentment toward the Jews when their claims are not satisfied.[73]

Singer also examines the reparation demands by African Americans. Some understand those demands as a call for redress of past injustice, whereas others see them as a "refusal to grow up." The result, evident in the volatile affirmative action debates, is that "calls to repair the current effects of past injustice are met with derisory denials that continuing injustice exists and that the problems of African Americans are now purely of their own making." As Singer observes about the mixed healing potential in both situations, the "very thing that restoration is intended to combat may be the result of the demand for restoration."[74]

In addition, even when individuals' psychic wounds are salved and there is no further victimization, reparation can mask lurking dangers. When reparation is little more than a monetary buy-off of protest, an assuaging of dominant group guilt without attitudinal and institutional restructuring, reparation can ultimately help perpetuate the institutional power structures and public attitudes that suppress freedom for those whom society views as different and vulnerable. Concerning these hidden risks of monetary reparations for Japanese American internees,

the "danger lies in the possibility of enabling people to 'feel good' about each other" for the moment, "while leaving undisturbed the attendant social realities" creating the underlying conflict.... redress and reparations could in the long term "unwittingly be seduced into becoming one more means of social control that attempts to neutralize the need to strive for justice."[75]

Notwithstanding legal and political objections and larger social concerns, reparation has been attempted with increasing frequency in recent years. Reparatory efforts include the United Church of Christ's monetary and land reparations to indigenous Hawaiians (nongovernmental reparations), the Florida legislature's monetary reparations for African American survivors of the Rosewood massacre (state and local government), the United States' reparations to Japanese Americans wrongfully interned during World War II (federal government), and the British government's monetary payments to New Zealand's Maoris (former colonial government). Pending reparation claims in the United States can be characterized as societal (including African Americans' claims for the continuing harms of slavery and Native Hawaiians' claims for the overthrow of the sovereign Hawaiian nation) and community based (including Korean American merchants' claims for burned stores and African Americans' claims of economic exploitation).

Studies of the sociopsychological effects of reparation for Japanese American internees and initial reports of other reparation efforts indicate significant benefits accruing to the beneficiaries.[76] One woman expressed how redress had at last "freed her soul." Other beneficiaries responded with a collective sigh of relief. Ben Takeshita, for instance, expressed the sentiments of many when he said that although monetary payment "could not begin to compensate . . . for his . . . lost freedom, property, livelihood or the stigma of disloyalty," it demonstrated the sincerity of the government's apology.[77]

Because of both the dangers and the transformative potential, the reparation dimension of interracial justice offers two insights into specific reparation efforts. One is normative: that acts of reparation by government or groups must result over time in a restructuring of the institutions and relationships that gave rise to the underlying justice grievance. Otherwise, as a philosophical and practical matter, reparations cannot be effective in addressing root problems of misuse of power, particularly in the maintenance of oppressive systemic structures, or integrated symbolically into a group's (or government's) moral foundation for responding to intergroup conflicts or for urging others to restructure oppressive relationships.

A second insight is descriptive: restructuring those institutions and changing societal attitudes will not flow naturally and inevitably from the reparations themselves. Dominant interests, whether government or private, will cast reparation in ways that tend to perpetuate existing power structures and relationships. Therefore, those benefiting from specific reparations need to draw on the material benefits of reparations and the political insights and commitments derived from their particular reparations process and join with others to push for bureaucratic, legal, and attitudinal restructuring—to push for material change. And their efforts must extend beyond their own repair.

This brings to mind a popular phrase, which I suggest inverting. Reparation can bridge the recognition and reconstruction dimensions of interracial justice if recipients "think locally and act globally": thinking locally to grasp the experiential lessons of power and value learned throughout the hands-on process of the reparation drive and acting globally to link with others different in culture or race but similar in efforts to restructure attitudes and institutions.

For racial communities, the four dimensions of interracial justice inquiry just described mean facing history, facing ourselves. And in the words of Rabbi Hillel, "If not now, when?"

# 9

# Apology and Reparations for Native Hawaiians

The story in chapter 3 of apology and reparations for Native Hawaiians continues. It is a story of reconciliatory effort of interest to African Americans, Latinas/os, Native Americans, and Asian Americans in San Francisco, Los Angeles, New York, Chicago, Seattle, Dallas, Houston, New Orleans, Washington, D.C., and Miami—wherever racial communities face colliding realities of intense interracial conflict and hopes for multiracial alliances.

What follows is not a complete social history. The story's sources are eclectic—interviews, personal observations, news articles, original documents, and scholarly publications. What follows (in this and the next two chapters) is an account of a race controversy viewed through a critical pragmatic lens. I shape the story in this fashion for two reasons. The first is to shed brighter light on the dynamics of struggle among communities of color to build right relationships through justice—stories of conflict, grievance, and healing too often told only in passing. The second reason is to illuminate the genesis and selective utility of the dimensions of interracial justice developed in earlier chapters.

## The Story Continues

*Apology*

The Asian American churches and Hawai'i Conference's apology and reparations proposals engaged church representatives at the 1993 Aha Pae'aina in a process of discernment. First in small groups and then as a whole, the church delegates discussed, debated, disagreed, and worshiped. After several rough days, they responded collectively to the continuing pain of Native Hawaiians. When all the Hawaiians in the large worship hall rose in answer to Rev. Lee's call, the conference delegates finally grasped the significance of, and approved, the apology and redress resolution.

The 1993 Aha Pae'aina consensus resolution marked the conference's awakening: "We, the delegates . . . approach our Native Hawaiian sisters and brothers with humility and gratitude as we have become aware of their anger and pain, highlighted by the 100th anniversary of the illegal overthrow of the Hawaiian Nation."[1] The resolution incorporated key aspects of the Asian American churches' apology resolution, particularly its call for reparations. It directed the Hawai'i Conference to apologize formally to Native Hawaiians for its predecessor's participation in the overthrow of the Hawaiian nation. It also instructed the conference to form the Hawai'i Apology Task Force to determine appropriate redress in furtherance of reconciliation.

A year-long task force study followed. In May 1994, the study culminated in a formal apology service at the Mauna 'Ala Chapel on the grounds of the Royal Mausoleum. There, Rev. Norman Jackson, head minister of the Hawai'i Conference and a Native American, apologized to Native Hawaiians for "the unjust involvement of [the Hawai'i Conference's] ancestor, the Hawaiian Evangelical Association, and for the unjust action of some of the officers of that body in the illegal overthrow of the Hawaiian Nation."[2] Rev. Jackson referred to the apology service as a time for confession "for our failure to assume responsibility for the consequences of [our ancestors'] acts, for the reality that surrounds us now." The assumption of that responsibility now "calls for . . . [a] reconstruct[ion] [of] our history, to know that there is no objective or neutral corner from which to read or write history."

To ground the conference apology, Rev. Jackson described historical particulars, citing an "unholy wedding of cross and flag" that immobilized the "colonized soul." The "creation of dependency, of shame, of the absence of self-confidence, and the internalizing of a will to judge, deny and avoid one's own culture is as wounding as any historical event." Rev. Jackson recognized that the church had made "no gesture to evaluate the theology that required a people to deny their culture and spirituality" and that "there [was] no acknowledgment of the drastic departure of Native Hawaiians from the membership of the [Hawaiian Evangelical Association] immediately following the Overthrow." He also admitted that words of apology are sometimes inadequate: "For some, [the] apology was much too little, and came much too late. For others, it was not necessary, and perhaps, offensive."

At the Mauna 'Ala service, several Native Hawaiians spoke candidly about Hawaiian suffering. Native Hawaiian leader Mililani Trask spoke of "a wound in the heart of [Hawaiian] people." Others explained those wounds in the context of present-day Hawaiian life. Dr. Kekuni Blaisdell, a Native Hawaiian physician, described the pain in social and physical terms: "[Na] Kanaka Maoli remain malalo, at the bottom, with the shortest life expectancies, with the highest rates of disease, highest rates of dropouts from our schools, highest rates for incarceration in our jails." Still others spoke about the need to heal this pain. "Today we are all able to come and cleanse that wound. [It is a] time for confession, but most important, a time for reconciliation."

Because of the pain and the desire for healing, and recognizing that an apology without acts of repair can be mere words, Rev. Jackson concluded the apology service by committing the conference to redress: "We have identified the depth of our need to confess in our faith. We have offered this service as an act of beginning reconciliation. And we commit our Conference to engage in redress." He also cautioned, however, about undue expectations. "We do not know what resources we will be able to make available for redress. As of now, all we have is the mechanism in place to begin."

*The Initial Plan for Redress*

Over the next year, the task force prepared an initial redress plan that proposed land and monetary reparations.[3] The plan acknowledged that all people are part of the same religious body but that a part of the body was "in pain and in hurt"—including hurt "crying out" from the desecration of Hawaiian culture and land described by Alice Zenger and Lehua Napoleon in chapter 3.

When one part is hurting and in pain, we are to share in that pain as well. . . . Let us not continue to allow a part of us [to] continue in pain and hurt. . . .

[W]e believe a spirit of alienation arising out of deep pain and rage exists within the Native Hawaiian community, within and outside the church. We have heard it in the testimonies of individual Hawaiian leaders. We have seen it in the faces of members in churches.[4]

The redress plan also observed that considerable energy had been spent by some "proving" the complicity of missionary families in the illegal overthrow and that an "equally vehement conviction by others [had] led to a denial of responsibility." Rather than endlessly "debate the history of the overthrow," the plan acknowledged that "a misunderstanding of the [church's] mission resulted in mission as triumphism, the identification of the gospel with one culture. This resulted in cultural genocide, coercive assimilation, historic shame, and loss of land for people of non-Western culture." The plan then expressed a desire for reconciliation— to "bridge the chasm of hurt." By seeking justice through redress, it said, "we want to heal the hurt. We want to make tangible . . . our desire that the harm caused by the alienation be righted."

When the plan was presented for formal approval at the conference-wide 1996 Aha Pae'aina, the response was decidedly mixed. Some Hawaiians expressed approval and supported the plan as justice long over-due. Others questioned the propriety of any apology and reparations on grounds that no wrong had been done. A well-known Hawaiian-Chinese entertainer supported the original missionaries. If it had not been for the missionaries, he said, "many of us would be lost."[5] A Hawai'i Conference Foundation trustee, citing fiduciary responsibilities, indicated that he "would do all in my power to prevent the distribution" of Hawai'i Conference endowment funds.[6]

Still others expressed strong disapproval of the reparations process itself. Concerned about the lack of community participation, several conference members requested more time to develop the plan to avoid "rushing into everything without input from our [Hawaiian] people." Several groups, including members of the Hawai'i Ecumenical Coalition, picketed the Aha Pae'aina session, asserting that the task force had failed "to receive input from the community." Dr. Blaisdell opposed the plan because the "Kanaka Maoli in most need" had not been substantially involved in developing the redress plan. He pointed out that "the process had not been pono, that is, not fair, not just." He called for the conference to "scrap the current Redress Plan and begin over again."[7]

Some Native Hawaiians believed that redress should more fully benefit the larger Hawaiian community, and not primarily the conference churches. Others felt that benefits should flow only to the sovereignty organizations who helped negotiate the 1993 United Church of Christ denominational apology.[8] Still others cautioned against expecting the Hawai'i Conference to cure one hundred years of Hawaiian suffering. The O'ahu island leader of Ka Lahui Hawai'i, the largest Hawaiian sovereignty organization, observed that "real redress can only come from the United States and the State [of Hawai'i]."[9]

With strong support from the task force, the conference board, and the Hawaiian churches and despite calls from opposing quarters to reject the redress plan altogether or to postpone decision making pending further study, the 1996 Aha Pae'aina approved the plan by consensus.

*Reparations*

Thereafter, the task force reconvened as the Redress Implementation Committee and tackled the details of reparations—contacting targeted recipient churches, performing title searches, and identifying legal restrictions on potential land transfers.[10] The committee identified eligible Hawaiian churches and held community meetings with churches throughout the Hawai'i Conference. After considerable discussion and in support of the principle of Native Hawaiian self-determination, the committee decided to place no restrictions on the use of the contemplated land or monetary grants. During this phase of the reparations process, Hawaiian clergy expressed concern about the inadequate involvement of the larger Hawaiian community.

The committee's final Redress Plan acknowledged that although the monetary reparations were significant, money alone would "not solve all that is not right in the Native Hawaiian community." It described redress as not as compensation for all losses or injuries but, rather, as an "act of apology and the expression of a desire for reconciliation."[11]

In this spirit, the Redress Plan committed $1 million to the Puʻa Foundation to benefit the Native Hawaiian community in general, augmenting the $1.25 million from the United Church of Christ's national instrumentalities. Conference monetary reparations also included $1 million to the Association of Hawaiian Evangelical Churches (AHEC), a formally recognized association in the conference, as well as $1.5 million in grants to individual Hawaiian churches that were in existence at the time of the 1893 overthrow.

In addition, the plan called for the transfer of six valuable parcels of land on five islands to Hawaiian churches and the Puʻa Foundation, and it provided for in-kind contributions of facilities, furniture, fixtures, equipment, personnel, and services to the Puʻa Foundation and AHEC. In July 1997, following the Hawaiʻi Conference Board's approval, reparations ceremonies were held at each Hawaiian church throughout the state.

Rev. Kaleo Patterson, a key supporter and critic of the apology and reparations package, captured it best. The redress efforts, however imperfect, "represent a major turning point in the church . . . [and] a beginning of the process of reconciliation."[12] What the church did was extraordinary. It apologized to the Native Hawaiians for its participation in the overthrow of the sovereign Hawaiian nation and made significant extensive land and monetary reparations. As Patterson acknowledged, the Hawaiʻi Conference was the first entity "to put its principles regarding Kanaka Maoli into practice."

## Reconciliation?

### Interracial Justice Inquiry

Is this ongoing story of intergroup grievance and redress an account of reconciliation? Are these efforts—and similar efforts in the United States, like the Southern Baptists' apology to African Americans for the denomination's support of slavery—helping unlock the deep pain of grievance and restore relationships? What insight might be drawn by other groups seeking reparations for the present wounds of historical injustice, particularly African Americans?

Let's take stock of the immediate responses. The conference's acts of apology and reparation have stirred deep emotions. The process was both painful and uplifting. It marked points of beginning transformation for many conference officials and Hawaiian church members. At a reparations service on Moloka'i in 1997, Rev. Carole Keim, head of the conference, apologized to four Hawaiian congregations and presented redress checks. Amid tears throughout, the moderator for one of the churches expressed forgiveness in the simplest terms: "On behalf of Native Hawaiians in our churches, I accept your apology and forgive."[13] After the service, a church member told Rev. Keim that she was initially opposed to redress and still had doubts about reparations, "but I can see how redress has helped so many."

Has the conference redress effort also begun to engender collective forgiveness by the broader Native Hawaiian community? Some Hawaiian leaders continue to support conference redress as beginning a rapprochement. Others denounce it as exclusionary and demand a fresh start. From varying vantage points, many sense that the conference and Hawaiian community have embarked on a halting and difficult journey—a journey of considerable yet unrealized healing potential, a journey likely to require rethinking and alteration along the way.

Answers to the main question—whether there will be long-term reconciliation within and beyond the church polity—await further contemplation and action.

How, then, at this moment, do we move beyond visceral responses to gain a deeper, more nuanced understanding of the Hawai'i Conference's and Asian American churches' four-year efforts to reconcile with Native Hawaiians? How do we assess analytically, guide conceptually, and remake practically (where needed) these and other similar justice efforts? The dimensions of interracial justice, I suggest, provide critical, pragmatic tools for interrogating, guiding and remaking.

Agency concepts of simultaneity and differential racialization provide a starting point. These concepts underscore the importance of separately examining a group's many relationships. Although the conference focused its healing efforts on two primary relationships (the Hawai'i Conference and Native Hawaiian churches, the conference and the broader Native Hawaiian community), the reconciliation process also encompassed two others (the Asian American churches and the Native Hawaiian churches, the Asian American and the Native Hawaiian communities in general). By locating the particulars of reconciliation in sociohistorical context, interracial justice inquiry assesses how in varying ways these relationships influenced, and were affected by, the conflictual and emotional reparatory process.

### The Hawai'i Conference and the Native Hawaiian Churches

The reconciliatory efforts concentrated on the relationship between the conference (as both the regional representative of the denomination and an entity composed of 120 congregations) and the conference's forty-seven Hawaiian churches. Interracial justice inquiry into the particulars and setting of redress efforts highlights the potential for long-term healing in that relationship.

For more than one hundred years, this relationship had been marked by contradiction—by Hawaiian church loyalty to the denomination and, at the same time, a Hawaiian sense of spiritual brokenness. Two-thirds of the polity's Native Hawaiian members left in anger immediately after the overthrow. Those that remained loyal continued to feel the sting of betrayal. For many Hawaiian church members, this contradiction buried their grievances against the conference. Without saying so, the Hawaiian church members quietly grieved not only over the loss of Hawaiian life, land, culture, and self-governance but also over the conference's betrayal of Hawaiian trust.

Membership in a moral community depends on validation by other community members: we are people only through other people. Conflicts over day-to-day matters and deeper grievances erect obstacles to validation, producing enmity and mistrust and dismembering community relationships. Dismemberment is what occurred when white American members of the conference's predecessor betrayed Hawaiian church members (most of whom were loyal to the church and Queen Lili'uokalani) by leading the overthrow and when white and Asian American church members later advanced socially and economically while "disregarding the suffering of Na Kanaka Maoli." The conference's apology to the Native Hawaiian churches started re-membering the community, a "painful re-membering, literally of being mindful again, of what we were and had as members and, at the same time, what we have jeopardized or lost by virtue of our offensive . . . action."[14] Part of that re-membering was recalling; part seeking forgiveness; part contemplating performative acts of repair. Seen in this way, the conference apology and the Asian American churches' apology proposal were a special kind of enacted story whose remedial potential stemmed from its acceptance of responsibility for racial harms, expression of contrition, and acts of reparation.

How did the Hawai'i Conference and Asian American church leaders enact the story of reconciliation? On what "shared definitions of the violation, its severity, history, and implications?"[15] Engendering what responses?

The conference performed the story in several parts over four years. It told the story of recognition, repentance, and reparation at many formal and informal gatherings to an array of church and community audiences. It reinforced that telling through written communications (reports, newsletters, bulletins) and informal meetings.

The story first emerged publicly through Rev. Sherry's 1993 denominational apology to the broader Hawaiian community. The apology was based on a lengthy, detailed, self-critical historical study by the denomination—a study published and widely distributed.[16] The Hawai'i Conference followed the denominational apology with its consensus resolution at the 171st Aha Pae'aina, setting the conference redress process in motion. It was at this polity gathering that Rev. Kekapa Lee called on his brothers and sisters in pain to stand; it was there that non-Hawaiians, four hundred or so, appeared to grasp for the first time and at a collective gut level the deep continuing pain of the church's Hawaiian people.

The solemn 1994 Mauna 'Ala apology service formally conveyed to Hawaiian church and community leaders the conference's contrition and acceptance of responsibility. There, drawing from the denominational historical study, Rev. Jackson acknowledged the "unjust involvement" of the conference's predecessor in the overthrow and the church's "failure to assume responsibility" for the ensuing deterioration of Hawaiian culture and life. His apology, and the Redress Plan a year later, thereby recognized church agency and accepted responsibility for resulting harms—the "identification of the gospel with one [white American] culture [that] resulted in cultural genocide [and] coercive assimilation."[17]

Although current members of the Hawai'i Conference were not personally responsible for "committing the crime," they inherited the responsibility for healing the breach in the present-day relationship: "We were not alive then, but our antecedents in the faith were, and the institution known as the Hawaiian Evangelical Association (HEA) is alive today as the Hawai'i Conference United Church of Christ. . . . Let us not continue to allow a part of us [to] continue in pain and hurt."[18] The conference thus accepted responsibility for harms that its ancestors had inflicted and for its own complicity in allowing the wounds to fester. Equally important, it also accepted responsibility for contributing to the healing of Hawaiian social and spiritual brokenness, regardless of its precise origins.

The Mauna 'Ala service was transforming for some. Genie Keanu, a Hawaiian church member, announced eloquently a new beginning for relations in the polity:

As we think of our experiences together let us consider them as different flowers woven together to form a lei. We have had many fragile blossoms in our lei, blossoms that were bruised by the hurts caused by those who came before us. It is time to close off that lei. It is time to put it aside. It is time for us to begin today to weave a new lei, a lei of healing.[19]

Rev. Jackson acknowledged that the polity was engaged in "reconstruct[ing] our history"—remaking the story of "our future together."

After two more years of intense study and debate, the conference adopted the Initial Redress Plan at the 1996 Aha Pae'aina, again recognizing Hawaiian people's continuing pain and committing to a specific plan of reparations. A year later, the conference held a reparations-reconciliation service at the Mokuaikaua Church in Kona. Janet Fujioka, president of the Hawai'i Conference Board, retold the apology story to the Hawaiian churches and four hundred Aha Pae'aina delegates, conveying the importance of redress to spiritual healing of all at the conference. Fujioka also read aloud the names of each of the forty-seven Hawaiian churches receiving redress. A powerful moment. Many tears.

The story's enactment in 1997 ended intimately. In midsummer, each Hawaiian church receiving monetary or land reparations held a reconciliation service. At each service, a conference board member presented the reparations, explained to congregation members the larger purposes of redress, and reiterated the conference's desire for reconciliation. One board member wrote shortly after her presentation, "There was heartfelt acceptance of the apology and many tears were shed." And another: "There were 'lump in throat' moments during the presentation." A Hawaiian church on the island of Kaua'i responded the day after the presentation with a letter of appreciation to the Hawai'i Conference. In the letter, the Waimea congregation indicated it would be discussing how to best use the reparations money to bring about "real reconciliation."[20]

The service at Kaumakapili Church on O'ahu in August was significant. Several of the church's members had participated actively in the denominational and conference redress processes. At the service, Kahu (pastor) David Ka'upu preached on olelo mihi (acts of forgiving, literally "tearless crying"). Congregation members followed with careful recitations of historical events and the redress process. Then on behalf of the conference, Rev. Wallace Fukunaga addressed the one hundred Hawaiian church members in attendance. As he presented the reparations payment, Rev. Fukunaga, an Asian American, expressed the conference's desire for reconciliation grounded in "unconditional love. We come to make peace with you, our brothers and sisters. We apologize [for the deep pain] . . . and we ask your forgiveness."[21]

Kaumakapili church moderator Mark Patterson's response conveyed great emotion and revealed the complexity of redress. His response was at once embracing and cautious, acknowledging the past and looking to the future. "I accept your gift of love, on behalf of the kupuna (elders) so we never forget what they went through; on behalf of the keiki (children), the hope for our future." He then added, "I also accept knowing that there is a burden now to be carried"—for the church and conference to reach out to the greater Hawaiian community to heal the wounds there. Significantly, Patterson's words of acceptance signaled openness and warmth, beginning rapprochement, but did not express forgiveness. Genuine forgiveness and meaningful transformation in a relationship take time. Whether collective forgiveness is forthcoming, Patterson seemed to be saying, may well be influenced by how the church and conference together carry their burden of continued healing efforts.

In this ceremony and others like it, the Hawaiian churches' open, emotional responses to the apologies and the conference's presentation of reparations evinced an encounter and exchange of pain along with the beginnings of release, of letting go. Has there been collective forgiveness by the members of the Hawaiian churches in response to these attempts to do justice? Has the relationship been transforming? The wound healed? Has reconciliation begun? Early indications—for example, the Kaumakapili Church—are that "it's a strong start, but only a start."

Is this beginning rapprochement likely to last? To mature? The answers, interracial justice inquiry suggests, may lie in the long-term effects of reparations. Are reparations contributing to attitudinal and institutional reordering? Are reparations making a difference in the tenor and structure of the conference's relations with its Hawaiian churches (and relations between Hawaiian and non-Hawaiian churches and between the conference and the larger Hawaiian community)? Words of transformation, without concrete reminders of change, tend to fade from collective memory.

From the start, the Asian American churches envisioned reparations for Native Hawaiians to foster material changes in institutional structures and collective attitudes. Their call for multimillion-dollar reparations challenged the Hawai'i Conference to move beyond words and to incorporate into the consensus apology resolution an active commitment to repair.[22] The goal—not justice said, but justice done.

The conference endeavored to do justice by offering monetary and land reparations to the Hawaiian churches that left the denomination as a result of the overthrow or that remained in the denomination despite it. The conference also made unrestricted $1 million reparations payments each to the Association of Hawaiian Evangelical Churches (AHEC) (a collective of Hawaiian churches in the Hawai'i Conference) and to the Pu'a Foundation (for the benefit of the larger Hawaiian community), along with the transfer of two valuable parcels of land to the foundation (the improved lands and building at one site are valued at more than $500,000). Finally, the conference committed administrative aid to AHEC and the foundation in their work with the Hawaiian churches and community.

Will all, or any, of these reparatory efforts enhance day-to-day working relationships and attitudes? Will the Hawaiian and Asian American churches work more often and more closely together on conference affairs, community service projects, and programs to improve social and economic conditions of Hawaiian community life? Will the conference's mainly white American churches participate in Hawaiian church–sponsored workshops on Hawaiian sovereignty? Will the many churches work together to break down Hawai'i's myriad racial stereotypes, to examine and undo damaging cultural images of one another?

Several churches are planning to use the reparations money for social services or Hawaiian education programs. Others are hoping to undertake projects aimed specifically at advancing reconciliation within and beyond the conference. Whether collective attitudes and institutional structures change for the better, and whether reparations contribute affirmatively to those changes, may well determine the next chapter in the conference— Hawaiian churches' story of reconciliation through redress.

### The Hawai'i Conference and the Hawaiian Community

This story is linked to another. Recognizing that the Hawaiian churches were part of the broader Hawaiian community and that the Hawaiian community had suffered cultural, economic, and spiritual harm traceable to the overthrow, the conference and the Asian American churches also sought to begin healing the breach between the church and the broader Hawaiian community.

Rev. Sherry's denominational apology (to fifteen thousand people at

Iolani Palace, where the 1893 coup occurred) and the Hawai'i Conference's Mauna 'Ala apology service (to seventy-five Hawaiian leaders and church representatives) reached out to both the Hawaiian churches and the larger Hawaiian community. These ceremonies, linked to the conference's commitment to continue repairing the damaged relations between the church and the Native Hawaiians, moved some Hawaiian community leaders. Mililani Trask, the kia'aina, or governor, of Ka Lahui O Hawai'i, sensed the beginnings of reconciliation. "There isn't a template for reconciliation, there is a process . . . [Although] we can't foresee the four corners of what reconciliation will evolve to be, . . . we can certainly do something together on this historic day. And that is [to] begin reconciliation, by joining our hearts together in a ceremony of prayer."[23]

*Mutual Engagement.*   Despite these beginnings, some perceived limitations, or flaws, in the conference's process for healing the larger Hawaiian community's wounds. They criticized the conference and its task force on two grounds: failing to communicate clearly the conference's healing priorities (creating undue expectations in the larger community) and failing to engage fully the nonchurch part of the Hawaiian community in the conference's process of repair.

The reconstructive dimension of interracial justice inquiry is helpful here. If the conference's sole goal was to heal relations in the church and thereby remake the church's interior story, then focusing heavily on the Hawaiian church–conference relationship was appropriate. But if the goal was also to remake the conference's relationship with the Hawaiian community, then meaningful engagement with the broader Hawaiian community was essential. Reconstructing a damaged relationship is aided by joint critical interrogation of grievances (their particulars and context) and the joint remaking of the intergroup narrative. Without mutual engagement, there can be no common efforts.

Moreover, forgiveness is relational. Reconciliation emerges over time from those common efforts, give and take, apologize and forgive. The absence of mutual engagement prevents both sides from undergoing acts of disarmament—the relinquishing of power over another in exchange for the cleansing of old wounds, the complex process of unlocking painful bondage to liberate the present from the past.[24]

To what extent did the conference and the Hawaiian community engage? The conference solicited participation from the Hawaiian community. Following the 1993 Aha Pae'aina consensus apology resolution, its task force met several times in different places to gain input from Hawaiian churches and community groups about the impending apology. After the Mauna 'Ala apology service, the task force held open meetings about reparations across the state. And in 1996, after approval of the Initial Redress Plan, the reconstituted Redress Implementation Committee sponsored meetings with Native Hawaiian churches and the broader community to determine the details of the plan.

For some Hawaiian community leaders outside the church, however, the conference's efforts to elicit nonchurch Hawaiian community participation were grudging. Both apology services were attempts at unilateral repair; the community meetings offered opportunities for input but not meaningful participation. Neither facilitated mutual engagement. At its September 1996 meeting, in response to criticisms about lack of community participation, the Redress Committee expressed a desire to reconnect with the Hawaiian community groups. It did so while cautioning that their contributions, though valued for redress implementation, would not alter the substance of the already-approved Redress Plan. "We are inviting input, but not change in the redress plan, so that they do not come with expectations which we cannot fulfill."[25]

From the conference's vantage point, there were several earlier opportunities for active Hawaiian community participation in the reparations process, and some members of the Hawaiian community participated in devising the Redress Plan. In addition, some pointed out that the larger Hawaiian community was itself fractured and spoke in many, often conflicting, voices. Organizations disagreed with one another on a variety of redress issues—as reflected in competing reparations demands, ranging from full conference compensation for all post-overthrow injuries to conference monetary payments to only those groups that lobbied for the denominational apology.

Regardless of these differences, from the perspective of some Hawaiian community leaders, what remained important was the reality of continuing Native Hawaiian frustration with feelings of disengagement. These feelings led to questions about the conference's sincerity. Hawaiian leaders "suspect[ed] that the church was not really interested in reconciliation, but only in 'saving face.' "

Those community leaders urged the conference to "scrap the current Redress Plan and begin over again so that it will be pono by involving right from the start those Kanaka Maoli who are in most need so that these Kanaka Maoli will not only be involved in the planning but also involved in the implementation of the plan."[26] Others requested more time to revise the Redress Plan: "We want to do what is 'pono' by not rushing into everything without input from our people."[27] This sense of missing engagement—miscast as simply a lack of input—appeared to "mute [the conference's] call for 'spiritual renewal' " and undermine the potential for Hawaiian community forgiveness.

Hawaiian community perceptions of the conference's failure to fully engage translated into political resistance. Community members adopted adversarial strategies, and Hawaiian groups publicly protested the adoption of the Redress Plan. Those actions made a strong political statement: Hawaiian political groups are integral to any settlement of Hawaiian grievances. In the language of reconciliation, those groups asserted the Hawaiian community's power not only by making demands but also by withholding forgiveness. Owing to the conference's limited capacity to repair socioeconomic as well as cultural wounds of the larger Hawaiian community, however, the long-term effect of this public act of empowerment is uncertain.

On one level, these difficulties of mutual engagement reflect a shortcoming in the conference's efforts, a failure of Hawaiian groups to organize and seize opportunities, or both. On another level, the difficulties reflect the dynamics of a group-to-group apology—where group representatives interact on behalf of sometimes vaguely defined amalgams of people, and sincerity and healing emotion are often difficult to discern. At both levels, the Hawaiian community's limited sense of processual engagement enhanced the importance of the substance of reparations offered.

*Dilemma of Reparation.* Hawaiian community criticisms about conference redress exacted a price, a toll paid from the possibility of reconciliation. Criticisms about process evolved into complaints about substance.

The main substantive complaint centered on the adequacy of the reparations. For some, the reparations did not substantially address the Hawaiian community's wounds traceable to the overthrow. They criticized conference redress as the left hand giving to the right. They called for the transfer of all land held by the church to Hawaiian community organizations. Some even called, impractically, for return of "ceded lands" (the more than 1 million acres held in trust by the state government). Still others demanded reinstatement of the Hawaiian kingdom: "I believe your effort should be going into reinstating what was stolen. . . . we all agree that a kingdom was stolen and we want it back."

At bottom, what these community spokespersons appeared to be after was reparation akin to full compensation for the many diverse parts of the Hawaiian community. "The redress plan as proposed does not address the need for just compensation for the racism and greed that missionaries of the time were responsible for. . . . the proposal ignores the fact that . . . descendants of the missionaries have, and continue to reap profits from the wrongdoings of the original missionaries."[28]

Restitution for all Hawaiian losses, tangible and intangible, however, lay well beyond the conference's reach. A conference commitment to full compensation would have been illusory, and the internal resistance it engendered likely would have doomed any redress package. Task force leaders thus acknowledged that the conference could contribute only in limited fashion to healing the hundred-year-old wounds of Native Hawaiians. "Monetary grants will not compensate for the terrible losses sustained. No sum can make up for the loss of freedom or sovereignty. The award serves a largely symbolic function." Through the recognition of wrongdoing and harm, contrition and symbolic yet material redress, the conference and Asian American church leaders attempted to commence, not complete, healing the breach in their relationship with Hawaiian community.

The Hawaiian community's dissatisfaction and the conference's responses—a seeming stalemate—were cast in terms of the adequacy of reparations. That debate can be revisited, and perhaps in the future recast, in terms of the dilemma of reparation. As observed earlier, inherent in reparation efforts are dual realities. If thoughtfully conceived, offered, and administered, reparations can be transformative. They can help change material conditions of group life and send political messages about societal commitment to principles of equality and justice. But when reparations stimulate change, they generate resistance. Proponents suffer a backlash from those desirous of preserving the racial status quo. Thus, when reparations are significant enough to aid in healing relational breaches, they also tend to inflame old wounds and to trigger regressive reactions. This is the dilemma of reparation.

The dilemma, the dual realities, played out in the conference redress. Serious discussion of reparations raised a host of fears. Amid the fractious debate at the 1993 Aha Pa'aina, some conference delegates called for a halt to the process in order to stop the bleeding. Both missionary descendants and Hawaiian church members expressed fears of tearing apart the conference by reopening (and not healing) one-hundred-year-old wounds. Others hinted at possibilities for renewed betrayal—in which the conference would regain the Hawaiian churches' trust, revisit the pain, and then, because of an internal backlash, once again disappoint. Still others worried about reinforcing negative stereotypes; Hawaiians were still unable lift themselves up.

In addition to revealing the angst of the reparation process—a fear of replicating the very injuries that redress designed to heal—the dilemma of reparation also partially explains the disappointed expectations of some Hawaiian community leaders. Those leaders criticized the conference redress priorities by saying, in effect, why them and not us, why so much for the churches and so little for the community?

The transformative potential of specific reparations is thus linked, ironically, to dissatisfaction. At best, reparations advance a process of repair. Every reparations effort, of political and financial necessity, is limited. Offering reparations to someone to repair certain wounds usually means not offering reparations (or not enough reparations) to someone else for their wounds. The offer of reparations to one group creates hopes, or even expectations, in others that their redress claims (even if distinct) will be realized. The notion of "repair" itself tends to generate outsized expectations of large-scale healing. Yet the reparations offered to one group may stretch the resources or political capital of the giver, thereby precluding reparations (or enough reparations) for others in the short run. By their very dynamic, even when important to the recipients, reparations are bound to disappoint others. And if expectations are high, this disappointment can translate into renewed feelings of betrayal.

*Material Change.* The reparation dimension of interracial justice offers no quick escapes from the dilemma. It does, however, suggest long-term paths. It does not argue for complacency—an "oh well" response to criticism that specific reparations are inadequate or misdirected. Rather, it directs inquiry into the effects of reparations: whether, for example, the conference's symbolic/material reparations over time encourage attitudinal changes and institutional restructuring sufficient for collective forgiveness by the Hawaiian community. If not, then rethinking and re-acting are in order. This inquiry into reconciliatory possibilities thus directs our attention to the forward-looking realm of material change.

Reconciliation is complex. It turns in part on material changes in the relationship over time. Acknowledging this, after presenting reparations to the Hawaiian churches, the Redress Implementation Committee posed a key question to the conference and the broader Native Hawaiian community: "What's next?" As Rev. Kuroiwa put it: "We [at the conference] are not washing our hands . . . [reparations is] a step in the process."[29] Indeed, Kuroiwa stressed the importance of extending the conference's reparatory work beyond "the church helping the church." Rev. Patterson focused the "what next" question on changes in structures and attitudes. "We can't just apologize and assume all the structures and attitudes will change. You gotta go back and revisit your policies."[30]

The funding ($1 million) of the Association of Evangelical Churches and the creation, the funding ($3.5 million plus land), and operation of the Pu'a Foundation embody the conference's effort to translate redress into Hawaiian community empowerment by revisiting "structures and policies." AHEC is an entity of the conference, and its resources will be used for the betterment of Hawaiian churches. Its mission, however, also includes betterment of the Hawaiian community. The Pu'a Foundation is a community-based organization whose goal is to initiate and support Hawaiian community programs in education, economic development, and social services. But the foundation's operations are currently stalled by disputes over structure and conference control.[31] It is too soon to tell whether attitudes and the social structure will change. Early indicators point to both possibilities and problems.

*Asian American Churches and Native Hawaiian Churches, Asian Americans and Native Hawaiians*

Asian American church leaders played an influential role throughout the reconciliation process.[32] They led discussions about redress before the 1993 Aha Pae'aina, sponsored the Asian American churches' apology resolution, chaired the Apology Task Force, aided the Redress Implementation Committee, and officiated at several reparation services on behalf of the conference.

Why the active leadership role of Asian Americans? The Asian American churches' apology resolution acknowledged historical and contemporary interracial realities. It recognized the "destruction of Native Hawaiian culture and the struggles of Na Kanaka Maoli" and noted that many Asians had "benefited socially and economically . . . at the expense of justice for Native Hawaiians."[33] Furthermore, it admitted that "mutual misunderstanding and mistrust" had resulted in the "use of stereotypes and caricatures to demean and dehumanize." The resolution also focused reconciliation around healing the hurt of Native Hawaiians: "We . . . will no longer ignore the anguish of our Native Hawaiian sisters and brothers. . . . [P]ublic acts of contrition are necessary . . . ' to begin a process of repentance, redress and reconciliation for wrongs done.' "

Most important, the resolution recognized Asian American agency and accepted responsibility for Asian American complicity in the subordination of Native Hawaiians. In the decades after the illegal overthrow of the Hawaiian kingdom, Chinese Americans and Japanese Americans began to acquire a limited degree of mobility and political power, eventually working their way off the plantations while continuing to live under the yoke of the white oligarchy. In 1954, a long-brewing political revolution triggered by an alliance of Japanese Americans, progressive whites, and unions radically altered the distribution of power in Hawai'i. Thereafter Asian Americans began to acquire greater political power even while white Americans continued to dominate the upper levels of big business and the media.[34]

Asian Americans aligned themselves with white Democrats and union leaders, both embracing and reforming the white oligarchy's institutional norms and practices. In so doing, Asian Americans used politics and law to shake Hawai'i's underclass free from the grip of the oligarchy, opening up schools, government, and social organizations to those formerly excluded. At the same time, they sometimes redeployed oppressive systemic structures—institutional structures once used by the oligarchy to subordinate Asian Americans and Hawaiians. Asian Americans, thus, were sometimes liberatory—pushing for social economic justice in health care, employment, and civil rights. At other times, however, they appropriated lands reserved for Hawaiian homesteading, limited access to government jobs along ethnic and political lines, and engaged in land speculation for personal profit. The Asian American churches' resolution admitted this dissonant reality. In effect, it apologized and accepted responsibility for Asian Americans' partial redeployment of oppressive institutional structures.

From the vantage point of interracial justice, the Asian American church clergy's efforts were both limited and significant. Those efforts were limited by the discordance among Asian American church members, including fierce disagreements about Hawaiian history and Asian American agency. Rev. Wong's passionate testimony at the 1993 'Aha Pae'aina, narrowly delimiting Asian American identity and responsibility, is an example—indeed, as Rev. Wong pointed out, most present-day, self-defined Hawaiians are the products of intermarriage with Asian and white Americans.[35] These and other struggles over recognition and responsibility (without even reaching questions of reconstruction and reparation) attest to the difficulties of interracial justice undertakings, even in a well-defined, moderate-sized polity.

The Asian American clergy's efforts were significant also because the Asian American churches sought to face their group history in subtle, self-critical fashion. Through the resolution and their subsequent leadership in the conference redress process, the clergy and their supporters acted—performed—on that self-critique. They announced their acceptance of responsibility for Asian American complicity in the subordination of Hawaiians. They acknowledged that the constrained nature of Asian American agency did not attenuate this responsibility. And their acceptance of responsibility and their suggestion of reparations for Native Hawaiians, which initially was ridiculed as impractical, opened a dialogue among the Hawai'i Conference's churches and jump-started the local process of reconciliation. Through words and acts, the Asian American churches challenged Asian Americans in Hawai'i both to do justice and to seek means for social, political, and economic advancement without becoming agents of oppression.

Is that challenge leading to healing between the Asian American and Native Hawaiian churches? Between the Asian American and Native Hawaiian communities? Will it preclude a repetition of the university newspaper editorial and cartoon by Asian American students that, in arguing against scholarships for Hawaiian students, disparaged Hawaiians culturally? Will it contribute to affirming responses to Alice Zenger's cry for help in the recovery of Hawaiian homelands or to Lehua Napoleon's call to stop the "annihilation of our culture, religion and way of life?" Will it help transform the image of Asian Americans as settlers "ignorant of or hostile to Hawaiian history and claims?" Possibly. Possibly not. It is too soon to tell. The answers may well turn on the continuing efforts by the Asian American and Hawaiian communities to build bridges. Some of those efforts have already begun. The Honolulu chapter of the Japanese American Citizens League, for instance, resolved to support Hawaiian sovereignty and formed workshops to talk with Hawaiian community leaders about sovereignty issues.

After one reparations service, I spoke with Hawaiian church members. Some looked puzzled when I asked about the impact of redress on Hawaiian and Asian American church relations. Others noted that "it was good what they [Asian American clergy] did." One person spoke passionately about how "it's time for Hawaiians and Asians to stop the suspicion. This is a start."

## Concluding Thoughts

What do these reconciliatory efforts—the obstacles, risks, achievements, and potential—have to offer other racial communities in post–civil rights America? In particular, what aid might African Americans find in seeking reparations for the wounds of slavery and Jim Crow segregation?

The conferencewide consensus at the 1993 Aha Pae'aina sought to re-make relationships within the conference, as well as between the conference and the broader Native Hawaiian community. It did so by making a formal commitment "to address past and present injustices affecting Native Hawaiian people." Rev. Kuroiwa, chair of the task force and primary author of the Asian American churches apology resolution, explained that the conference needed to apologize "because there was an injustice done historically . . . if the church is going to be a just church, we need to address the injustice."[36] The Initial Redress Plan reiterated this: "There can be no reconciliation without justice."[37] The goal of reconciliation through justice thus served as a fundamental principle guiding the acts of apology and reparation.

Interracial justice embraces this notion of reconciliation through restorative justice. It entails hard acknowledgment of the historical and contemporary ways in which racial groups harm one another, along with affirmative redress of justice grievances and the rearticulation and restructuring of current relations. The specific dimensions of interracial justice address restoration through interrogation of and action on justice grievances underlying immediate conflicts. This interrogation and action are integral part of a larger "complex process of 'unlocking' painful bondage, of mutual liberation"—a mutual liberation that "frees the future from the haunting legacies of the [distant and recent] past."[38] It is this larger complex process that links interracial justice to healing, and healing to reconciliation.

The denominational and Hawai'i Conference apologies to the Hawaiian churches were repeated and deepened over a four-year period. Every Hawaiian church member had the opportunity to hear the apology publicly from conference leadership and to experience the apology personally through the individual church services. Those apologies recognized deep Hawaiian suffering, analyzed history with a critical eye, accepted responsibility, and expressed contrition.

In concert with the performative acts of apology, the conference and its Hawaiian churches undertook a three-year, painstaking process of reparation. This process recognized that when the grievances were strong and wounds deep, justice required more than an apology, that reconciliation took more than words. The reparations offered by the conference went well beyond the symbolic. The land and monetary grants were sufficiently large to affect conditions of racial group life.

Equally important, the conference—in person through its leaders—presented the reparations and apologized directly to each Hawaiian church and its members. The forty-seven separate reparations services across the state—one for each Hawaiian church—transformed what could have been an impersonal group-to-group apology into an intimate, personal experience for most. Several Hawaiian churches, struggling for years, appear to be experiencing spiritual rejuvenation. For them and others, the conference reparations demonstrated commitment and care in its efforts to repair the breach.

Yet forgiveness takes time. Some Hawaiian churches expressed forgiveness. Others accepted the apology and reparations with appreciation but were not ready to forgive, to release the conference and themselves from one hundred years of pain. For them, reparations marked a midpoint, not the end, of the reconciliation process in the conference.

This difficult but important process of reconciliation in the Hawai'i Conference bears a striking resemblance to the United Church of Canada's 1986 apology to its native churches. I summarize here Nicholas Tavuchis's account. To heal wounds inflicted by the church on its native members—including the banning of native language, culture, and spiritual practices—the church council, at its annual meeting, after hard debate and a three-hundred-to-twelve vote, apologized to its native churches.

In our zeal to tell you about Jesus Christ, we were blind to your spirituality. We imposed our civilization on you as a condition for accepting our gospel. As a result, we are both the poorer. We are not what God meant us to be. These are not just words. It is one of the most important actions ever taken by the church. We ask you to forgive.[39]

Judged by most indicators, the apology—particularly its language and the way it originated—appeared to be more than a self-serving gesture. It showed that the "overwhelming majority of the United Church leaders and delegates came to believe that past wrongs against their native co-religionists had poisoned their relationships and that a contrite, public apology was essential to heal the wounds."

The initial reaction of the National Native Church council was "great happiness" and a "deep sense of liberation." After two years of contemplation, however, the new All-Native Circle Conference offered a more subtle response to the apology—a response similar in important respects to Mark Patterson's response to the Hawai'i Conference apology and presentation of reparations at the Kaumakapili Church ceremony. The All-Native Circle Conference representatives warmly acknowledged the apology but declined to accept it. The church had been instrumental in oppression, they said, and "these are difficult things to heal." From Tavuchis's vantage point, the native speakers "served to credit the apology with good will without disregarding the gravity of past and recent indignities by forgiving too easily or quickly and thus releasing the church from the consequences of what it had done and condoned." Forgiveness might be forthcoming, but not easily or quickly. It had yet to be fully earned. (Recall Pat Williams's suggestion in chapter 2, that African Americans politely hand back any U.S. apology-only for slavery).

Might reparations have hastened the United Church of Canada's reconciliation with its native churches? A longer period of church self-study (the apology decision-making process took two weeks)? A joint church–Native Conference critique (the apology process was unilateral)? Repeating the apology to a variety of native audiences throughout the area (the apology was given once)?

Assessed against this apology, the Hawai'i Conference and Asian American churches' redress process earns good marks. In terms of recognition, responsibility, reconstruction, and reparation, in terms of Hawaiian church responses after four years, the reconciliatory words spoken and acts undertaken reflect depth and breadth. They signal a potential for releasing the haunting legacies of the past, for the long-term healing of relationships in the polity.

What about the conference's relationship with the larger Hawaiian community? With Asian Americans and Native Hawaiians? As discussed, the impact of the conference redress on these relationships beyond the church polity is much more difficult to assess. The larger communities are diffuse; deep engagement between group representatives is difficult; interactions are often symbolic; and the conference's reparatory capacity is limited.

And yet, the conference and Asian American and Hawaiian leaders did take concrete steps. The long-range effects of reparations may be a key. The conference's contributions to the AHEC and the Puʻa Foundation, although not nearly enough for some, were substantial nonetheless. It may well be that the practical and symbolic import of a group-to-group apology may lie not in its words of contrition but in the remedial and reparatory work it accomplishes. Indeed, will the justice process repair the harms, heal the wounds? Will it create new problems or resurrect old ones? The only certainty at this juncture is that future efforts will be crucial. As the conference's Redress Committee asked in the summer of 1997, "What's next?"

# 10

## The Hat Shop Controversy

### African Americans and Asian Americans in Los Angeles

The following story differs in many respects from the United Church of Christ and Asian American churches apologies to Native Hawaiians. Like the PNT grocers story described in the prologue, this story about African Americans and Asian Americans emerged from recent neighborhood conflicts between individuals that escalated into a tense interracial controversy. It also reflects largely failed private and institutional efforts at rapprochement. Interracial justice inquiry unravels some of the immense difficulties, and possibilities, of healing both interpersonal and intergroup wounds on the rough terrain of grievance and neighborhood politics.

### The Los Angeles Hat Shop

*Confrontation and Escalation*

In January 1996 Rev. Lee May, an African American pastor of the First AME Church in Pasadena, walked into a South Central Los Angeles hat and wig store owned by fifty-three-year-old Korean American In-Suk Lee.[1] Rev. May had just officiated at a funeral and was wearing a formal black suit and tie. According to May, he was about to ask for assistance when "one of the owners, I assume, came to me and said they were sorry, it was a store for women only. . . . Women only. Women only. No men. No men."

According to Lee, Rev. May "kept walking around the store picking up different hats and putting them down." His presence appeared to make an African American woman customer nervous. She was about to open her purse to make a purchase and then hesitated. A friend of Lee's husband who was visiting the store, Mr. Kim, told Rev. May that "this is a women's store." An argument ensued, during which Kim threatened to call the police. Lee told Rev. May: "No. No. We don't want to do that. I just wish you would leave. I'm getting a headache." Lee's husband did not participate in the exchange because of the hearing loss he had suffered during the rebellion-riot four years earlier. Rev. May left in anger, leaving his business card and promising that he would be back: "This is not the end of this."

Lee's friends initially attributed the incident to a breakdown in communications. Rev. May perceived the situation differently: He was a victim of "a blatant act of discrimination. All I know is that all three [Asians] were united in wanting me to leave the store." He thereafter contacted the Brotherhood Crusade, a African American community organization dedicated to black community empowerment and fair treatment. In February the crusade sent a dozen black men to the store, none of whom was served. (It is unclear why service was refused). The crusade then gathered thirty protesters to picket Lee's store. Lee closed her shop and left. The crusade framed the dispute as an African American and Korean American conflict and demanded a public apology to Rev. May as well as a meeting with the store owners. It threatened a prolonged boycott.

### Apology and Rejection

Lee thereafter composed a letter with the aid of her pastor, Rev. Sang-Won Shin.[2] In the letter Lee apologized to Rev. May. "I want to apologize to you from the bottom of my heart that last time you dropped by our store as a customer, I inadvertently allowed an unfortunate incident to happen." In addition, Lee conveyed that "Mr. Kim has said that he deeply regrets what he did and wants to seek your forgiveness." Lee added that she wanted to follow Rev. May out of the store and apologize but did not want to make her husband's friend lose face.

Rev. May refused to forgive Kim or Lee, calling the apology "insufficient." He instead demanded a public apology and a meeting with Lee in order to culturally sensitize her. The crusade spokesperson agreed, emphasizing the harm not only to Rev. May but also to the African American community: "It has to be a public apology to Rev. May and the community because she publicly embarrassed him and degraded him" as an African American.

Rev. May's demands initially went unanswered. Rev. Shin, pastor of Lee's church, explained Lee's avoidance of May in cultural and gendered terms: "For a woman of Lee's age and background to meet face-to-face with non-Korean males in this context is unthinkable." Lee's self-imposed isolation also stemmed from the physical, mental, and financial strain and the unwanted media attention. Having already lost another business during the 1992 rebellion-riot, and fearful of further confrontations with the crusade, Lee decided to abandon her hat store business permanently: "I'm too weary and afraid to continue."

### Resolution and Disintegration

On the day of the storefront picket, people concerned about the dispute contacted Marcia Choo of the Asian Pacific American Dispute Resolution Center of Los Angeles.[3] Choo, a Korean American, tried to mediate the dispute over the next four months. Lee's increasing reluctance to participate actively in the dispute resolution processes, however, hindered Choo's efforts. Retreating from the media frenzy, Lee disconnected her phone, thereby minimizing contact with Choo and others.

During the subsequent impasse, Rev. Leonard Jackson and Yohngsohk Choe intervened.[4] Rev. Jackson and Rev. May are ministers of the same denomination; Choe is a leader of the community group Koreatown–West Adams Public Safety Association. Rev. Jackson and Choe negotiated a meeting between Rev. May and Lee. Rev. Jackson indicated that Rev. May was "more than glad" to meet with Lee: "That's what he wanted all along."

Almost a half a year after the store confrontation and months after Lee closed her store, Rev. May and Lee met in a two-hour private session at Lee's church. The meeting ended on an apparent high note, with the two hugging, holding hands, and praying. The intermediaries and Rev. May announced the formation of a sister-church tie between the Rev. May's and Rev. Shin's congregations, as well as other "positive programs," including scholarships for black students.

Although some held high hopes for a public reconciliation, the ensuing press conference fell far short of expectations.[5] Lee reluctantly agreed to attend—the intermediaries persuaded her it was the only way to bring closure. The common ground identified in Rev. May's and Lee's private meeting proved illusive in the public spotlight; African American and Korean American supporters disagreed openly about the substance of the accord. Brought from her sickbed to what amounted to a public ceremony, Lee exhibited considerable physical and emotional distress. During the conference she cried and hid her face behind papers.

Several issues of seeming importance were not addressed at the press conference. Neither Rev. May nor Lee fully acknowledged the hurts of the other. Neither acknowledged deeper grievances that some African Americans and Korean American merchants held against each other—grievances and the resulting distrust that apparently underlay the hat store customer-proprietor interaction and transformed it into a full-blown interracial conflict that far transcended the initial dispute. No one at the public ceremony fully addressed what appeared to be central to the escalation of the dispute—the stock stories and historical roots of clashes between inner-city Korean store owners and African American customers across the country.

Despite Lee's obvious distress at the press conference and the unaddressed issues at the controversy's core, media representatives reported a rapprochement, casting the public event in an overwhelmingly favorable light. The media reported the healing of African American and Korean American rifts in Los Angeles. Reporters announced the reconciliation event to be a success and, with little follow-up, declared the dispute "resolved."[6]

*Postscript*

Weakened by a heart condition and the protracted struggle, Lee never reopened her store. She relocated to a small border town near Mexico. Appearing on a radio talk show, Rev. May commented that if Korean American shopkeepers are afraid of crime where they do business, they should move.[7] In the end, the hat shop controversy joined numerous other interracial conflicts in which minorities find themselves "on an isolated space, thrown into battle, fighting for no real prize."[8] During the dispute, Rev. Shin posed a simple question that captured the angst: "Who is gaining from this?"[9]

Somewhat ironically, the controversy appeared to build interminority cooperation among some of those attempting to facilitate its resolution. Representatives of the Brotherhood Crusade and the Asian Pacific American Dispute Research Center cooled past tensions and forged a better working relationship. Frustrated by the deadlock, a Korean radio station started a weekly call-in program, "Listening to African-American Voices," featuring a black guest "from all walks of life."[10] The first guest on the show was Rev. Jackson. (Rev. May also appeared on the show, generating two hundred calls from listeners nationwide). During his appearance, Rev. Jackson expressed his support for the program and suggested that black radio stations participate. "If you want to get rid of the infection, you have to cut deep and it will hurt," he said, "Frank talk is good for both communities. . . . The question is: does it heal clean?"

## Reconciliation?

Indeed, the questions for Korean American and African American communities in South Central Los Angeles are, did they cut deep and did the wounds heal clean?

*Interracial Justice Overview*

How are we to think about this resolution of the hat shop controversy? Was it reconciliation? Or false grace? Was it genuine healing? Or a media concoction?

How did the apparent rapprochement affect Rev. May and Lee? The African American and Korean American communities? Were the underlying interracial justice grievances addressed, let alone redressed? Of what significance were these healing efforts to future interracial interactions? To alliance forging and coalition building? In Los Angeles and elsewhere?

On one level, the hat shop conflict and "reconciliation" is a tale of missed opportunities. Lee let Rev. May leave her store without an immediate apology; May rejected Lee's initial apology; and the public healing ceremony, the press conference, ended in confusion. On a deeper level, the hat shop dispute reveals conflictual (and perhaps typical) efforts to build relationships between individuals and between their racial communities. Instead of catharsis, Lee and Rev. May appeared to deepen their personal anguish. Instead of airing, redressing, and reframing intergroup grievances, they appeared to leave interracial tensions in limbo. As in other cases of interracial conflict, their inability to achieve mutual liberation meant little interracial transformation. In the end, neither May nor Lee or the African American and Korean American organizations could answer Rev. Shin's question: "Who's gaining from this?"

The effort by Lee and Rev. May and their intermediaries reflected their shared desire to put the dispute behind them. Why did honest efforts by well-intentioned individuals ultimately fail to bring about both interpersonal and interracial healing? The interracial justice dimensions, I suggest, sharpen the inquiry into these questions and illuminate initial responses. These dimensions provide an approach to critically examining, assessing, and, where appropriate, reconfiguring ongoing intergroup healing efforts like those of Lee and Rev. May.

Rev. May and Lee were caught in a bewildering swirl of accusations, rejoinders, and countercharges. Amid the turmoil, two distinct potential healing moments emerged—the first when Lee apologized by letter shortly after the incident, and the second when Lee and Rev. May met privately under the guidance of intermediaries and then held a ceremonial press conference.

*The Apology Debacle*

Once the dust settled from the in-store conflict and the subsequent storefront protest, the first significant opportunity for interracial healing arose when Lee sent her formal apology letter to Rev. May. Realizing her mistake in allowing her husband's friend to order Rev. May out of the store, Lee admitted, "I should have apologized no matter how Mr. Kim might take it . . . I reacted too late."[11] Why did Lee's admission of personal error and expression of contrition fail to engender forgiveness?

Lee, of course, apologized several months after the incident and under the threat of a boycott—raising the specter of apology as a commodity rather than a sincere expression of contrition. In addition to possible insincerity, however, Lee's initial efforts suffered from several shortcomings. Reconstructive inquiry characterizes apologies as speech acts, as performance. That performance usually has the greatest impact when experienced directly.[12] Lee desperately sought to avoid direct contact with Rev. May and hoped that the formal apology letter would end matters. "Will the apology be the end of it," she asked. "Or will they keep coming back?"[13] However sincere her apology and however valid her cultural justifications for avoiding a confrontation, the impersonal written mode of the apology may well have undermined its effectiveness.

In turn, Rev. May's outright rejection of Lee's private apology and his insistence on contrition expressed publicly to the African American community indicated that he remained, at least at the time, unmoved to forgive. Rev. May explained his insistence and his willingness to accept negative repercussions for Lee in terms of improved Korean American treatment of African Americans. "Even if she closed the store, I'm still pursuing the [issue]," he maintained. "I'm trying to make some good out of it. I am trying to make other Koreans more sensitive to African Americans."[14] By imposing on Lee the burdens of reconciliation and by defining "good" to mean benefit to African Americans, Rev. May at the time was unable to appreciate the change of heart—his willingness to forgive —necessary for healing.

In response, Lee expressed her fatigue and anxiety about the impasse. "Sometimes I'm so weary I just think to myself 'I'll be liberated from all this trial when I die.' We made a mistake, but is it something that cannot be forgiven?"

A failure of recognition thus marked the first healing moment. To what extent did Rev. May and Lee see into the woundedness of each other and critically examine the specific circumstances, larger socioeconomic context, stock stories, and cultural representations informing their dispute? The answer—very little. From the information available, it appears that Lee, Rev. May, and their supporters failed to explore seriously and articulate publicly the complex intergroup dynamics of their dispute. The lack of rigorous critical examination of both the particulars/contextual and structural/discursive aspects of the Korean-black framing of the controversy severely hampered their initial reconciliatory efforts.

More specifically, Lee's written apology acknowledged the inappropriateness of Mr. Kim's action and Lee's inaction. Rev. May's response also addressed the circumstances of his exclusion from the hat store. Weaving the particulars of their interpersonal interaction into an apology and response, however, was not nearly enough to bring about intergroup healing. The dispute had already escalated (through the crusade's participation and the media coverage) from an interpersonal conflict into an interracial controversy.

Neither Rev. May nor Lee or their backers publicly identified the interracial context. The racial demographics and political economy of the area and the class and gender of the principals, factors in the controversy, went largely unexplored. Also overlooked was the connection of the hat shop conflict to others in the local area and region. How, for example, did images of friction between Korean and African Americans in most major cities rapidly heat the in-store conflict into an interracial conflagration?[15]

Perhaps it was too early for probing interrogation; everyone's emotions were too raw. Perhaps there was no helpful discursive framework. Perhaps the supporters had other agendas. Rather than a joint critical interrogation of intergroup grievances, Lee, despite apologizing to Rev. May, balked at serving as the scapegoat for all the wrongs of Korean store owners; Rev. May, hoping to do "some good," insisted on teaching Korean American merchants a lesson.

Inquiry into group responsibility sheds more light on this shaky foundation of apology. To what extent did Rev. May and Lee accept appropriate responsibility for harm to each other's racial communities? Lee failed to acknowledge any responsibility for racial injury or to accept any responsibility for healing interracial wounds. "Why does this have to become a big racial issue?" she complained. "If something like this had happened among Koreans, this wouldn't be a problem at all. We might exchange a few harsh words, but that would be end of it."[16] Lee could not understand Rev. May's racial complaint or the depth of his anger. Lee seemed caught in her own confusion and anxiety about the boycott and could not comprehend "what she did to deserve this." Lee's sense of hopelessness arose in part from her inability to recognize her contribution to the African American community's sense of racial injury. Mediator Choo's attempt to help Lee understand that sense of woundedness was misinterpreted by Lee as siding with Rev. May.

Portraying herself as a victim of Rev. May's intransigence, Lee discounted his feelings of indignation as well as the anger of inner-city blacks at continuing discrimination. A Blackwatch Movement leader and organizer of several Korean American store boycotts, echoed the sentiments of many inner-city blacks who view Koreans as the next self-serving immigrant group to step on them: "We buy fruits, leather, jewelry, they sell us vegetables, repair our shoes, dry clean our clothes but they have no respect for us."[17] A casual remark further describes the reason for the anti-Korean animus: "I've been discriminated against by white people all my life, so I'll be damned if I let this Korean discriminate against me." These angry feelings of continuing black subordination—this time by a nonwhite racial group—were likely intensified by looming African American worker concerns about apparent job and housing displacement by growing numbers of Latina/o immigrants in Southern California.[18]

By misunderstanding Rev. May's hurt and ignoring the sources of African American anger, Lee exposed herself to criticism as a "typical" Korean American—an immigrant who fails to appreciate the psychological and material advantages that some members of her group enjoy over blacks burdened with a two-centuries-long legacy of slavery and who refuses to recognize current discrimination against African Americans. Under these circumstances, Rev. May's demand that Lee's apology publicly acknowledge the racialized nature of his injury appears understandable.

At the same time, Rev. May also cast himself as the sole victim, a portrayal that appeared to obscure his at least partial responsibility for Lee's economic and racial injuries. Rev. May discredited Lee's fears, just as she discounted his anger. Rev. May initially failed to grasp the depth of Lee's suffering from the destruction of her other store and her husband's hearing loss. Rev. May's anger and sense of victimization, it seems, limited his capacity to empathize with the hopes, pain, and struggles of Lee and other Korean American immigrants in South Central.

His anger also seemed to detract from the recognition of economic realities, that inner-city minority merchants often are buffeted by the dual winds of harsh outside corporate practices (credit, pricing, goods, transportation) and white racism. By effectively declaring his treatment by Lee an outrage against the African American community and by not publicly acknowledging Lee's personal history, the gender and cultural dynamics of the conflict, or the problems of Korean American merchants, Rev. May narrowly framed the dispute as Korean racism against blacks. This framing absolved Rev. May of personal responsibility for any racialized harms and in effect denied African American agency.

How could both Rev. May and Lee see themselves as sufferers and not the agents of the other's pain? Differential agency and simultaneity provide clues. Those concepts explain how both Lee and Rev. May, in differing ways and without acknowledging it, wore the hats of victim and perpetrator. Inquiry into the setting and the details of the controversy reveals that each wielded distinct, if subtle, forms of "power over" the other.

South Central Los Angeles is a borderland site where new immigrants settle and come into contact with American-born blacks. For many experiencing severe economic problems, interracial conflict is viewed as a zero-sum game in which one racial group can be a winner only if others are losers. Although African Americans have acquired some political power in Los Angeles, Asian Americans and Latinas/os, the area's fastest-growing racial groups, are demanding greater political participation. These groups are seen increasingly by some African Americans as competitive threats.[19]

Amid the changing demographics and shifting power among racial communities in the South Central borderland, Rev. May and Lee and their respective communities possessed a power enlivened and constrained in multiple ways. Simultaneity, a key aspect of constrained agency, explains how in the hat shop controversy African Americans and Asian Americans possessed power over each other in different arenas, even though each group was disadvantaged in differing ways by continuing white dominance over many spheres of inner-city social and economic life.

A group engages in relationships in many settings, with power flowing in several directions. A group may be positioned with "power over" in one relationship in one setting and with lesser power in the same relationship in a different setting. Each setting in turn is formed by alignments with other groups and ongoing interactions based on gender, race, class, immigrant status, sexual orientation, and culture.

Lee's ownership of the hat store, for example, gave her economic power over Rev. May. She controlled a resource giving her material advantages over many of her inner-city customers and appeared comparatively empowered financially in relation to Rev. May. By contrast, in the public arena, as a respected African American male community leader with media access and political contacts and as an English speaker, Rev. May possessed power over Lee. Although Lee possessed power over May in the confines of her store, she was comparatively disadvantaged in the larger community as an immigrant from Korea, a woman, and a non–native English speaker, even while both Korean and African communities continued to face various forms of white racism.

In particular, Rev. May's alignment with the Brotherhood Crusade, with its reputation for nonviolent economic pressure, enhanced Rev. May's public power over Lee. With May's approval, the crusade used civil rights strategies for resisting white dominance against a Korean immigrant woman merchant (confrontation, publicity, moral and legal demands). Although often effective historically in white-black civil rights struggles, their use here raised a key question. Was it appropriate to deploy those strategies against members of another racial group that continues to suffer many forms of discrimination?

That question is multifaceted, with varying responses. But consider: The protest and the threat of a prolonged boycott not only resulted in the closure of Lee's hat shop—a loss to the African American community—it also failed to address the underlying interracial grievances and socioeconomic conditions that exacerbated the initial conflict. Even though the tactic captured the attention of Korean American communities, it failed to advance materially the interests of neighborhood African Americans and failed to facilitate even a beginning interracial rapprochement.

In these differing ways, Lee and Rev. May were simultaneously privileged and subordinated, empowered and disempowered. If they had sought genuine reconciliation after exercising racialized and gendered power over each other, both would be obligated to accept responsibility for the harms inflicted and to take active steps toward rebuilding some degree of trust between their racial communities.[20] By not engaging in this kind of subtle interrogation of agency and responsibility, however, both Rev. May and Lee maintained entrenched victim positions. In doing so, they undermined any potential for personal and group transformation during the first healing moment.

### Healing or False Grace?

During the second potential healing moment, the private meeting and press conference, Rev. May and Lee moved more purposefully toward healing. With the help of intermediaries behind closed doors, Rev. May and Lee appeared to establish common ground. "Pastor May is a good, warm man of God, after all," Lee declared to the media after the private meeting. "He prayed for my health and for my husband's hearing problem."[21] Rev. May and Lee scheduled a press conference to publicly memorialize their newfound understandings. As described earlier, however, the press conference was a disaster. Why did this second round of reconciliatory efforts show more promise than the first but end similarly?

Reconstruction and reparation inquiry focus on affirmative steps toward redressing underlying grievances and rebuilding the relationship—steps toward restorative justice. What ameliorative steps did Lee and Rev. May take to redress both personal and intergroup wounds? To what extent did they alter group attitudes and the structure of African American and Korean American relations? Did the hugs and smiles signal a fundamental transformation or simply a temporary salve?

The private meeting arranged by Choe and Rev. Jackson broke the impasse and appeared to initiate personal healing for both Rev. May and

Lee. What did they discuss? Clearly, they talked about their personal hurts. Lee appeared to gain an appreciation of Rev. May as an African American community leader concerned about Korean-black relations. Rev. May appeared to rethink his view of Lee as a villain, and his prayer for Lee and her husband during the private meeting displayed sensitivity to Lee's pain. By meeting in a nonadversarial setting, Rev. May and Lee seemed to open themselves to each other. The private session, at least temporarily, alleviated their interpersonal tension. "It's not so difficult to iron out misunderstanding when you sit down and just talk quietly," said Choe.

But by the time of that meeting, the controversy's "misunderstanding" extended far beyond Rev. May and Lee's hat shop argument. During this second potential healing moment, did Rev. May and Lee grapple with the broader socioeconomic backdrop of their dispute? Did they address publicly the underlying interracial grievances that transformed the in-store interactions into something much larger—a Korean–African American controversy? Was their private reconciliation based only on an interpersonal exchange or also on an informed public commitment to help heal the breach in Los Angeles between Koreans and blacks, a breach widened by their conflict?

The failure of the public ceremony, marked by the heated interchange between Rev. May and Lee's supporters, Lee's emotional breakdown, her subsequent move to another city, and May's later critical comments about Korean merchants reveal little interracial understanding. Most important, they belie a fractured foundation for intergroup healing.

Part of the problem may have been the dynamics of a public apology.[22] Many of the common pitfalls—remaining silent, challenging factual interpretations, denying allegations—materialized at the press conference. In addition to the troublesome dynamics of publicizing the apology, however, something more of substance seemed amiss. Interracial justice inquiry provides a glimpse.

However sincere, performative acts such as apologies and expressions of forgiveness, without some joint remaking and retelling of the intergroup story, are not likely to promote sustained interracial healing. Lee and Rev. May, it appears, could not remake the intergroup narrative because they and their intermediaries did not, even during the second potential healing moment, unravel the stock stories of grievance told by one group about the other, stories of grievance fueling a hat shop dispute into an interracial fire. They did not critically challenge each story's "facts," its methodology, its damaging cultural depictions of the other, its tendency to universalize negative traits, and its contribution to group subordination.

More specifically, Rev. May and Lee and their supporters did not publicly critique popular cultural portrayals of Koreans as rude, aloof, and condescending. Nor did they unpack stories about government financial incentives for Korean immigrants that enable Koreans Americans to take over predominantly black communities (some accounts name the exact dollar amount given to each Korean immigrant on arrival). Nor did they jointly challenge cultural depictions of black youths as violent gangbangers and adults as lazy and untrustworthy. These stock stories perpetuate suspicion and disrespect in inner-city encounters. They also appear to have played parts in transforming the hat shop confrontation into an interracial controversy—from Lee's initial perception of Rev. May as a possible threat to her business to May's portrayal of Lee as a financially well-off, oppressive store owner.

These stock stories and the cultural images they conveyed likely had an incendiary effect on the May-Lee conflict, an effect intensified by recent history in Korean-black relations in Los Angeles—which also remained publicly unacknowledged during the second potential healing moment. In 1991, Korean store owner Soon Ja Du shot and killed fifteen-year-old African American Latasha Harlins. Du's no-jail sentence following her conviction for manslaughter sparked outrage. In *The Sentinel*, an African American newspaper, the theme of initial coverage of the shooting was Korean "disrespect" of blacks, a theme that was transformed into "black injustice" upon Judge Joyce Karlin's sentencing of Soon Ja Du to a fine and community service. This transition "was accompanied by the construction of Soon Ja Du as an archetypal Korean merchant utilizing economic and political influence to collaborate with those in positions of power against the interests of African Americans, as represented by Harlins's death."[23] This media theme implicated Korean Americans in the judicial system's apparent double standard for blacks and aligned Korean Americans with continuing white dominance. For many blacks, Soon Ja Du's sentencing became a symbol of racial injustice.

By contrast, the *Korea Times*'s coverage initially focused on black crime and its impact on Korean Americans. Soon Ja Du was cast as an immigrant struggling to survive economically in a crime-ridden African American neighborhood, a symbol of Korean immigrants trying to make ends meet in America. After the strident African American reaction to Du's sentencing, the fear of retaliatory racial attacks transformed the *Korea Times*'s theme from the Korean immigrant struggle into the African American scapegoating of Korean Americans.

Adding to the fear of retaliation were *The Sentinel*'s letters to the editor charging Korean Americans with "pushing African Americans out of the picture" (a charge also levied increasingly by blacks against Latinas/os in Los Angeles). One letter protested the inclusion of a Korean American in a poster of America's racial groups commemorating Martin Luther King Jr. Day. The letter stated that African Americans "are being pushed out of the picture. Immigrants are displacing Blacks economically and politically. And according to the poster, our very presence is next."[24] Rev. May's plan to train Lee in cultural sensitivity similarly played into images of Korean Americans as strange social delinquents in need of instruction on the way things are done in America. This image, replayed by supporters at the press conference, tapped into stock stories of Asian Americans as incomprehensible and intrusive—forever foreigners.

But what about Rev. May's and Lee's efforts at institutional reordering? At their private meeting they agreed to start a sister-church relationship and to commence other Korean-black programs, including scholarships for black students.[25] These actions reflect limited but meaningful strides toward a "shift of focus from conceptions of power over someone toward power as ability or capacity, to power to do something."[26] Scholarships, for example, aim to elevate disadvantaged youths by removing financial obstacles to higher education. Establishing formal ties between community organizations opens lines of communication and places both groups on common social footing. Both actions embody Rev. Jackson's view of reparation as ongoing process: "This [reconciliation] is a real blessing. . . . It's just the kind of thing we need to keep on doing."[27]

Despite the good intentions, both reparation proposals withered. The sister-church proposal failed to rise above "surface and shallow rhetoric—especially since there was no dissecting of the misunderstanding." The plan for black scholarships also proved illusory; Lee's financial losses foreclosed that possibility. A spokesperson for the Multi-Cultural Collaborative in Los Angeles observed that black scholarships are frequently promised as part of the immediate resolution of an interracial dispute and that in many instances, the promise is simply forgotten. Only occasionally is it fulfilled. In either situation, the promise approximates a commercial transaction—"A price to pay for doing business in a black neighborhood."[28]

In assessing this second potential healing moment, ethical notions of responsibility are useful. They enjoin one racial community from advancing at the expense of another. They also direct a group failing that initial responsibility, a group that denigrates or disables another, to redress the resulting harms. According to these notions, both Lee and Rev. May bore responsibility for interrogating how stock stories, and the harms those stories ostensibly justified, advanced their group's interests at the expense of the other. In light of the heightened interracial tensions in the area, Rev. May and Lee were also responsible for jointly reconstructing a new narrative based on interracial cooperation and trust. Neither, on their own or through the mediators, made lasting headway on these difficult tasks.

## The Future?

So how are we to think about this resolution of the hat shop controversy? The questions posed earlier persist.

What were the effects on Rev. May and Lee? For the African American and Korean American communities? Were the underlying interracial justice grievances addressed, let alone redressed? Of what significance were these healing efforts to future interracial interactions? To alliance forging and coalition building? In Los Angeles and elsewhere? In the largest sense, was it reconciliation?

As with the United Church of Christ apology to Native Hawaiians, key relationships warrant careful attention. Unlike the church–Native Hawaiian situation, in which the relationships were between groups (that is, interactions largely among group representatives), the May-Lee reconciliatory effort involved one interpersonal relationship between the principals to the dispute (May and Lee) and one group-to-group relationship (African Americans and Korean Americans).

On an interpersonal level, when Rev. May and Lee met outside the media glare, without political organizations, they related as caring, wounded individuals. Judging from its immediate aftermath, empathy for personal hurts, sincere apologies, and forgiveness characterized the meeting.

That interpersonal rapprochement, however, was not enough to engender intergroup healing. The May-Lee conflict widened the already yawning chasm between Los Angeles's African American and Korean American communities. Reconciliation could no longer be just interpersonal—between Rev. May and Lee as customer and store owner. They both had become (Lee involuntarily) representatives of their communities. Reconciliation for Rev. May and Lee meant also addressing the breach between their racial communities. Although Rev. May and Lee tended to the interpersonal in their private meeting, they and their supporters did not tend to the interracial in the public ceremony. The warm feelings of the private meeting quickly dissipated in public because their closed-door reconciliation did not lay the foundation—in the ways discussed earlier—for healing raw intergroup wounds.

Thus although the media characterized the public ceremony as interracial reconciliation, heated disagreements between Rev. May's and Lee's supporters and May's later comments and Lee's relocation to another town indicated otherwise. As one observer noted, "nothing really happened to heal the larger racial wounds inflicted." Critical social analysis of the historical and contemporary roots of interracial grievances went largely unarticulated. Racial misconceptions remained. Without a newly framed intergroup narrative, outsiders to the relationship aligned themselves with either Rev. May or Lee according to their own interests in a effort to mold public understanding of the dispute and alter the distribution of political power. Without acknowledgment of the deep interracial grievances undergirding the controversy and without recognition of the difficulties of group healing, the media polished the dispute into a shining illusion of interracial reconciliation.

Under these circumstances, it is not surprising that neither Lee nor Rev. May appeared to gain much insight into the dynamics for rebuilding broken intergroup relations. It is also not surprising that the public ceremony failed to produce genuine expressions of contrition and forgiveness; that despite the warm personal feelings at the private meeting, the ceremony failed to offer mutual release for both Rev. May and Lee and their racial communities.

In sum, interracial justice inquiry illuminates these reconciliatory efforts. Rev. May and Lee and their intermediaries sought, but largely failed, to achieve interracial justice—a hard acknowledgment of the ways in which racial groups harm one another, along with affirmative redress of past grievances with present-day effects. They tried in piecemeal fashion to rebuild damaged relationships using words of redress and reconciliation (apology, forgiveness). But they failed to locate those words in a larger framework of restorative justice. Instead, unintentionally and in varying ways, they talked past the dynamics of group healing and undermined prospects of intergroup reconciliation.

Yet for those attempting to mediate the May-Lee dispute and address Korean American and African American tensions, something productive, a glimmer of possibility, emerged. For Rev. Shin, despite the problems and setbacks, the conflict "offered a valuable forum to establish ties with African American and other non-Korean churches."

What lies ahead?

Without meaningful reconciliation, African American and Asian American relations in the millennium are likely to be, in Yogi Berra's words, déjà vu all over again. Consider again the PNT grocers boycott described in the prologue. In important respects, that controversy involving a Vietnamese American merchant and African American church and political leaders in inner-city New Orleans mirrors the hat shop controversy in Los Angeles. Despite differences in locale, the Asian American ethnic group and the battleground (the federal court), the similarities are unmistakable. Perhaps the most revealing similarity is the immense difficulty and importance of racial communities working to achieve restorative justice.

# 11

# Truth and Reconciliation

## South Africa 1998

After massive internal resistance and unanimous international disapproval, including economic sanctions, leaders of the black African National Congress (ANC) and the white National Party agreed to hold democratic elections in South Africa. Thereafter, the newly elected ANC
leaders dismantled racist apartheid political structures. The suffering of
apartheid, however, remained. South Africa's justice minister, Dullah
Omar, a former ANC negotiator, described that suffering in terms of
anguish, despair, and bitterness.

Apartheid created mutual suspicion, hatred and at times on the part of victims a
desire for revenge and vengeance. As the nation begins to heal from the wounds
of apartheid, the anguish, despair and bitterness have become more visible and
sometimes indelible. To be able to move forward South Africa has had to come
to terms with the painful reality that characterises its past.[1]

## Post-Apartheid South Africa: Truth and Reconciliation

After the fall of apartheid, Nelson Mandela joined hands with F. W. de
Klerk and declared, "Let's forget the past! What's done is done!"[2] Mandela, head of South Africa's new government and former prisoner of de

Klerk's white National Party regime, sent a clear message: Reconciliation between whites and blacks, and among various black South African groups, is a fundamental first step toward rebuilding the nation.[3]

Among his first presidential acts, Mandela signed the Promotion of National Unity and Reconciliation Bill, which established the Truth and Reconciliation Commission.[4] Headed by Nobel Peace laureate Archbishop Desmond Tutu, the seventeen-member commission includes psychologists, lawyers, and scholars selected by experts and appointed by Mandela. The commission is composed of three committees with distinct but related functions: the first function is to investigate gross violations of human rights; the second, to consider amnesty for those who confess to political crimes; and the third, to recommend reparations for victims.[5]

Justice Minister Omar, author of the bill, observes that in creating the Truth and Reconciliation Commission, "we have grappled with how to deal with our past as part of a total constitutional and political settlement for our country." This settlement included an agreement for binding democratic elections; a new constitution authorizing democratic government at national, provincial, and local levels; a constitutional bill of rights; a constitutional court; dissolution of all apartheid structures; and finally, amnesty for political abuses supporting or resisting apartheid. The settlement's aims were to establish the principles of accountability and rule of law, generate respect for human dignity, and develop a human rights culture while providing some measure of justice.[6]

According to Omar, given the political changes and these social goals, the commission's paramount task is to initiate a healing process that encourages genuine reconciliation among the races. "There is a need for understanding, but not for vengeance, a need for reparation, but not for retaliation."[7] Commission proponents believe that healing is achievable and that South African society can move beyond the social and psychological injuries of apartheid if those who inflicted racial wounds acknowledge the suffering and accept appropriate responsibility. The commission's work is deemed especially important by many in light of the perceived failure of South Africa's courts and criminal laws to bring apartheid abusers to justice—as evidenced by the acquittal of the former apartheid defense minister Magnus Malan and others on charges of ordering a massacre in a black township.[8]

A first step in the commission's process is storytelling by those phys-ically and emotionally scarred. For Archbishop Tutu, the catharsis of per-sonal storytelling is as necessary to South Africa's healing as the broader legal and governmental changes. "The consequences of apartheid cannot be wiped away simply by democratic decision-making structures or even by large sums of money for housing, education, health, and job creation." Saths Cooper, director of the Family Institute in Johannesburg, agrees, maintaining that "a broad commission allowing victims to articulate their suffering is essential for reconciliation. 'The degree of hurt, bitterness, and anger is still palpable. No amount of legislation will remove that.' "[9]

A second step in the commission's process is acknowledgment of harm by wrongdoers. The commission "hopes to encourage political criminals on all sides to confess in detail to their acts." Criminal confessions are fostered by assurances of amnesty, offering "perpetrators of human-rights abuses a kind of giant national plea bargain."[10] Their stories and apolo-gies, commission proponents hope, will lead to a sense of closure for those who suffered. Commission supporters believe that perpetrator sto-rytelling and amnesty will also prevent protracted litigation and adversity in reconstructing the nation.

With the storytelling by both perpetrators and those suffering, Arch-bishop Tutu echoes Justice Minister Omar's view of the commission and emphasizes that the commission's goal is reconciliation, not retribution. Telling stories is a beginning step toward forgiveness and, therefore, na-tion building. "It's realpolitik, this forgiveness thing. It's not just some-thing in the realm of religion or the spiritual. If [retributive] justice is your last word, you've had it. You've got to go beyond it."[11] According to Tutu, retributive justice is "largely Western. The justice we hope for is restorative of the dignity of the people."[12] This kind of restorative justice is reflective of the African notion of *ubuntu*, or "interconnectedness." Ubuntu is the idea that no one can be healthy when the community is sick. "Ubuntu says I am human only because you are human. If I un-dermine your humanity, I dehumanize myself." It characterizes justice as community restoration—the rebuilding of the community to include those harmed or formerly excluded.

Assessed from the vantage point of interracial justice, the commission's stated purpose and overall structure appear salutary. The commission's goal is to promote reconciliation through interracial healing, and its structure is designed to facilitate intergroup healing by filling a psychological gap left by legal and political reforms formally abolishing apartheid. That gap, according to interracial justice, is characterized by a need for recognition (survivor storytelling and perpetrator confessions of wrongful acts), for acceptance of responsibility, and for reconstructive acts (perpetrator apologies, victim forgiveness), and reparation. The commission's functions, in concept, address those needs.

Contrary to critics' initial fears, the commission's work in practice has not opened the floodgates to demands for revenge or exorbitant compensation.[13] Some participants appear satisfied with having their suffering acknowledged.[14] However, others worry about empty apologies, that storytelling about personal trauma and words of apology alone are unlikely to lead to meaningful reconciliation. Those who suffered need to perceive an apology as complete and sincere, with the former aggressors recognizing the historical roots of present hurts and accepting responsibility for the harm inflicted. For many, the acknowledgment and the apology must also be accompanied by meaningful social structural and attitudinal changes. They worry that apology without reparation will lead to cheap reconciliation, in which the words are warm but the relationship is cold.

Because of these concerns, a pivotal question raised by interracial justice inquiry is whether the commission's work will unlock painful bondage and result in the kind of mutual liberation that fosters the rebuilding of relationships—genuine reconciliation. What is the impact of victim storytelling, of perpetrator confessions? Is reconciliation possible without some form of punishment? If the objective of perpetrator confessions is amnesty rather than contrition, will reconciliation prove illusory? Is a crucial realpolitik issue the adequacy of funding for reparations to repair the heart of apartheid's devastation (in terms of education, health, socioeconomic, and political status for blacks)? Without it, will South Africa's future be one of healing or of haunting injustice? Interracial justice inquiry raises these questions about the commission's agenda while affirming the many beneficial aspects of the commission's work.

## Realpolitik: Storytelling, Confession, and Amnesty

The commission embarked on its mission in 1995, its regional hearings providing victims of human rights abuses a public forum for denouncing the specific atrocities of apartheid. Nohle Mohapi testified about her husband, Mapetla, who apparently was tortured to death in prison in 1976. Nohle refused to believe the official story that Mapetla hanged himself in his cell. The authorities later detained and tortured Nohle as the widow of an accused terrorist. "I was full of hate when my husband died. . . . I hated them for the oppression. . . . Now I want to share the difficult times."[15] Most important for Nohle, "I want the people to hear today what happened, and my children, I want them to know that their father did not kill himself." Hearing the truth enables people to move forward; "life must continue."[16] Mzukisi Mdidimba expressed similar sentiments in different words. "When I have told stories of my life before, afterward I am crying, crying, crying, and felt it was not finished. This time, I know what they've done to me will be among these people and all over the country. I still have some sort of crying, but also joy inside."[17]

This kind of commission storytelling is key to reconciliation. Those whose screams fell on deaf ears now have an opportunity for the world to hear their pain. Storytelling of this sort may be the only way for perpetrator groups to recognize the others' pain while enabling those suffering to transcend it. It facilitated personal and collective mourning by people like Nohle Mohapi and Mzukisi Mdidimba; it enabled them to work through their loss and the losses of black South Africa.

Others participated in the commission hearings to seek healing through symbolic reparations. Mothers wanted tombstones for dead children; families wanted loved ones' remains for proper burial.[18] Ncediwe Mfeti's husband Phindile, a student at the University of Natal, disappeared in 1987. She told the commission that the last time she heard his voice, he called to tell her about some new jeans. Since that day, she has tried desperately to solve the mystery of his disappearance. She requested only that the commission locate his body: "Even if he was burned. If only I could get a little bone or ashes that were his."[19]

In these ways, the commission provided a formal, solemn forum where "different stories, different memories, and different histories can emerge as the basis for an inclusive nation-building exercise."[20] While recognizing the therapeutic effect of such testimony, however, Mandela cautioned that survivor storytelling is only the beginning of the healing process. For expressions of pain to move the country toward reconciliation, white and black South Africans need to accept appropriate responsibility for those hurts, as both individuals and group agents.

With this in mind, the commission in 1996 asked the perpetrators of human rights abuses to confess in the interest of healing—the payoff for which might be indemnity from prosecution and civil liability. Understandably, the amnesty provisions of the Promotion of National Unity and Reconciliation Act were, and continue to be, controversial. These provisions were included in the act despite great misgivings by negotiators for the African National Congress. In terms of realpolitik, however, amnesty was the fulcrum for the National Party's agreement to hold democratic elections and, in effect, to abolish apartheid. The transition from apartheid to a democracy in South Africa did not result from military victory by black South Africans. Rather, it emerged from a negotiated settlement. In exchange for a nonviolent transition to democracy, the people of South Africa, of necessity, agreed to political amnesty.

Justice Minister Omar summarized it in this way: As the "struggle against apartheid ... escalated, it became increasingly ... clear ... that there was no possibility of victory or defeat by either side to the conflict in the immediate future." The National Party, which controlled the government at the time of the settlement,

would not have agreed to democratic elections and the introduction of this democratic constitution without the provision for amnesty. . . . The choice before us was to have peace in our country or to continue the war. . . . One must locate the question of amnesty in the context of the total settlement in our country.[21]

Amnesty was the price the people of South Africa paid to attain national peace and begin healing.

For the commission, perpetrator stories, even those told under a promise of amnesty, are integral to joint understandings of past justice grievances underlying continuing racial tensions and to a fashioning of new narratives about current relationships. "Talk of reconciliation is shallow and fruitless without a careful and thoroughgoing investigation of the difference that divides the nation."[22] A common historical memory constructed by victims, perpetrators, and collaborators is central to national reconstruction.

The commission's work is continuing. Because of the controversy surrounding amnesty and because of the intensifying calls for reparations and changes in socioeconomic conditions, the prognosis for the commission's work, in terms of long-term interracial reconciliation, is split between the potential for extraordinary success and dispiriting failure. Although the commission productively addressed one important aspect of interracial justice—the need for recognition through storytelling—the next phase of the commission's work has been characterized by fits and starts, successes and failures.

Whether the commission's work will ultimately generate a collective sense of justice done, of mutual liberation from pain and guilt and genuine interracial healing, is a question open to speculation. Confessional testimony before the commission, assessed in a framework of interracial justice, reveals why.

### F. W. de Klerk, Ex-President of the Former Ruling National Party

In August 1996 F. W. de Klerk, former president of South Africa's National Party, appeared before the commission. Several years earlier, de Klerk presided over the formal dismantling of apartheid. He is credited for his cooperative workings with Mandela; both received the 1993 Nobel Peace Prize. In his testimony, de Klerk apologized for apartheid and for human rights abuses. His thirty-page summary of government policies and practices, including the apology, however, omitted most of the details, and his outright denial of any knowledge of who carried out the human rights abuses was booed from the floor. De Klerk diminished the National Party's responsibility for apartheid by describing the party's actions as "unconventional," by denying personal knowledge of gross human rights violations, and by pointing the finger of guilt not only at the African National Congress but also at white racist policies and practices worldwide. As a counterpoint to his apology, de Klerk stated that blacks had "benefited enormously" from South Africa's white supremacist policies, citing better schools, housing, and hospitals and "greater wealth."²³

De Klerk's see-no-evil stance belied his position as leader of the National Party. He refused to recognize both the horrific suffering inflicted by apartheid (to empathize) and the specific acts of the National Party agents in furtherance of white supremacy (to acknowledge the particulars of oppression and their sociohistorical context). The tenor of de Klerk's apology and his grudging acknowledgment of the National Party's role in apartheid abuses enabled observers to characterize his testimony as "disingenuous and def[ying] belief," "an insult to any audience's intelligence," and "another chorus of that universal song, 'I'm sorry, but it wasn't my fault, and everybody else was doing it, and we weren't the only bad guys, and they were worse.' "²⁴

De Klerk's apology followed the testimony of hundreds of survivors of apartheid. Their stories of murder, torture, rape, and other human rights abuses contrasted starkly with de Klerk's characterization of former National Party leaders as men of honor who were simply "mistaken" in their apartheid policies. "I retain my deep respect for our former leaders. In the context of their time, circumstances and convictions they were good and honourable men, though history has shown that, as far as the policy of apartheid was concerned, they were deeply mistaken."²⁵

Agency analysis of de Klerk's terse National Party apology reveals its inadequacy. While acknowledging the "deeply mistaken" governmental "policy of apartheid," de Klerk eschewed critical sociolegal interrogation of the dominant white minority's actions and the privileges it received through apartheid. Most important, his apology failed to acknowledge the National Party members' agency concerning human rights violations and the long-term disabling institutional constraints imposed on black self-definition and self-development. According to de Klerk's implicit logic: no agency, therefore no responsibility, and no need to express collective remorse.

From most observer accounts, de Klerk's apology was empty—a minimalist, insincere effort to satisfy the commission's call. Without the threat of rigorous commission cross-examination, de Klerk appeared to accede to the requirements of form (apology) without conceding anything meaningful in substance (recognition). Despite the commission's aims and efforts, de Klerk's apology, combined with former President Botha's later refusal to testify,[26] offered little if any basis for forgiveness and transformation—for the mutual liberation essential to restoring broken relationships.

Indeed, some South Africans wondered how black South Africans can "grant forgiveness to monsters who simply list their atrocities and expect amnesty without contrition." "I lost my entire family after our home . . . was bombed," said a black woman whose husband and four children were burned beyond recognition by a government hit-squad attack. "To me, knowing who did it or who gave the orders will not change a thing, especially the fact that those who destroyed my life will not face the wrath of the law."[27]

"There is no feeling of forgiveness in my heart. There is no constitutional duty placed on me to forgive," said Marius Schoon, a white antiapartheid activist whose wife and daughter were killed by a letter bomb meant for him. The former police officer who admitted to sending the bomb planned to confess formally before the commission in return for amnesty. "Only if [those guilty of torture and murder atone for their crimes] can there be true national reconciliation," said Rajee Gopal Vandeyar, a "colored" antiapartheid activist severely beaten and tortured by police. "To forgive these people is asking a lot." The widow of Steve Biko, who died in prison of police-inflicted injuries, summarized her feelings about the value of confessional testimony: "Peace would be brought by having my husband next to me right now."[28]

For some black South Africans, those reactions inflamed suspicions that many white South Africans tolerated major political changes only because they were allowed to retain property and privilege without expressing contrition or accounting for past misconduct. Winnie Mandela articulated that frustration in a eulogy that contributed to her removal from the new government's cabinet. Many blacks, she said at a constable's funeral, were upset with the slowness of the transition and believed that the new government was more interested in appeasing whites in the interest of hollow reconciliation than in facing the realities of continuing discrimination and racism against blacks.[29]

*Thabo Mbeki, Deputy President of the ANC and the*
*Current Government*

Thabo Mbeki's apology presented a stark contrast. He apologized on behalf of the African National Congress for human rights violations committed by ANC members primarily against black South Africans during the ANC's liberation fight. Mbeki was the first person testifying to extend a direct apology to the survivors and families of victims. In an extensive self-study, detailing the many injuries inflicted by the ANC, Mbeki admitted to "grisly human rights violations" and apologized for the ANC's actions. He indicated that the ANC and its leaders, now in power in the new South African government, accepted collective responsibility for those actions.[30] At the same time, Mbeki carefully framed the context of the ANC apology. He distinguished abuses by freedom fighters from those of defenders of apartheid, noting that ANC abuses occurred in an otherwise "just war"—"it would be morally wrong and legally incorrect to equate apartheid with the resistance against it."[31]

In terms of group agency, Mbeki's apology reflected the ANC's quest for governmental stability from a position of emergent power. The apology nevertheless appeared to be far more than a bid for political consolidation; it also exhibited the ANC's commitment to reconciliation—to rebuilding relations not only between whites and blacks but also among blacks. It showed this latter commitment by recognizing the ANC's wrongful actions during its liberation struggles and the resulting suffering of black South Africans—that is, by acknowledging that a group with some degree of power could be simultaneously oppressed and oppressive. It also demonstrated this commitment by reaching out to those harmed and their families.

Mbeki's apology reached out in specific ways. The apology document answered many questions asked by South Africans wondering about missing loved ones. The document described the identities of hundreds killed or missing and detailed the bombings and attacks in which civilians were inadvertently killed. The document also included previously concealed internal reports describing the "horrific living conditions and mistreatment at former ANC military training camps."[32] A reporter who observed the testimony of 140 witnesses highlighted the significance of Mbeki's reconstructive act: "The depths of pain and anger are still there. . . . [But m]ost of them have said effectively, 'we need to know what's happened, who was involved and then we're prepared to forgive.' "[33] By providing specific details and offering victims' stories to facilitate mourning, the ANC acknowledged the particulars of the harms inflicted and accepted responsibility (delimited by political circumstances) for healing. By making the effort to let people know what happened to whom, by recognizing harm and accepting responsibility, the ANC laid the beginnings of a foundation for forgiveness, for black-on-black healing.

The juxtaposition of de Klerk's minimalist apology and Mbeki's revelatory apology is jarring. Mandela anticipated their contrasting approaches two years earlier when he cautioned: "The freedom fighters were asked to disclose what offenses they have committed, we would like also the defenders of apartheid to disclose what offenses they have committed."[34]

## Mangosuthu Buthelezi, Head of the Zulu-Based Inkatha Freedom Party and Home Affairs Minister

Zulu nationalist leader Mangosuthu Buthelezi, prime minister of the newly created Bantustan of KwaZulu, apologized to the ANC on behalf of the Zulu-based Inkatha Freedom Party. In a 769-page apology document, Buthelezi expressed abhorrence for bloodshed and observed that Inkatha Party members had been drawn into violence. Although denying any personal role in apartheid violence, Buthelezi then apologized on behalf of the Inkatha Party, saying he was "sorry for any hurt [he had] caused the ANC leadership" in supporting the apartheid regime. Buthelezi's apology acknowledged some degree of responsibility for those hurts while recognizing the difficulty of preventing future conflicts. "I know that because we are human beings, and therefore sinners, that we shall hurt each other even tomorrow. I nevertheless apologise for the past hurts."[35] In addition to the apology, Buthelezi listed 422 Inkatha Party leaders killed since 1985 and demanded that the commission investigate and explain these killings: "Nowhere else in the world could killing on such a grand scale go unchallenged and unexplained."[36]

Although some observers perceived his apology as superficial at best, from the vantage point of interracial justice, Buthelezi's apology to the

ANC was significant, not so much for the specific words of apology, but for the historical importance of the performative act of acknowledgment. Over the last decade, the fierce rivalry between the ANC and the Inkatha Party resulted in twenty thousand deaths. The violence subsided only in May 1996 with the signing of a peace pact. Moreover, the Inkatha Party opposed the formation of the commission and initially refused to participate in its proceedings, citing the commission's bias favoring the ANC. Indeed, in his testimony, Buthelezi voiced continued misgivings about the commission's work: "We believed and we continue to believe that the commission as currently composed . . . will neither reveal the truth nor bring the reconciliation we so desperately need in this land."[37] Buthelezi nevertheless appeared before the commission, acknowledged the Inkatha Party's partial responsibility for apartheid violence, and apologized to the ANC. Under these circumstances, Buthelezi's appearance itself, supported by his words, reflected a desire to begin a process of intraracial reconciliation and a willingness to accept some responsibility for healing.

Buthelezi's ambivalence toward the commission resurfaced eight months after his testimony, when an Inkatha Party spokesperson again criticized the commission for its ANC bias. Although consistent with prior criticisms, the timing of this one—coinciding with criticisms by others about the commission's progress—clouded the somewhat improved relations between the ANC and the Inkatha Party. In response, Dr. Alex Boraine, the commission's acting chair, and an ANC member, decried the lack of cooperation by a "major constituency" and worried about the impact of Inkatha Party's resistance on the commission's final recommendations.[38]

### The Confession of Steve Biko's Killers

In addition to organizational confessions, the commission heard testimony about specific human rights violations. For example, in January 1997 the commission announced that five former policemen seeking amnesty had confessed to the 1977 murder of black antiapartheid activist Steve Biko. Biko, head of the Black Consciousness movement, had spoken openly and harshly against apartheid. After his arrest, the police beat him into near unconsciousness. Denied medical attention, Biko was driven naked 750 miles to Pretoria where he died in a jail cell. Thousands mourned at his funeral.[39]

At the inquest, the police major testified that Biko hit his head on a wall during a scuffle, and the inquest examiners determined that the police were not responsible for Biko's death. The medical exoneration of the police triggered international outrage. In 1997 the police involved sought legal amnesty for what their lawyer euphemistically called "an interrogation gone wrong." The officers came forward as evidence of their guilt mounted.

The police confessions were important to the commission's legitimacy. Commission critics had grown increasingly restive about the failure of the reconciliation process to elicit genuine confessions from high-profile white South Africans or from whites involved in notorious abuses. After numerous testimonials by those suffering and de Klerk's tepid apology, the police confessions on the high-profile Biko case lent some semblance of balance to the commission's work.

The confessions, however, also triggered opposition. The police had one apparent goal in confessing: to avoid legal responsibility for their crimes. They did not recognize the suffering they inflicted or acknowledge why their acts amounted to human rights abuses. They expressed no contrition and offered no amends. Biko's family strongly opposed amnesty. Biko's son said he would feel "cheated if they walk away being granted amnesty and applauded by the world as heroes." A year before the officers applied for amnesty, the Biko family filed suit challenging the commission's power to grant amnesty, arguing unsuccessfully that amnesty robbed the victims and their families of their constitutional right to seek justice through legal redress.[40]

In practice, and possibly because of situations such as this, the commission has carefully limited the amnesty program. Early on, Archbishop Tutu declared, "blanket amnesty is out." To obtain amnesty, a perpetrator must show that he committed a politically motivated crime. The commission therefore carefully scrutinized all amnesty applications. Although it had received more than 5,500 amnesty applications and had processed over 800 by May 1997, the commission had granted only 39 (denying 797).[41]

As revealed by the response to Biko's killers' confessions and as predicted by the interracial justice inquiry into responsibility and reconstruction, neither the political necessity for amnesty nor its limited operation erased the survivors' need for the perpetrators' contrition. Although the survivors' stories and the perpetrators' testimony are essential to reconciliation, more is needed. Repairing the damaged relationship between the racial groups "requires that the victimizers accept responsibility for their acts or those of their predecessor governments and people, recognize the injustice done, and in some way ask forgiveness of the victims" and undertake reparatory action.[42]

Biko's killers' confessions, like de Klerk's apology, failed to do this in meaningful fashion. The confessions reflected little recognition of group agency and acceptance of responsibility for apartheid abuses; failed to acknowledge the benefits to whites and harms to blacks of South Africa's former legalized racial hierarchy; and did not clearly commit whites to redefining and restructuring intergroup relations.

## Changes in Group Attitudes and Societal Structures: Repairing the Wounds

Midway through the commission's process, during the amnesty hearings, some black South Africans expressed intense criticism of the inadequacy of victim stories and perpetrator confessions. Many white perpetrators had benefited materially from apartheid. Amnesty would not only relieve them of civil and criminal liability; it would also preserve their ill-gotten gains. Given the political necessity of amnesty, black South Africans began asking for something tangible in exchange. As a basis of meaningful reconciliation, they demanded material change in living conditions and the building of black-controlled economic institutions. The reconstruction and reparation dimensions of interracial justice highlight the reasons for these demands.

Organizations from the housing, development, poverty, social services, legal, education, and human rights sectors demanded that in addition to human rights abuses, the "Truth Commission should probe socioeconomic violations." The University of the Western Cape's Community Law Centre, the Development Action Group, and the Legal Resources Centre cautioned "that [the commission] will not fulfill its legal obligations unless it includes in its work certain violations of socioeconomic rights."

According to these organizations, apartheid policies (including urban planning, influx control, group areas, and bantu education) were responsible for severe socioeconomic injuries to most black South Africans. Victim stories and perpetrator testimony may address personal trauma, but they do not repair socioeconomic harms. At a March 1997 commission-sponsored forum, witness after witness called for the commission to focus its work on economic justice.[43] For these South African blacks, changes in social attitudes and economic structures are essential. Until the victims of apartheid experience a material improvement in daily living and working conditions, there will be little racial healing.

The concerns voiced by these groups speak to the importance of reparation. Specific reparations are a tangible expression of a group's desire to redress historical justice grievances. They can be a catalyst for social and economic restructuring. When reparatory acts aim to rebuild intergroup relations through attitudinal changes and institutional restructuring, reparation can be transformative. Reparation addresses group rather than individual claims and therefore focus on removing substantive barriers to group liberty and equality—in education, housing, medical care, employment, cultural preservation, and political participation.

Despite the dismantling of apartheid political structures, economic and social barriers remain. Without reparation to uplift those injured, postapartheid reconciliation may be impossible. Recognizing this reality, Justice Minister Omar opined that the commission's Reparation and Rehabilitation Committee "is undoubtedly one of the most important committee[s] in the overall process of trying to bring about maximum justice for victims."[44] Midway through the commission's hearing process, the ANC took an even stronger stance: reparation is essential to healing. "Unless there are meaningful reparations [by the perpetrators], the process of ensuring justice and reconciliation will be flawed."[45] Speaking on behalf of apartheid victims, a South African black eloquently humanized this focus on reparation: "We don't want [the perpetrators] to be locked up in jails. We don't want them to suffer as we and our families did. We don't want to respond to evil by being evil." For her, healing would be best accomplished by monetary reparations from the perpetrators. "The best way for perpetrators of apartheid atrocities to demonstrate their commitment to reconciliation would be to contribute financially to the families of victims." Monetary reparations are one way to close the huge gap in wealth between whites and blacks created by apartheid's economic and political structures. The "inequalities will not make it easy to heal the wounds of the victims as they are still suffering the pain of not only loosing [*sic*] their loved ones but also their bread-winners."[46]

In June 1996 the commission's Reparation and Rehabilitation Committee recognized the pressing need for interim reparations. The committee adopted the Policy Framework for Urgent Interim Reparations Measures for the socioeconomic reordering of society. The framework made policy recommendations for substantial governmental (but not private) reparations, to compensate individual survivors of human rights violations as well as "all the communities whose dignity was destroyed through a systematic machinery of human rights violations and state neglect."[47]

The committee expressly directed policymakers toward a reparation program built on principles of redress, restitution, rehabilitation, restoration, and reassurance of nonrepetition. The recommended policy framework focused on five categories of reconstruction: (1) care for those suffering emotionally, (2) medical care, (3) financial assistance for those in dire need, (4) access to education, and (5) symbolic remembrances. The recommendations identified specific measures to address these needs, set out eligibility criteria, and outlined methods of implementation.

The committee's principles, needs categories, and recommendations are directed toward the kind of material social structural change likely to foster a willingness to forgive—to reconcile. First, meaningful apologies and reparations, including restitution, rehabilitation, and restoration, are reconstructive keys to group healing. Second, principles of restitution, rehabilitation, and restoration focus on changes in societal attitudes and institutional structures. Last, the reframing of a new narrative about the interracial relationship concentrates on ending legislative and administrative policies resulting in human rights violations.

Although the Interim Framework's principles and recommendations are salutary, their implementation will require huge resources and the creation of bureaucratic structures. Consistent with the settlement between the ANC and the National Party, the commission did not suggest reparatory payments by white beneficiaries of apartheid. Instead, it requested an initial appropriation of $675 million from parliament. Funding of that request for reparatory work may be key to material change in racial conditions and, therefore, reconciliation. Owing to the already shaky South African economy, an appropriation close to full funding over the next several years will be difficult. Knowing this, other countries have offered to contribute to victim compensation.[48]

The commission's push for substantial reparations could lead to real change. But there is a risk. Because of financial and other realpolitik limitations, the commission's ambitious reparation and rehabilitation plan could prove illusory—leading to what Dietrich Bonhoefer called "cheap grace," or false reconciliation. With the reparatory framework in place and publicized, the people of South Africa may feel good for the moment, and South Africa may look good internationally. But without adequate funding and a supporting infrastructure, the plan may deliver less than promised in terms of direct help to individuals and alter little in terms of social attitudes and socioeconomic conditions. In addition, the reparation process itself could generate a social and political backlash against blacks by resentful white South Africans—white South Africans have already given up political power, so why should they also have to suffer further deterioration of the national economy? The dilemma of reparation inherent in efforts such as this remains: whether the reparation process will eventually lead to repair or will instead prolong victimization and aggravate intergroup racial wounds, sometimes for generations.

## What's Next?

The commission's work demonstrates the significant possibilities and severe problems of interracial reconciliation on a societal level. Unlike the hat shop and PNT grocers controversies (which started with interpersonal conflicts in neighborhood locales) and unlike the United Church of Christ apology to Native Hawaiians (which focused initially on restoring interracial relations in a Hawai'i church polity), the commission's healing mission touches multiple relationships across space, time, and cultures. Reconciling racially to rebuild a country is fraught with difficulty—and promise.

Interracial justice inquiry reveals some of the obstacles and possibilities. Although race controversies are rarely subject to orderly scrutiny, thoughtful inquiry into each of a controversy's four dimensions—recognition, responsibility, reconstruction, and reparation—offers at least partial illumination of the prospects for interracial healing.

Most evident from the commission's efforts to date are two realities. First, racial reconciliation is messy, conflictual, and time-consuming. It cannot be achieved quickly, neatly, or painlessly, by unilateral decisions, with resort to healing bromides. Second, a sincere apology and some form of reparation are often necessary for reconciliation. Yet they may not be enough if societal attitudes and institutional structures do not change. If those with power intend to retain their power over others and their attendant privileges, then no apology will lead to genuine reconciliation— the kind of mutual release that transforms the relationship and liberates it from the legacies of the distant or recent past.[49]

In light of these realities, how will the commission's work play out over time? For South Africans, what will be the long-term effect of the apologies conveyed? The reparations bestowed? The amnesty granted? What lessons are there for contemplated race apology strategies in the United States? How do we assess and evaluate them? The answers to these questions are still wide open.

Some South Africans are hopeful. Henrik Van der Merwe, founder of the Centre for Intergroup Studies in South Africa, displays guarded optimism. He is encouraged by the commission's work and by multiracial grassroots efforts to reconstruct South African society. From his vantage point, the commission's healing work and the daily one-on-one interracial interactions he observes are building a foundation for a new society, a future in which blacks and whites share a common language, culture, and history.[50]

Despite the commission's success in attracting public recognition of survivors' suffering and perhaps because of its difficulty in procuring meaningful confessions with contrition, the commission's work still receives strong criticism from both ends of the political spectrum. Some perceive only the downside of the dilemma of reparation: the public airing of old hurts stirs resentments that impede peaceable relations. "If anything, it's had [a negative] effect. I see no signs of the truth, followed by catharsis followed by healing. I think that is the sheerest mythology." Instead, these critics believe that storytelling forces open old wounds and interrupts healing. Apartheid hurt South Africans of all colors, they argue. In the interest of peace, all citizens of the new society should simply forget the past and focus on immediate, concrete concerns about employment, education, and the like.[51]

Some take the "forget and forgive" argument a step further. They assert that every white South African who benefited from white privilege under apartheid shares some responsibility for the suffering it caused. Given such universal white culpability, it would be practically impossible to bring every individual "responsible" for apartheid to justice. And since justice is an impossibility, they argue, the goal should simply be peace.

At the other end of the spectrum, some argue that peace is impossible without justice and that justice is impossible without reparation and a change in attitude and behavior on the part of former oppressors. Griffith Mxenge, a prominent ANC civil rights lawyer, was murdered by apartheid police who recently were granted amnesty for their crime. According to his brother Churchill, "People who are hurt and bleeding [cannot] simply . . . forget about their wounds and forget about justice . . . that is not normal. That doesn't happen. Unless justice [in the courts] is done it's difficult for any person to think of forgiving." A South African reporter, bothered by the tepid apologies and amnesty without contrition, similarly observed, "Precisely because reconciliation has not been earned, it functions as nothing more than a bandage that splits as soon as there is any pressure applied to it."[52]

Together, the laudatory observations and the criticisms of the commission's work reveal the subtleties of the intergroup dynamics at play. Different relationships are affected in different ways. One significant relationship is white on black. De Klerk's minimalist apology, Biko's killers' confession without contrition, white backlash, and meager white involvement suggest that present-day black-white reconciliation rests on a tenuous foundation—a bandage ready to split. Whereas black spectators packed the commission hearings, white attendance was sparse. Many whites apparently perceived the commission's work as a "black thing." Alex Boraine, the acting commission chair, warned that white South Africans' "disappointingly poor" participation could impede national healing.

Indeed, white South African leaders contribute to this impediment. They admit the inappropriateness of apartheid yet disclaim responsibility for its injuries because they never participated directly in apartheid abuses. When the president of Mozambique visited the South African parliament, the parliament speaker apologized on behalf of all South Africa for the suffering that apartheid inflicted on its neighbor country. White members of de Klerk's National Party jeered. Their spokesperson complained, "When are we going to be done with all this recrimination? For how long are we going to hear that we did this and that and the other? I was not the architect of apartheid. I got it. Basically, we are the ones who dismantled it, who moved away from it."[53] His statement revealed the sentiments of some and perhaps many white South Africans who did not actively support apartheid human rights abuses. Because they feel no guilt for causing direct harm and overlook the racial benefits they enjoyed during apartheid, they feel no obligation to redress black suffering. By denying group agency and by aligning themselves with de Klerk's position, those South Africans support continuing white refusal to acknowledge responsibility for the racial harms of apartheid.

In this setting, de Klerk's halfhearted apology and the Biko killers' perfunctory confessions raise serious doubts about the potential for a "forgiving-forgiven transaction in the present and future politics" of South Africa.[54] Black and white South Africans of goodwill, of course, will build constructive relationships, relationships no doubt aided not only by the fall of apartheid but also by the commission's work. But with the leadership's resistance to large-scale white repentance (through the acknowledgment of harm) and contrition (the acceptance of responsibility and a commitment to repair), the prospects for genuine (as distinguished from media sound-bite) black-and-white reconciliation appear dim.

More difficult to discern at this point is black-on-black reconciliation. Two relationships are prominent: the ANC's relationship to the Inkatha Party and the ANC's relationship to the black populace.

Mbeki's and Buthelezi's testimonies cautiously signaled reconciliatory beginnings for the ANC and the Inkatha Party. Those beginnings ad-dressed very real past and continuing hostilities. The town of Bhambayi is emblematic of that black-on-black enmity. Once the settlement from which Mahatma Gandhi organized nonviolent protest among the Indians of South Africa, Bhambayi is now bitterly divided, even among members of the same tribe. A recent visitor observed how "over the last decade the community . . . has been torn apart by violence—murders, house-burnings, rapes—in a bitter war between one side, which is ANC-run and the other, which supported the Inkatha Freedom Party."[55]

By spelling out the ANC-inflicted injuries against black South Africans (including Inkatha Party members) and by apologizing to survivors and families of victims, Mbeki confessed that the ANC at times deployed against blacks the structures and strategies of oppression used by govern-ment forces against the ANC. Because of ANC's access (albeit limited) to economic resources and public communication channels, some ANC members oppressed black dissidents and terrorized other poor black South Africans even while those ANC members resisted oppressive apart-heid institutions and policies. With Mbeki's confession, the ANC psycho-logically disarmed itself and renounced symbolically its power over other black South Africans. This disarmament conveyed what appeared to be genuine desire for intraracial reconciliation.

Similarly, Buthelezi's initial willingness to work with an ANC-run gov-ernment evinced a desire for peaceful handling of black-on-black griev-ances. Moreover, his apology to the ANC, despite his initial opposition to the commission, reflected some degree of commitment to end subju-gation among black South Africans. Buthelezi's apology for the Inkatha Party's support of apartheid, although halting, also appeared sincere, cau-tiously laying another cornerstone in the foundation for reconciliation among South African blacks. The Inkatha Party's later renewed criticism of the commission's bias toward the ANC may well have chipped or even cracked that cornerstone, typifying the volatile, unpredictable dynamics of intraracial rapprochement. If Inkatha Party members continue to feel wronged by the ANC—whether in past interactions or as a result of current commission bias—they will likely mourn perceived ANC human rights abuses indefinitely.

The commission's effect on the ANC's relationship with the black populace is the most difficult to assess. Black South Africans continue to hold the ANC and its leaders in high regard. After all, they were their liberators. The ANC's confession of and apology for specific human rights abuses against blacks in its "just war" against apartheid appear to resonate with blacks generally. Whether the ANC can successfully shift from liberator to administrator is critical, it appears, to long-term relations with the black populace. The ANC maintains a shaky grasp on political power while attempting to fund and administer reparations and to restructure South African society socially and economically. Whites maintain partial control over both the civil government and the military, and the new government has limited administrative experience in managing a nation.[56]

In the larger picture, with vision and courage, South Africa has undertaken the monumental task of racial healing. Whether its commission's work will engender restorative justice—the repairing of the wounds of the community by reintegrating those at its margins—is an open question. What is evident is that the often wrenching reconciliatory process has helped heal some but not others, that some groups have grasped the opportunity for beginning rapprochement and others have not. As for the prospects of a long-term transformation, to date, amid the fits and starts, successes and failures, kudos and criticisms, collective reframing has yet to occur concerning "what happened," "who is responsible," and "how we are to get on with the new South Africa." A new societal narrative that both acknowledges the past and transcends it is still in the making. Whether new collective memories will lead to forgiveness and a release of the "haunting legacies of the past"—repair—is the question of South Africa's future.

The unlocking of painful bondage and the mutual liberation of all South Africans will likely require more than survivors' storytelling, confessions without contrition, and tepid apologies. When those suffering see material change in socioeconomic conditions and institutional structure, when some form of meaningful reparation is forthcoming, then those long disenfranchised in South Africa may sense a kind of justice that liberates, that contributes to intergroup healing, to restoring the community—*ubuntu*.

# Epilogue

Spring 1998 witnessed three notable racial events. First, the Eisenhower Foundation released the report of its study of racial conditions in contemporary America. The report, entitled the *Millennium Breach*, found stark social and economic divisions between blacks and whites. It concluded that the racial breach would remain, and possibly worsen, without affirmative public- and private-sector measures to repair the damage to the material conditions (jobs, eduction, health, housing) of the lives of America's racial minorities, particularly African Americans.

Second, President Clinton stood at the door to the main slave-trade fort in Senegal, Africa, and condemned the inhumanity of historical European and American slavery. He called for racial reconciliation. Third, in community meetings across the United States, people of diverse races met to "talk story"—sometimes openly, sometimes dogmatically—about racial wounds and healing.

Viewed collectively, these events painted a racial landscape marked by both continuing racial divisions and a desire among many for peaceable and productive relations. They highlighted the importance of white-on-black and also white-on-color and color-on-color interactions. And they underscored the need to repair damage not only to racial group members but also to communities—and to the country.

How, then, do we get along? How can we "do justice" in order to heal the racial wounds, to reconcile, as a step toward peaceable and productive relations here and abroad? These are the race questions for the new millennium.

# Notes

Notes to Prologue

1. According to the Nguyens, "Mr. Narcisse attacked Tihn Nguyen, the minor son of Tho Nguyen, with a crow bar; Mr. Nguyen came to his son's defense with a baseball bat; Mr. Narcisse began beating Mr. Nguyen with the crow bar, and another of Mr. Nguyen's sons, Kevin Nguyen came to his father's defense with a gun, which was not fired." The Nguyens asserted that the altercation began when Narcisse told an African American teenager that he should not associate with Nguyen's son, Tihn, because Tihn was Vietnamese. Narcisse maintained that the Nguyens attacked him without provocation. Complaint for Injunctive Relief and Request for Temporary Restraining Order p. 3, *Ngyuen v. Neighborhood Committee for Justice* (E.D. La. 1996) (No. 96-2099) (hereafter cited as Complaint).

For reports on the genesis and escalation of the dispute, see Tara Young, "Tensions Explode at Store, Spawn Protest," *New Orleans Times-Picayune*, May 30, 1996, p. B1; Tara Young, "Fighting over Crumbs: Cultures Clash at Corner Store," *New Orleans Times-Picayune*, July 3, 1996, p.1; "Boycotted Store Reopens amid Tensions, *Baton Rouge Sunday Advocate*, July 14, 1996, p. 5B. The PNT grocers story recited here is based on these and similar reports and on available firsthand information; it is not a complete historical account.

2. Complaint, p. 6.

3. Tara Young, "New Orleans Crowd Vows to Banish Store," *New Orleans Times-Picayune*, June 15, 1996, p. B1.

4. Letter from Willye Jean Turner, Neighborhood Committee for Justice, to Oliver Thomas, councilman, city of New Orleans, June 5, 1996.

5. Complaint, p. 5. See also Tara Young, "Suit Claims Economic Terrorism," *New Orleans Times-Picayune*, June 21, 1996, p. B1.

6. The Nguyens' attorney characterized the altercation and ensuing boycott as "mostly personal" and "more economically based." Telephone interview with Dan Zimmermann, attorney for the Nguyens, April 28, 1996. Dr. Thiem Dang, president of the Vietnamese American Association in New Orleans, thought the altercation was an "isolated incident" resulting from "a misunderstanding on

both sides." A spokesperson for the Committee for Justice characterized the issue as one of "respect." Young, "Fighting over Crumbs," p. A1.

7. Young, "Fighting over Crumbs," p. A1.

8. The legal process proved inhospitable to rethinking New Orleans's race relations—relations strained by high levels of poverty in black communities, white flight, and growing Vietnamese American populations. "Most of the have nots are black and most of the haves are white." "What Are Your Feelings about Race Relations in Our Area, after Watching Events Unfold in Los Angeles, and Where Do We Go from Here?" *New Orleans Times-Picayune*, May 2, 1992, p. A19.

The Vietnamese immigrant population in the south has steadily increased over the last twenty years. Dr. Luyen Cao observes that this growth, combined with misinformation about them (such as stories that Catholic charities supplies down payments for their houses) hinders Vietnamese assimilation. Nikita Stewart, "Vietnamese Fear Anti-Refugee Campaign: Push to House New Immigrants in Other Areas Seen as Threat," *Louisville Courier-Journal*, November 15, 1994, p. 1A.

9. Muhammad Yungai, "Blacks Still Seek Empowerment," *New Orleans Times-Picayune*, June 30, 1996, p. B6.

10. Order Denying the Plaintiffs' Motion to Enforce the Settlement Agreement at 6, *Nguyen v. Neighborhood Committee for Justice* (E.D. La. 1996) (No. 96-2099) (concluding that the Nguyens breached the agreement, thereby absolving the committee and church of their obligations).

11. Historically, blacks occupied the lowest position in Louisiana's racial hierarchy. Creoles—people of mixed French, Indian, and African ancestry—were accorded privileges that positioned them between blacks and whites. The "specification of Creole was equally a creation of law and social policies unique to Louisiana that granted, policed, and maintained a system of racial caste and hierarchy." Peter Kwan, "Unconvincing," 81 *Iowa L. Rev.* 1557 (1996); Arnold R. Hirsch and Joseph Logsdon, *Creole of New Orleans: Race and Americanization* (1992). Although Vietnamese Americans are among the nation's poorest minorities, they are often seen as occupying an "in between" position in the racial hierarchy once held by Creoles. See Young, "Fighting over Crumbs," p. A1.

Resentment against Vietnamese immigrant entrepreneurs is reflected in violent southern conflicts between Vietnamese and nonimmigrants. In 1981, Ku Klux Klan members terrorized Vietnamese fishermen on the Texas Gulf Coast. Philip Zelikow, editorial, *Fort Worth Star-Telegram*, May 14, 1995, p. 2. According to the U.S. Justice Department in Houston, there has been an increasing number of "violent confrontations between Vietnamese fishermen and the Ku Klux Klan, between Vietnamese merchants and black customers and between Vietnamese and Latino residents of the same condominium." One newspaper reported that in Houston, which has one of the largest Vietnamese communities in America, "black people rate their relationship with Asians as worse than their relationship with white people." Jonathan Tilove, "Racial, Ethnic Map Grows More Complex:

Houston Strives to Keep Order, *New Orleans Times-Picayune*, December 29, 1996, p. A14.

12. Tara Young, "Peace Breaks Out: Neighbors Welcome Grocers," *New Orleans Times-Picayune*, September 10, 1996, p. B1.

13. Tara Young, "Raising Strength: Prayer Service Promotes Healing, Ethnic Groups Come Together," *New Orleans Times-Picayune*, November 29, 1996, p. B3.

14. Ibid. See also Robert Miller, "Prayer Service Bolsters Unity," *New Orleans Times-Picayune*, December 15, 1996, p. 1C.

## Notes to Introduction

1. I use the word *interracial* narrowly here to denote relations among nonwhite racial groups, and by *nonwhite racial groups* I mean groups or communities of color. Those commonly recognized racial groups include African Americans, Asian Americans, and Native Americans (including Native Hawaiians). I also treat Latinas/os as a racial group, even though Hispanic/Latina/o has been defined by the U.S. Census and other legal directives as an ethnic group (racially either white or nonwhite). See Lawrence Wright, "One Drop of Blood," *New Yorker*, 1993, pp. 46–47. By doing so, I am acknowledging the social and political construction of racial and ethnic categories. See Michael Omi and Howard Winant, *Racial Formation in the United States*, 2d ed.,(1994), p. 55. For this reason, I also recognize the significance of white as a racial category and use the term *multiracial* to denote interactions among racial groups, including white Americans.

Racial and ethnic classifications also are sometimes gendered. Latino, for instance, is used as both a general group reference and a designation for male group members; Latina refers to women group members. Thus Latina/o is a general group reference that acknowledges the gendered dimension of racial and ethnic identity.

2. Julio Laboy, "Koreans and Hispanics Build Ties in Los Angeles," *Wall Street Journal*, January 29, 1997, p. CA2. Recent multiracial coalitions formed to address specific social, economic, or political issues of common concern include the MultiCultural Collaborative (working on affirmative action and school reform in Watts); AGENDA (Action for Grassroots Empowerment and Neighborhood Development Alternatives) (South Central Los Angeles African American/Latina/o coalition working on economic-social justice and youth organizing); Metropolitan Alliance (addressing needs of working-class communities in Los Angeles); APALC of Southern California (providing Los Angeles Asian Pacific American communities with multilingual legal services and civil rights advocacy); and New York Immigration Coalition (NYIC) (more than thirty organizations coordinating multiracial voter registration programs); Women on the Move to Eliminate Racism (addressing racism in education, job training and employment, law enforcement, child and health care).

3. Coalitions formed specifically to address interracial tensions and to build intergroup relations include a joint effort by the Korean American Coalition and the National Association of Latino Elected and Appointed Officials (strengthening ties to handle intergroup tensions); Blacks and Jews in Conversation (judges' and lawyers' workshops for Jewish and black students to discuss race); and Black-Korean Mediation Project (joint project of civic and professional organizations emphasizing understanding and cooperation between black and Korean communities in New York City).

Coalitions that initially formed around specific issues and later were transformed into coalitions to address intergroup tensions include the Civil Rights Consortium; Western Justice Center Foundation in Pasadena (initially an alternative dispute resolution project of ninth circuit judges now focusing on interracial conflict resolution); Asian Pacific American Dispute Resolution Center (mediating services for conflicts within Asian Pacific American communities and interracial conflicts).

4. Paula D McClain and Joseph Stewart Jr., "Can We All Get Along?" in their *Racial and Ethnic Minorities* in *American Politics* (1995), p. 126.

5. David Roediger, *Towards the Abolition of Whiteness: Essays on Race, Politics, and Working Class History* (1994), p. 1.

6. Norman Matloff, "Asians, Blacks and Intolerance," *San Francisco Chronicle*, May 20, 1997, p. B-1.

7. Sally Merry and Neal Milner, *The Possibility of Popular Justice: A Case Study of Community Mediation* in *the United States* (1993).

8. Catharine MacKinnon, "From Practice to Theory, or What Is a White Woman Anyway?" 4 *Yale J.L.* and *Feminism* 13 (1991).

9. This idea of the "Rs" of intergroup healing came up at a workshop of the Facing History and Ourselves program in Brookline, Massachusetts, in April 1997. The workshop, following a conference on collective memory and violence, identified more than twenty "Rs" as conference themes. The title to chapter 8 of this book borrows from the program's name.

10. Geiko Mueller-Fahrenholz, *The Art of Forgiveness: Theological Reflections on Healing and Reconciliation* (1997), pp. 5, 25.

11. Dana Takagi, *Retreat from Race: Asian Americans and Affirmative Action* (1993).

12. Lisa Lowe, "Heterogeneity, Hybridity, Multiplicity: Marking Asian American Differences," *Diaspora* 1 (1991): 24, 31.

## Notes to Chapter 1

1. See, for example, Michael C. Thornton and Robert J. Taylor, "Intergroup Attitudes: Black American Perceptions of Asian Americans," *Ethnic and Racial Studies* 11 (1988): 474 (addressing the "escalating antipathy" between "blacks and Asian Americans" and suggesting "a better understanding of how these two

populations [now] view each other"); S. M. Miller, "Coalition Etiquette: Ground Rules of Building Unity," *Soc. Pol.* 47 (1983): 14 (suggesting codes of behavior to foster intergroup understanding to aid in coalition building); Kenneth J. Meier, "Cooperation and Conflict in Multiracial School Districts," *Journal of Pol.* 53 (1991): 1123. See generally James Jennings, ed., *Blacks, Latinos, and Asians in Urban America* (1994); R. Radhakrishnan, "Culture as Common Ground: Ethnicity and Beyond," *Melus* 5 (1987): 14.

2. See, for example, Armando Navarro, "The South Central Los Angeles Eruption: A Latino Perspective" 19 *Amerasia Journal* 19 (1993): 69, 83 ("Latinos must also participate in the formation of multiethnic/racial coalitions which are predicated on the inclusion of all groups and segments who share a common interest in the rebuilding of SCLA and Los Angeles"); Rodney E. Hero, "Multiracial Coalitions in City Elections Involving Minority Candidates," *Urban Affairs Quarterly* 25 (1989): 342, 349 (noting that some political observers assume that shared political concerns will bring blacks and Hispanics together as "likely allies in urban politics"); Edward T. Chang, "Jewish and Korean Merchants in African American Neighborhoods: A Comparative Perspective," *Amerasia Journal* 19 (1993): 2, 18 ; Ella Stewart, "Communication between African Americans and Korean Americans: Before and after the Los Angeles Riots," *Amerasia Journal* 19 (1993): 23, 46.

3. See Daryl Harris, "Generating Racial and Ethnic Conflict in Miami: Impact of American Foreign Policy and Domestic Racism," in Jennings, *Blacks, Latinos, and Asians in Urban America*, p. 80; Lisa C. Ikemoto, "Traces of the Master Narrative in the Story of African American/Korean American Conflict: How We Constructed 'Los Angeles,' " 66 *S. Cal. L. Rev.* 1581, 1584 (1993); Reginald Leamon Robinson, " 'The Other against Itself': Deconstructing the Violent Discourse between Korean and African Americans," 67 *S. Cal. L. Rev.* 15, 28–31 (1993) (describing monopoly capitalism and the narrative of "white America and its social institutions" as integral to the "violent discourse" between Koreans and African Americans).

4. For recent works looking beyond structural factors and examining intergroup grievances and racial identity politics from the vantage points of communities of color, See Karen Umemoto, "Blacks and Koreans in Los Angeles: The Case of LaTasha Harlins and Soon Ja Du," in Jennings, *Blacks, Latinos, and Asians in Urban America*, p. 95; Manning Marable, "Building Coalitions among Communities of Color: Beyond Racial Identity Politics," in Jennings, *Blacks, Latinos, and Asians in Urban America*, 29. See also Mari J. Matsuda, "Beside My Sister, Facing the Enemy: Legal Theory out of Coalition," 43 *Stan. L. Rev.* 1183 (1991); Trask, "Coalition-Building."

5. Jonathan Tilove, "Minorities Fighting Each Other for Power—Many Ready to Abandon Idea of Rainbow Coalitions, *New Orleans Times-Picayune*, December 8, 1996, p. A20.

6. Ibid. See also Rodolfo F. Acuna, *Anything but Mexican: Chicanos in Contemporary Los Angeles* (1996), p. 139 (describing the "politicization of the 'other' " and the effect of changing demographics and economics on conflicts among African Americans, Chicanos, and Asian Americans).

7. Benjamin Pimentel, "Asian Americans' Awkward Status—Some Feel Whites Use Them as 'Racial Wedge' with Others," *San Francisco Chronicle*, August 22, 1995, p. A1.

8. Alejandro Portes and Alex Stepick, *City on Edge: Transformation of Miami* (1996).

9. *Ho v. San Francisco Unified School District*, No. C-94-2418 (N.D. Cal. 1994).

10. Rick DelVecchio, "Unusual Lawsuit Stirs Racial Questions in Oakland," *San Francisco Chronicle*, August 13, 1996, p. A15; Tilove, "Minorities Fighting Each Other for Power."

11. First Amended Complaint for Declaratory and Injunctive Relief for Violations of 42 U.S.C. sec. 1983, *Ho v. San Francisco Unified School District*, No. C-94-2418 (N.D. Cal. 1994) (hereafter cited as Amended Complaint); Memorandum Decision and Order p. 8, *Ho v. San Francisco Unified School District*, No. C-94-2418 (N.D. Cal. 1994).

12. See Consent Decree, *San Francisco NAACP v. San Francisco Unified School District*, 576 F. Supp. 34, 53 (N.D. Cal. 1983); Henry Der, "The Asian American Factor in the Affirmative Action Debate: Victim or Shortsighted Beneficiary of Race-Conscious Remedies," in *Leap—Common Ground: Perspectives on Affirmative Action* (1996).

13. See *People v. Hall*, 4 Cal. 399 (1854). See also Tomas Almaguer, *Racial Fault Lines* (1994).

14. Amended Complaint, p. 3.

15. Mamie Huey, "Chinese Americans Have Bone to Pick with Consent Decree," *Asianweek*, January 27, 1995, pp. 5, 8.

16. These kinds of arguments have received considerable public attention. See Richard Herrnstein and Charles Murray, *Bell Curve: Intelligence and Class Structure in American Life* (1994) (construing IQ test information to mean that Asian Americans and whites are innately more intelligent than African Americans and Latinas/os); Dinesh D'Souza, *End of Racism* (1995) (arguing the cultural superiority of descendants of Asia and Western Europe, particularly in comparison with African Americans).

17. Plaintiffs' Memorandum of Points and Authorities in Opposition to Defendant's Motion to Dismiss, at 10, *Ho v. San Francisco Unified School District*; Mamie Huey, "NAACP Sides with SF School District in Ongoing Lowell Saga," *Asianweek*, January 20, 1995, p. 5.

18. Huey, "Bone to Pick," pp. 5, 8.

19. Frank H. Wu, "Behind the GAO Report," *Asianweek*, December 22, 1995,

p. 11 (reporting on white neoconservative politicians' use of Asian Americans to argue for abolishing affirmative action).

20. See Der, "Asian American Factor," p. 4. As a basis for comparison, a study of the 1994 entering freshman class at UCLA found that if students were admitted on "academic criteria alone," the number of Asians would increase (42.2 to 51.1 percent), as would the number of whites (30.7 to 42.7 percent), and the number of Hispanics (20 to 5 percent) and blacks (7.1 to 1.2 percent) would decline sharply. See Andrew Hacker, "Goodbye Affirmative Action," *New York Review of Books*, July 11, 1996, p. 21.

21. See Louis Harris Research, *Taking America's Pulse: The Fall Report of the National Conference Survey on Intergroup Relations* 1994) (commissioned by the National Conference of Christians and Jews). The poll found that almost half of all blacks and Latinas/os believe that Asian Americans are "wary, suspicious, and unfriendly toward non-Asians" and "unscrupulously crafty and devious in business." Thirty-five percent of Asians and 24 percent of African Americans think that "Latinos lack ambition and drive to succeed." Thirty-one percent of Asian Americans and 26 percent of Latinas/os agree that "African-Americans want to live on welfare."

22. See Dana Takagi, *Retreat from Race: Asian-American Admissions and Racial Politics* (1992), p. 139. In a 1995 press release accompanying a General Accounting Office report on college admissions prepared at his request, Congressman Dana Rohrbacher reiterated the Asian/black rationale for eliminating affirmative action: "Young Asian Americans are being victimized by quota-based college admissions policies designed to benefit *preferred minority groups.* . . . The education establishment's race-obsessed admissions doctrine demonstrably discriminates against Asian Americans." Wu, "Behind the GAO Report," p. 11 (emphasis added). The "preferred minority groups" that Rohrbacher clearly was referring to were African Americans and Latinas/os.

23. See Takagi, *Retreat from Race*. The Berkeley controversy started with Asian American complaints about a hidden quota limiting admissions of Asian Americans. The administration's investigation determined that the decline was the result of a "series of deliberate policy changes . . . instituted [by the university] . . . knowing that they would reduce Asian American freshman enrollment at Berkeley" (p. 34). Conservative politicians and commentators, initially uninterested in Asian American civil rights, tried to shift the terms of the debate from Asian American exclusion in admissions to a general attack on affirmative action. See, for example, Dinesh D'Souza, *Illiberal Education* (1991). A naturalized citizen from India, D'Souza aligned Asians with whites against African Americans and Latinas/os. As Takagi observes, "Whereas Asian American organizations accused . . . officials of discrimination against Asians in order to protect whites, neoconservatives charged . . . discrimination was a matter . . . between blacks and Asians" (p. 139).

24. For a more developed discussion of the *Ho* case, See Eric K. Yamamoto,

"Critical Race Praxis: Race Theory and Political Lawyering Practice in Post–Civil Rights America," 95 *Mich. L. Rev.* 821 (1997).

25. John Dawson, *Healing America's Wounds* (1995); Geiko Muller-Fahrenholz, *The Art of Forgiveness* (1997); Donald Shriver, *An Ethic for Enemies: Forgiveness in Politics* (1995); Robert Schreiter, *Reconciliation: Mission and Ministry in a Changing Social Order* (1992); Gregory Baum and Harold Wells, eds., *The Reconciliation of Peoples: Challenge to the Churches* (1997). See also Willis H. Logan, ed., *The Kairos Covenant* (1988); Spencer Perkins and Harold Rice, *More Than Equals: Racial Healing for the Sake of the Gospel* (1993). For related scholarship that is not theologically based see Harlon L. Dalton, *Racial Healing: Confronting the Fear between Blacks and Whites* (1995); Joseph V. Montville ed., *Conflict and Peacemaking in Multiethnic Societies* (1990).

26. Nicholas Tavuchis's *Mea Culpa* (1991) is a significant recent work outside the theological realm, as he develops a "sociology of apology and reconciliation." His theory, like those of recent theological works, does not focus on interracial grievances.

27. See, for example, Study Circles Resource Center, "Toward a More Perfect Union in an Age of Diversity," *Focus on Study Circles: The Newsletter of the Study Circles Resource Center* 8 (2), Spring 1997.

28. See Richard W. Brislin, *Cross-Cultural Encounters* (1981); Bruce E. Barnes, "Conflict Resolution across Cultures: A Hawaii Perspective and a Pacific Mediation Model," *Mediation Quarterly* 12 (1994): 117; Isabelle R. Gunning, "Diversity Issues in Mediation: Controlling Negative Cultural Myths," *Journal of Disp. Resol.* (1995): 55; Dale Bagshaw, "Whose Idea of Fairness: Examining the Impact of Culture on the Mediation Process," in *Second International Mediation Conference— Mediation and Cultural Diversity* (January 1996); Study Circles Resource Center, "Toward a More Perfect Union."

29. Virstan B. Y. Choy, "From Surgery to Acupuncture: An Alternative Approach to Managing Church Conflict from an Asian American Perspective," *Congregations* 16 (November/December 1995).

30. Gregory Baum, "A Theological Afterword," in Schreiter, *Reconciliation of Peoples*, pp. 184, 189; Montville, *Reconciliation*.

31. Jeff Chang, "Race, Class, Conflict and Empowerment: On Ice Cube's 'Black Korea,'" *Amerasia Journal* 19 (1993): 87, 99, n. 2 .

32. Korean American reporter John Lee described to an Asian American columnist the difficulty of collaborating with an African American reporter on the Soon Ja Du–Latasha Harlins story. Lee described their apparent inability to engage in a careful analysis of the event— "We argued about it. It was very emotional"— and how this contributed to their newspapers' distortion of African American– Korean American conflicts. The columnist viewed the reporters' difficulties as "symptomatic of the ways their respective communities regarded the incident." Guy Aoki, "Racial Coverage," *Rafu Shimpo*, May 7, 1997, p. 3.

33. See Elizabeth Martinez, "Beyond Black and White: The Racisms of Our Time," *Soc. Just.* 20 (1993): 22; Yamamoto, "Critical Race Praxis," p. 889.

34. It also overlooks white relations with nonblack people of color. While this relationship is also jurisprudentially important (see, for example, *Hernandez v. New York*, 500 U.S. 352 [1991], allowing the white attorney to use peremptory juror challenges to eliminate Hispanic jurors), I focus on interminority group, or interracial, relations.

35. Fred L. Pincus and Howard J. Ehrlich, eds., *Race and Ethnic Conflict: Contending Views of Prejudice, Discrimination, and Ethnoviolence* (1993); Aspen Institute Berlin/Carnegie Endowment for International Peace, *Unfinished Peace: Report of the International Commission on the Balkans* (1996).

36. See Bill Ong Hing, *Remaking Asian America through Immigration Policy, 1850–1990* (1993), p. 2 (nativistic responses to Asian immigration); Will Kymlicka, *Multicultural Citizenship* (1995) (focusing on American and Canadian Indians); Eric K. Yamamoto, "Rethinking Alliances: Agency, Responsibility and Interracial Justice," 3 *UCLA Asian Pac. Am. L. J.* 33 (1995) (justice grievances among communities of color); Almaguer, *Racial Fault Lines* (racial hierarchy); "Los Angeles— Struggles toward a Multiethnic Community," *Amerasia Journal* 19 (1993) (examining conflictual relations among African Americans, Asian Americans, and Latina/o Americans).

37. James H. Johnson Jr. and Melvin L. Oliver, "Interethnic Minority Conflict in Urban America: The Effects of Economic and Social Dislocations," in Pincus and Ehrlich, *Race and Ethnic Conflict*, p. 194; William Julius Wilson, *Truly Disadvantaged* (1987).

38. See, for example, George J. Borjas, "Immigrants, Minorities and Labor Market Competition," *Indus. and Labor Rel. Rev.* 40 (1987): 382; Ivan Light and Edna Bonacich, *Immigrant Entrepreneurs: Koreans in Los Angeles* (1988).

39. Joe R. Feagin and Clariece Booher Feagin, "Theoretical Perspectives in Race and Ethnic Relations," in Pincus and Ehrlich, *Race and Ethnic Conflict*, p. 29.

40. Almaguer, *Racial Fault Lines*; David O. Goldberg, *Racist Culture* (1993).

41. Angela P. Harris, *What We Talk about When We Talk about Race* (forthcoming).

42. Third Amended Complaint for Monetary, Declaratory and Injunctive Relief, *United Minorities Against Discrimination v. City and County of San Francisco*, No. C-91-2350, at 1–5, 9, 10, 12, 18, 21, 22 (N.D. Cal. November 9, 1994).

43. Defendants' Response to Plaintiffs' Statement of Facts, *United Minorities*, at 7 (January 27, 1995); Plaintiffs' Supplemental Brief in Opposition to Defendants' Motion for Summary Judgment, *United Minorities*, at 7 (May 15, 1995).

44. Stipulation and Protective Order, *United Minorities*, at 2 (March 29, 1994).

45. Jim Impoco, "California Tries to Give Back the Tired and Poor," *U.S. News and World Report*, November 21, 1994, p. 42; "Cops Promise Action on

Asian 'Mug Book,' " *San Francisco Chronicle*, August 2, 1991, p. A24; Torri Minton, "Quiet Marin Confronts Hate Crimes / National Study Sees Rise in Violence against Asians," *San Francisco Chronicle*, November 29, 1995, p. A13; Candy Kit Har Chan, "Equitable Admissions," *Asianweek*, January 26, 1996, p. 11. For a historical analysis of anti-Chinese sentiment, see Hing, *Remaking Asian America*, p. 139.

46. See Don T. Nakanishi, "A Quota on Excellence? The Asian American Admissions Debate," in Don T. Nakanishi and Tina Yamano Nishida, eds., *Asian American Educational Experience* (1995), pp. 273, 280; Bill Wong, "Sweet and Sour," *Asianweek*, January 26, 1996, p. 6 (describing the "cold shower for S.F. euphoria" over the appointment of Chinese American Fred Lau, including the "racially charged contretemps" following his appointment); Alethea Yip, "Among the Supremes: Judge Ming Chin Appointed to California Supreme Court," *Asianweek*, February 2, 1996, p. 9.

47. Mari J. Matsuda, "We Will Not Be Used," 1 *Asian Am. Pac. Is. L. J.* 79 (1993).

48. See Samuel Cacas, "Minority Lawyers Organize against California Save Our State Initiative," *Asianweek*, September 2, 1994, p. 1; "New Coalition Formed to Address Racism in Southern California," *Rafu Shimpo*, June 12, 1992, p. 1; Ben Q. Limb, "New York Launches Black-Korean Mediation Project," *Napaba Lawyer*, October 1994, p. 7.

49. See, for example, Frank Wu, "At Lowell High, Who Is Equal to Whom?" *San Francisco Chronicle*, September 21, 1994, p. A23; Jack Miles, "Blacks Versus Browns," *Atlantic Monthly*, October 1992, p. 41; Jeffrey Schmatz, "Miami's New Ethnic Conflict: Haitians vs. American Blacks," *New York Times*, February 19, 1989, p. 1.

50. The plaintiffs are employing statutes, Title VII, and 28 U.S.C. Sec. 1983, originally designed for black minority victims' claims against white majority perpetrators. The plaintiffs' rhetoric ignores interracial interactions and instead somewhat tortuously refers to defendants' agents as "neither African American nor Hispanic." Third Amended Complaint, pp. 12, 14–22.

51. 509 U.S. 630 (1993).

52. For a view of the historical legal and practical relevance of this distinction, see *Adarand Contractors, Inc. v. Pena*, 115 S.Ct. 2097 (1995) (Stevens, J., dissenting).

53. *Shaw*, 509 U.S. at 631.

54. 115 S. Ct. 2097 (1995) (Scalia, J., concurring).

55. I use the term *de facto prohibition* because the Court majority's position is, in effect, one of color blindness. While Justices Scalia and Thomas argue for a complete ban on racial classifications, *Adarand*, 115 S. Ct. at 2118–19, the Court majority's formal position is that all racial classifications are subject to strict scrutiny and that a classification will survive such scrutiny only under compelling circumstances. *Shaw v. Hunt*, 116 S. Ct. 1894 (1996) (hereafter cited as *Shaw II*).

The judicial reality, however, has been that strict in theory is fatal in fact. The majority's de facto acceptance of color blindness as constitutional doctrine is revealed in two ways. The first is Justice Sandra O'Connor's stated goal of "eliminat[ing]" governmental use of "racial stereotypes" and her apparent equating of racial stereotypes with the recognition of race. *Shaw I*, 509 U.S. at 647. See also *Bush v. Vera*, 116 S.Ct. 1941 (1996). The second, as Justice John Paul Stevens points out in his *Shaw II* dissent, is that the plaintiffs "claimed [a] violation of a shared [citizens'] right to a color-blind districting process" and that the claim emanates "from the Court's unarticulated recognition of a new substantive due process right to 'color-blind' districting itself." *Shaw II*, 116 S.Ct. at 1909–10 (Stevens, J., dissenting).

56. Alexandra Natapoff, "Trouble in Paradise: Equal Protection and the Dilemma of Interminority Group Conflict," 47 *Stan. L. Rev.* 1059, 1062 (1995); Selena Dong, "Too Many Asians": The Challenge of Fighting Discrimination against Americans and Preserving Affirmative Action," 47 *Stan. L. Rev.* 1027 (1995). Alexandra Natapoff traces the Supreme Court's treatment of interminority conflicts from *United Jewish Organizations of Williamsburgh v. Carey*, 430 U.S. 144 (1977), *Regents of University of California v. Bakke*, 438 U.S. 265 (1978), *City of Richmond v. J.A. Croson Co.*, 488 U.S. 469 (1989), *Shaw I*, 509 U.S. 630, through *Johnson v. De Grandy*, 114 U.S. 2647 (1994) to gain insight into "issues of race-based redistribution, political process, and intergroup conflict that seem to most concern the Court." Natapoff, "Trouble in Paradise," pp. 1065–79.

57. *Shaw*, 509 U.S. at 643.

58. The Court's recent rulings in *Adarand, Shaw I,* and *Croson* implicitly adopt this line of reasoning. For critique of the impact of the Court's de facto color-blindness rulings in these cases, see Thomas Ross, "The Richmond Narratives," 68 *Tex. L. Rev.* 381 (1989) (critiquing *Croson*); Morton J. Horwitz, "The Supreme Court, 1992 Term—Foreword: The Constitution of Change: Legal Fundamentality without Fundamentalism," 107 *Harv. L. Rev.* 30 (1993) (*Shaw*); Jen-L-Wong, "*Adarand Contractors, Inc. v. Pena*: A Color-Blind Remedy Eliminating Racial Preferences," 18 *U. Haw. L. Rev.* 939 (1996) (*Adarand*).

59. In 1989 Mari Matsuda suggested that race jurisprudence attend to differences in racial and ethnic groups in terms of power and political participation. See Mari J. Matsuda, "Public Response to Racist Speech: Considering the Victim's Story," 87 *Mich. L. Rev.* 2320, 2341 (1989). Of the recent articles addressing the topic, several were published in 1993 following the South Central Los Angeles uprising, with the remainder in 1995. See Yamamoto, "Rethinking Alliances"; Charles R. Lawrence III, "Foreword: Race, Multiculturalism, and the Jurisprudence of Transformation," 47 *Stan. L. Rev.* 1 (1995); Bill Ong Hing, "In the Interest of Racial Harmony: Revisiting the Lawyer's Duty to Work for the Common Good," 47 *Stan. L. Rev.* 910 (1995); Natapoff, "Trouble in Paradise"; Paul Brest and Miranda Oshige, "Affirmative Action for Whom?" 47 *Stan. L. Rev.* 855 (1995);

Deborah Ramirez, "Multicultural Empowerment: It's Not Just Black and White Anymore," 47 *Stan. L. Rev.* 957 (1995); Dong, " 'Too Many Asians,' "; Bill Ong Hing, "Beyond the Rhetoric of Assimilation and Cultural Pluralism: Addressing the Tension of Separatism and Conflict in an Immigration-Driven Multicultural Society," 81 *Cal. L. Rev.* 863 (1993); Ikemoto, "Traces of the Master Narrative"; Robinson, " 'The Other against Itself' "; Sumi K. Cho, "Korean Americans vs. African Americans: Conflict and Construction," in Robert Gooding-Williams, ed., *Reading Rodney King / Reading Urban Uprising* (1993), p. 196.

60. Natapoff, "Trouble in Paradise"; Ramirez, "Multicultural Empowerment"; Hing, "Racial Harmony"; Yamamoto, "Rethinking Alliances"; Robinson, " 'The Other against Itself.' "

61. See, for example, Lawrence, "Race, Multiculturalism."

62. Baum and Wells, *Reconciliation of Peoples*, p. vii.

63. See Margaret M. Russell, "De Jure Revolution?" 93 *Mich. L. Rev.* 1173, 1175 (1995) (calling for a "theoretics of practice" as part of critical race theory).

64. See Manning Marable, *Beyond Black and White: Transforming African American Politics* (1995); bell hooks, *Killing Rage: Ending Racism* (1995).

65. George M. Fredrickson, "Far from the Promised Land," *New York Review of Books*, April 18, 1996, pp. 16–18.


## Notes to Chapter 2

1. Harlon Dalton, *Racial Healing: Confronting the Fear between Blacks and Whites* (1995).

2. See Arthur Kleinman, *The Illness Narratives: Suffering, Healing and the Human Condition* (1989).

3. David Morris, *Culture of Pain* (1991).

4. Dalton, *Racial Healing*, p. 97 (quoting Frederick Douglass).

5. John Dawson, *Healing America's Wounds* (1995).

6. See Eric K. Yamamoto, "Race Apologies," 1 *Iowa J. Gender, Race & Just.* 47 (1997) (cataloging national and international trends of race apologies).

7. Courtland Milloy, "Texaco Taps a Deep Well of Racism," *Washington Post*, November 10, 1996, p. B01; Jeff Chang, "Race, Class, Conflict and Empowerment: On Ice Cube's 'Black Korea,' " *Amerasia Journal* 19 (1993): 87, 96–97.

8. Adrienne Knox, "Rutgers Acts to Upgrade Racial Ties," *Star Ledger*, June 10, 1995, p. 1.

9. Gary L. Carter, "Southern Baptist Convention Apologizes to Blacks for Its History of Racism," *Baltimore Sun*, June 21, 1995, p. 5D; Mary Rourke, "Lutherans and Jews Working Hard to Overcome," *Buffalo News*, July 15, 1995, p. A8; Greg Wiles, "Church Setting up Foundation for Hawaiians," *Honolulu Advertiser*, June 10, 1995, p. A1.

10. Jim Specht, "Clinton Signs Apology for Hawaii Overthrow," *Gannet News*

*Service*, November 23, 1993, p. 3; "Rosewood Survivors Finally Get Apology to Pay Rampage Victims," *News & Observer*, April 9, 1994, p. A5; Michael D'Orso, *Like Judgment Day: Ruin and Redemption of a Town Called Rosewood* (1996). See Yamamoto, "Race Apologies."

11. How are apology and reparation ceremonies structured? Chapters 8 through 11 offer detailed accounts. John Dawson's description of a Native American apology ceremony provides a preview. The "healing conference" was organized by the Reconciliation Coalition, created by Dawson and others to address racial healing for the Native American survivors of U.S. racial violence. The Northern Arapaho, Northern Cheyenne, and Kiowa nations participated. At the outset, a carefully researched statement itemized specific injustices. Representatives from groups responsible for violence then expressed their remorse and asked for forgiveness. A representative of the Denver mayor's office said, "I feel ashamed . . . on behalf of the Mayor and the City Council of Denver, I wish to extend my profound apologies for this legacy of lies, theft and death." According to Dawson, the responses to confessions were deeply moving. Native Americans had grown weary of grieving and yearned for resolution. Arnold Hedly, who represented the Northern Arapaho, said he had forgiven his oppressors and hoped for a harmonious future. Cheyenne Sylvester Knows-His-Gun suggested new beginnings, "Belatedly, we welcome you to Indian country. This great land belongs to all and we welcome you to this country" (Dawson, *Healing America's Wounds*, p. 155).

12. Peter Baker, "President May Consider Apology for Slavery," *Buffalo News*, June 16, 1997, p. A1.

13. *CNN Both Sides with Jesse Jackson* (CNN radio broadcast, June 22, 1997) (President Clinton).

14. "Congressmen Urge Apology for Slavery," *Baltimore Sun*, June 13, 1997, p. 9A.

15. *ABC Nightline* (ABC News television broadcast, June 18, 1997); *CNN Newsnight* (CNN television broadcast, June 22, 1997).

16. Patricia J. Williams, "Apologia Qua Amnesia," *The Nation*, July 14, 1997, p. 10.

17. Lori S. Robinson, "The Price of Slavery," *Honolulu Advertiser*, June 21, 1997, p. B1.

18. See Yamamoto, "Race Apologies," p. 6.

19. Eric K. Yamamoto, "Friend, Foe or Something Else: Social Meanings of Redress and Reparations," 20 *Denv. J. Intl. L. & Pol.* 223, 227 (1992).

20. D'Orso, *Like Judgment Day*, p. 322.

## Notes to Chapter 3

1. Initial Plan for Redress for the Hawai'i Conference UCC to Na Kanaka Maoli, 174th 'Aha Pae'aina, Central Union Church, June 10–15, 1996, "Chronology of Events," p. 2.

2. The Hawai'i Conference of the United Church of Christ is fairly described as multiracial. Church congregations in the conference reflect a diversity of races, and several individual churches identify their members as predominantly of a particular race and culture. The churches' race/ethnicity includes Japanese/Japanese American, Chinese American, Korean American, Samoan American, and Native Hawaiian, among others. Other churches have a predominantly white American membership. Interview with Rev. Wallace Ryan-Kuroiwa, senior pastor, Nu'uanu Congregational Church, in Honolulu, October 7, 1994.

3. Motion 5 of the 171st annual meeting of the Hawai'i Conference of the United Church of Christ: "A Vision of a New Day: Promoting Solidarity and Reconciliation through an Act of Apology," in *Ho'olokahi, 171st Aha Pae'aina*, June 15–19, 1993, Hawai'i Conference United Church of Christ, pp. 81–82 (hereafter cited as Asian American Apology Resolution). See also Andrew Walsh, "Congregational Influences in Hawaii (1820–1893)," pp. 37–40 (1993) (prepared for the president of United Church of Christ to evaluate the propriety of an apology).

4. Jeff Chang, "Lessons of Tolerance: Rethinking Race Relations, Ethnicity and the Local through Affirmative Action in Hawaii" (1994) unpublished paper.

5. Interview with Rev. Wallace Ryan Kuroiwa, senior pastor, Nu'uanu Congregational Church, Honolulu, June 16, 1993. Rev. Kuroiwa and attorney Arthur Goto were the principal drafters of the apology resolution. Rev. Kuroiwa later chaired the Hawai'i Conference's Task Force of Reparations, and Mr. Goto served as a member. Because of my legal work supporting Japanese American World War II internees, I was asked early on by the Asian American clergy group to review the draft apology-reparations resolution and contribute my views on the apology project. From 1996, as an associate conference minister of the Hawai'i Conference, my spouse, Joan Ishibashi, assisted the conference's Redress Implementation Committee.

6. Rev. Richard Kamanu, Transcript of Proceedings, 'Aha Pae'aina, June 19, 1993, Hawai'i Conference United Church of Christ (hereafter cited as Proceedings), p. 3. Several people presenting testimony similarly recounted these views.

7. Until 1997, the U.S. Census and other federal agency directives legally designated Asian Americans and Native Hawaiians as part of the same race—"Asian and Pacific Islander." In 1997 Native Hawaiians achieved recognition as a separate racial category—Native Hawaiian and Pacific Islander. See Lawrence Wright, "One Drop of Blood," *New Yorker*, July 25, 1994, p. 47.

8. Testimony of Dean Fujii (reading letter from Rev. Richard Wong), Proceedings, p. 5. The transcript of Rev. Wong's letter contains the phrase "invasion with Native Hawaiians." My sense, from my personal recollection and the context of the letter, is that the transcriber misheard the word *relations* and substituted *invasion*. The quotation in the text of this essay therefore substitutes *relations*, in brackets.

9. Rev. Kekapa Lee, Proceedings, p. 11.

10. Initial Plan for Redress of Hawai'i Conference UCC to Na Kanaka Maoli, 174th 'Aha Pae'aina, Central Union Church, June2010–15, 1996, "First Component: Redress by Conveyance of Land," pp. 9–12, and Exhibit A.

11. "Beyond our cultural difference, the legal history of Hawaiians places us in a separate category from that of immigrants to Hawai'i. Hawaiians are the only people who have legal and historical rights to lands in Hawai'i based on aboriginal occupation." Haunani-Kay Trask, "Coalition-Building Building Natives and Non-Natives," 43 *Stan. L. Rev.* 1197, 1205–6 (1991).

12. These concepts are discussed in more detail in chapter 5. See also George Cooper and Gavan Daws, *Land and Power in Hawaii* (1985) (depicting second-generation Japanese Americans and third- and fourth-generation Chinese Americans' use of state government positions and rhetoric of land reform to acquire wealth through often surreptitious land transactions and developments); Eric K. Yamamoto, "Rethinking Alliances: Agency, Responsibility and Interracial Justice," 3 *Asian Pac. Am. L. J.* 33, 48 (1995).

13. Trask, "Coalition-Building," p. 1205.

14. Michael Haas, *Institutional Racism: The Case of Hawai'i* (1992), pp. 2, 111–12.

15. Cooper and Daws, *Land and Power*, p. 428 (quoting Rev. Akaka's opposition to the Hawai'i Land Reform Act).

16. Kim Muranaka, "Merit-Based Waiver, Not Backhanded Gift," *Ka Leo o Hawai'i*, August 25, 1993, p. 4.

17. In recounting these stories, I am writing through the lens of my own cultural heritage and experience. My grandparents emigrated from Japan to Hawai'i in the early 1900s to work on the plantations. I thus am a third-generation Japanese American, or *sansei*. My experiences and those of my ancestors in Hawai'i differ, therefore, from those of many Native Hawaiians.

18. *A Broken Trust*, Report of the Hawaii Advisory Committee to the United States Commission on Civil Rights (1991), p. 29 (citing Hawaiian Homes Update Forum, Honolulu, September 6, 1988, pp. 153–55).

19. Lilikala Kame'eleihiwa, *Native Land and Foreign Desires — Pehea la e Pono Ai?* (1992), pp. 23–32.

20. Davianna Pomaika'i McGregor, *Pele vs. Geothermal: A Clash of Cultures* (1990), pp. 3–4; Linda S. Parker, *Native American Estate: Struggle over Indian and Hawaiian Lands* (1989), pp. 8–10.

21. See Walsh, "Congregational Influences"; Melody McKenzie, ed., *Native Hawaiian Rights Handbook* (1991), p. 12, citing Kuykendall, *The Hawaiian Kingdom 1874–1893* (1967), p. 608. See also Neil M. Levy, "Native Hawaiian Land Rights," 63 *Cal. L. Rev.* 848, 861–66 (1975).

22. *A Broken Trust*, p. 17; Susan C. Faludi, "Broken Promise: How Everyone Got Hawaiians' Homelands except Hawaiians," *Wall Street Journal*, September 9, 1991, p. A-2.

23. *A Broken Trust*, p. 39.

24. Native Hawaiians Study Commission, *Report on the Culture, Needs, and Concerns of Native Hawaiians* (1983), pp. 102–4.

25. See Michael Kioni Dudley and Keoni Kealoha Agard, *A Hawaiian Nation II: A Call for Hawaiian Sovereignty* (1990), p. 117, and *He Alo a He Alo: Face to Face, Hawaiian Voices on Sovereignty* (1993), p. 167.

26. See Haunani-Kay Trask, *From a Native Daughter: Colonialism and Sovereignty in Hawaii* (1993), pp. 31–32.

27. Act of March 18, 1959, Pub. L. No. 86-3, 73 Stat. 4, as amended by Act of July 12, 1960, Pub. L. No. 86-624, subsec. 41, 74 Stat. 422; Haw. Const. Art. XII, secs. 1 and 2.

28. See *A Broken Trust*,; Office of State Planning, *Report on Federal Breaches of the Hawaiian Home Lands Trust, Part I* (1992); *Federal-State Task Force Report on the Hawaiian Homes Commission Act* (1983).

29. Eric K. Yamamoto, Moses Haia, and Donna Kalama, "Courts and the Cultural Performance: Native Hawaiians' Uncertain Federal and State Law Rights to Sue," 16 *U. Haw. L. Rev.* 1 (1993).

30. *A Broken Trust*, p. 29 (quoting Alice Zenger).

31. *Morton v. Mancari*, 417 U.S. 535 (1974); *Rice v. Cayetano*, 963 F. Supp. 1547 (Haw. 1997); Jon Van Dyke, "The Constitutionality of the Office of Hawaiian Affairs," 7 *U. Haw. L. Rev.* 63 (1985). But see Stuart Minor Benjamin, "Equal Protection and the Special Relationship: The Case of Native Hawaiians," 106 *Yale L. J.* 537 (1996).

32. The memorandum claimed to "expressly overrule" an August 27, 1979, Interior Department opinion finding a trust relationship between the United States and Native Hawaiians pursuant to the Hawaiian Homes Commission Act. Thomas L. Sansonetti, solicitor, U.S. Department of the Interior, "The Scope of Federal Responsibility for Native Hawaiians under the Hawaiian Homes Commission Act," January 19, 1993, p. 2.

33. Grover Cleveland, *Intervention of U.S. Government in Affairs of Foreign Friendly Governments*, Message to Congress, December 18, 1893, U.S. Congress House Report No. 243, 53rd Cong., 2d sess., December 21, 1893 ("The military occupation of Honolulu by the United States . . . was wholly without justification").

34. Senate Joint Resolution 335, *Senate Congressional Record*, S177346-47 (1992).

35. *Pele Defense Fund v. Paty*, 837 P.2d 1247 (Haw. 1992); *Public Access Shoreline Hawai'i v. Nansay, Inc.*, 900 P.2d 1313 (Haw. 1993).

36. Haas, *Institutional Racism*, p. 248.

37. Jonathan Y. Okamura, "Why There Are No Asian Americans in Hawaii: The Continuing Significance of Local Identity," 135 *Social Process in Hawaii* 161, 172–73 (1994).

38. Ibid. p. 172 (citing Franklin Odo, "The Rise and Fall of the Nisei," *Hawaii Herald*, August–November 1984 [describing this myth]).

39. See generally Bill Ong Hing, *Making and Remaking Asian America through Immigration Policy 1850 to 1990* (1993).

40. Yamamoto, "Rethinking Alliances," p. 52, n. 118.

## Notes to Chapter 4

1. Sally Falk Moore, "Treating Law as Knowledge: Telling Colonial Officers What to Say to Africans about Running 'Their Own' Native Courts," 26 *Law & Soc. L. Rev.* 11, 43 (1992).

2. "Anti-Asian Sentiment on the Rise: Group Finds Hate Crimes in Region Increased 113%," *San Jose Mercury News*, August 3, 1995, p. 3B.

3. See Derrick Bell, *Faces at the Bottom of the Well: The Permanence of Racism* (1992); Thomas Byrne Edsall and Mary D. Edsall, *Chain Reaction: The Impact of Race, Rights, and Taxes on American Politics* (1992); Douglas Massey and Nancy A. Denton, *American Apartheid: Segregation and the Making of the Underclass* (1993).

4. Dinesh D'Souza, *The End of Racism* (1995).

5. Martha Minow, "Partial Justice," in Martha Minow and Austin Sarat, eds., *The Fate of Law* (1991), p. 17 (observing "shifting alignments" and "new debates about rights, about the rule of law, about foundations for belief and the nature of truth, and about the relations between individuals and society"). See also Kwame Anthony Appiah and Henry Louis Gates Jr., "Editors' Introduction: Multiplying Identities," in Kwame Anthony Appiah and Henry Louis Gates Jr., eds., *Identities* (1995); Roy L. Brooks, *Integration or Segregation: A Strategy for Racial Equality* (1996).

6. Bill Ong Hing, "Beyond the Rhetoric of Assimilation and Cultural Pluralism: Addressing the Tension of Separatism and Conflict in an Immigration-Driven Multiracial Society," 81 *Calif. L. Rev.* 863 (1993).

7. Richard Herrnstein and Charles Murray, *The Bell Curve Intelligence and Class Structure in American Life* (1994); Thomas Sowell, *Civil Rights: Rhetoric or Reality?* (1984).

8. Andrew Hacker, *Two Nations: Black and White, Separate, Hostile, Unequal* (1992). See K. Anthony Appiah, "Identity, Authenticity, Survival: Multicultural Societies and Social Reproduction," in Amy Guttman and Charles Taylor, eds., *Multiculturalism: Examining the Politics of Recognition* (1994).

9. Empirical studies conclude that "middle-class blacks continue, despite affirmative action, to suffer from racial discrimination. Far from being paranoid or oversensitive, they are in fact more likely to encounter face-to-face prejudice and unfair treatment than are lower-class African Americans" who are less likely to have troubling contacts with white competitors or superiors. Jennifer Hochschild, *Facing up to the American Dream: Race, Class and the Soul of Nation* (1995), p. 42;

Joe R. Feagin and Melvin P. Sikes, *Living with Racism: The Black Middle-Class Experience* (1994); Rodolfo F. Acuna, *Anything but Mexican: Chicanos in Contemporary Los Angeles* (1996); Hing, "Beyond the Rhetoric."

10. Fred L. Pincus and Howard J. Ehrlich, "The Study of Race and Ethnic Relations," in Fred L. Pincus and Howard J. Ehrlich, eds., *Race and Ethnic Conflict* (1994), p. 3.

11. For insight into coalition problems and possibilities among communities of color, see K. Anthony Appiah and Amy Guttman, *Color Conscious: The Political Morality of Race* (1996); Eric K. Yamamoto, "Rethinking Alliances: Agency, Responsibility and Interracial Justice," 3 *UCLA Asian Pac. Am. L. J.* 221 (1995); James Jennings, ed., *Blacks, Latinos, and Asians in Urban America* (1994). Also part of that landscape are the scholarly critiques of and political efforts to build economic power by racial minorities. See William Julius Wilson, *The Truly Disadvantaged: The Inner City, the Underclass and Public Policy* (1987); Martin Carnoy, *Faded Dreams: The Politics and Economics of Race in America* (1994); Cornel West, *Race Matters* (1993); Hochschild, *Facing up to the American Dream*.

12. *R.A.V. v. City of St. Paul*, 505 U.S. 377 (1992).

13. Iris Marion Young, *Justice and the Politics of Difference* (1991), p. 39.

14. Ibid. p. 41.

15. Mari J. Matsuda et al., *Words That Wound: Critical Race Theory, Assaultive Speech, and the First Amendment* (1993), p. 5.

16. Steven Gregory, "Race, Rubbish, and Resistance: Empowering Difference in Community Politics," in Steven Gregory and Roger Sanjeki, eds., *Race* (1994).

17. U.S. Commission on Civil Rights, *Racism in America and How to Combat It*, Clearinghouse Publication, Urban Series No. 1, January 1970, p. 2.

18. Hochschild, *Facing up to the American Dream* (quoting U.S. Department of Labor report).

19. Edward Barnes, "Can't Get There from Here," *Time*, February 19, 1996, p. 33.

20. Ibid. (quoting Warren Galloway, head of Buffalo's Operation Push).

21. Ibid. pp. 37–38. I combine Young's use of oppression (the inhibition of group self-development) and domination (the inhibition of group self-determination) and call that combination *oppression*.

22. Ibid. pp. 58–59, 62. According to Young, these grievances and their consequences are revealed in five concrete ways. Exploitation (profit making by owners off the labor of unfairly treated workers), marginalization (exclusion from the system of labor), and powerlessness (lack of participation in decisions affecting conditions of daily existence) are three. These occur by virtue of the social divisions of labor and adversely affect group self-development and self-determination. Cultural imperialism (the "universalization of a dominant group's experience and culture, and its establishment as the norm") and systemic violence ("violence . . . directed at members of a group simply because they are members

of that group") are the other two. When combined, they lead to cultural domination.

23. Robert J. C. Young, *Colonial Desire: Hybridity in Theory, Culture and Race* (1995), p. 54.

24. Robert Post, ed., *Law and the Order of Culture* (1991), p. vii. See also Guyora Binder, "Beyond Criticism," 55 *U. Chi. L. Rev.* 888, 906 (1988).

25. John O. Calmore, "Critical Race Theory, Archie Shepp, and Fire Music: Securing an Authentic Intellectual Life in a Multicultural World," 65 *S. Cal. L. Rev.* 2129, 2182–83 (1992), quoting Clifford Geertz, *The Interpretation of Cultures* (1973), p. 89. See also Renato Rosaldo, *Culture and Truth: The Remaking of Social Analysis* (1989), p. 26.

26. Adeno Addis, "Individualism, Communitarianism, and the Rights of Ethnic Minorities," 67 *Notre Dame L. Rev.* 615, 658 (1992).

27. Susan K. Serrano, "Rethinking Race for Strict Scrutiny Purposes: Yniguez and the Racialization of English Only," 19 *U. Haw. L. Rev.* 221 (1997).

28. Susan Orenstein, "Affirmative Action in the Negative," *California Lawyer* 46, 48 (August 1995).

29. Charles Lawrence III, "The Id, the Ego, and Equal Protection: Reckoning with Unconscious Racism," 39 *Stan. L. Rev.* 317, 323 (1987). See also Jody David Armour, *Negrophobia and Reasonable Racism* (1997) (examining unconscious racism against African Americans).

30. 174 F. 834 (C.C.D. 1909).

31. Linda Hamilton Krieger, "The Content of Our Categories: A Cognitive Bias Approach to Discrimination and Equal Employment Opportunity," 47 *Stan. L. Rev.* 1161, 1187–89, 1199 (1995).

32. David A. Wilder, "Perceiving Persons as a Group: Categorization and Intergroup Relations," in David L. Hamilton, ed., *Cognitive Processes in Stereotyping and Intergroup Behavior* (1981), p. 213.

33. Krieger, "The Content of Our Categories," p. 1192.

34. Albert Memmi, *The Colonizer and the Colonized* (1965).

## Notes to Chapter 5

1. Martha Minow, *Making All the Difference* (1991), p. 173 (suggesting a social relations approach to understanding the construction of difference among social groups).

2. Motion 5 of the 171st annual meeting of the Hawai'i Conference of the United Church of Christ: "A Vision of a New Day: Promoting Solidarity and Reconciliation through an Act of Apology" (hereafter cited as "Asian American Resolution"), in Lokahi 171st Aha Pae'Aina, June 15–19, 1993, Hawai'i Conference United Church of Christ, pp. 81–82.

3. Reginald Leamon Robinson, " 'The Other against Itself': Deconstructing the

Violent Discourse between Korean and African Americans," 67 *S. Cal. L. Rev.* 15 (1993); Selena Dong, " 'Too Many Asians': The Challenge of Fighting Discrimination against Asian Americans and Preserving Affirmative Action," 47 *Stan. L. Rev.* 1027, 1031 (1995); "California Immigrants Fear Hatred Set Free by Prop. 187," *Honolulu Star Bulletin*, December 12, 1994, p. A9.

4. Jeff Chang, "Lessons of Tolerance: Rethinking Race Relations, Ethnicity and the Local through Affirmative Action in Hawaii," 1, 12 (1994) (paper presented at the annual meeting of the Association for Asian American Studies).

5. Susan Stanford Friedman, "Beyond White and Other: Relationality and Narratives of Race in Feminist Discourse," *Signs* 3 (Autumn 1995): 33.

6. Ibid. pp. 2, 3, 28; Michael Omi and Howard Winant, "On the Theoretical Status of the Concept of Race," in Cameron McCarthy and Warren Crichlow, eds., *Race, Identity and Representation in Education* (1993), p. 7.

7. Michael Omi and Howard Winant, *Racial Formation in the United States,* 2d ed. (1994), pp. 19–60.

8. See Nathan Glazer and Daniel Patrick Moynihan, *Beyond the Melting Pot: The Negroes, Puerto Ricans, Jews, Italians and Irish of New York City,* 2d ed. (1970).

9. In its neoconservative form, reworked ethnicity theory is rooted in the "European immigrant analogy"—a belief that immigrants of color face identical circumstances faced earlier by white European immigrants and that success or failure at assimilation can be attributed to internal group traits. Omi and Winant, *Racial Formation,* p. 21; Ian Haney-Lopez, "The Social Construction of Race: Some Observations on Illusion, Fabrication, and Choice," 29 *Harv. C.R.–C.L. L. Rev.* 1, 21–24 (1994) (criticizing ethnicity theory's employment of the immigrant analogy and its de-emphasis on racial barriers).

10. Mary C. Waters, *Ethnic Options* (1993), pp. 156, 158 ("Whites with a symbolic ethnicity [such as Italian American] are unable to understand the everyday influence and importance of skin color and racial minority status").

11. Dinesh D'Souza, *The End of Racism: Principles for a Multiracial America* (1995).

12. Richard Herrnstein and Charles Murray, *The Bell Curve: Intelligence and Class Structure in American Life* (1994) (attributing differences in intelligence among racial groups, measured by IQ tests, to genetic differences).

13. George M. Fredrickson, "Demonizing the American Dilemma," *New York Review of Books,* October 19, 1995, pp. 10, 12 (reviewing D'Souza's *The End of Racism*).

14. Robert Blauner, *Racial Oppression in America* (1972), pp. 83–85.

15. Robert Blauner, a strong proponent of internal colonialization theory in the 1970s, linked third world peoples with racial minorities in the United States and described American internal colonialism in terms of American conquest and hegemony over racial groups within North American borders. See ibid., p. 12.

16. Omi and Winant, *Racial Formation,* pp. 36–47 (the nation-based paradigm

retains an "explanatory framework based on race" but addresses racial formation issues inadequately through a "distorted 'national' lens"); Haunani-Kay Trask, *From a Native Daughter: Colonialism and Sovereignty in Hawaii* (1993); Gary Peller, "Race Consciousness," 1990 *Duke L. J.* 758 (1990) (describing African American nationalism movements).

17. Edna Bonacich, "A Theory of Middlemen Minorities," 38 *Amer. Soc. Rev.* 583 (1973).

18. Robinson, " 'The Other against Itself,' " pp. 73, 110.

19. Richard H. McAdams, "Cooperation and Conflict: The Economics of Group Status Production," 108 *Harv. L. Rev.* 1003, 1029, 1077 (1995) (breaking from traditional law and economic analyses of race discrimination to account for status-production values and impacts).

20. Pat Chew, "Asian Americans: The "Reticent" Minority and Their Paradoxes," 36 *Wm. and Mary L. Rev.* 1 (1994). In a national survey, 46 percent of the Asian Americans polled indicated that they personally had experienced serious discrimination.

21. Lisa Ikemoto, "Traces of the Master Narrative in the Story of African American / Korean American Conflict: How We Constructed 'Los Angeles,' " 66 *S. Cal. L. Rev.* 1581 (1993).

22. See generally Patrick Williams and Laura Chrisman, eds., *Colonial Discourse and Post-Colonial Theory* (1994), pp. 1–20. See Trask, *Native Daughter*, p. 133 (describing neocolonialism as a "continuing Western influence, located in flexible combinations of the economic, the political, the military and the ideological (but with an over-riding economic purpose").

23. The term *postcolonial* thus has two main meanings. *Post-colonial*, with a hyphen, is used to denote time, space, and structure—that is, a formerly colonized society that has been decolonized or is in the process of formal decolonization. *Postcolonial*, with or without the hyphen, is also used to describe "the critique of colonialist knowledge and representation of subject populations." Postcolonial theory in this sense is a critique of largely Western European methods of knowledge production and cultural representation concerning colonized "others," methods that not only excluded those others from participation in the colonial polity as subjects but also supported external control over foreign territories. Vijay Mishra and Bob Hodge, "What Is Post(-)Colonialism?" in Patrick Williams and Laura Chrisman, eds., *Colonial Discourse and Post-Colonial Theory* 276 (1994) (" 'Post-colonial' thus becomes something which is 'post' or after colonial"); Edward Said, *Orientalism* (1978) (pathbreaking discourse analysis of occidental West creation of the "orient"); Edward Said, *Culture and Imperialism* (1994) (describing the continuing effects of Western imperialism through cultural oppression); Patrick Williams and Laura Chrisman, "Colonial Discourse and Post-Colonial Theory: An Introduction," in their *Colonial Discourse and Post-Colonial Theory*, p. 2. ("Colonial discourse analysis and post-colonial theory are

thus critiques of the process of production of knowledge about the Other"). But see Bernard Lewis, *Islam and the West* (1993) (criticizing Said's notion of an "invented" orient); Aijaz Ahmad, *In Theory* (1992) (criticizing Said's over-simplification of the dichotomy of East and West).

24. See Michel Foucault, *Madness and Civilization* (1961) (connecting discourse with power); Said, *Orientalism* (using Foucault's discourse theory of power to analyze "orientalism"); Ngugi wa Thiong'o, "The Language of African Literature," in Williams and Chrisman, *Colonial Discourse and Post-Colonial Theory*, p. 435; Sara Suleri, "Woman Skin Deep: Feminism and the Postcolonial Condition," *Critical Inquiry* 18 (1992): 756; Gayatri Chakravorty Spivak, "Who Claims Alterity?" in Barbara Kruger and Phil Marian, eds., *Remaking History* (1989). Compare Anne McClintock, *The Angel of Progress: Pitfalls of the Term "Post-Colonialism"* (1992), p. 294 (observing that the misuse of the concept of postcolonialism results in disguising structures of colonialism and warning about scholars' focus on time rather on power in defining postcolonial).

25. Frederick Cooper, "Conflict and Connection: Rethinking Colonial African History," *American Historical Review* 99 (1994): 1519, 1533, 1540.

26. Rey Chow, *Writing Diaspora: Tactics of Intervention in Contemporary Cultural Studies* (1993), pp. 16–17.

27. Lisa Lowe, "Heterogeneity, Hybridity, Multiplicity: Marking Asian American Differences," *Diaspora* 1 (1991): 24, 31.

28. Ibid. pp. 29–31, discussing Frantz Fanon, *The Wretched of the Earth*, trans. Constance Farrington (1963) (Algerian resistance to French colonialism).

29. Michael Lerner and Cornel West, *Jews and Blacks* (1995), p. 9 (quoting and interpreting a passage from the Torah and citing Freud's use of the repetition compulsion idea). In the Torah's "do not oppress as you are oppressed" injunction, Lerner sees the challenge and possibility of healing and genuine transformation, citing Jews' newfound safety in America and a concomitant new responsibility for addressing the struggles of African Americans.

30. Martha Minow, *Not Only for Myself: Identity, Politics and Law* (1997), pp. 53, 54 (citing Margaret Beale Spender, Michael Cunningham, and Dean Phillips Swanton, "Identity as Coping: Adolescent African American Male's Adaptive Responses to High Risk Environments," in Herbert W. Harris, Howard C. Blue, and Ezra E. H. Griffith, eds., *Racial and Ethnic Identity: Psychological Development and Creative Expression* (1995), pp. 31, 49.

31. Early postcolonial theory appeared both to celebrate the agency of those colonized—their politics constituted an "autonomous domain"—and to deny its existence—"They cannot represent themselves; they must be represented." Ranajit Guha, "On Some Aspects of the Historiography of Colonial India," *Subaltern Studies* 1 (1982): 3. More recent work, however, recognizes a limited, or constrained, form of agency. The subordinated can "speak" and thereby at least partially define themselves in relation to dominant powers and other groups, but

only through cracks in the dominant discourse and often only in fractured, oppositional ways. Gayatri Spivak, "Can the Subaltern Speak?" in Cary Nelson and Lawrence Grossberg, eds., *Marxism and the Interpretation of Culture* (1988) (positing a minimalist or nonexistent voice of the subordinated in traditional discourse but recognizing a capacity for ad hoc rewriting of social texts through calculated acts of resistance); Gyan Prakash, "Subaltern Studies as Postcolonial Criticism," *American Historical Review* 99 (1994): 1475; Williams and Chrisman, *Colonial Discourse and Post-Colonial Theory*, p. 4.

32. Haney-Lopez, "The Social Construction of Race," p. 47.

33. Postcolonial theory is susceptible to criticism on the grounds that its focus on the colonialist cultural representations of colonial subjects and on the resistance by those subjects tends to ignore the dynamics of intergroup power (and conflict) among nondominant groups, or the exercise of agency in intergroup relations. Postcolonial theory may also be susceptible to the related criticism that it is insufficiently attentive to the salience and complexity of racial difference. Postcolonial theory, like colonialism and nationalism theories, tends to homogenize racial groups, focusing on common oppression by white-controlled social and political structures. Finally, as insufficiently attentive to intergroup power and racial differentiation, postcolonial theory may be criticized for underdeveloping notions of racial group responsibility in the exercise of intergroup power.

34. Trina Grillo and Stephanie Wildman, "Obscuring the Importance of Race: The Implication of Making Comparisons between Racism and Sexism (or Other -isms)," 1991 *Duke L. J.* 397 (1991). See also Martha R. Mahoney, "Whiteness and Women, in Practice and Theory: A Reply to Catharine MacKinnon," 5 *Yale J. L. & Feminism* 217 (1993) (critiquing Catharine MacKinnon's responses to charges of gender essentialism); Catharine MacKinnon, "From Practice to Theory, or What Is a White Woman Anyway?" 4 *Yale J. L. & Feminism* 13 (1991).

Grillo and Wildman warn that the use of suffix "-isms" to describe forms of subordination (sexism, racism) creates the illusion that all patterns of domination are the same. The danger, according to Grillo and Wildman, is that "someone subordinated under one form may feel no need to view himself/herself as a possible oppressor, or beneficiary of oppression, within a different form. For example, white women, having an-ism that defines their condition—sexism, may not look at the way they are privileged by racism. They have defined themselves as one of the oppressed." Grillo and Wildman, "Obscuring the Importance of Race," p. 34.

35. Mahoney, "Whiteness and Women," pp. 222, 230.

36. Ibid., p. 230. Feminist scholars have addressed the question of women's agency outside the context of race. See, for example, Kathryn Abrams, "Ideology and Women's Choices," 24 *Ga. L. Rev.* 761 (1990); Lucinda Finley, "The Nature of Domination and the Nature of Women: Reflections on Feminism Unmodified,"

82 *NW. U. L. Rev.* 352 (1988); Stephanie M. Wildman, "The Power of Women," 2 *Yale J. L. & Feminism* 435 (1990); Christine A. Littleton, *"Feminist Jurisprudence: The Difference Method Makes,"* 41 *Stan. L. Rev.* 727 (1989).

37. Mahoney, "Whiteness and Women," p. 247. See Angela P. Harris, "Race and Essentialism in Feminist Legal Theory," 42 *Stan. L. Rev.* 581 (1990); Marlee Kline, "Race, Racism and Feminist Legal Theory," 12 *Harv. Women's L. J.* 11 (1989); Elizabeth Spelman, *Inessential Woman: Problems of Exclusion in Feminist Thought* (1988).

38. Patricia Hill Collins, *Black Feminist Thought* (1991), pp. 225–26.

39. Friedman, "Beyond White and Other," p. 5.

40. Thomas Wartenberg, *Forms of Power: From Domination to Transformation* (1990). An "agent" or social actor refers to either an individual or a group "capable of performing actions" (p. 76). My focus is on group agency. "Central agents" means the two or more agents directly involved in a relationship. The term *central* distinguishes the agents of the focal relationship from "outside agents," or agents outside the central relationship who exert influence on it. Within the central relationship, I term one agent the *first* agent and the other the *second* (or *third*, etc.) agent. The terms *first* and *second* agent imply some differential racial status and power between agents. I do not use terms such as "dominant and subordinate" agents, as Wartenberg does, because those terms presuppose a relationship of domination. Whether a relationship of differential status and power, often shifting and changing, is one of domination, and therefore warrants some form of reformation and possibly rectification, is the focus of inquiry, not its premise.

Finally, the term *field* has special meaning. Wartenberg compares a social field with a magnetic field whose reality "lies in its alteration of the space surrounding the magnet in such a way that the motion of any susceptible object is affected" (p. 74). The mere presence of an agent with power alters the social space for acting occupied by other agents.

41. Ibid. pp. 141–45, 148.

42. Ibid. p. 164.

43. Omi and Winant, *Racial Formation*, p. 55.

44. Michael Omi, "Out of the Melting Pot and into the Fire: Race Relations Policy," in *The State of Asian America: Policy Issues to the Year 2020* (1993), p. 203.

45. See Yen Espiritu, *Asian American Pan-Ethnicity* (1992). See also Howard Winant, *Racial Conditions* (1994), p. 59.

46. Omi, "Out of the Melting Pot," pp. 203, 207.

47. Chew, "Asian Americans," p. 26. Chew also cites other "variables including religion, age, socioeconomic status, occupation, place of residence in their country of origin and in the United States, and reason for immigration" (p. 26).

48. Trask, *Native Daughter*, pp. 24, 96 (describing Native Hawaiian demands for self-determination).

49. Jeff Chang, "Race, Class, Conflict and Empowerment: On Ice Cube's 'Black Korea,' " *Amerasia. J.* 19 (1993): 87, 102–3.

50. Robert Stauffer, "Real Politics," *Honolulu Weekly*, October 19, 1994, p. 4. See also Michael Haas, *Institutional Racism: The Case of Hawaii* (1993), p.18.

51. Trask, *Native Daughter*, p. 77 (Hawai'i's constitution requires that the beneficiaries of Hawaiian homelands and ceded lands trusts have at least 50 percent Hawaiian blood).

52. "Asian American Resolution," pp. 81–82.

53. Chang, "Black Korea." See also Eric K. Yamamoto, "Friend, Foe or Something Else: Social Meanings of Redress and Reparations," 20 *Denv. J. Int'l L. & Pol'y* 223, 232 (1992).

54. Cornel West, "Black Leadership and the Pitfalls of Racial Reasoning," in Toni Morrison, ed., *Race-ing Justice, En-Gendering Power: Essays on Anita Hill, Clarence Thomas, and the Construction of Social Reality* (1992), pp. 396–97. See also Cornel West, *Race Matters* (1993), pp. 28–29 (describing "prophetic moral reasoning"); Anthony E. Cook, "Beyond Critical Legal Studies: The Reconstructive Theology of Dr. Martin Luther King Jr.," 103 *Harv. L. Rev.* 985 (1990).

55. Ken Adelman, "The Drama of Rectifying History," *San Diego Union and Tribune*, April 6, 1994, p. B6 (quoting Havel).

56. Charles R. Lawrence III, "The Id, the Ego, and Equal Protection: Reckoning with Unconscious Racism," 39 *Stan. L. Rev.* 317, 325–26 (1987).

57. John Dawson, *Healing America's Wounds* (1995), p. 30.

58. Stephanie M. Wildman and Adrienne D. Davis, "Language and Silence: Making Systems of Privilege Visible," 35 *Santa Clara L. Rev.* 881 (1995).

59. Dawson, *Healing America's Wounds*, pp. 150, 224, 230.

## Notes to Chapter 6

1. Robert A. Williams Jr., Keynote Address, Western Law Teachers of Color Conference, La Jolla, Calif., March 1996; Robert A. Williams Jr., "Vampires Anonymous and Critical Race Practice," 95 *Mich. L. Rev.* 741 (1997).

2. Gerald P. Lopez, *Rebellious Lawyering: One Chicano's Vision of Progressive Law Practice* (1992).

3. Luke Cole, "Empowerment as the Key to Environmental Protection: The Need for Environmental Poverty Law," 19 *Eco. L. Q.* 619, 648, 654 (1992).

4. Eric K. Yamamoto, "Critical Race Praxis: Race Theory and Political Lawyering Practice in Post–Civil Rights America," 95 *Mich. L. Rev.* 821 (1997).

5. E. Allan Lind and Tom R. Tyler, *The Social Psychology of Procedural Justice* (1988).

6. Critical theory, broadly described, produces four inquiries. The "critical" dimension to the inquiry demands critical social analysis: (1) the recognition that existing social identities and arrangements are not necessarily rational, natural or

inevitable, thus offering possibilities for social action for subordinated groups; (2) an account of the historical and cultural conditions that shape the point of view of social actors, thus acknowledging that actors may be differently situated and have differing vantage points from which they view the social world; (3) an examination of power and societal structures (political, economic, religious, social), thereby illuminating the connections between power and the construction of knowledge and between the use of knowledge and oppression or liberation; and (4) the scrutiny of social meanings attached to dynamic categories (such as race, African American, equality) and frameworks (such as legal liberalism, neoconservatism, Marxism), thereby recognizing ways that context imbues categories and frameworks with social significance and linking individuals and groups to social structures. See generally Craig Calhoun, *Critical Social Theory* (1995); Mari J. Matsuda et al., *Words That Wound: Critical Race Theory and the First Amendment* (1993) , p. 7 (describing key aspects of critical race theory).

7. See Cass R. Sunstein, *Legal Reasoning and Political Conflict* (1996) (describing legal reasoning as it is practiced).

8. The ways in which legal theorists, for example, can engage are varied, including advising political organizations; litigating or consulting with litigation teams; supervising law students challenging institutional actions; lobbying legislative and administrative bodies on behalf of specific organizations; cultivating relations with journalists covering community justice issues; writing op-ed essays; writing critical sociolegal analyses on specific issues for organizational newsletters; drafting legal briefs; doing legal historical research for community groups; training lay lawyers; and giving issue and strategy presentations to community groups.

9. Michael Omi and Howard Winant, *Racial Formation in the United States* (1994), p. 72 (describing racial formation as having representational and social structural components).

10. Rev. Robin Petersen and Lou Ann Parsons, *United Church Board for World Ministries, See-Judge-Act: Pastoral Planning for a Prophetic Church* (1993), pp. 5, 22–27, 32–35.

11. See Richard Rorty, *Contingency, Irony, and Solidarity* (1989); Cornel West, *Prophetic Pragmatism* (1988); Cornel West, *The American Evasion of Philosophy* (1990); Margaret Jane Radin, "The Pragmatist and the Feminist," 63 *S. Cal. L. Rev.* 1699 (1990). Martha Minow and Elizabeth Spelman, "In Context," 63 *S. Cal. L. Rev.* 1597 (1990); Joseph William Singer, "Property and Coercion in Federal Indian Law: The Conflict between Critical and Complacent Pragmatism," 63 *S. Cal. L. Rev.* 1821 (1990). For an insightful treatment of a "realistic approach to sociolegal theory," see Brian Z. Tamanaha, *Realistic Socio-Legal Theory: Pragmatism and a Social Theory of Law* (1997).

12. See, for example, Richard A. Posner, "Legislation and Its Interpretation: A Primer," 68 *New. L. Rev.* 431 (1989); Richard A. Posner, "What Has Pragmatism to Offer Law?" 63 *S. Cal. L. Rev.* 1653 (1990).

13. Steven Walt, "Some Problems of Pragmatic Jurisprudence," 70 *Tex. L. Rev.* 317, 330–31 (1991).

14. Mari J. Matsuda, "Pragmatism Modified and the False Consciousness Problem," 63 *S. Cal. L. Rev.* 1763, 1768 (1990).

15. Paulo Freire, *Pedagogy of Oppressed* (1974), p. 52.

16. Phillip Berryman, *Liberation Theology* (1987), pp. 5–7, 86.

17. Lucinda M. Finley, "Breaking Women's Silence in Law: The Dilemma of the Gendered Nature of Legal Reasoning," 64 *Notre Dame L. Rev.* 886, 888 (1989); Deborah L. Rhode and Martha Minow, "Reforming the Questions, Questioning the Reforms: Feminist Perspectives on Divorce Law," in Stephen D. Sugarman and Herma Hill Kay, eds., *Divorce Reform at the Crossroads* (1990); Deborah Maranville, "Feminist Theory and Legal Practice: A Case Study on Unemployment Compensation Benefits and the Male Norm," 43 *Hastings L. J.* 1081 (1992); Amy E. Hirsch, "Income Deeming in the AFDC Program: Using Dual Track Family Law to Make Poor Women Poorer," 16 *N.Y.U. Rev. L. & Soc. Change* 713 (1988-89).

18. Elizabeth Schneider, "The Dialectic of Rights and Politics: Perspectives from the Women's Movement," 61 *N.Y.U. L. Rev.* 589 (1986); Vicki Schultz, "Telling Stories about Women and Work: Judicial Interpretations of Sex Segregation in the Workplace in Title VII Cases Raising the Lack of Interest Argument," 103 *Harv. L. Rev.* 1749 (1990); Mary Jane Mossman, "Feminism and Legal Method: The Difference It Makes," in Martha A. Fineman and Nancy S. Thomadsen, eds., *At the Boundaries of Law* (1991), p. 283; Trina Grillo, "The Mediation Alternative: Process Dangers for Women," 100 *Yale L. J.* 1545 (1991).

19. Cole, "Empowerment as the Key," p. 648; Sheila Foster, "Race Matters: The Quest for Environmental Justice," 20 *Eco. L. Q.* 721 (1993). See also Anthony V. Alfieri, "Reconstructive Poverty Law Practice: Learning Lessons of Client Narrative," 100 *Yale L. J.* 2107 (1991); Christopher P. Gilkerson, "Poverty Law Narratives: The Critical Practice and Theory of Receiving and Translating Client Stories," 43 *Hast. L. J.* 861 (1992).

20. Angela P. Harris, "Foreword: The Jurisprudence of Reconstruction," 82 *Cal. L. Rev.* 741 (1994).

21. See generally Richard Delgado, ed., *Critical Race Theory: The Cutting Edge* (1995); Kimberlè Crenshaw et al., eds., Critical Race Theory: The Key Writings That Formed the Movement (1995); Robert L. Hayman Jr., "The Color of Tradition: Critical Race Theory and Postmodern Constitutional Traditionalism," 30 *Harv. C.R.–C.L. L. Rev.* 62 (1995).

22. See Yamamoto, "Critical Race Praxis" (describing the practical turn in critical race theory and its limitations).

23. Harris, "Jurisprudence of Reconstruction," p. 779.

24. Derrick A. Bell, *And We Are Not Saved* (1987), p. 5; Giradeau Spann, *Race against the Court* (1993).

25. Patricia J. Williams, *The Alchemy of Race and Rights* (1991), pp. 146–65.

26. Derrick A. Bell, "*Brown v. Board of Education* and the Interest Convergence Dilemma," 93 *Harv. L. Rev.* 518 (1980).

27. *Shaw v. Reno*, 509 U.S. 630, 657 (1993).

28. Angela P. Harris, What We Talk about When We Talk about Race (forthcoming).

29. David B. Wilkins, "Practical Wisdom for Practicing Lawyers: Separating Ideals from Ideology in Legal Ethics," 108 *Harv. L. Rev.* 458, 471 (1994); Cass R. Sunstein, "Incommensurability and Valuation in Law," 92 *Mich. L. Rev.* 779 (1994).

30. Eric K. Yamamoto, "Efficiency's Threat to the Value of Accessible Courts for Minorities," 25 *Harv. C.R.–C.L. L. Rev.* 341 (1990).

31. *Adarand Constructors, Inc. v. Pena*, 63 U.S.L.W. 4523 (1995); *Miller v. Johnson*, 63 U.S.L.W. 4726 (1995); *Capitol Square Review and Advisory Board v. Pinette*, 63 U.S.L.W. 4684 (1995); *Missouri v. Jenkins*, 515 U.S. 70 (1995).

32. See *Watson v. Fort Worth Bank and Trust*, 487 U.S. 977 (1988); *Patterson v. McLean Credit Union*, 491 U.S. 164 (1989); *Wards Cove Packing Co. Antonio*, 490 U.S. 642 (1989); *St. Mary's Honor Center v. Hicks*, 113 S. Ct. 2742 (1993). Congress rejected aspects of Patterson and Wards Cove through the 1991 Civil Rights Act. Pub. L. No. 102–66, sec. 2, 105 Stat. 1071 (1991). See also *City of Richmond v. J. A. Croson Co.*, 488 U.S. 469 (1989) (invalidating a construction minority set-aside ordinance and subjecting state affirmative action programs to the strict judicial scrutiny); *Shaw v. Reno*, 509 U.S. 630 (1993) (invalidating state voter redistricting plan that purposely created two African American majority districts).

33. *Shaw*, 509 U.S. at 543 (Stevens, J., dissenting).

34. Martha Minow, introduction to Susan Richards Shreve, ed., *Outside the Law: Narratives on Racial Justice in America* (1997).

35. David Roediger, *Towards the Abolition of Whiteness: Essays on Race, Politics, and Working Class History* (1994), p. 1.

36. See generally Haunani-Kay Trask, "*Coalition-Building between Native and Non-Natives*," 43 *Stan. L. Rev.* 1197 (1991).

37. Jeff Chang, "Race, Class, Conflict and Empowerment: On Ice Cube's 'Black Korea,'" *Amerasia Journal* 19 (1993): 87, 93–96.

38. David M. Trubek, The Handmaiden's Revenge: On Reading and Using the Newer Sociology of Civil Procedure," 51 *Law & Contemp. Probs.* 111, 124 (1988).

39. Frank Michelman, "The Supreme Court and Litigation Access Fees: The Right to Protect One's Rights," 1973 *Duke L. J.* 1153, 1172–73 (identifying litigation process values of dignity, participation, deterrence [or social welfare], and effectuation).

40. Much of the following discussion, including the citations, is taken more or less verbatim from part of an earlier work: Eric K. Yamamoto, Moses Haia,

and Donna Kalama, "Courts and the Cultural Performance: Native Hawaiians' Uncertain Federal and State Law Rights to Sue," 16, *U. Haw. L. Rev.* 1 (1994).

41. Gerald Torres and Kathryn Milun, "Translating Yonnondio: By Precedent and Evidence: The Mashpee Indian Case," 1990 *Duke L. J.* 625, 628.

42. Sally E. Merry, "Law and Colonialism," 25 *Law & Soc. Rev.* 889, 892 (1991).

43. See William Felstiner, Richard Abel, and Austin Sarat, "The Emergence and Transformation of Disputes: Naming, Blaming, Claiming," 15 *Law & Soc. Rev.* 631 (1980–81); Lynn Mather and Barbara Ygnvesson, "Language, Audience and the Transformation of Disputes," 15 *Law & Soc. Rev.* 775, 780 (1980–81); Bryant Garth, "Power and Legal Artifice: The Federal Class Action," 26 *Law & Soc. Rev.* 237, 240 (1992).

44. Mather and Ygnvesson, "Language, Audience," p. 780. See also Judith Resnik, "On the Bias: Feminist Reconsiderations of the Aspirations for Our Judges," 61 *S. Cal. L. Rev.* 1877 (1988).

45. Mather and Yngvesson, "Language, Audience," pp. 778–79. See also Richard Delgado, "Legal Storytelling: Storytelling for Oppositionists and Others: A Plea for Narrative," 87 *Mich. L. Rev.* 2411 (1989).

46. 26 *Cong. Rec.* 1885 (1894). See also Nell Jessup Newton, "Indian Claims in the Courts of the Conqueror," 41 *Am. U. L. Rev.* 753, 760–61; Robert A. Williams Jr., "Encounters on the Frontiers of International Human Rights Law: Redefining the Terms of Indigenous Peoples' Survival in the World," 1990 *Duke L. J.* 660; S. James Anaya, "The Rights of Indigenous Peoples and International Law in Historical and Contemporary Perspective," 1989 *Harv. Indian L. Symp.* 191 (1990).

47. Newton, "Indian Claims," p. 760.

## Note to Part 3

1. "Right relationships are those that honor mutual human worth, that redress past wrong so far as injuries are able to be redressed, and in which steps have been taken so that neither fear nor resentment play dominant roles." Sally Engle Merry and Neal Milner, *The Possibility of Popular Justice* (1995), p. 361.

## Notes to Chapter 7

1. Harlon Dalton, *Racial Healing: Confronting the Fear between Blacks and Whites* (1995), pp. 96, 97.

2. Stephen Landsman, *Adversarial Justice* (1987).

3. See Cass R. Sunstein, "Incommensurability and Valuation in Law," 92 *Mich. L. Rev.* 779 (1994).

4. James Boyd White, *Heracles' Bow* (1985), p. 42.

5. Philip Selznick, *The Moral Commonwealth* (1992), pp. 434, 435.

6. See Kimberlè Crenshaw, "Race, Reform and Retrenchment: Transformation

and Legitimation in Antidiscrimination Law," 101 *Harv. L. Rev.* 1331 (1988) (contrasting process equality with substantive equality in constitutional law); Paul R. Dimond, "The Anti-Caste Principle—Towards a Constitutional Standard for Review of Race Cases," 30 *Wayne L. Rev.* 1 (1993) (ascertaining an anticaste constitutional principle for race cases).

7. Judicial remedies also encompass, in limited fashion, the concept of prohibition—enjoining specific institutional acts when monetary compensation is deemed inadequate.

8. Linda Krieger, "The Content of Our Categories: A Cognitive Bias Approach to Discrimination and Equal Employment Opportunity," 47 *Stan. L. Rev.* 1161 (1995).

9. *Hansberry v. Lee*, 311 U.S. 32 (1940).

10. Lorraine Hansberry, *To Be Young, Gifted and Black*, adapted by Robert Nemiroff (1969).

11. Patricia Williams, "Alchemical Notes: Reconstructing Ideals from Deconstructed Rights," 22 *Harv. C.R.–C.L. L. Rev.* 401, 430, 433 (1987).

12. See David Augsburger, *Conflict Mediation across Cultures* (1992), p. 259 (describing reconciliation and the "many faces of forgiveness" in diverse cultural settings).

13. Harold Wells, "Theology of Reconciliation," in Greg Baum and Harold Wells, eds., *The Reconciliation of Peoples: Challenge to the Churches* (1997), pp. 1, 2, 3–14. Wells cites verses from the Judeo-Christian Bible informing a theology of reconciliation: Deut. 6:4–5; Lev. 16:20–22 (Atonement), 19:18; Ps. 137:9, 85:10; Isa. 32:15–17, 11:2–9; Jer. 6:14–15 (Hebrew Vision); Matt. 9:13, 18:21–22, 5:23, 28, 39, 44, 45, 25:30 (Justification),7:1 (Universality of Sin), 8:5–10, 10:45, 22:40; Luke 18:10–14, 19:9, 7:47 (Grace), 10:29–37, 15:11–32, 17:17, 4:26–27 (Teaching and Deeds of Jesus), 18:10–14; Rom. 3:23, 3:10–12; John 1:29, 8:7, 2 Cor. 5:19, 20; He. 7:27; Eph. 2: 8–9. Gregory Baum, Wells's coeditor, observes that this scriptural reading supporting a theology of reconciliation is not traditional. This "ministry [of reconciliation] is a bold undertaking . . . [and the] authors [of the book] realize that the church's theological tradition offers very little wisdom on the social meaning of reconciliation." Baum also observes that the book's authors agree that "reconciliation is an ambiguous theological term" (Gregory Baum, "A Theological Afterword," in *Reconciliation of Peoples*, pp. 184, 188).

14. Willis H. Logan, ed., *The Kairos Covenant* (1988), p. 16, emphasis in the original.

15. James Cone, *Martin and Malcolm and America: A Dream or a Nightmare* (1991), p. 78.

16. Donald W. Shriver, *An Ethic for Enemies* (1995), p. 182, quoting Martin Luther King. See also Martin Luther King Jr., *Strength to Love* (1963), p. 49; Cornel West, *Prophesy and Deliverance* (1982).

17. Strictly interpreted, atonement means reconciliation between God and

humans through the death of Jesus. Harold Wells observes that "today the theology of atonement has become extremely controversial," with some finding the idea of divinely inspired sacrifice "unintelligible" or "immoral." While acknowledging the critiques, Wells rejects the "doctrine of atonement as religiously and culturally antiquated." Finding broader meaning, he argues that atonement speaks to a "persistent need" across cultures to sacrifice to make up for sins—a "recognition that our evil deeds cannot be taken lightly. Reconciliation is costly" (Wells, "Theology of Reconciliation," pp. 9–10).

18. "Black Men Heed Unity Call," *San Francisco Chronicle*, October 17, 1995, p. 1.

19. Jim Forest, "A Dialogue on Reconciliation in Belgrade," in Baum and Wells, *Reconciliation of Peoples*, pp. 110, 116–17.

20. Fumitaka Matsuoka, *Out of Silence: Asian American Churches* (1994), p. 131. See also Sang Hyun Lee, "Pilgrimage and Home in the Wilderness of Marginality: Symbols and Context in Asian American Theology," *Princeton Seminary Bulletin* 49 (1995).

21. Joseph V. Montville, "The Healing Function in Political Conflict Resolution," in J. D. Sandole and Hugo van der Merwe, eds., *Conflict Resolution Theory and Practice: Integration and Application* (1993), p.115 (discussing the teachings on reconciliation of Vietnamese Zen Buddhist master Thich Nhat Hanh). See also Sivio E. Rillipaldi, "Zen-Mind, Christian-Mind, Empty Mind," *J. Ecumen. Studies* (winter 1982): 69–84; Daisetz T. Suzuki, *Zen and Japanese Culture* (1969).

22. Jer. 3 and Deut. 10.

23. Baum, "A Theological Afterword," p. 188 (describing the Kairos Document's charges of complicity in apartheid by liberal Christian churches); John W. de Gruchy, "The Dialectic of Reconciliation," in Baum and Wells, *Reconciliation of Peoples*, pp. 16, 21.

24. Logan, *The Kairos Covenant*, p. 9.

25. Wells, "Theology of Reconciliation," p. 4 (recalling statements by white South African heads of state). Gregory Baum criticizes conservative Catholic bishops in Latin America, who accused liberation theology of pitting the rich against the poor and thereby sinning against church unity, of preaching a "reconciliation that does not demand structural change in the social order; their theology allows the rich to keep their power and privilege." Baum, "A Theological Afterword," p. 188).

26. Dietrich Bonhoeffer, *The Cost of Discipleship* (1984), pp. 35 ff.

27. Jer. 3 and Deut. 10; Michael Lerner and Cornel West, *Jews and Blacks* (1995), p. 9; Logan, *The Kairos Covenant*; James Cone, *Black Theology and Black Power* (1969).

28. See generally Vamik D. Volkan, "An Overview of Psychological Concepts," in *The Psychodynamics of International Relationships* (1990), p. 43.

29. Vamik D. Volkan, *The Need to Have Enemies and Allies* (1988), p. 155;

David M. Noer, *Healing the Wounds* (1993), p. 5; Robert Jay Lifton, *The Protean Self: Human Resilience in an Age of Fragmentation* (1993); Judith Lewis Herman, *Trauma and Recovery* (1992); John E. Mack, "The Psychodynamics of Victimization," in *The Psychodynamics of International Relationships* (1990).

30. Vamik D. Volkan, "Psychoanalytic Aspects of Ethnic Conflict," in Joseph V. Montville, ed., *Conflict and Peacemaking in Multiethnic Societies* (1990), p. 90; Michael A. Hogg and Dominic Abrams, *Social Identifications: A Social Psychology of Intergroup Relations and Group Processes* (1988); John H. Harvey, *Embracing Their Memory: Loss and the Social Psychology of Storytelling* (1996).

31. Geiko Mueller-Fahrenholz, *The Art of Forgiveness* (1997), pp. 28, 36.

32. Hiroshi Wagatsuma and Arthur Rosett, "The Implications of Apology: Law and Culture in Japan and the United States," 20 *Law & Soc. Rev.* 461 (1986).

33. See generally White, *Heracles' Bow*; Arnold Schuchter, *Reparations: The Black Manifesto and Its Challenge to White America* (1970); Johan Galtung, *Solving Conflicts: A Peace Research Perspective* (1989); Eric K. Yamamoto, "Friend, Foe or Something Else: The Social Meanings of Redress and Reparations," 27 *Denv. J. Int'l. Law & Pol.* 223 (1992).

34. Elazar Barkan, "Payback Time: Restitution and the Moral Economy of Nations," *Tikkun*, September 19, 1996, p. 52.

35. Lynne Duke, "Witness to a Celebration," *Washington Post*, July 10, 1994, p. W8.

36. Tina Rosenberg, "Recovering from Apartheid," *New Yorker*, November 18, 1996, p. 90 (quoting Tutu). Ubuntu is a Xhosa proverb: *umntu ngumuntu ngabantu* (a person is a person through persons). Charles Villa-Vincencio, "Telling One Another Stories," in Baum and Wells, *Reconciliation of Peoples*, pp. 30, 38. In describing *ubuntu*, Tutu explained that "you must do what you can to maintain this great harmony, which is perpetually undermined by resentment, anger, desire for vengeance. That's why African jurisprudence is restorative rather than retributive." Mark Gevisser, "Profile: Tutu's Test of Faith," *Africa News Service*, April 12, 1996 (quoting Tutu).

37. Mari J. Matsuda, "Looking to the Bottom: Critical Legal Studies and Reparations," 22 *Harv. C.R.C.–L. L. Rev.* 323, 391 (1987).

38. Rosenberg, "Recovering from Apartheid," p. 90.

39. Jon M. Van Dyke and Gerald Berkley, "Redressing Human Rights Abuses," 20 *Denv. J. Int'l Law & Pol.* 243, 266 (1992) (recognizing that the protection of group rights has been steadily increasing in recent years).

40. Jennifer M. L. Chock, "One Hundred Years of Illegitimacy: International Legal Analysis of the Illegal Overthrow of the Hawaiian Monarchy, Hawai'i's Annexation, and Possible Reparations," 17 *U. Haw. L. Rev.* 463, 495 (1995).

41. Stephen T. Boggs and Malcolm Naea Chun, "Ho'oponopono: A Hawaiian Method of Solving Interpersonal Problems," in Karen-Ann Watson-Gedeo and Geoffrey M. White, eds., *Conflict Discourse in Pacific Societies* (1990), p. 123. See

also Marg Huber, "Mediation around the Medicine Wheel," *Mediation Quarterly* 10 (1993): 355 (describing the Native American medicine wheel as a model for contemporary group healing).

42. E. Victoria Shook, *Ho'oponopono: Contemporary Uses of a Hawaiian Problem-Solving Process* (1985), pp. 11, 46. See also Karen Ito, "Ho'oponopono, to Make Right: Hawaiian Conflict Resolution and Metaphor in the Construction of a Family Therapy," *Culture, Medicine & Psychiatry* 9 (1989): 201.

43. The ho'oponopono process is described in the following way: "Once the proper climate is set, the leader focuses on the specific problem. The hala, or transgression is stated. Hala also implies that the perpetrator and the person wronged are bound together in a relationship of negative entanglement called hihia" (Shook, *Ho'oponopono*, p. 11). After working through the hala, the parties engage in mahiki, or "talk story." Controlled by a community leader to prevent outbursts and misunderstandings, the mahiki focuses on the "transgression and its consequences: bad feelings, strained relationships, misfortune, illness" (Boggs and Chun, "Ho'oponopono," p. 131; Shook, *Ho'oponopono*, p. 11). An essential attribute of the "talk story" is sincerity (*oia'i'o*), implying emotional truth, as well as the outward expression of inward feelings. Another attribute related to sincerity is mutual understanding, a meeting of minds and spirit, a sharing of mana'o. Following mahiki is mihi. *Mihi* is a "sincere confession of wrongdoing and the seeking of forgiveness" with the aspiration of severing (*oki*) the negative entanglements (*hihia*) to bring back balance to the relationship.

44. Philmer Bluehouse and James W. Zion, "Hozhooji Naat'aanii: The Navajo Justice and Harmony Ceremony," *Mediation Quarterly* 10 (1993): 327–34. See also Larissa Behrendt, *Aboriginal Dispute Resolution* (1995) (dispute resolution practices in traditional and contemporary aboriginal societies).

45. Ronald J. Fisher, "Generic Principles of Resolving Intergroup Conflict," *Journal of Social Issues* 50 (1994): 47.

46. John O. Calmore, "Racialized Space and the Culture of Segregation: 'Hewing a Stone of Hope from a Mountain of Despair,' " 143 *U. Pa. L. Rev.* 1233 (1995) (applying Fisher's scheme to multiracial conflicts and coalitional efforts in Los Angeles).

47. John Dawson, *Healing America's Wounds* (1995).

48. Ibid. pp. 26, 30, 135–36.

49. Montville, "The Healing Function," p. 112.

50. Donald Hope, "The Healing Paradox of Forgiveness," *Psychotherapy* 24 (1987): 240, 241.

51. Montville highlights three components of victimhood: "a history of violent traumatic aggression and loss; a conviction that the aggression was unjustified by any standard; and an often unuttered fear on the part of the victim group that the aggressor will strike again at some feasible time in the future" (Montville, "The Healing Function," pp. 113, 119).

52. Shriver, *An Ethic for Enemies*, p. 9.
53. Ibid. p. 164.

## Notes to Chapter 8

1. Harlon Dalton, *Racial Healing: Confronting the Fear between Blacks and Whites* (1995), p. 65. See also Sally Engle Merry and Neal Milner, *The Possibility of Popular Justice* (1995), p. 361; John Paul Ledarach and Ron Kraybill, *The Paradox of Popular Justice: A Practitioner's View* (1995), pp. 357–78.

2. E. Allen Lind and Tom Tyler, *The Social Psychology of Procedural Justice* (1988).

3. See also Eric K. Yamamoto, "Rethinking Alliances: Agency, Responsibility and Interracial Justice," 3 *UCLA Asian Pac. Am. L. J.* 33, 65–69 (1995) (sketching group healing concepts drawn from disciplines of law, theology, social psychology, political theory, and indigenous practices).

4. Geiko Mueller-Fahrenholz, *The Art of Forgiveness: Theological Reflections on Healing and Reconciliation* (1997), pp. 5, 25.

5. See generally Dalton, *Racial Healing* (using healing metaphor in discussing racial conflict); Rhonda V. Magee, "The Master's Tools, From the Bottom up: Response to African American Reparations Theory in Mainstream and Outsider Remedies Discourse," 79 *Va. L. Rev.* 863, 879 (1993) ("Opening old wounds [is] necessary to cure current ills").

6. Arthur Kleinman, *The Illness Narratives: Suffering, Healing, and the Human Condition* (1989).

7. David Morris, *The Culture of Pain* (1991).

8. See generally Toni Massaro, "Empathy, Legal Storytelling, and the Rule of Law: New Words, Old Wounds?" 87 *Mich. L. Rev.* 2099 (1989) (describing empathy, legal justice and the "call to context").

9. Charles Villa-Vicencio, "Telling One Another Stories: Toward a Theology of Reconciliation," in Greg Baum and Harold Wells, eds., *The Reconciliation of Peoples: Challenge to the Churches* (1997), p. 31.

10. James Cone, *God of the Oppressed* (1995), pp. 102–3.

11. David Mura, *Where the Body Meets the Memory* (1995) (describing his father's difficult choice, while on a pass from the interment camp, to sit in the front of the bus).

12. Mueller-Fahrenholz, *The Art of Forgiveness*, p. 26.

13. Massaro, "Empathy."

14. See Nancy Abelman and John Lie, *Blue Dreams* (1996) (describing how the media framed blacks [poor, inner city, welfare] and Korean Americans [culturally different, model minority entrepreneurs] as "antipodal minorities" and how this framing displaced the focus on socioeconomic causes for the rebellion-riot).

15. Richard Delgado, "Legal Storytelling: Storytelling for Oppositionists and

Others: A Plea for Narrative," 87 *Mich. L. Rev.* 2411 (1989); Eric K. Yamamoto, Moses Haia, and Donna Kalama, "Courts and the Cultural Performance: Native Hawaiians' Uncertain Federal and State Law Rights to Sue," 16 *U. Haw. L. Rev.* 1 (1994).

16. Reginald Leamon. Robinson, " 'The Other Against Itself': Deconstructing the Violent Discourse between Korean and African-Americans," 67 *S. Cal. L. Rev.* 15 (1993).

17. *People v. Superior Court of Los Angeles County* (Soon Ja Du), 5 Cal. App. 4th 822 (1993).

18. See Anthony E. Cook, "Beyond Critical Legal Studies: The Reconstructive Theology of Dr. Martin Luther King, Jr.," 103 *Harv. L. Rev.* 985 (1990).

19. Dalton, *Racial Healing*, pp. 137–39, 155–56, 162.

20. Charles R. Lawrence III and Mari J. Matsuda, *We Won't Go Back: Making the Case for Affirmative Action* (1997), p. 192.

21. Carnegie Endowment for International Peace, *Unfinished Peace: Report of the International Commission on the Balkans* (1996).

22. See Iwona Irwin-Zarecka, *Frames of Remembrance: The Dynamics of Collective Memory* (1994).

23. Joseph V. Montville, "The Healing Function in Political Conflict Resolution," in Dennis J. D. Sandole and Hugo van der Merwe, eds., *Conflict Resolution Theory and Practice: Integration and Application* (1993), p. 112. What Montville does not provide as part of this second stage is a conceptual basis for assessing the extent to which the group is "responsible" for harm experienced by another group's members.

24. John Dawson, *Healing America's Wounds* (1995), pp. 103, 135, 262 (asserting that the healing process includes confession, repentance, reconciliation, and restitution).

25. Jack E. White, "Texaco's High-Octane Racism Problems," *Time*, November 25, 1996, p. 33.

26. Ramon Lopez-Reyes, "The Demise of the Hawaiian Kingdom: A Psycho-Cultural Analysis and Moral Legacy (Something Lost, Something Owed)," 18 *Haw. Bar J.* 3, 19 (1983).

27. Catherine Peck, "The Palestinian Center for Rapprochement between People," in Baum and Wells, *Reconciliation of Peoples*, p. 96.

28. Charles R. Lawrence makes this general point in his analysis of Ice Cube's "Black Korea" rap. Lawrence and Matsuda, *We Won't Go Back*.

29. Cornel West, "Black Leadership and the Pitfalls of Racial Reasoning," in Toni Morrison, ed., *Race-ing Justice, En-Gendering Power: Essays on Anita Hill, Clarence Thomas, and the Construction of Social Reality* (1992), pp. 396–97.

30. Mueller-Fahrenholz, *The Art of Forgiveness*, p. 26.

31. Rafael Moses, "Acknowledgment: The Balm of Narcissistic Hurts," *Austin Riggs Center Review* 3 (1990): 5–6.

32. See Charles R. Lawrence III, "The Id, the Ego, and Equal Protection: Reckoning with Unconscious Racism," 39 *Stan. L. Rev.* 317, 322 (citing S. Freud, *The Ego and the Id*, in vol. 3 of *The Standard Edition of the Complete Psychological Works of Sigmund Freud*, ed. J. Strachey (1951), p. 19.

33. Betty Winston Baye, "Time to 'Walk the Walk,' " *Louisville Courier Journal*, June 22, 1995, p. 13A (comment made concerning the Southern Baptist apology to African Americans for the church's racism).

34. Different cultures shape performative steps differently. See, for example, Hiroshi Wagatsuma and Arthur Rosett, "The Implications of Apology: Law and Culture in Japan and the United States," 20 *Law & Soc. Rev.* 461 (1986) (describing Japanese and American cultural differences and the effect of those differences on approaches to dispute resolution).

35. Nicholas Tavuchis, *Mea Culpa: A Sociology of Apology and Reconciliation* (1991), p. 8.

36. Ibid. p. 18.

37. Mark O'Keefe and Tom Bates, "Sorry about That," *Portland Oregonian*, July 23, 1995, p. F01.

38. Letter by Rev. Shin Asami, quoted in Dawson, *Healing America's Wounds*, pp. 261–62.

39. Wagatsuma and Rosett, "The Implications of Apology," pp. 248, 496.

40. Ibid. pp. 462, 464, 492.

41. Ibid. pp. 462, 473, 492.

42. O'Keefe and Bates, "Sorry about That," p. F01. Elazar Barkan also suggests that even in cases without the redistribution of resources, the injured group that receives a public apology or open admission of guilt at a minimum "benefits from the . . . recognition of its victimization and of its previously ignored history, which consequently becomes part of global history" (Elazar Barkan, "Payback Time: Restitution and the Moral Economy of Nations," *Tikkun*, September 19, 1996, p. 52).

43. Marla Dickerson, "Who's Sorry? In Their Rush for Repentance," *Detroit News*, July 16, 1995, p. B4.

44. Tavuchis, *Mea Culpa*, pp. 7, 23.

45. Ann Calhoun, "A World of Empty Apologies," *Honolulu Advertiser*, July 24, 1995, p. A6.

46. Dawson, *Healing America's Wounds*, p. 148.

47. Yvonne Park Hsu, " 'Comfort Women' From Korea: Japan's World War II Sex Slaves and the Legitimacy of Their Claims for Reparations," 2 *Pac. Rim L. & Pol'y J.* 97, 128 (1993) (quoting Tanabe).

48. Tavuchis, *Mea Culpa*, p. 109.

49. David W. Augsburger, *Conflict Mediation across Cultures: Pathways and Patterns* (1992), p. 283. See also Donald W. Shriver Jr., *An Ethic for Enemies: Forgiveness in Politics* (1995), p. 178.

50. Mueller-Fahrenholz, *The Art of Forgiveness*, pp. 5, 25.

51. Ibid. p. 26.

52. Ibid. p. 28.

53. Paulo Freire, *Pedagogy of the Oppressed* (1974), pp. 28, 125.

54. Hannah Arendt, *The Human Condition* 244 (1963).

55. Augsburger, *Conflict Mediation*, pp. 277, 280, 283 (quoting Kaunda). Augsburger uses the terms "true forgiveness" and "reconciliatory forgiveness" interchangeably.

56. Villa-Vicencio, "Telling One Another Stories," p. 34 (citing Hans-Georg Gadamer, *Truth and Method* [1988], p. 272).

57. Jerome Bruner, The *Culture of Education* (1996). Bruner's multidisciplinary work on cultural psychology is controversial. For an insightful account, See Clifford Geertz, "Learning with Bruner," *New York Review of Books*, April 10, 1997, p. 22.

58. Dalton, *Racial Healing*, p. 156.

59. Lopez-Reyes, "The Demise of the Hawaiian Kingdom," p. 19.

60. S.J. Res. 19, 103d Cong., 1st sess., 107 Stat. 1510 (1993).

61. Moses, "Acknowledgment," pp. 4, 6.

62. Barkan, "Payback Time," p. 52. According to Barkan, groups may also engage in negotiating restitution because of political pressure or exhaustion from prolonged conflict. Restitution is a "matrix of guilt and mourning, atonement and national revival."

63. Montville, "The Healing Function," p. 115.

64. Lopez-Reyes, "The Demise of the Hawaiian Kingdom," p. 6. For an insightful inquiry into sorrow and suffering, see Elizabeth V. Spelman, *Fruits of Sorrow* (1997).

65. Mari Matsuda, "Looking to the Bottom: Critical Legal Studies and Reparations," 22 *Harv. C.R.–C.L. L. Rev.* 323, 391, 393–94 (1987). See also Magee, "The Master's Tools," p. 913 ("Reparations would be powerful symbols of white group responsibility for the continued degradation of African American life and culture").

66. Manning Marable, *Race, Reform, and Rebellion: The Second Reconstruction in Black America—1945–1990*, 2d ed. (1991), pp. 6, 24.

67. Magee, "The Master's Tools," p. 879 (subcommittee members' comment on Conyers's reparations study bill, "Commission to Study Reparation Proposals for African Americans Act," H.R. 1684, 102 Cong., 1st sess. [1991]).

68. See Tong Yu, "Reparations for Former Comfort Women of World War II," 36 *Harv. Int'l L. J.* 528, 539 (1995).

69. John Stevens Keali'iwahamana Hoag, "The Moral, Historical and Theoretical Framework for Restitution and Reparations for Native Hawaiians," April 28, 1995 (unpublished paper), p. 19. Elazar Barkan observes that injured groups often seek to achieve a more moderate goal than full retroactive justice, such as lessen-

ing conflict or improving their economic condition (Barkan, "Payback Time," p. 52).

70. John de Gruchy, "The Dialectic of Reconciliation: Church and the Transition to Democracy in South Africa," in Baum and Wells, *Reconciliation of Peoples*, p. 26.

71. Matsuda, "Looking to the Bottom," pp. 373–88. Matsuda has thoughtfully refuted the narrow common law-based objections. I address the larger idea of group responsibility in chapter 5 and so will not repeat Matsuda's analysis here.

72. Joseph Singer, "Reparation," April 10, 1997 (unpublished manuscript), pp. 2–3.

73. Alex Bundy, "Gypsies Demand Compensation for Suffering during Holocaust," *Honolulu Advertiser*, August 4, 1997, p. A10.

74. Singer, "Reparation," pp. 3, 4.

75. Eric K. Yamamoto, "Friend, Foe or Something Else: Social Meanings of Redress and Reparations," 20 *Denv. J. Int'l. Law. & Pol.* 223–24, 232 (1992).

76. Ibid. pp. 224, 227.

77. Tavuchis, *Mea Culpa*, p. 107 (quoting Ben Takeshita).

## Notes to Chapter 9

1. Exhibit B, "Initial Plan for Redress of the Hawai'i Conference of United Church of Christ to Na Kanaka Maoli, Halawai Ho'omana: A Service of Confession, Reconciliation and Commitment to Redress," June 10–15, 1996, resolution adopted at the 1993 annual meeting of the Hawai'i Conference (hereafter cited as Exhibit B), p. 2 .

2. "Initial Plan for Redress of the Hawai'i Conference of United Church of Christ to Na Kanaka Maoli, Halawai Ho'omana: A Service of Confession, Reconciliation and Commitment to Redress," June 10–15, 1996 (hereafter cited as "Initial Plan for Redress"), pp. 3–4.

3. Ibid. pp.. 9–16.

4. Ibid. pp. 5–8.

5. Community speakers at the 174th 'Aha Pae'aina, June 10–15, 1996, pp. 16–17 (comment attributed to Leon Siu).

6. Ibid. p. 18 (comment attributed to Wil Sanborn, former Hawai'i Conference Foundation trustee).

7. Ibid. pp. 5, 7, 10 (comments attributed to Kawehiokalaninuieamaumau Kanui, Momi Segario, and Kekuni Blaisdell); Kaleo Patterson, "Stumbling on the Path to Redress," *Ho'ike i Ka Pono*, Winter 1996/97, p. 2.

8. Ibid. p. 10 (redress should be "given to the greater native public"), p. 19 ("the only beneficiaries of the land should be the members of those sovereignty organizations that helped negotiate the 1993 Apology"). See also Letter from Reverend Tuck Wah K. Lee to Janet Fujioka, chairperson of the Hawai'i Confer-

ence of the United Church of Christ, December 2, 1996 (suggesting contributing all redress lands to a sovereign Hawaiian nation upon formal recognition).

9. Ibid. p. 9 (comment attributed to Keali'i Gora).

10. Hawai'i Apology Task Force Hawai'i Conference of the United Church of Christ, Meeting Recap., August 7, 1996, p. 2.

11. "Initial Plan for Redress," p. 7.

12. Patterson, "Stumbling," p. 2.1.

13. Interview with Carole Keim, Interim Hawai'i Conference of the United Church of Christ Minister, in Honolulu, July 30, 1997.

14. Nicholas Tavuchis, *Mea Culpa: A Sociology of Apology and Reconciliation* (1991), p. 8.

15. Ibid. pp. 57–58.

16. Andrew Walsh, "Congregational Influences in Hawai'i (1820–1893)," in *New Conversations* (United Church Board for Homeland Ministries, Spring 1993), pp. 23–43.

17. "Initial Plan for Redress," p. 8.

18. Ibid. pp. 5–6.

19. Exhibit B, p. 14.

20. Letter from Sue Kaneshina, Keawala'i Congregational Church, July 27, 1997; letter from Edith Kapiko, Waiola Church Lahaina, July 13, 1997; letter from Jo Douglass, Moderator, Waimea United Church of Christ, July 21 1997.

21. These are my personal recollections of the reparations ceremony at Kaumakapili Church on August 24, 1997.

22. Marla Dickerson, "Who's Sorry? In Their Rush for Repentance," *Detroit News*, July 16, 1995, p. B4.

23. Exhibit B, pp. 10–11 (comment attributed to Mililani Trask).

24. Geiko Mueller-Fahrenholz, *The Art of Forgiveness: Theological Reflections on Healing and Reconciliation* (1997), p. 25.

25. Hawai'i Apology Task Force, p. 1.

26. Community speakers, p. 5 (comment by Kekuni Blaisdell).

27. Ibid. p. 7 (comment by Kawehi Kanui).

28. Ibid. p. 17 (comment by Jose Luis Morin).

29. Interview with Rev. Wallace Ryan Kuroiwa, Nu'uanu Congregational Church, Honolulu, March 26, 1997.

30. Interview with Rev. Kaleo Patterson, Kaumakapili Church, Honolulu, March 25, 1997.

31. Some community leaders worry about undue conference influence on the board because three of the six members of the board are United Church of Christ members, though the board chair is not.

32. Rev. Kuroiwa drafted the initial Asian American churches' apology resolution and chaired the Hawai'i Apology Task Force.

33. Motion 5 of the 171st annual meeting of the Hawai'i Conference of the

United Church of Christ: "A Vision of a New Day: Promoting Solidarity and Reconciliation through an Act of Apology," in Ho'o lokahi, 171st Aha Pae'aina, June 15–19, 1993, Hawai'i Conference United Church of Christ, pp. 81–82.

34. Lawrence Fuchs, *Hawaii Pono* (1970).

35. Eric K. Yamamoto, "Rethinking Alliances: Agency Responsibility and Interracial Justice," 33 *UCLA Asian Pac. Am. L. J.* 34, 43 (1995).

36. Interview with Rev. Kuroiwa.

37. "Initial Plan for Redress," p. 7.

38. Mueller-Fahrenholz, *The Art of Forgiveness*, pp. 5, 25.

39. Tavuchis, *Mea Culpa*, pp. 113–14.


## Notes to Chapter 10

1. The account of the hat shop encounter and its aftermath is drawn primarily from news articles and selected interviews and is not a complete history of the controversy. "Citing Bias Against Minister, Blacks Picket and Close Korean Hat Shop in Los Angeles," *Jet*, June 17, 1996, p. 39; "Central Los Angeles: Activists Demand Apology from Shopkeeper, Threaten Boycott," *Los Angeles Times*, February 14, 1996, p. B5; K. Connie Kang, "One Incident Reverberates in Two Worlds: 'I Should Have Apologized,' " *Los Angeles Times*, February 15, 1996, p. B1 (hereafter cited as "Should Have Apologized"); Andrea Ford, "One Incident Reverberates in Two Worlds: 'You're Afraid of Me,' " *Los Angeles Times*, February 15, 1996, p. B1.

2. K. Connie Kang, "Korean Closes Store That Blacks Picketed in Dispute: Hat Shop Owner Says She Apologized and Asked Forgiveness of Minister Who Was Refused Service. But He Says He Will Pursue the Issue to Culturally 'Sensitize' Her," *Los Angeles Times*, May 22, 1996, p. B1 (hereafter cited as "Korean Closes Store").

3. Telephone interview with Marcia Choo, Asian Pacific American Dispute Resolution Center of Los Angeles, February 7, 1997.

4. K. Connie Kang, "Black Pastor, Korean Shop Owner Resolve Racial Incident," *Los Angeles Times*, June 2, 1996, p. B1 (hereafter cited as "Racial Incident Resolved").

5. Richard Winton and K. Connie Kang, "Pastor Transferred in Probe of Unauthorized Mortgages," *Los Angeles Times*, April 1, 1997, p. B3; interview with Choo.

6. Recalling her experience with the hat shop dispute, Choo indicated that the press sometimes failed to provide accurate accounts of the dispute. "Almost any situation worsens as soon as the press gets wind of it. One reason for this is that there are always gaps in the stories they tell, and the public tends to fill in these gaps on their own" (interview with Choo).

7. K. Connie Kang, "Airing Differences in Bid for Harmony Radio: Korean-Language Call-in Show Features Black Guests and Frank Discussions about Cul-

tural Tensions," *Los Angeles Times*, July 22, 1996, p. B1 (hereafter cited as "Airing Differences").

8. Jeff Chang, "Race, Class, Conflict and Empowerment: On Ice Cube's 'Black Korea,' " 19 *Amerasia Journal* 87, 101 (1993).

9. Kang, "Korean Closes Store," p. B1.

10. Kang, "Airing Differences," p. B1.

11. Kang, "Should Have Apologized," p. B1.

12. Nicholas Tavuchis describes the significance of a personal apology: "The energizing medium [orality] . . . cannot be ignored or underestimated. . . . There is . . . nothing as effective and unsettling as having to address in person someone we have wronged, no matter how much a culture stresses writing" (Nicholas Tauvichis, *Mea Culpa: A Sociology of Apology and Reconciliation* [1991], p. 23.

13. Ford, "One Incident," p. B1.

14. Kang, "Korean Closes Store," p. B1.

15. For a description of other conflicts, see Yumi Wilson and Christian Miller, "Mace Fracas Accents Ethnic Gaps: As East Bay Diversifies, Tensions Grow," *San Francisco Chronicle*, March 22, 1993, p. A11; Meg Kissinger, "Beauty Island Rhetoric Stays Hot: Protests Continue in Wake of Fire as Mayor Calls for Non-Violent Resolution," *Milwaukee Journal Sentinel*, May 4, 1996, p. 1; Gracie Bonds Staples, "Black, Asian Tension Lingers: Almost Two Years after the Slaying of an African-American by a Korean-American Store Owner in South Fort Worth, Efforts to Improve Race Relations Have Little Lasting Effect Despite Some Progress," *Fort Worth Star-Telegram*, May 12, 1996, p. 29.

16. Ford, "One Incident," p. B1.

17. Chang, "Race, Class," p. 99, citing Vinette K. Pryce, "Carson and 'Black-watch' to Boycott Koreans on MLK Day," *New York Amsterdam News*, December 28, 1991, p. 82.

18. See Colloquy, "Our Next Race Question: The Uneasiness between Blacks and Latinos," *Harper's*, April 1996, p. 55 (discussion between Jorge Klor de Alva and Cornel West about African American and Latina/o tensions).

19. Karen Umemoto, "Blacks and Koreans in Los Angeles: The Case of La-Tasha Harlins and Soon Ja Du," in James Jennings, ed., *Blacks, Latinos, and Asians in Urban America* (1994), p. 95; Rodolfo F. Acuna, *Anything but Mexican: Chicanos in Contemporary Los Angeles* (1996).

20. The latent gender issues in the hat shop incident also were lost in the public uproar. Once the hat shop controversy escalated into a citywide race drama, few remembered that the incident began with an African American woman customer apparently hesitating to make her purchase when Rev. May entered the store. Rev. May initially framed the conflict in gendered and raced terms. "It's a case where the man [Kim] is threatened by and has a fear of African American males. He wants African American women to come in and support his business and to deny African American males. Seems he has a great fear of African

American men and his business is in an African American neighborhood" (Kang, "Should Have Apologized," p. B1).

21. Kang, "Racial Incident Resolved," p. B1.

22. Tavuchis aptly describes the pitfalls of translating a personal apology into a public ceremony. "Whatever . . . the social relationship . . . going public provides fresh opportunities for displays of pride . . . [and] turns all parties into performers. In an attempt to counter imputations of . . . stigmatized membership status, save face, and avoid self-incrimination . . . [parties] may resort to a number of defensive rhetorical strategies . . . [including] remaining silent, denying the allegations, challenging the validity of facts or interpretations . . . attempting to withdraw the matter from public discussion" (Tavuchis, *Mea Culpa*, p. 53).

23. Umemoto, "Blacks and Koreans," p. 101.

24. Ibid. p. 105.

25. Lee did not offer, and May did not demand, monetary compensation. Although Rev. May had a possible civil rights claim, he chose to "get some kind of audience" with the store owners instead of filing a legal complaint (Ford, "One Incident," p. B1).

26. Angela Harris, "Foreword: The Jurisprudence of Reconstruction," 82 *Cal. L. Rev.* 741, 781 (1994).

27. Kang, "Racial Incident Resolved," p. B1.

28. Telephone interview with Joe Hicks, executive director, Multi-Cultural Collaborative, February 12, 1997.


## Notes to Chapter 11

1. Dr. Dullah A. M. Omar, Address to the Twelfth National Human Rights and Justice Conference, Harvard University, April 10, 1997. Other countries in Europe, Latin America, Asia, and Africa have emerged from dictatorships and are facing similar issues of transitional justice.

2. Mark Gevisser, "Can South Africa Face Its Past?" *The Nation*, June 26, 1995, p. 916 (hereafter cited as "Face Its Past"). See generally Adrien K. Wing, "Towards Democracy in a New South Africa," 16 *Mich. J. Int'l L.* 689 (1995) (describing the transition from apartheid to a constitutional democracy); Ziyad Motala, *Constitutional Options for a Democratic South Africa: A Comparative Perspective* (1994); Leonard Thompson, *A History of South Africa* (1990) (describing apartheid segregation laws); John Dugard, *Human Rights and the South African Legal Order* (1978) (describing "security" laws resulting in detention, torture, and death with process protections).

3. The use of the terms *black* and *white* here greatly simplifies South Africa's complex system of racial classifications. *Nonwhite* might be a more accurate term than *black* for describing the many people oppressed by the white National

Party's apartheid regime. With this in mind, I nevertheless use *black* because, in the context of South African apartheid, black stood for more than a racial designation; it also signaled political opposition. The account of the Truth and Reconciliation Commission deals with the wounds of apartheid and resistance to it.

4. Kenneth Christie, "South African Truth Commission Performs Vital Role," *Straits Times*, April 25, 1996, p. 39. See generally Priscilla B. Hayner, "Fifteen Truth Commissions—1974 to 1994: A Comparative Study," *Human Rights Quarterly* 16 (1994): 597 (describing truth commissions in countries throughout the world).

5. Alexandra Zavis, "Panel Faces Truth, Fear, and Anger: Apartheid's Past Is Confronted," *Houston Chronicle*, March 2, 1996, p. 23; Arno Mayer, "South Africa Begins Digesting the Apartheid Era," *Deutsche Presse-Agentur*, December 3, 1995.

6. Omar, Address.

7. Robert Block, "Apartheid Sinners Confront the Truth," *The Independent* (London), May 19, 1995, p. 14.

8. Lee Michael Katz, "South Africa Opens Wounds to Heal Wrongs of Past," *USA Today*, October 21, 1996, p. 13A (describing the "controversial decision" that "stunned South Africa" and quoting Archbishop Tutu as saying "acquittal in a criminal court says nothing about the moral guilt or innocence of the individual concerned").

9. John Battersby, "South Africans Weigh Exposing Apartheid Crimes," *Christian Science Monitor*, May 18, 1994, p. 1.

10. Tina Rosenberg, "Recovering from Apartheid," *New Yorker*, November 18, 1996, p. 87.

11. Mark Gevisser, "South Africa Profile: Tutu's Test of Faith," *Mail & Guardian* (Johannesburg), April 12, 1996 (hereafter cited as "Test of Faith").

12. Rosenberg, "Recovering from Apartheid," p. 90. For insightful discussions of legal narratives, their effects, and limitations, see Toni Massaro, "Empathy, Legal Storytelling, and the Rule of Law: New Words, Old Wounds?" 87 *Mich. L. Rev.* 2099 (1989).

13. Rex Merrifield, "South African Truth Probe Still Viewed with Skepticism," Reuters, Ltd., May 12, 1996; "Victims Testify in Bid for Healing," *Calgary Herald*, April 16, 1996, p. A6; Dele Olojede, "Long Road to Reconciliation: Probe into Apartheid's Horrors May Bring Truth, but Not Justice," *Newsday*, April 16, 1996, p. A16.

14. Katz, "South Africa Opens Wounds," p. 13A (quoting Archbishop Tutu about public storytelling, "you can see some of the healing is happening").

15. "Victims Testify in Bid for Healing."

16. Olojede, "Long Road to Reconciliation."

17. Rosenberg, "Recovering from Apartheid," p. 92.

18. Merrifield, "South African Truth Probe."

19. Robert Block, "When the Truth Is Too Hard to Bear," *The Independent* (London), April 17, 1996, p. 10.

20. Charles Villa-Vicencio, "Telling One Another Stories," in Harold Wells and Gregory Baum, eds., *The Reconciliation of Peoples: Challenge to the Churches* (1997), p. 31.

21. Omar, Address.

22. Villa-Vicencio, "Telling One Another Stories."

23. Linda Goyette, "Leadership Is Knowing When to Say You're Wrong," *Montreal Gazette*, August 23, 1996, p. B5; Bob Drogin, "Apartheid Abuses: De Klerk Pleads Ignorance," *Los Angeles Times*, August 22, 1996, p. A4 (hereafter cited as "Apartheid Abuses").

24. "Time Present, Time Past: Mr. de Klerk's Apology Does Not Go Far Enough," *Guardian* (London), August 23, 1996, p. 012; Goyette, "Leadership," p. B5.

25. Roger Matthews, "De Klerk Apologizes for South Africa's Past," *Financial Times*, August 22, 1996, p. 6.

26. Former South African President Pieter Wilem Botha announced to the commission in late November 1996 that he would not participate in its proceedings, apologize for anything, or apply for amnesty. Botha, who disagreed with the creation of the commission, indicated that he was not guilty of anything, particularly "blatant murder," and stated that the commission's proceedings would develop into a "persecution" of Afrikaners. Botha reportedly cast Afrikaners as victims of both earlier British imperialism and current selective punishment. As de Klerk did, Botha observed that Afrikaners did not invent or import racism to South Africa and suggested probing human rights violations by the African National Congress ("South Africa's Ex-President Botha Will Not Apply for Amnesty," *Deutsche-Presse Agentur*, November 21, 1996).

27. Gevisser, "Test of Faith"; Gumisai Mutume, "South Africa—Politics, Truth Will Out, Next Year," *Inter-Press Service*, November 30, 1995.

28. Olojede, "Long Road to Reconciliation"; "Anti-Apartheid Activists Tell of Beatings and Torture," *Agence France-Presse*, July 24, 1996; "Widow Visits Prison Where South Africa Activist Died in 1977," *Dallas Morning News*, September 11, 1995, p. 4A.

29. Gevisser, "Face Its Past." Even Archbishop Tutu appeared to concede partially this point as a matter of survival politics. "The perpetrators are still in the security forces and part of the civil service. Those people have the capacity of destroying this land. . . . If there were not the possibility of amnesty, then the option of a military upheaval is a very real one" (Rosenberg, "Recovering from Apartheid," pp. 89–90).

30. Drogin, "Apartheid Abuses." See generally Wing, "Towards Democracy," pp. 706–8 (describing South African political organizations and their participation

in postapartheid reconstruction); Nicholas Haysom, "Democracy, Constitution-alism, and the ANC'S Bill of Rights for a New South Africa," *Social Justice* 18 (1991): 40. Thabo Mbeki later acknowledged and received amnesty for political abuses as an ANC leader (se "Amnesty Given to 43 People," Truth and Reconcil-iation Commission, November 28, 1997).

31. *All Things Considered:* "Former South African Leader Apologizes for Abuses" (National Public Radio broadcast, August 24, 1996). While acknowledg-ing this distinction, Archbishop Tutu clashed openly with ANC officials "who don't think that their members need to seek amnesty since whatever they did under apartheid was justified as part of the struggle for freedom" (Rosenberg, "Recovering from Apartheid," p. 92).

32. Bob Drogin, "ANC Admits Rights Abuses," *Los Angeles Times*, p. A16.

33. Merrifield, "South African Truth Probe."

34. "Mandela Appeals for National Reconciliation and Building of Mutual Trust," SABC-TV television broadcast, Johannesburg, April 30, 1994.

35. Michael Hamlyn, "Zulu Nationalist Leader Chief Mangosuthu Buthelezi Demanded Thursday That South Africa's Truth and Reconciliation Commission Investigate the Killings of 422 Leaders of His Inkatha Party," *Agence France-Presse*, September 5, 1996; Inigo Gilmore, "Buthelezi Says Sorry to ANC for Years of Inkatha Violence," *Times* (London), September 6, 1996.

36. "Truth Commission Vows to Protect Apartheid Era Abusers," *African News Service*, September 16, 1996.

37. Hamlyn, "Zulu Nationalist Leader."

38. "Statement by Dr. Alex Boraine on the IFP," Truth and Reconciliation Commission, July 21, 1997. The Inkatha Party continues to shift its alignments throughout the reconciliation process. Its violent relationship with the ANC ended with the peace pact and Buthelezi's apology. Perhaps because of the ANC's rise to power and its apology for ANC abuses, the Inkatha Party adopted a conciliatory posture at the outset of the commission's hearings. Recent Inkatha Party criticism indicates a repositioning in relation to the commission and ANC critics. By adding its voice to the criticism, the Inkatha Party appeared to be distancing itself from the ANC and its members.

The commission's actions tend to refute charges of an ANC bias. In June 1997, the commission granted amnesty to the convicted murderers of prominent ANC civil rights lawyer Griffith Mxenge.

39. "Police Admit Biko Killing," *Facts on File World News Digest*, February 13, 1997, p. 96-F2.

40. Christiane Amanpour and Judy Woodruff, "Twenty Years after Biko's Death, His Killers Step Forward," *CNN Worldview*, Transcript #97022010V18, February 20, 1997; Hugh Dellios, "6th South African Cop Seeks Amnesty in Biko's Death; Officials Hope Truth Finally Will Come Out," *Chicago Tribune*, February 12, 1997, p. 8.

41. "News Release," Truth and Reconciliation Commission, May 4, 1997; "Statement," Truth and Reconciliation Commission, May 6, 1997.

42. Joseph V. Montville, ed., *Conflict and Peacemaking in Multiethnic Societies* (1990), p. 538.

43. "Truth Commission Should Probe Socio-Economic Violations," *South African Press Association*, March 28, 1997; "TRC to Host Forum on Economic Justice and Reconciliation," *South African Press Association*, March 14, 1997.

44. Omar, Address.

45. John Yeld, "Apartheid Profiteers 'Must Pay Reparation,'" *Africa News Service*, May 12, 1997.

46. "Make Perpetrators Pay for Misdeeds," *South African Press Association*, March 28, 1997.

47. "Policy Framework for Urgent Interim Reparation Measures," Truth and Reconciliation Commission, September 14, 1996.

48. Beatrice Khadige, A Year on, South Africa's Truth Body Uncovers Atrocities, Heals Wounds," *Agence France-Presse*, April 14, 1997.

49. Harlon Dalton, *Racial Healing: Confronting the Fear between Blacks and Whites* (1995).

50. Henrik Van der Merwe, Address to the University of Hawai'i, March 4, 1997.

51. Merrifield, "South African Truth Probe."

52. Rosenberg, "Recovering from Apartheid," p. 88; Gevisser, "Face Its Past."

53. Gevisser, "Face Its Past."

54. Donald W. Shriver Jr., *An Ethic for Enemies: Forgiveness in Politics* (1995), p. 219.

55. Timothy Garton Ash, "The Curse and Blessing of South Africa," *New York Review of Books*, August 14, 1997, p. 8.

56. Van der Merwe, Address.

# Index

# About the Author

Eric K. Yamamoto is a professor of law at the William S. Richardson School of Law, University of Hawai'i at Manoa, and is a graduate of the Boalt Hall School of Law, University of California at Berkeley. He is an award-winning teacher and writes in the areas of civil litigation procedure and racial justice.

In the mid-1980s, prior to law teaching, Professor Yamamoto served as co-counsel to Fred Korematsu in the *coram nobis* litigation successfully reopening the infamous World War II Japanese American internment case *Korematsu v. U.S.* Much of his current civil rights and community law work and writing build on that experience.